THE MAKING OF THE CHINESE CIVIL CODE

The Chinese Civil Code (2020) is the first civil code in mainland China since 1949. As well as consolidating existing civil legislation, the Code incorporated a number of doctrinal and structural changes that are significant both in and beyond China. The chapters in this volume demonstrate the extent of European influence on Chinese civil law and also show how Chinese law innovates, building upon those influences. The book shares insights from both the key Chinese scholars who were directly involved in the drafting process and veteran Western scholars who study Chinese private law.

HAO JIANG is Assistant Professor of Comparative Private Law at Bocconi University. He has written about Chinese, European, and American private law from a comparative perspective. He also writes about contract theory. With James Gordley, he co-authored the *Introduction to the Comparative Study of Private Law* (2021).

PIETRO SIRENA is Professor of Civil Law, European Private Law, and Comparative Private Law at Bocconi University, where, since 2018, he has served as Dean of the Law School. He also serves on the Executive Committee of the European Law Institute (ELI) and as Director of the Società Italiana per la Ricerca nel Diritto Comparato (SIRD). In 2022, he was elected President of the Society of European Contract Law (SECOLA) and, in 2018, as associate member of the Académie International de Droit Comparé (AIDC).

THE MAKING OF THE CHINESE CIVIL CODE

Promises and Persistent Problems

Edited by

HAO JIANG

Bocconi University

PIETRO SIRENA

Bocconi University

CAMBRIDGE UNIVERSITY PRESS

CAMBRIDGE
UNIVERSITY PRESS

Shaftesbury Road, Cambridge CB2 8EA, United Kingdom

One Liberty Plaza, 20th Floor, New York, NY 10006, USA

477 Williamstown Road, Port Melbourne, VIC 3207, Australia

314–321, 3rd Floor, Plot 3, Splendor Forum, Jasola District Centre, New Delhi – 110025, India

103 Penang Road, #05–06/07, Visioncrest Commercial, Singapore 238467

Cambridge University Press is part of Cambridge University Press & Assessment, a department of the University of Cambridge.

We share the University's mission to contribute to society through the pursuit of education, learning and research at the highest international levels of excellence.

www.cambridge.org
Information on this title: www.cambridge.org/9781009336635

DOI: 10.1017/9781009336611

First published 2023
First paperback edition 2025

A catalogue record for this publication is available from the British Library

Library of Congress Cataloging-in-Publication data
Names: Jiang, Hao (Law teacher), editor. | Sirena, Pietro, editor.
Title: The making of the Chinese Civil Code : promises and persistent problems / edited by Hao Jiang, Università Commerciale Luigi Bocconi, Milan; Pietro Sirena, Università Commerciale Luigi Bocconi, Milan.
Description: Cambridge, United Kingdom ; New York, NY : Cambridge University Press, 2023. | Includes index.
Identifiers: LCCN 2023018198 | ISBN 9781009336642 (hardback)
Subjects: LCSH: Civil law–China–Codification.
Classification: LCC KNQ500 .M37 2023 | DDC 346.51–dc23/eng/20230703
LC record available at https://lccn.loc.gov/2023018198

ISBN 978-1-009-33664-2 Hardback
ISBN 978-1-009-33663-5 Paperback

To Huimin, Ethan, and my parents. Thank you for letting me be me.

To the late Gabriele Crespi Reghizzi (1941–2022) for working to contribute to this volume until the very last moment of his life.

—H. J.

To the memory of Cesare Massimo Bianca (1932–2020) and Rodolfo Sacco (1923–2022), unparalleled forerunners of comparative legal thinking and shining models of commitment to academic life.

To the late Gabriele Crespi Reghizzi (1941–2022) for his friendship, generosity, and kindness.

—P. S.

CONTENTS

List of Tables ix
List of Contributors x
Preface xiii
Acknowledgements xv
List of Abbreviations xvi

1 The Making of a Civil Code in China: Promises and Perils of a New Civil Law 1
HAO JIANG

2 Personality Rights in China's New Civil Code: A Response to Increasing Awareness of Rights in an Era of Evolving Technology 41
WANG LIMING AND XIONG BINGWAN

3 *Force Majeure* or Change of Circumstances: An Enduring Dichotomy in Chinese Law? 77
LIU QIAO

4 Article 580 (2) of the Chinese Civil Code: Can Chinese Folk Medicine Cure Serious Illness? 94
HAN SHIYUAN

5 Contractual Consent in the New Chinese Civil Code 114
CATHERINE VALCKE

6 The Security Interests in Chinese Law: Some Nuances 131
LEI CHEN

7 Chinese Tort Law in the Era of the Civil Code 153
DING CHUNYAN

8 Causation in the Chinese Civil Code: A Comparative Law Appraisal 179

MARTA INFANTINO AND WEIWEI WANG

9 The Aims of Tort Law across China and the West 197

MAURO BUSSANI

10 Classifying the Passive Appreciation of Separate Property during Marriage in the Chinese Civil Code: A Legal and Economic Analysis 214

JIAN HE

11 The Rule of Law in Traditional China 235

JAMES GORDLEY

12 The Private Law Influence of the Great Qing Code 249

ZHANG TAISU

13 The New Validity Rules in Chinese Civil Code and Chinese State-Owned Enterprises' Freedom in Contracting: One Step Too Far 269

HAO JIANG AND ANTONIA VON APPEN

14 Chinese Civil Law and Soviet Influences: What Is Left? 292

GIANMARIA AJANI

15 The Connections between Roman Law and Chinese Civil Law: Traditions, Innovations and Environmental Protection 308

ENRICO TOTI

Index 325

TABLES

7.1 Torts based on presumed fault liability under the TLB 165
7.2 Torts based on strict liability under the TLB 166
7.3 The imputation system under the TLB 169
7.4 The multi-tier liability system under the TLB 170
7.5 The SPC's judicial interpretations regarding the TLB (May 2020 to December 2021) 174

CONTRIBUTORS

GIANMARIA AJANI, Professor of Law, University of Turin, Italy

MAURO BUSSANI, Professor of Law, University of Trieste, Italy, and Adjunct Professor of Law, University of Macau, S.A.R. of the P.R. of China

LEI CHEN, Chair Professor in International Arbitration and Chinese Law, Durham University, UK

DING CHUNYAN, Professor of Law, City University of Hong Kong, China

JAMES GORDLEY, W. R. Irby Chair Professor in Law, Tulane University, New Orleans, LA, USA

HAN SHIYUAN, Professor of Law, Tsinghua University, Beijing, China

JIAN HE, Associate Professor of Law, Peking University, Beijing, China

MARTA INFANTINO, Associate Professor of Comparative Private Law, University of Trieste, Italy

HAO JIANG, Assistant Professor of Comparative Private Law, Bocconi University, Milan, Italy

LIU QIAO, Professor of Law, City University of Hong Kong, China

ENRICO TOTI, Professor of Chinese Law, Roma Tre University, Italy

CATHERINE VALCKE, Professor of Law, University of Toronto, Canada

ANTONIA VON APPEN, PhD candidate, Department of Legal Studies, Bocconi University, Milan, Italy

WANG LIMING, Professor of Law, Renmin University of China, Beijing, China

WEIWEI WANG, practising lawyer, Trieste, Italy

XIONG BINGWAN, Associate Professor of Law, Renmin University of China, Beijing, China

ZHANG TAISU, Professor of Law, Yale Law School, New Haven, CT, USA

PREFACE

The passage of the Chinese Civil Code was a monumental event both for China and the international community. Yet, it is a daunting task to present a scientific account of the Code to a readership in and out of China. In fact, it is difficult for private law experts in the West to understand Chinese law without context if they only rely upon a superficial reading of the text. It is also difficult for Chinese scholars to understand their own law if they only seek internal explanations for incompatible yet coexisting doctrines that were likely the products of legal transplants from different sources. Moreover, any civil law would have to serve the socio-economic context in which it operates.

Therefore, we decided to approach Chinese Civil Code through comparative law and cross-disciplinary research. The vision of this book, as pointed out in Chapter 1, is to trace the root cause of a number of persistent problems such as the tensions between the rise of private law and the dominant state sector, the contradictions among legal transplants, the incompatibility between doctrinal innovations and the existing structure, and the clash between distributive justice – the foundation of Chinese moral philosophy – and commutative justice – the foundation of Western private law. In this regard, we owe a debt to Rodolfo Sacco's *Legal Formants* or *Formanti Giuridici.*

We are incredibly fortunate to have gathered a group of leading scholars to join this endeavour from mainland China, Hong Kong, Italy, Germany, the United Kingdom, and the United States. They are not only extremely diverse in origin but, more importantly, in expertise and methodology.

In fact, we went far beyond what is in the text. The breadth of expertise involved allowed us to carefully examine the core doctrinal changes through a comparative view and take a close look at the ideological, historical, sociological, and philosophical dimensions of Chinese civil law. Specifically, we invited contributors to explain the development of Chinese law through the lens of Soviet law (Gianmaria Ajani,

Chapter 14), evaluate the applicability of liberal rules to state-owned enterprises (Hao Jiang and Antonia von Appen, Chapter 13), assess the sheer positive effect of codification in the Qing dynasty (Zhang Taisu, Chapter 12), and present the Confucian model of rule of law (James Gordley, Chapter 11). They also critically evaluated some fundamental doctrines in civil law such as change of circumstances (Han Shiyuan, Chapter 4; Liu Qiao, Chapter 3), security interests (Lei Chen, Chapter 6), and causation (Marta Infantino and Weiwei Wang, Chapter 8). Mauro Bussani (Chapter 9) offered a pluralistic view of tort law and explained why we should absolutely take the aim or societal function of torts into consideration when we assess the black-letter law. Ding Chunyan (Chapter 7) demonstrated how the doctrinal system of tort law has been transformed under the new Code. Wang Liming, the main architect of the Chinese Civil Code, along with Xiong Bingwan, presented a persuasive account of why personality rights law deserves an independent status in modern civil law (Chapter 2). Enrico Toti (Chapter 15) made a surprising connection between the procedural rules in Roman law and the green principle in Chinese Civil Code. Our deepest gratitude goes to all of them.

ACKNOWLEDGEMENTS

Material that has previously appeared in the following articles has been reproduced in this book with the permission of the relevant journals.

Hao Jiang. 'The Making of a Civil Code in China: Promises and Perils of a New Civil Law' (2021) 95 *Tulane Law Review* 777, www.tulanelawreview.org/pub/volume95/issue4/the-making-of-a-civil-code-in-china-promises-and-perils-of-a-new-civil-law-6622b.

Hao Jiang and Antonia von Appen. 'The New Validity Rules in Chinese Civil Code and Chinese State-Owned Enterprises' Freedom in Contracting: One Step Too Far' (2022) *Chinese Journal of Comparative Law* Volume 10, Issue 3, https://doi.org/10.1093/cjcl/cxac024.

Wang Liming and Xiong Bingwan. 'Personality Rights in China's New Civil Code: A Response to Increasing Awareness of Rights in an Era of Evolving Technology' (2021) 47 *Modern China* 37, https://doi.org/10.1177/0097700420977826.

ABBREVIATIONS

BGB	Bürgerliches Gesetzbuch
CCC	Chinese Civil Code
ECL	Economic Contract Law
GPCL	General Principles of Civil Law
ISPs	internet service providers
NPC	National People's Congress
NPCSC	National People's Congress Standing Committee
PRC	People's Republic of China
ROC	Republic of China
SASAC	The State-Owned Assets Supervision and Administration
SOE	state-owned enterprises
SPC	Supreme People's Court
TLB	Book on Tort Liability
TLL	Tort Liability Law
TVE	township and village owned enterprise

1

The Making of a Civil Code in China

Promises and Perils of a New Civil Law

HAO JIANG

The Civil Code of the People's Republic of China (the Code) was enacted on May 28, 2020, and became effective on January 1, 2021, as the first civil code in Communist China.[1] Half a century of codification efforts finally resulted in this much-anticipated code. It utilizes state-of-the-art codification techniques and presents a number of innovative features unique to China.

In its concise 1,260 articles, the Code is divided into seven books: General Provisions, Property Rights, Contracts, Personality Rights, Marriage and Family, Inheritance, and Tort Liabilities. In a break with civilian traditions, the Code divides obligations into contracts and torts,[2] and it absorbs the law of unjust enrichment into the book on contracts as quasi-contracts.[3] Moreover, a book on the law of personality stands on its own and includes an enumerated list of personality rights protected by Chinese law.[4] These articles on personality rights focus on privacy and data protection in an effort to keep the Chinese civil law up to date so that it can tackle the legal challenges posed by the advancement of technology.

Much progress has been made with the adoption of the Code, but there are problems that need to be addressed for this civil code to be ultimately successful. Some of these problems come from the tensions between the rise of private law and the dominant state sector, the

[1] "中华人民共和国主席令 第四十五号" ["Order of the President of the People's Republic of China No. 45"] (signed by Xi Jinping, President of the People's Republic of China, May 28, 2020) (2020) *Standing Comm. Nat'l People's Cong. Gaz.* (Civil Code Special Issue) 1.

[2] See "中华人民共和国民法典" ["Civil Code of the People's Republic of China"] (promulgated by the Nat'l People's Cong., May 28, 2020, effective Jan. 1, 2021), pts. III, VII (2020) *Standing Comm. Nat'l People's Cong. Gaz.* (Civil Code Special Issue) 2.

[3] See ibid., arts. 985–88.

[4] See ibid., arts. 989–1039.

contradictions among legal transplants, the incompatibility between doctrinal innovations and the existing structure, and the clash between distributive justice – the foundation of Chinese moral philosophy – and commutative justice – the foundation of Western private law. I argue that solutions to some persistent problems require structural change in the Chinese economy, doctrinal innovation and clarification, and conscientious acceptance of a law that is based upon philosophical ideas that differ from traditional Chinese moral philosophy.

1.1 Introduction: Some Persistent Problems

China is certainly the last major civilian jurisdiction to adopt a civil code. In 1991, James Gordley predicted that Western private law would "govern nearly the entire world" when China adopts its civil code.[5] That statement was true. Chinese private law has been Westernized for a long time, yet China did not have a civil code until recently. In the year 2020, after seventy years of communism, China finally enacted a civil code. In my view, the delay does not reflect a lack of diligence on the part of the legislature and legal scholars but rather arose from some fundamental problems that needed to be resolved before a coherent and functional code could be drafted. Though the pre-communist Civil Code of the Republic of China (ROC) was a modern and sophisticated one, it was based on private ownership and a capitalist market.[6] When a pure socialist regime was established in 1949, the legitimacy of the ROC's Code disappeared.[7] However, after the economic reform of the late 1970s, a state-led capitalist economy reintroduced a socialist market

[5] James Gordley, *The Philosophical Origins of Modern Contract Doctrine* (Oxford: Oxford University Press, 1991), p. 1.

[6] The Nationalist government of China promulgated the Civil Code of the Republic of China in 1929, which was modeled on the German Civil Code and included five books: General Principles, Obligations, Property, Family, and Successions. Hao Jiang, "Chinese Tort Law: Between Tradition and Transplants," in M. Bussani and A. Sebok (eds.), *Comparative Tort Law: Global Perspectives* (Cheltenham: Edward Elgar, 2015), pp. 385, 392. This civil code is still in use in Taiwan

[7] According to socialist legal theories, ownership of the means of production was exclusively in the hands of the State. Even means of subsistence, the resources necessary for people's daily consumption, could not be traded on the market. See "中央政法干部学校民法教研室" ["Civ. L. Teaching & Rsch. Section, Cent. Pol. & Legal Cadres' Sch."], "中华人民共和国民法基本問题" ["Basic Issues of the Civil Law of the People's Republic of China"] (1958) 26, 129.

economy and, most importantly, private ownership.[8] Nevertheless, additional difficulties came to light in using private law to regulate the life of private citizens.

First, there is a theoretical difficulty in applying Western private law to a partially state-owned economy. According to the 'will' theories of explaining legal doctrine that were developed in the West in the nineteenth century, a party was bound by what they willed and only what they willed.[9] That theory was hard to reconcile with the long-standing idea that contracts should be fair – to use the language of Aristotle, that they should do commutative justice – and it created theoretical difficulties in explaining private law.[10] When this theoretical foundation was borrowed in China, the problems were exacerbated, especially when state ownership was involved. Courts are often misled by will theories and refuse to examine whether a contractual transaction was in fact an effort to strip state assets.[11] This problem might be exacerbated further by a progressive structural change adopted by the Code that significantly modernizes Chinese private law. Following the German tradition, the Code unifies the rules governing the voidability of contracts and of civil juristic acts, which were previously in conflict, under one set of rules in the General Provisions of the Code that deals with all civil juristic acts, including contracts.[12] Moreover, the Code no longer treats state interests any differently from private interests and eliminates the power of the State to declare the nullity of a contract.[13]

[8] See discussion in Section 1.3.

[9] See, e.g., James Gordley, *Foundations of Private Law: Property, Tort, Contract, Unjust Enrichment* (New York: Oxford University Press, 2006), p. 14; Randy E. Barnett, "A Consent Theory of Contract" (1986) 86 *Columbia Law Review* 269, 272 (explaining that a contract is enforceable because the promisor has chosen to commit himself). For a historical development of will theories, see James Gordley and Hao Jiang, "Contract as Voluntary Commutative Justice" (2020) *Michigan State Law Review* 725, 728–37.

[10] Aristotle saw contracts as voluntary acts of commutative justice and torts as involuntary acts of commutative justice. See Aristotle, *Nicomachean Ethics* (Terence Irwin trans., 2nd ed.) (c. 384 BCE) (Indianapolis: Hackett, 1999), pp. 72–73.

[11] See generally Hao Jiang, "Freedom of Contract under State Supervision" (2016) 7 *George Mason Journal of International Commercial Law*, 202 (demonstrating the incoherence arising from China's adoption of Western contract theory).

[12] See "中华人民共和国民法典" ["Civil Code of the People's Republic of China"] (promulgated by the Nat'l People's Cong., May 28, 2020, effective January 1, 2021), arts. 143–57 (2020) *Standing Comm. Nat'l People's Cong. Gaz.* (Civil Code Special Issue) 2; see also ibid., art. 133 (defining "civil juristic act").

[13] See "中华人民共和国合同法" ["Contract Law of People's Republic of China"] (promulgated by the Nat'l People's Congress, March 15 1999, effective October 1, 1999), art. 52

Furthermore, conflicting legal transplants need to be harmonized and clear rules established in order to minimize the danger of contradictions within the Code. For example, courts seem to be at odds as to whether recovery for pure economic loss is permitted by Chinese tort law. Before the enactment of the Code, article 2 of the Chinese Tort Liability Law (TLL), like section 823 of the German Civil Code, enumerated the rights protected in tort and excluded rights that are not rights of person and property.[14] As we shall see, German courts have concluded that a plaintiff cannot recover from pure economic loss.[15] Article 6 of the TLL, on the other hand, resembled articles 1240 and 1241 of the French Civil Code, which permit recovery so long as harm resulted.[16] French courts have held that a plaintiff can recover for pure economic loss.[17] The result in China was confusion and inconsistency in judicial decisions.[18] It is my impression that most judges have not faced the question of whether there should be liability for pure economic loss. They either do not see why the law should only protect rights of property and person or consider economic rights part of property rights. Judges who do face the question are unsure whether economic rights are protected by law.[19]

Following China's enactment of the Code, it looks like the French view has prevailed among the drafters, as evidenced by the new article

(1999) *Standing Comm. Nat'l People's Cong. Gaz.* (repealed 2021) 104; "中华人民共和国民法通则" ["General Principles of the Civil Law of the People's Republic of China"] (promulgated by the Nat'l People's Congress, April 12, 1986, effective January 1, 1987), art. 58 (repealed 2021), www.npc.gov.cn/wxzl/wxzl/2000-12/06/content_4470.htm [https://perma.cc/Y6X6-5N54]; see text accompanying notes 37–39.

14 See "中华人民共和国侵权责任法" ["Tort Liability Law of the People's Republic of China"] (promulgated by the Standing Comm. Nat'l People's Cong., December 26, 2009, effective July 1, 2010), art. 2 (2010) *Standing Comm. Nat'l People's Cong. Gaz.* 4 (repealed 2021); Bürgerliches Gesetzbuch [BGB] [Civil Code], § 823, www.gesetze-im-internet.de/bgb/__823.html (German).

15 See discussion in Section 1.4.5.

16 Tort Law of the People's Republic of China, art. 6; code civil [C. civ.] [Civil Code] arts. 1240–41 (French).

17 See, e.g., Cour de cassation [Cass.] [supreme court for judicial matters] 2e civ., June 12, 1987, Bull. civ. II, No. 128 (French) (recognizing the right to recovery for pure economic loss but denying recovery because the damage was too uncertain); Cass. 2e civ., February 21, 1979, Bull. civ. II, No. 56 (French).

18 See discussion in Section 1.4.5.

19 For example, one judge wrongly noted that pure economic loss is a common law concept not protected by Chinese law. "贺欣、萍乡市恒泰行房地产咨询评估有限公司房地产价格评估合同纠纷二审民事判决书" ["He Xin, Pingxiang City Hengtaihang Real Estate Consulting Appraisal Co., Ltd., Real Estate Price Appraisal Contract Disps., Civ. Judgment of Second Instance"] (2017).

1165.[20] Supposedly, this clear contradiction in the TLL ended as of 2021 when that law was superseded by the Code.[21] However, this significant change was not mentioned in either legislative or academic commentaries before the official passage of the Code. It was not even debated among academics. Indeed, two of the drafters have different opinions as to whether article 1165 has changed the law. Zhou Youjun, one of the drafters, is of the view that the law has not changed and that civil interests are exactly the interests previously listed in article 2 of the TLL.[22] Meng Qiang, the secretary of the drafting committee, stated in an email to the author that civil interests are to be broadly interpreted and that pure economic loss will receive more protection with time.[23] Clearly, the two positions are contradictory. There is no doubt that this barely noticed but fundamental change in Chinese tort law will continue to create significant confusion in practice.

Additionally, on a deeper level, philosophical ideals of private law that suit China need to be compatible with doctrinal rules. Western private law is based on the fundamental idea that justice in a dispute between private parties – as Aristotle would say, commutative justice – is distinct from the fairness of the distribution of wealth in society – as Aristotle would say, distributive justice.[24] Nevertheless, a concern for the distribution of wealth is supposed to be at the foundation of the Chinese legal system. Courts need clearer guidance as to how to reconcile such a direct conflict between the two. The prime example is a basis for liability in tort that is recognized in China but not in the West: what may be called

[20] "中华人民共和国民法典" ["Civil Code of the People's Republic of China"] (promulgated by the Nat'l People's Cong., May 28, 2020, effective January 1, 2021), art. 1165 (2020) *Standing Comm. Nat'l People's Cong. Gaz.* (Civil Code Special Issue) 2 ("The actor infringing upon civil rights and interests of others by fault and causing damage shall assume tort liability.").

[21] See ibid., art. 1260 (repealing the legal predecessors to the Code, including the TLL, when the Code took effect on January 1, 2021).

[22] Zhou Youjun (周友军), "民法典侵权责任编的制度发展" ["The Institutional Development of the Civil Code Book on Tort Liability"]; ("微信：网络法前沿") [WeChat: Frontiers Cyber L.] (June 2, 2020), https://mp.weixin.qq.com/s/dKpr6wAwqbZwl3C1KWQNtQ [https://perma.cc/E966-PP9X].

[23] Email from Meng Qiang, Professor of Law, Beijing Inst. of Tech., to author (June 11, 2020, 4:21 a.m.) (on file with author) [hereinafter Email from Meng Qiang, June 11]; Email from Meng Qiang, Professor of L., Beijing Inst. of Tech., to author (June 6, 2020, 11:06 p.m.) (on file with author).

[24] See Aristotle, *Nicomachean Ethics*, pp. 71–74.

"liability in equity."[25] According to the doctrine of liability in equity, once harm is done, the party that caused it is partially liable even though he was not at fault, provided that he is in a financial position to pay.[26] Whether to impose liability, however, rests at the discretion of Chinese judges.[27] This rule is not easy to square with the traditional grounds for liability in the West or with the idea that private disputes concern only commutative justice.

Moreover, doctrinal innovations can be a double-edged sword that need to be more carefully crafted to avoid conflicting or counterproductive results. The adoption of a book on personality rights is a prime example. Its adoption was based on the view that it is an independent set of laws that deserves its own space.[28] Nevertheless, when seeking relief, it only makes sense that the general provisions of tort law apply.[29] This situation raises several practical difficulties for parties seeking relief. If both tort law and personality rights law elements have to be met before a party can bring an action under personality rights law, it is unclear whether the innovation is actually making it easier to protect personality rights.

This chapter uses historical and comparative insights to showcase the tensions between the new Code and these pre-existing and persistent problems. As we shall see, the root cause of these persistent problems comes not only from legislative techniques but rather mostly from the Chinese economic structure and state ownership, conflicts between distributive justice – the foundation of Chinese moral philosophy – and commutative justice – the foundation of Western private law – and from the compatibility issues in legal transplants.

1.2 Some History

In 1949, when the People's Republic of China was founded following World War II and the Chinese Civil War, the Civil Code of the ROC was

[25] See Civil Code of the People's Republic of China, art. 1186 ("If the damage is through no fault of both the victim and the tortfeasor, the loss may be borne by both parties according to the law.").

[26] For a detailed discussion, see Section 1.5.1.

[27] Wang Liming (王利明), Zhou Youjun (周友军), and Gao Shengping (高圣平), 中国侵权责任法教程 [*Textbook on the Tort Liability Law of China*] (Beijing: 人民法院出版社, 2010), p. 167.

[28] See discussion in Section 1.4.1.

[29] This is a position that is endorsed by one of the drafters, Meng Qiang. See Email from Meng Qiang, June 11.

abolished along with the other codes and laws of the ROC. Massive nationalization of private ownership and the use of central planning to replace a private market took place in the 1950s.[30] Afterward, private ownership of the means of production was eliminated.[31] When private ownership was denied, it became hard to track the development of private law, and many would argue that the first thirty years of communist China was a lawless era in private law.[32]

As private ownership lost its legitimacy, it became hard to justify the existence of property law and tort law. Nevertheless, contracts and contract law could still exist to regulate the contractual dealings between government agencies and state-owned enterprises (SOEs).[33] Contracts were only allowed between government agencies and SOEs and for the sole purpose of implementing state economic policies and directives.[34] Such activities were regulated by governmental regulations rather than statutes. All economic activities undertaken with the motive of making a profit were deemed illegal.[35] As a result, the contracting process was heavily regulated, and little autonomy was left to the contracting parties.[36] State-owned enterprises were instructed to enter into a contract with an assigned counterpart on terms stipulated by the State.[37] They did not have an independent budget and were deprived of the autonomy to retain any profit.[38] As a result, no official law (neither statutes nor case law) dealing with private law was in place until the economic reform at the end of the 1970s. Thereafter, contractual transactions were regulated by different bodies of statutes depending on the identity of the parties

[30] For the history and economic logic in establishing state-owned enterprises and massive nationalization of the economy, see Justin Yifu Lin et al., *State-Owned Enterprise Reform in China* (Hong Kong: Chinese University of Hong Kong Press, 2002), pp. 20–28.

[31] See ibid.

[32] Jiang, "Freedom of Contract under State Supervision," pp. 215–23.

[33] "机关、国营企业、合作社签订合同契约暂行办法" ["Interim Measures for the Signing of Contracts by Government Agencies, State-Owned Enterprises, and Cooperatives"] (promulgated by the Fin. & Econ. Comm. Cent. People's Gov't Admin. Council, September 27, 1950, effective September 27, 1950), art. 1, CLI.4.159965 (http://PKULaw.com).

[34] See ibid. (stating that the purpose of the law is to facilitate business transactions between government agencies, state-owned enterprises, and village collectives to prevent unfaithful conduct that causes loss to a party and impairs the planned economy).

[35] See Jiang, "Freedom of Contract under State Supervision," pp. 235–38 (explaining that profiteering was deemed an illegitimate contracting goal).

[36] See ibid., pp. 218–19.

[37] Ibid.

[38] Ibid.

(domestic or foreign) and the types of transactions (technological or economic).[39] In 1986, legislation similar to a civil code with the title General Principles of Civil Law was adopted.[40] It supplied a framework for civil law in modern China, providing basic rules of property law, contract law, tort law, and unjust enrichment in only 156 articles.[41] Apparently, the coverage was not complete and many detailed rules were needed for a civil code of proper length.

Several failed attempts to codify Chinese civil law led to a piecemeal approach. Each book of the civil code was to be enacted separately, and a final codification ensured the consistency and coherence of the code. For example, Contract Law was enacted in 1999 to replace the three separate contract law statutes,[42] Property Law in 2007,[43] and Tort Liability Law in 2009.[44] Lastly, the General Provisions of Civil Law, now the first book of the Code, was enacted in 2017.[45] A draft civil code was released in

[39] The three separate contract law statutes were Economic Contract Law (1981), Foreign Economic Contract Law (1985), and Technology Contract Law (1987). "中华人民共和国经济合同法" ["Economic Contract Law of the People's Republic of China"] (promulgated by the Nat'l People's Cong., December 13, 1981, effective July 1, 1982) (repealed 1999), http://english.mofcom.gov.cn/aarticle/lawsdata/chineselaw/200211/20021100053738.html [https://perma.cc/8AE5-2MRK]; "中华人民共和国涉外经济合同法" ["Law of the People's Republic of China on Economic Contracts Involving Foreign Interests"] (promulgated by the Standing Comm. Nat'l People's Cong., March 21, 1985, effective July 1, 1985) (repealed 1999), www.npc.gov.cn/wxzl/wxzl/2000-12/06/content_4455.htm [https://perma.cc/QHG4-CXWH]; "中华人民共和国技术合同法" ["Law of the People's Republic of China on Technology Contracts"] (promulgated by the Standing Comm. Nat'l People's Cong., June 23, 1987, effective November 1, 1987) (repealed 1999), www.npc.gov.cn/wxzl/wxzl/2000-12/06/content_4484.htm [https://perma.cc/782B-DHMM].

[40] "中华人民共和国民法通则" ["General Principles of the Civil Law of the People's Republic of China"] (promulgated by the Nat'l People's Congress, April 12, 1986, effective January 1, 1987) (repealed 2021), www.npc.gov.cn/wxzl/wxzl/2000-12/06/content_4470.htm [https://perma.cc/Y6X6-5N54].

[41] See ibid.

[42] "中华人民共和国合同法" ["Contract Law of People's Republic of China"] (promulgated by the Nat'l People's Congress, March 15, 1999, effective October 1, 1999) (1999) *Standing Comm. Nat'l People's Cong. Gaz.* 104 (repealed 2021).

[43] "中华人民共和国物权法" ["Property Law of the People's Republic of China"] (promulgated by the Nat'l People's Congress, March 16, 2007, effective October 1, 2007) (2007) *Standing Comm. Nat'l People's Cong. Gaz.* 291 (repealed 2021).

[44] "中华人民共和国侵权责任法" ["Tort Liability Law of the People's Republic of China"] (promulgated by the Standing Comm. Nat'l People's Cong., December 26, 2009, effective July 1, 2010) (2010) *Standing Comm. Nat'l People's Cong. Gaz.* 4 (repealed 2021).

[45] "中华人民共和国民法总则" ["General Provisions of the Civil Law of the People's Republic of China"] (promulgated by the Nat'l People's Congress, March 15, 2017, effective October 1, 2017) (2017) *Standing Comm. Nat'l People's Cong. Gaz.* 191 (repealed 2021).

December 2019 and was subject to extensive public, academic, and legislative debate prior to its official enactment on May 28, 2020.[46]

1.3 Legitimatizing Private Law

In my view, the single most important feature of the Code is its effort to legitimatize private law. For the first time in the history of communist China, state and private interests are treated equally. The recognition of the legitimacy of private ownership interests has always been a major ideological hurdle in China's private lawmaking since the 1950s. The Chinese Constitution of 1954 actually set a clear goal to transform private ownership into socialist public ownership. Article 10 of the Constitution of 1954 provided: "The policy of the State towards capitalist industry and commerce is to use, restrict and transform them. The State . . . encourages and guides their transformation into various forms of state-capitalist economy, gradually replacing capitalist ownership with ownership by the whole people."[47]

Starting in 1954, government regulations required that private enterprises be converted into public-private joint ventures with the State.[48] In 1956, all private and individually owned enterprises were transformed into public private joint ventures, which soon became de facto SOEs.[49] By the end of that year, only 0.5 percent of private enterprises had not yet been formed into public-private joint ventures.[50] In 1957, 70 percent of industrial output was allocated through state planning, while the

[46] For a detailed timeline of the codification process, see the official legislative commentary, "关于 中华人民共和国民法典（草案）的说明" ["Notes on 'The Civil Code of the People's Republic of China (Draft)'"] (delivered by Wang Chen, vice chairman of the Standing Comm. Nat'l People's Congress, May 22, 2020) (2020) *Standing Comm. Nat'l People's Cong. Gaz.* (Civil Code Special Issue) 178.

[47] Constitution [Xianfa], art. 10 (1954).

[48] James Gordley et al., *An Introduction to the Comparative Study of Private Law* (2nd ed.) (Cambridge: Cambridge University Press, 2021), p. 578; Yifu Lin et al., "State-owned Enterprise Reform in China," pp. 26–27.

[49] Willy Kraus, *Private Business in China: Revival between Ideology and Pragmatism* (Erich Holz trans.) (Honolulu: University of Hawaii Press, 1991) pp. 54–55 ("[M]ixed enterprises would be directed and administered solely by the government . . . . [P]rivate owners had 'actually become state employees [*sic*].'" (quoting Private Business, China News Analysis [China News Analysis, Hong Kong, China], March 29, 1957, at 1, 1); Yifu Lin et al., "State-Owned Enterprise Reform in China," p. 27.

[50] Gordley et al., *An Introduction to the Comparative Study of Private Law*, p. 578.

remaining 30 percent was through sales contracts.[51] In the Chinese Constitution of 1975, the protection of private ownership was finally discarded, and only public ownership was inviolable.[52] After the economic reform at the end of the 1970s and the declaration of establishment of a socialist market economy, the ideology shifted toward protection of the private economy, and the law has followed suit. A 1988 amendment to the current Chinese Constitution, adopted in 1982, permitted "the private sector of the economy to exist and develop within the limits prescribed by law."[53] Further, the private sector of the economy was regarded as "a complement to the socialist public economy."[54] The status of the private economy was elevated to "an important component" of the economy in 1999.[55] In 2004, a constitutional amendment provided that private ownership is inviolable.[56] Today, the private economy makes up more than half of the Chinese economy,[57] and the commitment to protect private interests is absolutely critical to the growth of China. This commitment to equal protection of state and private interests is duly recognized by article 207 of the Code, which provides: "The property right of the State, the collectives, the individual persons and other obligees are protected equally by law, and no organizations or individuals shall encroach on it."[58]

1.3.1 State Interest in Contract Law

Contract is considered a subcategory of civil juristic acts in German-inspired civil law systems, including China. Supposedly, there is only one set of rules regulating validity of civil juristic acts that determines the

[51] Liang Huixing (梁慧星), "论我国合同法律制度的计划原则与合同自由原则" ["On the Plan Principle and Principle of Freedom of Contract in Our Contracting System"] (1982) 4 法学研究 [*China Journal of Law*], pp. 44–46.

[52] Xianfa art. 8 (1975).

[53] Xianfa amend., art. 1 (1988) (amending Xianfa art. 11 [1982]).

[54] Ibid.

[55] Xianfa amend., art. 16 (1999) (amending Xianfa art. 11 [1982]).

[56] Xianfa amend., art. 22 (2004) (amending Xianfa art. 13 [1982]).

[57] The private sector makes up 60 percent of the Chinese gross domestic product. Amir Guluzade, "The Role of China's State-owned Companies Explained," World Economic Forum (May 7, 2019), www.weforum.org/agenda/2019/05/why-chinas-state-owned-companies-still-have-a-key-role-to-play/ [https://perma.cc/67R2-B7JH].

[58] "中华人民共和国民法典" ["Civil Code of the People's Republic of China"] (promulgated by the Nat'l People's Cong., May 28, 2020, effective January 1, 2021), art. 207 (2020) *Standing Comm. Nat'l People's Cong. Gaz.* (Civil Code Special Issue) 2.

validity of contracts.[59] Traditionally, in China there have been inconsistencies and contradictory rules concerning the validity of contracts and civil juristic acts. Despite the presence of the same vitiating factors, whether a contract was voidable may have depended on the existence of a state interest. For example, under the 1986 General Principles of the Civil Law, vitiating factors such as fraud, duress, and mistake rendered a civil juristic act void.[60] In the 1999 Contract Law statute, the concept of relative nullity was first introduced to give the aggrieved party an option to keep the contract alive.[61] Vitiating factors then made a contract only voidable, which contradicts the General Principles of the Civil Law. Moreover, even within the Contract Law itself, there were tensions between article 52 and article 54.[62] Fraud and duress would render a contract merely voidable under article 54, but the contract would be void and null if fraud and duress harmed a state interest under article 52. As I have shown elsewhere, a state interest is not the public interest but is more likely to be the financial interest of SOEs, which only adds to the doctrinal uncertainties.[63]

The Code streamlines the rules concerning validity and eliminates the differences in the treatment of contracts and civil juristic acts. Now there is only one set of rules that deals with the validity of civil juristic acts, and

59 For example, the German Civil Code only provides one set of validity rules on mistake regarding civil juristic acts without having a different article for contracts. See BGB § 119, www.gesetze-im-internet.de/bgb/__119.html.

60 "中华人民共和国民法通则" ["General Principles of the Civil Law of the People's Republic of China"] (promulgated by the Nat'l People's Congress, April 12, 1986, effective January 1, 1987), art. 58 (repealed 2021).

61 "中华人民共和国合同法" ["Contract Law of the People's Republic of China"] (promulgated by the Nat'l People's Congress, March 15, 1999, effective Oct. 1, 1999), art. 54 (1999) *Standing Comm. Nat'l People's Cong. Gaz.* 104 (repealed 2021). For a historical discussion of the introduction of relative nullity in Western law and Chinese law, see Hao Jiang, "Enlarged State Power to Declare Nullity: The Hidden State Interest in the Chinese Contract Law" (2014) 7 *Journal of Civil Law Studies* 147, 149–56.

62 Article 54 provides that, as in Western jurisdictions, a party who was induced to enter a contract by fraud or duress may have it annulled or modified. (Contract Law of the People's Republic of China art. 54). Article 52 provides that a contact is "invalid" if "either party enters into the contract by means of fraud or coercion, undermining national interests ... social and public interests are undermined; or ... mandatory provisions of laws and administrative regulations are violated." Ibid., art. 52(1), (4)–(5).

63 See generally Jiang, "Freedom of Contract under State Supervision" (demonstrating the issues that arise from the freedom of contract granted to SOEs).

it applies to contracts as well.[64] According to the Code, illegality, sham transactions, and violation of good morals will render a civil juristic act null and void.[65] Victims of fraud, duress, mistake, and obvious unfairness have the option to rescind the civil juristic act by a claim before the court or arbitration institution.[66] Thus, the Code no longer has special rules that afford state interests greater protection. At least in its form, Chinese codification of private law has moved toward a body of law that does not subscribe to a particular political ideology and that levels the playing field between state and private enterprises. The only remaining state power to intervene in contractual autonomy is to secure emergency orders in times of disaster, such as COVID-19. The Civil Code adopted a provision that is similar to the Defense Production Act in the United States.[67] It requires the appropriate private parties to accept state production orders when a need arises for disaster relief or disease prevention.[68]

Nevertheless, on the negative side, without a significant reform of the corporate governance structure of SOEs, it is unclear whether the equal treatment of state and private interests will exacerbate the problem of stripping of state assets that previous laws tried to curb. After the establishment of SOEs and massive nationalization in the 1950s, a free market no longer existed.[69] The State took contractual autonomy away from SOEs and made the law paternalistic.[70] The end result was to make contract law a body of regulations that ensured the accurate documentation of state economic plans. Contractual autonomy was to be prevented. The State, through directives, decided whom to contract with, what to contract about, and the terms of the contract.[71]

These measures were necessary because, without a free and competitive market, the price no longer reflected value, and the profit no longer indicated managerial performance. Without effective market information, like indicators such as price and profits, the normal corporate

[64] "中华人民共和国民法典" ["Civil Code of the People's Republic of China"] (promulgated by the Nat'l People's Cong., May 28, 2020, effective January 1, 2021), arts. 143–51 (2020) *Standing Comm. Nat'l People's Cong. Gaz.* (Civil Code Special Issue) 2.

[65] Ibid., arts. 143–46.

[66] Ibid., arts. 147–51.

[67] Compare ibid., art. 494 with Defense Production Act, 50 U.S.C. § 4511.

[68] Civil Code of the People's Republic of China art. 494.

[69] See Joseph E. Stiglitz, *Whither Socialism?* (Cambridge, MA: MIT Press, 1994), pp. 110–11.

[70] See generally Yifu Lin et al., "State-owned Enterprise Reform in China" (describing the evolution of SOEs and the Chinese government's management of them).

[71] See generally Jiang, "Freedom of Contract under State Supervision" (discussing the State's interest in contract law).

governance mechanism fails. As Joseph Stigliz has pointed out, without functioning market competition, a rational incentive structure cannot be formed.[72] When the incentives between managers and SOEs cannot be aligned, the fear is that the managers will engage in transactions that would profit themselves rather than the State. Therefore, the State has to be more paternalistic to prevent managers from looting state assets. Logically, then, the law has to afford state assets more protection and avoid contracts that are harmful to SOEs in hindsight. Justin Yifu Lin, a prominent Chinese economist, has argued that SOEs can still succeed in the market economy without privatization, but the key is to subject SOEs to a competitive market without policy-induced burdens and soft budget constraints.[73]

In reality, both still exist. SOEs still carry out policy goals that are nonprofit driven, and SOE managers make business decisions that are in alignment with their political responsibilities.[74] Such decisions enhance the political legitimacy of the Communist Party of China and, at the same time, serve to advance the managers' bureaucratic careers.[75] As I have explained elsewhere:

> These decisions are not necessarily in the best commercial interest of the enterprises. Examples are managerial decisions to engage in major disaster relief efforts at the cost of the SOEs to gain political capital, overstaffing to lower the unemployment rates, providing essential services to the society at below market prices or listing overseas to attract political attention.[76]

On the other hand, in order for SOEs to survive, the State must provide direct and indirect subsidies. As a result, SOEs will continue to have information advantages over the State. A liberal law would encourage asset stripping. Take freedom of contract. In a 2013 case that concerned a dispute over the sale of a privatized former SOE, the court abstained from assessing the fairness of the price in a stock purchase agreement even when 69 percent of a RMB 3.8 million yuan company was sold for a mere

72 Stiglitz, "Whither Socialism?," p. 111.

73 See generally Yifu Lin et al., "State-owned Enterprise Reform in China" (arguing how SOEs can succeed without privatization).

74 Jiangyu Wang, "The Political Logic of Corporate Governance in China's State-owned Enterprises" (2014) 47 *Cornell International Law Journal* 631, 663–64; Jiang, "Freedom of Contract under State Supervision," p. 253.

75 Wang, "The Political Logic of Corporate Governance," pp. 666–69; Jiang, "Freedom of Contract under State Supervision," p. 253.

76 Jiang, "Freedom of Contract under State Supervision," p 253.

RMB 300,000 yuan.[77] When facing the potential harm to a state interest, the court expressly limited its role to examining the external forms of a commercial transaction rather than its substance.[78] The court prioritized the public policy to ensure the safety of the transaction over a paternalistic approach to curb asset stripping even when it could have rescinded the transaction under Contract Law article 52.[79] Here, freedom of contract allowed state assets to be sold to former state employees at a bargain.

With the new Code, it looks like the necessary legal steps have been taken. However, institutionally, SOEs still are involved in undertaking nonprofitable political tasks and at the same time benefit from the financial and policy support of the government. Again, it remains to be seen whether such a pro-transaction reform will lead to a potentially precarious outcome when a state interest is involved.

1.3.2 Public Landownership and Private Land Use Rights

When we talk about private law in the West, the premises we work from are that things are privately owned and that there is a free market in which people can trade things that are privately owned. Those premises, however, cannot be taken for granted in China. China has maintained a system of exclusive public land ownership but allows an extensive private land use right for the right-holders to exercise virtually all ownership rights.

The Theory

In China, private ownership of land and the means of production was abolished in the early 1950s.[80] Ownership was held exclusively by the State until the end of the 1970s when private ownership was reintroduced.[81] During this period, ownership rights were exercised by SOEs on behalf of the State in the form of rights of operational management.

77 See 夏云与江苏省演艺集团有限公司、南京大风创业投资管理有限公司股权转让纠纷一审民事判决书 [*Xia Yun* v. *Jiangsu Performing Arts Grp. Co., Ltd. & Nanjing Dafeng Venture Cap. Mgmt. Co., Ltd.*, First-instance Civil Judgment on Equity Transfer Disp.], (2013) Bai Shanf Chu Zi Di 231 Hao (2013)白商初字第231号) [(2013) Bai Shang Chu Zi No. 231] (Qinhuai Dist. People's Ct. of Nanjing City July 15, 2014).

78 Ibid.

79 Ibid.

80 See Yifu Lin et al., *State-owned Enterprise Reform in China*, pp. 20–23.

81 See above notes 49–53 and accompanying text.

Such a model represented a class-based theory of law and depended upon a planned economy. One of the ideas on which Western law has been built is that the law is impartial.[82] Supposedly, the law should apply to all and protect the interest of all regardless of social status. However, in Marxist theory, law is only the law of the ruling class and represents only the will of the ruling class.[83] Law, therefore, is a means that the ruling class alone uses to exploit the oppressed classes.[84]

According to Karl Marx, all the other elements in the society are superstructures based on economic conditions.[85] Law is a superstructure that is dependent on the economic basis of the society.[86] Therefore, legal relationships are "rooted in the material conditions of life,"[87] and law is the reflection of "the material production of a given society."[88] The forms and content of the law differ according to the economic conditions of the society. Law is defined as "a system (order) of social relations corresponding to the interests of the ruling class and protected by the organized force of this class (the State)."[89] According to the leading Soviet theorist Pashukanis, capitalist law was merely a reflex of the capitalism economic conditions rather than "a manifestation of justice."[90] Accordingly, private ownership is evil and exists to facilitate class exploitation.[91] It should be eliminated in a society where the proletariat becomes the ruling class.[92] Land should belong to the peasants rather than the landlords.

[82] See Vladimir Gsovski, "The Soviet Concept of Law" (1938) 7 *Fordham Law Review* 1, 2–3.

[83] Ibid., p. 3.

[84] Ibid.

[85] See generally Karl Marx, *A Contribution to the Critique of Political Economy* (N. I. Stone trans., 2nd German ed.) (Chicago: Charles H. Kerr & Co., 1904) (developing this theory).

[86] Gsovski, "The Soviet Concept of Law," 5.

[87] Ibid. (quoting Marx, *A Contribution to the Critique of Political Economy*, p. 11).

[88] Ibid. (quoting Karl Marx, Speech of Defence Before the Cologne Jury (February 9, 1849), as reprinted in Max Beer, "Further Selection from the Literary Remains of Karl Marx" (1923) 5 *Labour Monthly* 174, 175.

[89] Rukovodyashchiye Nachala Po Ugolovnomu Pravu RSFSR [Fundamentals of the Criminal Law of the RSFSR], Sobraniye Uzakoneniy i Rasporyazheniy Rabochego i Krest'yanskogo Pravitel'stva [SU] [Collection of Legalizations and Orders of the Workers and Peasants' Government] 1919, No. 66, Item 590, § 1, as translated in Gsovski, "The Soviet Concept of Law" at 8.

[90] Gsovski, "The Soviet Concept of Law," p. 10–11.

[91] Ibid., p. 12.

[92] Ibid., pp. 13–14 ("The government tried to be the only producer and distributor of commodities. It intended to do away with all private property.").

The Practice

Under this ideology, all land is publicly owned in China as land is either state-owned or owned by village collectives.[93] Still, based on the civilian concept of usufruct, a land use right was created that approximates land ownership. It is true that urban lands are owned by the State while rural lands are owned by village collectives.[94] Also, it is not legally permissible to assign land ownership.[95] On the other hand, houses can be owned by private parties and freely traded on the market.[96]

The tension between private house ownership and public land ownership created a distinct right: the land use right.[97] A land use right is a right of usufruct, which entitles a party to use, enjoy, and profit from the land.[98] There are various time limits that have been set for land use rights based on the purposes of the land use.[99] According to administrative regulations enacted in 1990, the time limit for the residential use is seventy years; the limit for industrial use is fifty years; the limit for uses for education, technology, culture, healthcare, and sports is fifty years; and the limit for tourism and commercial entertainment use is forty years.[100]

For the first time, the Code clarifies the legal consequences of the expiration of the time limits.[101] The usufruct of residential housing will be automatically renewed while renewal of other kinds of land use rights will follow separate statutes.[102] Thus, residential land use right holders will have a right that approximates full land ownership.

[93] "中华人民共和国土地管理法" ["Land Administration Law of the People's Republic of China"] (promulgated by the Standing Comm. Nat'l People's Cong., June 25, 1986, as amended by the Standing Comm. Nat'l People's Congress, August 26, 2019, effective January 1, 2020), art. 2.

[94] Ibid., art. 9.

[95] See ibid., arts. 2, 12.

[96] "中华人民共和国民法典" ["Civil Code of the People's Republic of China"] (promulgated by the Nat'l People's Cong., May 28, 2020, effective January 1, 2021), arts. 352–53 (2020) *Standing Comm. Nat'l People's Cong. Gaz.* (Civil Code Special Issue) 2.

[97] Land Administration Law of the People's Republic of China art. 10.

[98] Civil Code of the People's Republic of China art. 344.

[99] "中华人民共和国城镇国有土地使用权出让和转让暂行条例" ["Interim Regulations of the People's Republic of China Concerning the Assignment and Transfer of the Right to the Use of the State-Owned Land in the Urban Areas"] (promulgated by the St. Council, May 19, 1990, as amended by the St. Council, November 29, 2020, effective November 29, 2020), art. 12 (June 26, 1990) *St. Council Gaz.* 355.

[100] Ibid.

[101] Civil Code of the People's Republic of China art. 359.

[102] Ibid.

1.4 Doctrinal Innovations and Challenges

Much of the civil law infrastructure in China came from legal transplants. The Code is no exception. French, German, and Anglo-American influences are seen throughout the Code. The German concept of *Rechtsgeschäft* (civil juristic act) is the bedrock of the general theory of Chinese civil law, and the renowned French Civil Code articles 1240–41 (formerly articles 1382–83) form the basis of fault liability.[103] Surprisingly, common law doctrines that seemingly would not grow on civil law soil also made their way into the Chinese Civil Code. Moreover, several doctrinal innovations also showed Chinese ingenuity in the making of a different civil law.

1.4.1 Personality Rights

Perhaps the biggest structural innovation in the Code is an independent book on personality rights. Article 990 provides: "Personality rights shall refer to the rights of life, body, health, name (natural person or otherwise), portrait, reputation, honor, privacy, etc. to which a civil party is entitled."[104] One of the drafters praised this innovation as an illustration of Chinese ingenuity in making its own civil law and an implementation of the constitutional protection of human dignity.[105]

However, when seeking the protection of the Code on the basis of personality rights, one might encounter a practical problem: What will the basis of the claim be now? Supposedly, all the rights within the scope of personality rights are already protected by tort law.[106] Will a party still have a claim for violation of personality rights without resorting to tort law? Will a party still have such a claim when elements necessary for tort

[103] Code civil arts. 1240–41 (French); see Civil Code of the People's Republic of China art. 1165.

[104] Civil Code of the People's Republic of China art. 990.

[105] Zhou Youjun (周友军), "周友军：民法典人格权编评析" ["Compilation and Analysis of Personality Rights in the Civil Code"], Weixin (微信), "中国民商法律网" ["WeChat: China Civil & Commercial Law Network"] (June 8, 2020), https://mp.weixin.qq.com/s/wa91sGfuyMYTgZlU9SZECg [https://perma.cc/5UG8-KWVQ].

[106] See Liang Huixing (梁慧星), "深圳 '歌乐山大讲堂' 第50期" ["Shenzhen 'Geleshan Lecture Hall' Issue 50"]: "关于民法典分则编纂中的重大分歧" ["Regarding the Major Differences in the Compilation of the Separate Provisions of the Civil Code"] (December 15, 2019), CLI.A.0110643 (Chinalawinfo) (arguing against the need for a distinction between personality rights and tort law and criticizing the seemingly new requirement to claim both personality and tort rights now that personality rights is a separate book).

liability are lacking, such as subjective culpability or causation? Liang Huixing, a prominent scholar who opposed an independent book on personality rights, argued that parties will now have to establish claims under both tort law and personality rights law.[107] Wouldn't that make it harder to get relief?

One of the drafters explained after the Code was enacted that personality rights law would be directly applicable and sufficient in itself as the basis of claim (*Anspruchsgrundlage*).[108] But again, violation of personality rights is either part of tort law or not. If it is, is it beneficial to allow parties to circumvent tort law and obtain relief? If it is not, are we really going to allow relief when such a violation is not even considered a tort? When the question was posed in an email exchange to Meng Qiang, one of the drafters, he gave a perplexing account:

> Protection of personality rights has its own unique features that are independent of tort law and so it deserves to be on its own. But of course, in order to get relief under personality rights law, the elements of tort law need to be satisfied. It will not be harder for the plaintiff to get relief because the civil rights/interests under the Code are open-ended and allow the judges to be creative.[109]

In my view, such a response will only add to the confusion. First, by requiring the claim to satisfy tort law and personality rights law, it narrows the scope of protection by definition. Second, if the scope of rights is open-ended under the tort law, and civil rights and interests under the tort law totally cover personality rights, everyone could just use tort law instead of resorting to the book of personality rights. If that were the case, the book of personality rights becomes declaratory in nature only.

In recent months, advocates for this innovation argued that personality rights as an independent book would allow the Code to protect constitutional rights, such as the right to education, that it was not able to protect before.[110] The sudden revelation of a large cluster of cases, in which unqualified candidates intercepted admitted candidates' admission

107 Ibid.

108 Zhou Youjun, "Compilation and Analysis of Personality Rights in the Civil Code."

109 Email from Meng Qiang, June 11.

110 For example, a cluster of identity theft cases in college admissions were recently discovered. The Code has shown the roadmap for how to deal with them. Mugong Jun （慕公君）, "民法讲座｜冒名上大学居然一查一串，民法典对此已有初步亮" ["Civil Law Lectures | A Series of Investigations Have Been Made to Go to College Under the Pretense of a Fake Name"], 微信: 慕公法治论坛》 [WeChat: Mu Gong Rule

letters from colleges after the college entrance exam and used the victim's name to attend college, caught media and societal attention.[111] In these cases, rich families paid government employees to illegally intercept admission letters. The victims, not having received the acceptance letter, assumed that they did not get admitted to colleges and went into the workforce instead. The identity thieves would graduate from college, receive gainful employment, and live a prosperous life while the victims, who were usually from underprivileged backgrounds and could only have achieved success by attending college, struggled in life and could not have a middle-class job.

Supposedly, a wrong to one's right to one's name and honor had been committed, but it was a one-time offense. The damage permitted by law does not reflect decades of income disparity and difference in future career paths. It appears that the victims of the new cluster of cases only sought to plead with the colleges for a chance to start their college education more than a decade after their "supposed" graduation. No monetary damages have been sought so far. Still, the view of practitioners is that without resorting to a right to education, damages can only be nominal.[112] According to the commentators, the practice people had seen from the case *Qi Yuling* v. *Chen Xiaoqi* could be revived by the Code through the law on personality rights.[113]

In the case of *Qi Yuling*, considered the Chinese equivalent of *Marbury* v. *Madison*, the Chinese Supreme People's Court unprecedentedly imposed tort liability for the defendant's infringement of the right to receive education, which is a constitutional right.[114]

L.F.] (June 29, 2020), https://mp.weixin.qq.com/s/jErlgnNCunmALuivRFnc3g [https://perma.cc/3DLQ-PDAL].

111 Ibid.

112 Ibid.

113 Ibid.

114 齐玉苓与陈晓琪等以侵犯姓名权的手段侵犯宪法保护的公民受教育的基本权利纠纷案 [Qi Yuling v. Chen Xiaoqi etc., Case of Infringement of the Constitutional Protection of the Basic Rights of Citizens to Education by Infringing the Right of Name] (2001) Sup. People's Ct. Gaz. 158 (Shandong Higher People's Ct. 2001). A large amount of scholarly attention has been devoted to this case, the significance of which has been compared to that of *Marbury* v. *Madison* in the United States because, before this case, the Chinese Constitution was not cited as a source of authority in China. See, e.g., Robert J. Morris, "China's Marbury: Qi Yuling v. Chen Xiaoqi – The Once and Future Trial of Both Education & Constitutionalization" (2010) 2 *Tsinghua China Law Review* 273, 274–75.

In this case, the plaintiff Qi went to junior high school with the defendant Chen.[115] Both graduated in 1990 and took the same entrance exam in order to further their education at a vocational business school, with a guaranteed job upon graduation provided that they graduate.[116] Qi did well and was supposed to receive the notice of admission from the business school; however, Chen, who did not do well, conspired with her father, along with the junior high school, to intercept Qi's notice of admission without Qi's knowledge, and they forged documents that would allow Chen to use Qi's name to attend the vocational school.[117] Chen subsequently attended this vocational business school under Qi's name.[118] Chen graduated and started working at the Bank of China's local branch – the guaranteed employment.[119] Qi, since graduation from junior high school, struggled to find stable employment and had to work temporary jobs in factories.[120] Qi then discovered the identity theft by chance in 1998.[121]

After Qi discovered the identity theft, she immediately sued in tort for violation of her right to her name as well as for violation of the right to receive an education.[122] It was argued that the right to receive education was not a civil right, and the trial court only allowed her to recover for violation of her right to her name.[123] On appeal, the Higher People's Court of Shandong Province petitioned to the Supreme People's Court for an interpretation of whether violation of a constitutional right can be remedied by imposing civil liability since the right to receive an education is not a right enumerated by the General Principles of the Civil Law.[124] In its reply, the Supreme People's Court expressly stated that the infringement of the plaintiff's constitutional right to receive an education

[115] See *Qi Yuling* (2001) Sup. People's Ct. Gaz. 158.
[116] Ibid.
[117] Ibid.
[118] Ibid.
[119] Ibid.
[120] Ibid.
[121] See ibid.
[122] See ibid.
[123] See ibid.
[124] 最高人民法院关于以侵犯姓名权的手段侵犯宪法保护的公民受教育的基本权利是否应承担民事责任的批复, 法释[2001]25号 [Reply on Whether the Accused Shall Bear Civil Liability for the Infringement of the Citizen's Fundamental Rights of Receiving Education under the Protection of the Constitution by Means of Infringing the Right of Name, Judicial Interpretation No. 25 (2001)] (promulgated by the Judicial Comm. Sup. People's Ct., June 28, 2001, effective August 13, 2001) (May 1, 2001) Sup. People's Ct. Gaz. 152 (abolished 2008), translated in *Qi Yuling* v. *Chen Xiaoqi et al.*: "Judicial

had resulted in the damage, and therefore, Chen and the other defendants were civilly liable.[125] As a result, not only did Qi recover losses arising out of the damage to the right to name, which included the tuition needed to repeat the junior high, but she was also entitled to the consequential economic loss, which included all the money Chen earned under Qi's name, along with the moral damage.[126]

The case of *Qi Yuling* proved that Chinese courts were able to expand the protection of rights outside a seemingly definite list of rights to be protected by tort law. However, it should be noted that the Supreme People's Court's interpretation just mentioned above was overturned in 2008 by a Supreme People's Court notice stating that this 2001 interpretation "discontinued to be applicable."[127] This controversial issue regarding the enforceability of constitutional rights in tort seems to have been clarified by Zhou Youjun, a drafter of the Code, who has stated that public law rights are not within the "civil interests" protected by tort law under article 1164,[128] which provides: "This Part adjusts the civil relations arising from the infringement upon civil rights and interests."[129] Still, it remains to be seen whether a new cluster of *Qi Yuling* cases will be litigated and what the personality rights law might contribute.

1.4.2 Change of Circumstances

Change of circumstances is a doctrine that excuses contractual performance when performance will not serve the purpose of the contract or will be excessively expensive. It is a relatively new doctrine in the European civil codes but is becoming an increasingly crucial one in the post-pandemic world. In both English[130] and American

Interpretation by the Supreme People's Court" (July/August 2006) *Chinese Education & Society* 58.

125 Ibid.

126 *Qi Yuling* (2001) Sup. People's Ct. Gaz. 158.

127 See关于废止2007年底以前发布的有关司法解释(第七批)的决定, 法释 (2008) 15号 [Decision on Abolishing Some Judicial Interpretations (the Seventh Batch) Issued Before the End of 2007, Judicial Interpretation No. 15 (2008)] (promulgated by the Judicial Comm. Sup. People's Ct., December 8, 2008, effective December 24, 2008) (February 1, 2009) Sup. People's Ct. Gaz. 7.

128 Youjun, "The Institutional Development of the Civil Code Book on Tort Liability."

129 "中华人民共和国民法典" ["Civil Code of the People's Republic of China"] (promulgated by the Nat'l People's Cong., May 28, 2020, effective January 1, 2021), art. 1164 (2020) *Standing Comm. Nat'l People's Cong. Gaz.* (Civil Code Special Issue) 2.

130 See, e.g., *Krell* v. *Henry* [1903] 2 KB 740 (EWCA) at 742–43 (English).

law,[131] there is a doctrine of frustration of purpose that excuses a performance when an underlying condition or basic assumption of the contract ceases to exist, which renders the performance useless to the receiving party. Additionally, in American law, there is an impracticability doctrine that excuses contractual liabilities when it has become excessively difficult to perform.[132] A similar doctrine, disturbance of basis of transaction, or *Störung der Geschäftsgrundlage*, was enacted into German law in 2002 in section 313 of the German Civil Code.[133] French law only adopted change of circumstances in 2016.[134] Chinese law first adopted the doctrine through a Supreme People's Court's judicial interpretation in 2009.[135] The Code formally adopts two articles in dealing with change of circumstances. The first, article 533, resembles section 313 of the German Civil Code in which relief is given when the basis of transaction (*Geschäftsgrundlage*) is destroyed due to the occurrence of a noncommercial risk.[136] The second, article 580, excuses the duty to perform but not liability for damages when the purpose of the contract is frustrated.[137]

As in German law, the non-breaching party is always entitled to demand performance.[138] Sometimes, the non-breaching party will demand performance even when the performance has become pointless to both parties. In *Xinyu Co.* v. *Feng Yumei Store*, Feng Yumei demanded the return of a twenty-two square-meter store that she had purchased from the developer of a mall after the developer reclaimed it because the developer had rebranded the whole mall (6,000 square meters) for a

131 See, e.g., Restatement (Second) of Contracts § 265 (Am. L. Inst. 1981).

132 Ibid., § 261.

133 BGB § 313, www.gesetze-im-internet.de/bgb/__313.html. Before 2002, German courts used good faith under German Civil Code section 242 to excuse performances that had become too costly. See Gordley et al., *An Introduction to the Comparative Study of Private Law*, pp. 256–63.

134 See Code civil art. 1195.

135 最高人民法院关于适用《中华人民共和国合同法》若干问题的解释(二), 法释〔2009〕5号 [Interpretation II of the Supreme People's Court of Several Issues concerning the Application of the Contract Law of the People's Republic of China, Judicial Interpretation No. 5 (2009)] (promulgated by the Judicial Comm. Sup. People's Ct., February 9, 2009, effective May 13, 2009), art. 26 (July 1, 2009) Sup. People's Ct. Gaz. 13 (abolished 2021).

136 "中华人民共和国民法典" ["Civil Code of the People's Republic of China"] (promulgated by the Nat'l People's Cong., May 28, 2020, effective Jan. 1, 2021), art. 533 (2020) *Standing Comm. Nat'l People's Cong. Gaz.* (Civil Code Special Issue) 2.

137 Ibid., art. 580.

138 See ibid., art. 577.

different line of business such that the store Feng Yumei had purchased could no longer exist.[139] The developer was willing to pay damages, but Feng Yumei insisted on performance.[140] The court held that performance could be excused and damages awarded.[141] Even though the plaintiff was, in principle, entitled to performance, requiring it would result in an obviously unfair outcome.[142] The Code, based on this case, adopted this common-law–inspired doctrine of frustration of purpose in article 580. Still, this new doctrine does not function in the same way as in the common law. In the common law, frustration of purpose would result in the termination of contract, and the non-performing party would no longer be required to pay damages. Here, article 580 only operates to excuse a party from a demand for specific performance but not from the liability for damages.[143]

The new law creates a unique scenario. When a performance becomes useless or simply excessively expensive, the adversely affected party will have two options: they could seek to terminate the contract under article 533, or, if that fails, they could have a second bite at the apple by asking to be excused from performing the contract and pay damages instead. Clear standards will need to be established to distinguish these situations.

1.4.3 *Unconscionability*

A doctrine like that of unconscionability might have found its way into Chinese law. More or less a dead doctrine in English law,[144]

139 新宇公司与冯玉梅商铺买卖合同纠纷案 [*Xinyu Co.* v. *Feng Yumei Store*, A Disp. Involving a Contract for the Sale of a Shop] (June 10, 2006) Sup. People's Ct. Gaz. 37 (Nanjing Interm. People's Ct. 2004).

140 Ibid.

141 Ibid.

142 Ibid.

143 Civil Code of the People's Republic of China art. 580 ("If either party to a contract fails to discharge non-pecuniary liabilities or fails to discharge non-pecuniary liabilities according to contractual agreements, the other party may request the discharge, except under any of the following circumstances: (1) Where the discharge is legally or practically impossible; (2) Where the subject matter of the liabilities is not suitable for compulsory discharge or too expensive for discharge; or (3) where the relevant creditor fails to demand the discharge within a reasonable period of time. If the purpose of a contract cannot be achieved due to one of the circumstances of exception as stated in the preceding paragraph, the people's court or the arbitration institution may terminate the rights and obligations relations under the contract at the request of the parties, but this does not affect the liability for breach of contract.").

144 See Gordley et al., *An Introduction to the Comparative Study of Private Law*, pp. 197–98.

unconscionability is widely used in America.[145] It requires both procedural unconscionability – or bargaining inequality – and substantive unconscionability – or gross disparity. Unconscionability will only set aside a contract when both conditions are met. This doctrine also has found its way into Chinese law.

With the promulgation of the General Principles of the Civil Law in 1986, Chinese law adopted two doctrines that remedy unfairness: "obvious unfair[ness]" (显示公平) and the "exploitation of his unfavorable position" (趁人之危).[146] Under article 54 of the 1999 Contract Law statute, both of these factors made a contract voidable.[147] According to the Supreme People's Court's opinion on the General Principles of the Civil Law, "obvious unfairness" requires both subjective unfairness and objective unfairness, a distinction like that drawn in the United States in discussions of the doctrine of unconscionability.[148] Subjective unfairness concerns what in American law is often called "procedural unconscionability": one party exploits its bargaining advantages over the other.[149] Objective unfairness concerns only the disparity (or gross disparity) between price and value, which is similar to what is often called "substantive unconscionability" in American law.[150] Therefore, the two

145 See ibid., pp. 198–99; see, e.g., Restatement (Second) of Contracts § 208, § 208 reporter's note cmt. a (Am. L. Inst. 1981).

146 "中华人民共和国民法通则" ["General Principles of the Civil Law of the People's Republic of China"] (promulgated by the Nat'l People's Congress, Apr. 12, 1986, effective Jan. 1, 1987), arts. 58-59 (repealed 2021), www.npc.gov.cn/wxzl/wxzl/2000-12/06/content_4470.htm [https://perma.cc/Y6X6–5N54]; see also Gordley et al., "An Introduction to the Comparative Study of Private Law," p. 216 (discussing the development and treatment of the two doctrines).

147 See "中华人民共和国合同法" ["Contract Law of People's Republic of China"] (promulgated by the Nat'l People's Congress, March 15, 1999, effective October 1, 1999), art. 54 (1999) *Standing Comm. Nat'l People's Cong. Gaz.* 104 (repealed 2021).

148 "最高人民法院印发" "关于贯彻执行〈中华人民共和国民法通则〉若干问题的意见（试行）" 的通知, 法[办]发[1988]6号 [Notice of the Supreme People's Court on Issuing the "Opinions on Several Issues Concerning the Implementation of the 'General Principles of the Civil Law of the People's Republic of China' (for Trial Implementation)," Law [Office] Fa [1988] No. 6 (promulgated by Adjudication Comm. Sup. People's Ct., January 26, 1988, effective April 2, 1988) (June 20, 1988) Sup. People's Ct. Gaz. 16, para. 72 (abolished 2021).

149 See Restatement (Second) of Contracts § 208 cmt. d; see also Opinions on Several Issues Concerning the Implementation of the "General Principles of the Civil Law of the People's Republic of China" para. 72 (requiring one party to take advantage of the other's lack of experience).

150 See Restatement (Second) of Contracts § 208 cmt. c; see also Opinions on Several Issues Concerning the Implementation of the "General Principles of the Civil Law of the

doctrines seem to overlap. The leading Chinese contract law scholar Han Shiyuan has claimed that, despite the Supreme People's Court's opinion, judges applying the doctrine of "obvious unfairness" continued to require only either substantive unfairness or objective unfairness.[151]

During my time teaching at City University of Hong Kong, I interviewed Chinese judges in order to assess their understanding of the doctrine. These interviews showed a slightly different picture. Overwhelmingly, judges only considered objective unfairness or the fairness of price in determining "obvious unfairness." In applying the doctrine of "exploitation of one's vulnerability," judges required both procedural unfairness and substantive unfairness. As a result, parties had the incentive to plead obvious unfairness, a doctrine that is more general. A stock purchase agreement was avoided when a party paid RMB 3.9 million yuan for 49 percent of the shares of a company that was not even worth RMB 100,000 yuan. The court concluded that the "unreasonably high price" is "conclusive evidence of obvious unfairness" although no exploitation or fraud was found.[152] This practice might remind us of German law. Normally, under German law, both exploitation and disparity would be required in invoking section 138 of the German Civil Code.[153] Nevertheless, if the substantive unfairness is severe, that alone might set aside the contract under section 138 for violation of good morals.[154] However, the law on this point has changed in China.

People's Republic of China" para. 72 (requiring the rights and obligations of the parties to violate principles of fairness and equal value compensation).

[151] Han Shiyuan (韩世远), 合同法总论 [*The Law of Contract*] (Beijing: 法律出版,2018) (4th ed.), p. 292.

[152] 佟旭、梁泽丰股权转让纠纷二审民事判决书 [Tong Xu, Liang Zefeng, a Civ. Judgment of the Second Instance in an Equity Transfer Disp.] (粤01民终23863号) [Guandong 01 Min Zhong No. 23863] (Guangzhou Interm. People's Ct. March 16, 2018).

[153] BGB § 138, www.gesetze-im-internet.de/bgb/__138.html ("(1) A legal transaction which is contrary to public policy is void. (2) In particular, a legal transaction is void by which a person, by exploiting the predicament, inexperience, lack of sound judgment or considerable weakness of will of another, causes himself or a third party, in exchange for an act of performance, to be promised or granted pecuniary advantages which are clearly disproportionate to the performance.").

[154] For example, section 138 was triggered when a loan interest was set at a rate (45 percent) that was beyond all reasonable measure, even when there was no exploitation. It offended good morals or public policy because "an acceptance of it ha[d] an unhealthy influence on the capital market and also create[d] the danger of causing the financial collapse of the debtor." Bundesgerichtshof [BGH] [Federal Court of Justice], November 9, 1961, (1962) *Neue Juristische Wochenschrift [NJW]* 483 (German), as translated in Gordley et al., "An Introduction to the Comparative Study of Private Law," p. 209. The

In 2017, the General Provisions of Civil Law (now incorporated into the Code as the book General Provisions) merged the two doctrines into one called the doctrine of "obvious unfairness."[155] "Obvious unfairness" makes a contract voidable. It appears that both procedural unfairness (exploitation) and substantive unfairness (significant imbalance or gross disparity) are necessary to establish "obvious unfairness." Article 151 of the Code provides: "If one party exploits the other party's unfavorable or perilous position and lack of good judgment or other circumstances, resulting in a grossly unfair civil juristic act from its initiation, the injured party shall be entitled to apply with the people's court or arbitration agency to rescind the act."[156] But whether the change in the General Provisions will lead to a change in practice has yet to be seen. Han Shiyuan expects relief for "obvious unfairness" will still be given for substantive unfairness, which will depend on an objective standard.[157] According to Han Shiyuan, however, to give relief on that basis is a mistake.[158] He believes that Chinese law should be primarily concerned with relief for procedural unfairness.[159] In his view, to give relief for substantive unfairness through such doctrines as obvious unfairness and change of circumstances circumvents party autonomy and the principle

Reich Court of Justice had previously explained the use of section 138 requires both disproportion and offensiveness of the terms. Reichsgericht [RG] [Reich Court of Justice], March 31, 1936, 150 *RGZ* 1, as translated in Gordley et al., "An Introduction to the Comparative Study of Private Law," p. 205. ("A juristic act (*Rechtsgeschäft*) in which performance and counterperformance are strikingly disproportionate but in which the remaining elements of usury (§ 138, par. 2) are not present is invalid under § 138, par. 1 when, in addition to the disproportion, the party claiming the disproportionate advantage exhibits such a character that the juristic act, given its content, motive, and purpose, offends [good morals (*gute Sitten*)]. Under some circumstances, such a character may be inferred from the dis-proportion.").

155 "中华人民共和国民法典" ["Civil Code of the People's Republic of China"] (promulgated by the Nat'l People's Cong., May 28, 2020, effective January 1, 2021), art. 151 (2020) *Standing Comm. Nat'l People's Cong. Gaz.* (Civil Code Special Issue) 2; "中华人民共和国民法总则" ["General Provisions of the Civil Law of the People's Republic of China"] (promulgated by the Nat'l People's Congress, March 15, 2017, effective October 1, 2017), art. 151 (2017) *Standing Comm. Nat'l People's Cong. Gaz.* 191 (repealed 2021); see also Gordley et al., "An Introduction to the Comparative Study of Private Law," p. 216 (discussing the changes implemented by the General Provisions).

156 Civil Code of the People's Republic of China art. 151.

157 Han Shiyuan, *The Law of Contract*, p. 52; see also Gordley et al., *An Introduction to the Comparative Study of Private Law*, p. 216 (discussing Han Shiyuan's views on the new doctrine of obvious unfairness).

158 Han Shiyuan, *The Law of Contract*, p. 52.

159 Ibid.

of *pacta sunt servanda.*[160] Consequently, relief should be given only under exceptional circumstances.[161]

1.4.4 Effect-to-Be-Determined Contracts

The Code has filled certain legal vacuums. There is a class of otherwise properly formed contracts that do not have legal effect until a legal requirement is met.[162] Such contracts are called effect-to-be-determined contracts. They are to be distinguished from conditional contracts. In a conditional contract, both parties have the full capacity to contract and decided to subject the contract to a condition precedent.[163] Such a contract is binding from the moment that it is concluded. In contrast, effect-to-be-determined contracts are subject to the satisfaction of a condition required by law, without which there will be no legally binding contract.[164]

This type of contract often took the form of a Sino-foreign joint venture agreement. Traditionally, a joint venture agreement that involves a foreign party needed to be approved by state authority.[165] As a result, a contract that requires state approval will have no legal effect until such approval is obtained. In such contracts, there will normally be a clause that assigns the domestic party the obligation of obtaining such approval. The domestic party that has second thoughts would technically not be able to default on their contractual obligations since there is not yet a contract. Previously, this issue could only be resolved by case law. In a well-known 2009 Supreme People's Court case, the court held that parties are still bound by the contractual obligations to seek approval;

[160] Ibid.

[161] Ibid., p. 53.

[162] "中华人民共和国合同法" ["Contract Law of People's Republic of China"] (promulgated by the Nat'l People's Congress, March 15, 1999, effective October 1, 1999), arts. 47–48 (1999) *Standing Comm. Nat'l People's Cong. Gaz.* 104 (repealed 2021).

[163] See ibid., art. 45; see also Mo Zhang, *Chinese Contract Law: Theory & Practice* (2nd ed. 2019) (Leiden: Brill Nijdhoff), p. 195 (distinguishing conditions on the performance of a contract from conditions on the validity of a contract).

[164] See Zhang, "Chinese Contract Law," pp. 154–56, 185–86.

[165] "中华人民共和国中外合资经营企业法" ["Law of the People's Republic of China on Chinese-Foreign Joint Ventures"] (promulgated by the Nat'l People's Congress, July 1, 1979, as amended by the Nat'l People's Congress, September 3, 2016, effective October 1, 2016), art. 3 (repealed 2020), www.npc.gov.cn/zgrdw/npc/xinwen/2016-09/06/content_1997113.htm [https://perma.cc/8FTY-MUER].

such terms are binding even though contract itself is not yet effective.[166] Since January 1, 2020, the new Foreign Investment Law dropped state approval as a general requirement for Sino-foreign joint ventures.[167] Still, state approval is required for a joint venture to conduct business in a restricted industry or an industry that requires licensing,[168] so the same issue of when parties are bound is still relevant. To solve this issue, the Code has adopted the Supreme People's Court's approach in article 502.[169] According to article 502, a party can sue for breach of contract if the duty to seek approval is breached by the other party, even though the contract is not yet effective.[170] However, this could lead to a doctrinal difficulty, where contractual liability can be imposed when there has not been a contract.

1.4.5 Pure Economic Loss

Clarifications are needed in some key areas of the civil law. The most prominent one is the scope of protected interests in tort law. Every tort law system has to deal with a fundamental question: Are all legal rights to be protected by tort law? If one only looks at the wording of civil codes, one might be under the impression that there are tort law systems that protect all legal rights from being infringed, while other systems only protect a select list of rights enumerated in the civil code. Examples of these two positions can be found in the French and German civil codes. The French Civil Code provides:

> Any human action whatsoever which causes harm to another creates an obligation in the person by whose fault it occurred to make reparation for it . . .. Everyone is liable for harm which he has caused not only by his action, but also by his failure to act or his lack of care.[171]

[166] 广州市仙源房地产股份有限公司与广东中大中鑫投资策划有限公司、广州远兴房产有限公司、中国投资集团国际理财有限公司股权转让纠纷案 [*Guangzhou Xianyuan Real Estate Co., Ltd.* v. *Guangdong Zhongda Zhongxin Inv. Plan. Co., Ltd., Guangzhou Yuanxing Real Estate Co., Ltd., & China Inv. Grp. Int'l Fin. Mgmt. Co., Ltd.*] (August 1, 2010) Sup. People's Ct. Gaz. 27 (Sup. People's Ct. 2009).

[167] See "中华人民共和国外商投资法" ["Foreign Investment Law of the People's Republic of China"] (promulgated by the Nat'l People's Cong., March 15, 2019, effective January 1, 2020) (2019) *Standing Comm. Nat'l People's Cong. Gaz.* 348.

[168] See ibid., arts. 28–30.

[169] "中华人民共和国民法典" ["Civil Code of the People's Republic of China"] (promulgated by the Nat'l People's Cong., May 28, 2020, effective January 1, 2021), art. 502 (2020) *Standing Comm. Nat'l People's Cong. Gaz.* (Civil Code Special Issue) 2.

[170] Ibid.

[171] Code civil arts. 1240–41.

On the other extreme, the German Civil Code is very specific about the scope of rights protected. Section 823 provides: "A person who, intentionally or negligently, unlawfully injures the life, body, health, freedom, property or another right of another person is liable to make compensation to the other party for the damage arising from this."[172]

Strangely, the prior Chinese law, in TLL article 2 and article 6, appeared to have adopted both positions.[173] In the previous TLL, a German-inspired article 2 enumerated the list of rights protected under tort law,[174] and a French-inspired article 6 protected all civil interests.[175] The new Code has dropped article 2 and maintained article 6 (now Code article 1165),[176] seemingly endorsing the French approach. However, several drafters have confirmed that the law has not changed and that the civil interests protected include all those covered previously in article 2.[177] Others say that the term "civil interest" is to be "interpreted broadly and creatively by the judiciary."[178]

This leaves open an important question: whether pure economic loss will be remedied under the new Code. Pure economic harm is not a violation of an absolute right and is excluded from the enumerated list in German Civil Code section 823 and the Chinese TLL article 2,[179] but pure economic loss could still fall within the scope of civil interests in the new Code depending on how it is interpreted. Wang Liming, the principal drafter, gave a very confusing interpretation. He takes the German

172 BGB § 823, www.gesetze-im-internet.de/bgb/__823.html.

173 "中华人民共和国侵权责任法" ["Tort Liability Law of the People's Republic of China"] (promulgated by the Standing Comm. Nat'l People's Cong., December 26, 2009, effective July 1, 2010), arts. 2, 6 (2010) *Standing Comm. Nat'l People's Cong. Gaz.* 4 (repealed 2021).

174 Ibid., art. 2 ("For the purpose of this Law, 'civil rights and interests' refer to personal and property rights, including, inter alia, the right to life, right to health, right of name, right of reputation, right of honor, portraiture right, right to privacy, autonomy in marriage, guardianship, ownership, usufruct, security interest in property, copyright, patent, right to exclusive use of trademarks, right of discovery, equity interest and right of inheritance.").

175 Ibid., art. 6 ("The actor infringing upon civil rights and interests of others by fault shall assume tort liability.").

176 See "中华人民共和国民法典" ["Civil Code of the People's Republic of China"] (promulgated by the Nat'l People's Cong., May 28, 2020, effective January 1, 2021), art. 1165 (2020) *Standing Comm. Nat'l People's Cong. Gaz.* (Civil Code Special Issue) 2 ("The actor infringing upon civil rights and interests of others by fault and causing damage shall assume tort liability.").

177 Youjun, "The Institutional Development of the Civil Code Book on Tort Liability."

178 Email from Meng Qiang, June 11.

179 See BGB § 823 (German); Tort Liability Law of the People's Republic of China art. 2.

view that pure economic harm is not a violation of an absolute right that is protected under tort law; however, under exceptional circumstances, the loss can be remedied when it is foreseeable and when the damage is certain.[180] The same reasoning has been adopted by French courts when deciding whether recovery should be allowed for pure economic loss even though recovery is not barred by articles 1240 and 1241.[181] It almost looks like the nature of the harm does not matter. Physical or not, recovery is permitted so long as causation and damage can be proved.

The doctrinal uncertainty leads to confusion in practice, as virtually no judges are aware of the exclusionary rule for pure economic loss. I interviewed twenty-seven elite Chinese judges enrolled in the master and doctoral programs at City University of Hong Kong.[182] It was clear that even when the German approach was in the law, it never stopped the judges from awarding damages for pure economic loss, as in France. Overwhelmingly, with the exception of four judges, they either did not appreciate why the law should only protect the rights of property and person, or they considered economic rights part of a property right. For the judges who recognize pure economic harm, they do not know whether economic rights shall be protected by law, or they only recognize pure economic harm in one scenario and ignore the limitation in others. Not a single judge was able to identify pure economic loss in a survey I gave of four hypothetical cases. Overwhelmingly, judges would allow parties to recover from pure economic loss, citing article 6 instead of article 2.

A survey of the case law confirms my impression that judges do not understand pure economic loss. In the past decade, close to a hundred cases can be found where courts identified the issue of pure economic loss; however, less than half a dozen of them did so correctly.[183] Others

[180] Wang Liming et al., *Textbook on the Tort Liability Law of China*, at 60–63.

[181] See Cass. 2e civ., June 12, 1987, Bull. civ. II, No. 128 (denying recovery for pure economic loss when a man who was about to close a deal was injured, causing the deal to go sour, because the loss was "hypothetical"); Cass. 2e civ., February 21, 1979, Bull. civ. II, No. 56 (denying recovery for pure economic loss when both debtors were killed in an accident and the creditor could not collect the debt because the loss was "not ... direct").

[182] The transcripts of the interviews are on file with the author.

[183] See, e.g., 北京市天奇伟业市政工程有限公司与北京市南苑植物油厂财产损害赔偿纠纷二审民事判决书 [*Beijing Tianqi Weiye Mun. Eng'g Co., Ltd.* v. *Beijing Nanyuan Vegetable Oil Factory*, Civil Judgment of the Second Instance of a Prop. Damage Comp. Disp.], (2018) Jing 02 Min Zhong 4810 Hao (2018) 京02民终4810号) [(2018) Beijing 02 Min Zhong No. 4810] (Beijing Second Interm. People's Ct. May 31, 2018) Yuehua,

confused pure economic loss with physical loss or unforeseeable harm or mistakenly think that pure economic loss is recoverable.[184]

1.4.6 Communitarian Value

The prevailing view of property rights in the West is that such rights are absolute and exclusive.[185] Such a view is not accurate and does not explain doctrines such as nuisance and necessity. On the other hand, Chinese law reflects a different, communitarian value.[186] According to this value, property rights come with obligations and responsibilities that one cannot do away with. Lei Chen gave two good examples of how such values are implemented through distinct property doctrines in Chinese law.[187] One is rural collective landownership. In contrast with state ownership of land, village collectives own rural land.[188] The land use right to it can only be possessed by peasant families.[189] Neither the collective ownership of land nor the family-based land use right is absolute.[190] These rights are very limited but serve the purpose of ensuring every family will have the land for farming and housing.

The second example is the right of neighbors who allow owners of one neighboring property to cross over another for the use of "water,

First Instance Civ. Judgment on Tort Liab. Disp.], (2017) Yue 0224 Min Chu 615 Hao ([2017] 粤0224民初615号) [(2017) Guangdong 0224 Min Chu No. 615] (Renhua Dist. People's Ct. Apr. 13, 2018) (Bashou Anli (把手案例) [Lawsdata.com], Caipan Wenshu (裁判文书) [Judgment Documents]).

184 For example, the courts might think loss of profit due to property damage is a pure economic loss. See 中国人民财产保险股份有限公司唐山市分公司与鞠振华、唐山市路南合鑫货运有限公司等机动车交通事故责任纠纷二审民事判决书 [*People's Ins. Co. of China Tangshan Branch* v. *Ju Zhenhua, Tangshan Lunan Hexin Feight Co., Ltd.*, Second-instance Civ. Judgment for Liab. Disp. Over Motor Vehicle Traffic Accident], (2017) Jing Min Zhong 792 Hao ([2017] 京民终792号) [(2017)Jing Min Zhong No. 792] (Beijing Higher People's Ct. December 29, 2017).

185 Gordley et al., *An Introduction to the Comparative Study of Private Law*, p. 580.

186 Lei Chen, "Private Property with Chinese Characteristics: A Critical Analysis of the Chinese Law on Property of 2007" (2010) 18 *European Review of Private Law* 983, 995.

187 Ibid., pp. 995–97.

188 See "中华人民共和国土地管理法" ["Land Administration Law of the People's Republic of China"] (promulgated by the Standing Comm. Nat'l People's Cong., June 25, 1986, as amended by the Standing Comm. Nat'l People's Congress, August 26, 2019, effective Jan. 1, 2020), art. 9 (2019) *Standing Comm. Nat'l People's Cong. Gaz.* 805.

189 See ibid., arts. 9–10, 13; Chen, "Private Property with Chinese Characteristics," p. 996.

190 Chen, "Private Property with Chinese Characteristics," p. 996; see Land Administration Law of the People's Republic of China, arts. 9–10.

drainage, ventilation, utility service, electricity cable, sunlight, or access."[191] Unlike the doctrine of necessity, the exercise of this right does not depend upon the presence of an emergency.[192] Therefore, it covers rights that are wider in scope than the more restricted ones of a servitude or easement. So long as a community good can be established, neighbors can easily exercise this right on another's property without the consent of the land use right holder.

1.5 Chinese Traditional Values

1.5.1 Liability in Equity

In a country that has been run by its own set of social norms that were guided by imperial law and Confucianism for thousands of years, the legitimacy of the foreign laws imposed by political elites cannot be gained overnight. It is not surprising that certain rules that reflect traditional Chinese moral philosophy have become part of the modern law. Liability in equity is one prime example. Article 1186 of the Code provides for a liability without fault.[193] It states: "If the damage is through no fault of both the victim and the tortfeasor, the loss may be borne by both parties according to the law."[194] Under this rule, the defendant who is not at fault for causing a harm can be liable for a partial loss suffered by the victim. The defendant may be liable if the defendant has the financial capacity to pay and if the court deems it appropriate. The award of such damages is discretionary. This rule was originally a legal transplant from article 406 of the 1922 Russian Civil Code.[195] In contrast to its

[191] See Chen, "Private Property with Chinese Characteristics," p. 996; see also "中华人民共和国民法典" ["Civil Code of the People's Republic of China"] (promulgated by the Nat'l People's Cong., May 28, 2020, effective January 1, 2021), arts. 290–92 (2020) *Standing Comm. Nat'l People's Cong. Gaz.* (Civil Code Special Issue) 2 (granting these rights).

[192] See Chen, "Private Property with Chinese Characteristics," pp. 996–97; see also Civil Code of the People's Republic of China arts. 290–92 (granting these rights on the basis of neighborly need, not an emergency).

[193] Civil Code of the People's Republic of China art. 1186.

[194] Ibid.

[195] Grazhdanskiy Kodeks RSFSR 1922 Goda [Civil Code of the RSFSR of 1922], Izvestiia Vserossiĭskogo Tsentral'nogo Ispolnitel'nogo Komiteta Sovetov Rabochikh, Soldatskikh i Krest'ianskikh Deputatov [Izv. vTsIK] [Bulletin of the All-Russian Central Executive Committee of the Councils of Workers', Soldiers', and Peasants' Deputies], November 12, 1922, No. 256, art. 406 (repealed 1964), translated in Vladimir Gsovski, "Soviet Civil Law: Private Rights and Their Back-Ground under the Soviet Regime" (1948), pp. 15, 209.

widespread use in China, its application in Russian law was rare and confined to exceptional cases. As Vladimir Gsovski observed:

> Section 406 may apply only in exceptional cases where, in view of the property status of the defendant as compared with that of the plaintiff, it would appear extremely unjust to impose upon the person injured damage caused by the defendant. The court may in such cases impose upon the defendant the full damage or part of it.[196]

He further explained that, in imposing this liability, the Russian Supreme Court held that causation was essential and exempted the government from the application of the rule for the obvious reason that the government is always the deeper pocket.[197] The deeper resonance of this rule with Chinese traditional moral philosophy might explain its wide recognition in China.

The fault liability regime is a reflection of commutative justice, while liability in equity is a liability based on distributive justice – the foundation of the traditional Chinese legal system.[198] Commutative justice, which holds one person liable for the harm they cause another, depends on the objective, reasonable person standard and duty of care to determine whether they are liable.[199] In traditional China, the duty to compensate another depended on one's status as a property owner.[200] The idea was to share the loss evenly. As a result, negligence and fault sometimes became irrelevant in determining liability.

On the other hand, parties' social statuses became a factor in determining liability. Aiding the weak and restraining the strong has always been recognized as a sound governance policy in both governing the country and adjudicating cases. Even for robbers, robbing the rich to aid the needy (劫富济贫) was popularly considered heroic and

[196] Gsovski, "Soviet Civil Law," p. 527 (translating M. M. Agarkov et al., *Uchebnik Grazhdanskogo Prava* [*Civil Law Textbook*] [1938] 406).

[197] Ibid., pp. 527–28.

[198] See note 24 and accompanying text.

[199] See Gordley et al., *An Introduction to the Comparative Study of Private Law*, p. 519; Aristotle, *Nicomachean Ethics*, pp. 72–73.

[200] See Deng Feng, "Corrective Justice in Confucian Legal Tradition: A Nonexistent Concept" 5 (undated) (unpublished manuscript), www.lawschool.cornell.edu/international/clarke_program/conferences/upload/DengFeng.pdf [https://web.archive.org/web/20180619094229/lawschool.cornell.edu/international/clarke_program/conferences/upload/dengfeng.pdf].

commendable behavior for outlaws.[201] In the chapter on the law of punishment in the *Book of Han* (汉书), a leading historical account of the Western Han Dynasty, it was pointed out that a sound governance policy should suppress the strong and support the weak (抑彊扶弱).[202] Hai Rui, perhaps the most well-known judge in imperial China, commented on this philosophy in adjudicating cases that were not otherwise determinable:

> I suggest that in returning verdicts to those cases it is better to rule against the younger brother rather than the older brother, against the nephew rather than the uncle, against the rich rather than the poor, and against the stubbornly cunning rather than against the clumsily honest. If the case involves a property dispute, it is better to rule against a member of the gentry rather than the commoner so as to provide relief to the weaker side. But if the case has to do with courtesy and status, it is better to rule against the commoner rather than against the gentry: the purpose is to maintain our order and system.[203]

Where a harm that is not subject to strict liability is suffered but neither party was at fault, there would be no recovery in Western tort law. However, letting a victim bear the entire damage has never been the solution preferred by the distributive justice system embraced in China. Distributive justice promotes the even distribution of losses.[204] But what are the policy benefits in advancing distributive justice? Confucius gave the strong argument that "a family does not worry that it has little but that that little is unevenly apportioned [不患贫，而患不均].... Because with equitable distribution there is no real poverty [均无贫] ...."[205]

However, drafters are afraid that this rule is subject to abuse. They fear that judges will see this rule as an easy way out and find liability when other elements of a tort are not present. In a recent case, a doctor warned

[201] See Jie Fu Jipin (劫富济贫), "Rob the Rich and Help the Poor" ("在线新华字典") [Online Xinhua Dictionary], http://xh.5156edu.com/html5/276606.html [https://perma.cc/SKF2-2QFJ] (explaining that it is considered a positive term). Other similar variations of the phrase include "kill the rich and help the poor ("杀富济贫"), ibid.

[202] See Ban Gu (班固), Han Shu, *Xinfa Zhi* (*汉书: 刑法志*) [*Book of Han: Treatise on Punishment and Law*] (c. 36–111 CE).

[203] Ray Huang, *1587: A Year of No Significance: The Ming Dynasty in Decline* (New Haven: Yale University Press, 1981), p. 131 (translating Hai Rui (海瑞), 海瑞集 [*Hai Rui Collection*] in Chen Yizhong (陳義鍾) (ed.) (1962), p. 117.

[204] See Gordley et al., *An Introduction to the Comparative Study of Private Law*, p. 519; Aristotle, *Nicomachean Ethics*, pp. 71–74.

[205] See Confucius, *The Analects of Confucius* (Burton Watson trans.) (New York: Columbia University Press, 2007), p. 115 (c. 475–221 BCE).

a sixty-nine-year-old man not to smoke in the elevator, and a quarrel between the two resulted.[206] Ten minutes later, the old man died of heart attack. The doctor was sued for wrongful death. The trial court ruled that the doctor was not at fault and yet was partially liable based on liability in equity. The appellate court overruled the decision and held that the doctor was not liable because there was no causation.[207] This case caused widespread concern,[208] and its ripple effect led to a minor legislative change.

As a warning sign, the Code changed the wording of the article on liability in equity from imposing liability based on "actual circumstance" in the old TLL[209] to "according to law" in the new Code.[210] Supposedly, this change means that even though fault is not required, other elements requisite in finding liability are still needed.[211]

1.5.2 Duty to Act

What happens when the law clashes with Chinese traditional moral values such as treating the young and the elderly as your own and helping people in need? In China, it appears, as we will see in the following case, that when lawmakers see that the traditional values are in danger, the law is changed to protect them. As a result – paradoxically, it would seem – there is now no duty to act in Chinese law; if you act to rescue people in need, you are immune from liability.

206 田九菊、杨帆生命权、健康权、身体权纠纷二审民事判决书 [Tian Jiuju, Yanf Fan, Second-instance Civ. Judgments for Disps. over the Right to Life, Health, and Physical Rights] (2017) Yu 01 Min Zhong 14848 Hao ([2017] 豫01民终14848号) [(2017) Henan 01 Min Zhong No. 14848] (Zhengzhou Interm. People's Ct. January 12, 2018).

207 Ibid.

208 See, e.g., Yu Zhong (喻中), "人民日报：劝阻不当行为值得鼓励" ["People's Daily: Discourage Misconduct Deserve Encouragement"], *Renmin Wang* (人民网) (*People's Daily Online*) (January 24, 2018), http://opinion.people.com.cn/n1/2018/0124/c1003-29782419.html [https://perma.cc/5Z2Q-4MRR].

209 "中华人民共和国侵权责任法" ["Tort Liability Law of the People's Republic of China"] (promulgated by the Standing Comm. Nat'l People's Cong., December 26, 2009, effective July 1, 2010), art. 24 (2010) *Standing Comm. Nat'l People's Cong. Gaz.* 4 (repealed 2021).

210 "中华人民共和国民法典" ["Civil Code of the People's Republic of China"] (promulgated by the Nat'l People's Cong., May 28, 2020, effective January 1, 2021), art. 1186 (2020) *Standing Comm. Nat'l People's Cong. Gaz.* (Civil Code Special Issue) 2.

211 This position was confirmed by the author's discussions with one of the drafters, Meng Qiang, at an online conference hosted by City University of Hong Kong on June 8, 2020.

The case of Peng Yu[212] is well-known to every Chinese person thanks to the judge's elaborate factual and legal reasoning in finding liability in equity in a way that offended the traditional moral values of respecting the old and being a Good Samaritan when needed.

In 2006, Ms. Xu, a senior, was knocked over while trying to board a bus by someone getting off the bus. It was alleged that she was lying on the ground until Peng Yu, a twenty-six-year-old man who had just got off the bus, helped her up and took her to the hospital along with her family. At the hospital, Mr. Peng gave Ms. Xu RMB 200 yuan. Ms. Xu was diagnosed with a fracture in her left thigh bone and was hospitalized. She underwent hip replacement surgery. Later, Ms. Xu sued Mr. Peng for personal injury, including medical expenses, nursing fees, and nutrition fees, along with moral damages for her mental distress. She alleged that Mr. Peng was the person who knocked her down. Media attention was not drawn to the case until the end of the second session of the trial when Mr. Peng contacted the media arguing that he was a Good Samaritan who voluntarily helped Ms. Xu.[213] However, the court noted that Peng Yu did not mention this fact as a defense until that very moment.[214] However, the trial drew national attention and widespread criticism. The existence of the litigation itself offended the traditional Chinese virtues of being a Good Samaritan when help is needed, of respecting old members of society, and of aiding the needy. The public feared that, if the rescued were allowed to sue their rescuers for damages, nobody would assist others when in need.[215] A second wave of public anger was triggered when the presiding judge, in applying liability in equity, awarded Ms. Xu 40 percent of the physical injury.[216] Moral damages were denied as they could not be claimed under liability in equity.[217] Commentators were of the view that this "single most idiotic opinion in history written by the

[212] 徐XX诉彭宇人身损害赔偿纠纷案 [*Xu XX* v. *Peng Yu*, Pers. Injury Comp. Disp. Case], (2007) Gu Min Yu Chu Zi Di 212 Hao ([2007] 鼓民一初字第212号) [(2007) Gu Min Yi Chu Zi No. 212] (Gulou Dist. People's Ct. of Nanjing September 3, 2007).

[213] See, e.g., Nanfang Wang (南方网) [S. Net], "男子称扶摔倒老太反被告 被判赔4万(图)" [" Man Said He Helped the Fallen Old Lady Against the Defendant and was Sentenced to 40,000 (photos)"], Wangyi Xinwen (网易新闻) [*NetEase News*] (Septembe 6, 2007, 5:24 a.m.), http://news.163.com/07/0906/05/3NMDBNR600011229.html [https://web.archive.org/web/20150929222444/http://news.163.com/07/0906/05/3NMDBNR600011229.html].

[214] *Peng Yu* (2007) Gu Min Yi Chu Zi No. 212.

[215] See, e.g., Wang [S. Net].

[216] See Peng Yu (2007) Gu Min Yi Chu Zi No. 212; see, e.g., Wang [S. Net].

[217] Peng Yu (2007) Gu Min Yi Chu Zi No. 212.

judge sabotaged the moral virtues and civilization that have been upheld in China for five thousand years and led good human nature to evilness."[218]

The popular rejection of the result derived mainly from the fact that the judge applied common sense to exclude the possibility that the defendant sent the victim to the hospital and paid her medical expenses without having been involved in the accident. According to the judge, in contemporary Chinese society, no person of good heart would have sent an injured person whom he did not know to the hospital and paid the medical expenses out of his own pocket without having caused the injury. The judge reasoned:

> According to [the] defendant's statement, he was the first getting off the bus; as a matter of common sense, it is more likely that he was the one who collided with the plaintiff.
>
> If the defendant was simply being a Good Samaritan, he should have caught the actual tortfeasor rather than just helped the defendant up. Also, the defendant should have let the plaintiff's family take her to the hospital. It was not necessary for him to go to the hospital with the victim. What the defendant did was not consistent with the common sense of being a Good Samaritan.[219]

It was this "commonsense" judgment by the judge that triggered the anger of the public. Even though the socioeconomic situation has changed significantly from the time of the imperial dynasties, the public chose to believe that in modern Chinese society there are still helpers who adhere to Confucian teaching and who are willing to go out of their way to help those in need.

The court correctly found that none of the parties were at fault.[220] It also held that Peng caused the fall of Xu and, therefore, should be responsible for 40 percent of the damage according to the principle of liability in equity.[221]

In passing judgment over the collision between the two, the court applied the preponderance of evidence standard and denied the Good Samaritan argument. Among the facts the court considered were Peng's

[218] Shi Hanbing (时寒冰), "Most Idiotic Judgment in History Will Lead Human Nature To Evil," *Souhu: Shi Hanbing* (搜狐:时寒冰) (September 6, 2007, 7:27 p.m.), http://shihb.blog.sohu.com/62983452.html [https://perma.cc/N5U7-JVUU].

[219] See Peng Yu (2007) Gu Min Yi Chu Zi No. 212.

[220] See ibid.

[221] See ibid.

previous police statement admitting the collision between the two and denying that he knocked Xu down, the undisputed fact that Peng gave Xu RMB 200 yuan, and the fact that Peng did not bring the Good Samaritan defense until the second session of the trial. Peng's statement to the police and the fact that he gave her RMB 200 yuan were clearly more persuasive and reliable indicators of the collision between the two than the Good Samaritan defense that was not brought up in the first place. Whenever there is preponderance of evidence in proving the causation of the loss in the absence of fault, the liability in equity under the fairness principle is the appropriate forum to remedy such damage under the law. It was well within the judge's wide discretion in awarding damage in liability in equity cases according to the property statuses of the parties.[222]

Both parties appealed the decision, and an angry public demanded a retrial.[223] As a result, some high-ranking provincial government officials were said to be involved in the case, and eventually, the case was settled under mediation in the appeal.[224] The government reported to the public that the case had been peacefully resolved.[225]

After this incident, according to a survey conducted in 2013, 84.9 percent of the public responded that they would be hesitant to help a fallen elder.[226] In 2017, the Supreme People's Court in an official blog post sought to set the record straight and restore the public confidence in the judicial system.[227] According to the post, Peng Yu admitted that he

222 See Liming et al., *Textbook on the Tort Liability Law of China*, p. 175.

223 Hanbing, "Most Idiotic Judgment."

224 Qi Ming (亓鸣), "彭宇案"和谐"解决" ["Peng Yu Case Resolved 'Harmoniously'"], 瞭望东方周刊 [*Oriental Outlook Weekly*] (April 11, 2008), www.lwdf.cn/oriental/community/20080306112758706.htm [https://web.archive.org/web/20100325233353/http://www.lwdf.cn/oriental/community/20080306112758706.htm].

225 Cui Tong (崔彤), "质疑彭宇案秘密和解" ["Questioning the Settlement of the Peng Yu Case"], Zhong Guang Wang (中广网) [China Broadcasting Network] (March 17, 2008), www.cnr.cn/luntan/sytt/200803/t20080317_504737680.html [https://perma.cc/Y4DW-MULN].

226 Xing Nan (向楠) and Tang Lingyue (倘凌越), "84.9% 公众坦言扶不扶老人很纠结" ["84.9% of the Public Frankly Said That They Are Struggling to Support the Elderly"], *Zhong Qing Bao Xi* (中青报系) [*China Youth Daily*] (December 10, 2013), http://zqb.cyol.com/html/2013-12/10/nw.D110000zgqnb_20131210_2-07.htm [https://perma.cc/V97K-HCCX].

227 最高人民法院 [Sup. People's Ct.], "十年前彭宇案的真相是什么?" ["What Is the Truth About Peng Yu's Case Ten Years Ago?"], Weibo (微博) [*Weibo*] (June 15, 2017, 9:24 a.m.), www.weibo.com/3908755088/F7TWtpb3w?type=comment#_rnd1566948447042 [https://perma.cc/J4C2-6SWK].

was actually the person who injured the old lady by knocking her over. Those facts were supported by a police statement. The Supreme People's Court implored the public to restore the vanishing traditional value and to help people in need. Still, to deter victims from making false allegations toward the rescuer, the 2017 General Provisions of Civil Law exempted rescuers from liability even when they acted with gross negligence.[228] The Code adopted this rule in article 184, which provides: "Whoever voluntarily takes emergency rescue measures and causes losses to the party being rescued shall not bear any civil liability."[229]

1.6 Conclusion

The enactment of the Chinese Civil Code is groundbreaking, and much is to be expected from it. Still, the big question remains whether the codification solves some fundamental problems in Chinese private law that cannot be adequately addressed by legislative techniques.

The major problem of applying contract law to SOEs lies in the lack of competitiveness of the market conditions in which SOEs operate. The incentive incompatibility and information asymmetry between the managers of SOEs and the State led to the dilemma in policy: to allow full contractual autonomy and encourage self-dealing and stripping of state assets or to deny autonomy and stop using market information as the yardstick for corporate governance. Clearly, China has taken the first route. My view is that the solution to such problems requires a structural change in the Chinese economy that normalizes the status of SOEs as market players subject to normal market risks and competitions.

The Code's doctrinal innovations require clarifications from the courts and academia. The internal contradiction between article 2 and article 6 of TLL regarding the scope of rights protected by tort law could have been avoided had the drafters and the legal profession understood the structures they borrowed from French and German tort systems. On its face, the new Code solved this problem by dropping the list of enumerated rights, but it only seems more urgent to clarify the scope of "civil

[228] See "中华人民共和国民法总则" ["General Provisions of the Civil Law of the People's Republic of China"] (promulgated by the Nat'l People's Congress, March 15, 2017, effective October 1, 2017), art. 184 (2017) *Standing Comm. Nat'l People's Cong. Gaz.* 191 (repealed 2021).

[229] "中华人民共和国民法典" ["Civil Code of the People's Republic of China"] (promulgated by the Nat'l People's Cong., May 28, 2020, effective January 1, 2021), art. 184 (2020) *Standing Comm. Nat'l People's Cong. Gaz.* (Civil Code Special Issue) 2.

interests" and, specifically, whether pure economic harm is within the scope. Inconsistencies and confusions will necessarily result from the lack of a clear roadmap. A clear legislative decision siding with either French or German law would be better than being equivocal. Moreover, the failure of the Code to distinguish intention from negligence needs to be addressed. Clear doctrinal standards of mental culpability must be established in any successful system of tort law. The existence of such a distinction in academic literature and criminal law makes its absence in the Code inexcusable.

The creation of liability in equity as an integral part of the liability regimes corresponds to the idea of distributive justice in the Chinese imperial legal tradition and reflects the preexisting social norms that are still well-accepted in contemporary Chinese society. Still, the continued growth of the market economy will bring about a conscientious acceptance of a law that is based upon philosophical ideas that differ from traditional Chinese moral philosophy.

In the end, despite the Western influence and massive legal transplants, it is China's civil law. It is new, and it will be a different kind of civil law. The Chinese people will breathe life into this brand new code and make it Chinese. As Roscoe Pound, a legal consultant to the Chinese government, noted seventy years ago: "It is more likely that the people will make over the law imposed upon it than that the people will be made over."[230]

[230] Roscoe Pound, "Comparative Law and History as Bases for Chinese Law" (1948) 61 *Harvard Law Review* 749, 750.

2

Personality Rights in China's New Civil Code

A Response to Increasing Awareness of Rights in an Era of Evolving Technology

WANG LIMING AND XIONG BINGWAN

> Legal precepts have to be fitted to the life of the people they are to govern, not the life of the people fitted arbitrarily to the legal precepts.
>
> Roscoe Pound, 1948[1]

2.1 Introduction

The diffusion of new technologies has begun to raise serious concerns over the invasion of personal spheres. In a recent interview at Davos,[2] Professor Yuval N. Harari, a historian and futurologist, warned that human society is close to or already at the point where organizations such as biotech and infotech giants and governments are capable of systematically hacking millions of people. Once such data-controlling organizations obtain enough personal data and computing power, they can predict and even manipulate human decisions. This will ultimately create data "colonies," with the potential to undermine the ideas of individual freedom, free markets, and liberal democracy.

Though such a "colonial" situation is unlikely to appear in the next two or three decades or even after, the use of algorithms in a wide range of sectors in digital markets[3] has raised serious concerns about the

[1] Roscoe Pound, "Comparative law and history as bases for Chinese law" (1948) 61 *Harvard Law Review* (5) 749–62.

[2] Huawei, "Ren Zhengfei and Yuval Noah Harari at Davos" (2020), www.huawei.com/us/facts/voices-of-huawei/davos.

[3] Michal S. Gal and Niva Elkin-Koren, "Algorithmic consumers" (2017) 30 *Harvard Journal of Law and Technology*, 309–53; Gerhard Wagner and Horst Eidenmüller, "Down by algorithms? Siphoning rents, exploiting biases, and shaping preferences: Regulating the dark side of personalized transactions" (2019) 86 *Univ. of Chicago Law Rev.* 581–609.

protection of personal information and, in general, personality. Changing modern technologies are posing unprecedented risks to personal integrity, freedom, and dignity, which constitute legally significant interests that are often embedded in the branch of law now known as personality rights law.

The right to personality is primarily a civil law concept.[4] It generally means an aggregate of personal rights that are aimed at the protection of the integrity, freedom, and dignity of a person. It comprises corporeal rights, including one's rights to life, body, and health, and incorporeal rights, including one's rights to one's name, portrait, reputation, honor, privacy, and personal information. Legitimate personal interests (but not enumerated "personality rights") have also been recognized by China's courts on a case-by-case basis, such as the interests to mourn deceased family members, to protect one's sexual autonomy, and to defend against false imprisonment.[5]

China's profound social and economic development is leading the materially richer Chinese people to seek the fulfillment of their nonmaterial needs. This is unlike circumstances a decade ago, when the drafting

[4] Adrian Popovici, "Personality rights – a civil law concept" (2004) 50 *Loyola of Los Angeles Law Rev.* 349–51; Giorgio Resta, "Personnalité, Persönlichkeit, Personality: Comparative perspectives on the protection of identity in private law" (2014) 1 *European Journal of Comparative Law and Governance* (3) 215–43.

[5] In one case, a funeral parlor mistakenly delivered the wrong person's cremation urn to a family. This resulted in the family mourning with the ashes of another family's loved one. Thus, the family members felt that their personal spheres were damaged but they could not find an enumerated personality right (a so-called nominate personality right) to contain it. In this case, family members could claim against the funeral parlor for damages for harm to their personal dignity. Such cases are not rare (Zhejiang Online, "浙江在线, '浦江殡仪馆'张冠李戴'把骨灰盒搞错了" ("Pujiang funeral parlor mixed up cremation urns") 浙江在线, July 12, 2011, http://zjnews.zjol.com.cn/05zjnews/system/2011/07/12/017670401.shtml. In a case on sexual autonomy, the plaintiff filed a lawsuit against her ex-boyfriend whom she came to know through a dating website, where both the plaintiff and the defendant had stated that they were single in their profiles. The plaintiff, later pregnant with the defendant's child, had an abortion after learning that the defendant was actually married. She claimed, and the court agreed, that the defendant had violated her sexual autonomy by concealing his marital status (Beijing Court 北京市第二中级人民法院 (2016) 民事判决书京二中民终字第 11106号 [Civil judgment no. 11106] Beijing Second Intermediate Court). Finally, in a typical case involving false imprisonment, *Zhang Qun* (张群) v. *Foshanshi Xinyijia Supermarket Co., Ltd.* (佛山市新一佳百货超市有限公司), a customer was accused by a supermarket of stealing when she tried to leave the premises after paying for her purchases. After being searched and questioned by the supermarket, she sued the latter for infringing upon her personal freedom. The court ruled in her favor (Foshan Court 广东省佛山市中级人民法院 [2004] 民事判决书佛中法民一终字第 307号 [Civil judgment no. 307] Foshan Intermediate Court).

of the Tort Liability Law was still aimed mainly at addressing issues concerning people's subsistence.[6] China observers have pointed out a rising demand among the public for their "rights." However, in the pursuit of nonmaterial rights in China, the emphasis has been primarily on the relationship between individuals and the state, and the dimension of such rights vis-à-vis private parties in civil society has been little explored. Studies on this subject are typically centered on social grievances that stoke public outcry and "mass incidents," as public protests are euphemistically referred to in the Chinese context.[7] This exclusive attention to demands for political rights or the right to subsistence[8] has left many other emerging needs unaddressed, such as the need to honor personal integrity, freedom, and dignity among individuals.

The growing consciousness of personality rights, coupled with their vulnerability under modern technologies, has led to one of the most noteworthy innovations in China's new Civil Code, adopted by the National People's Congress on May 28, 2020.[9] The new Civil Code builds on classic civil codes (consisting of six books: general provisions, property rights, contract, marriage, succession, and tort liability) and adds to them a separate book on the protection of personality rights.[10] This step admittedly has not been free of academic controversy, regarding, in

[6] Jacques Delisle, "A common law–like civil law and a public face for private law: China's tort law in comparative perspective" in Chen Lei and C. H. van Rhee (eds.), *Towards a Chinese Civil Code: Comparative and Historical Perspectives* (Leiden: Martinus Nijhoff, 2012), pp. 353–94.

[7] Yanqi Tong and Shaohua Lei, "Large-scale mass incidents and government responses in China' (2010) 2 *International Journal of China Studies* 487–508; Feng Chen, "Subsistence crises, managerial corruption and labour protests in China" (2000) 44 *China Journal* 41–63; William Hurst and Kevin J. O'Brien, "China's contentious pensioners" (2002) 170 *China Q.* 345–60.

[8] Elizabeth J. Perry, "Studying Chinese politics: Farewell to revolution?" (2007) 57 *China Journal* 1–22; Elizabeth J. Perry, "Chinese conceptions of 'rights': From Mencius to Mao – and now" (2008) 6 *Perspectives on Politics* (1) 37–50.

[9] NPC (2020) The Civil Code of the People's Republic of China (English translation at www .pkulaw.com/en_law/aa00daaeb5a4fe4ebdfb.html?keyword=civil%20code (NPC [2020]).

[10] Unlike many classic civil codes, such as the German Civil Code, China's Civil Code does not have a chapter detailing the general provisions governing obligations. Instead, the general provisions of obligation that materially overlap with the general rules of contract (such as joint and several obligations, divisible and indivisible obligations, obligations involving third parties, performance, assumption, and subrogation of obligations) have been absorbed by the General Rules of the Book of Contract. See Zhu Hu, "朱虎 '债法总则体系的基础反思与技术重整" ("A fundamental reflection on and technical reconstruction of the general section of the Law of Obligation") (2019) 13 清华法学 (3) 126–42.

particular, whether such an unprecedented approach might lead to confusion over the structure of the code and to political disturbance within Chinese society.[11] However, as we argue in this chapter, the adoption of an independent book on personality rights is not "just a minor technical issue," as some academics have put it.[12] Rather, behind the technical structure of a separate book is a vigorous academic and legislative endeavor to respond to the growing consciousness of personality rights among the public and the ubiquitous technological risks they face in contemporary China, such as the widespread collection of facial geometry and biometric information by public and private entities, the disclosure of defaulters' information through apps such as TikTok and WeChat to coerce them to comply with court decisions, and the application of gene-editing tools on human embryos as a disease prevention measure.

Adapting the law to respond to new technologies is not a new phenomenon in legal history. The emergence of personality rights protection as an autonomous problem in the nineteenth century was a consequence of the introduction of photography in the press and commercial advertisements.[13] In response, both German legal scholars' construction of the

[11] Liang Huixing ("梁慧星 '中国民法典中不能设置人格权" ["The personality right can't be as a separated part in Chinese Civil Code"] [2016] 2 中州学刊 48–54) and other scholars have argued that the inclusion of a separate section on personality rights in the code violates the time-honored Pandectist system adopted by German Civil Code and others. Provisions in such a stand-alone section are merely declarative of personality rights that can fall within the scope of the General Provisions of the Chinese Civil Code, which enumerates all types of civil rights covered by the code. The protection of these rights ultimately depends on the concrete remedial provisions in the part on tort liability. However, there is a rich literature arguing that the new structure of the code is coherent. See, e.g., Wang Liming, "人格权的积极确权模式探讨 – 论人格权法与侵权法 之关系" ("On the active confirmation of personality rights: the relationship of personality rights law and tort liability law") (2016) 2 法学家 1–14; Wang Liming, "论人格权请求权与侵权损害赔偿请求权的分离" ("On the separation of the right to claim personality rights and the right to claim damages") (2019) 1 中国法学 224–43; Yang Lixin, "对民法典规定人格权法重大争论的理性思考" ("Some reflections on the big controversy over the inclusion of personality law in the civil code") (2016) 1 中国法律评论 90–106). Moreover, Professor Liang Huixing, a renowned civil law scholar in China who strongly opposed the separate book approach, held that such an approach follows the structure of the Civil Code of Ukraine and has repeatedly warned that this may lead to a "color revolution" in China similar to that in Ukraine in 2014.

[12] Chen Lei, "Debating personality rights protection in China: A comparative outlook" (2018) 26 *European Review of Private Law* (1) 31–55.

[13] Robert E. Mensel, "'Kodakers lying in wait': Amateur photography and the right of privacy in New York, 1885–1915" (1991) 43 *American Quarterly*. (1) 24–45.

paradigm of the "general right of personality" and American legal academics' advancement of the inviolable value of the "right to privacy" pointed to a defensive structure of personality rights mainly within the framework of tort law.[14]

However, today, more than ever before, human society has reached a tipping point of technological explosion. "Breakthroughs in biotech, physics, chemistry, neurology, and mathematics, as well as interdisciplinary and cross-domain innovations have built significant momentum for humanity's advancement."[15] Yet the challenges that this technological explosion poses to the protection of personality are quantitatively and qualitatively incomparable to the problems raised by photography in the nineteenth century.

For China, it has become crucial to reassess whether the defensive structure of personality rights protection under tort law remains the best legislative choice. As some scholars of comparative law have already pointed out, diffusing the entire body of personality rights issues into tort law is rather simplistic and reductionist because the sanctioning regime against the tortfeasor in tort law does not pay sufficient attention to a person's claim for respect. Social respect is essential to personal integrity and human dignity.[16] This paradigm can neither reflect social and economic evolution in a timely and effective manner nor serve to protect a wide range of proactive uses of personal attributes within contractual relationships.

The limits of the nineteenth-century defensive structure of personality rights protection under tort law to some extent led China to adopt an independent Book of Personality Rights in its recently adopted Civil Code. Such a book, if designed well, can encompass a wide range of personality interests and harms in the face of technological explosion, old and new, tangible and intangible, patrimonial and inalienable, tortuous and contractual, commercial and gratuitous, reactive and proactive, defensive and preventive, and so forth. As many jurisdictions are contemplating adapting their existing codes or designing new ones to keep

14 Konrad Zweigert and Hein Kötz, *An Introduction to Comparative Law* (Oxford: Oxford University Press, 1998), p. 688; Samuel D. Warren and Louis D. Brandeis, "Right to privacy" (1890) 4 *Harvard Law Review* (5) 193–220.

15 Huawei, "Ren Zhengfei."

16 Peter Schwerdtner, *Das Persönlichkeitsrecht in der deutschen Zivilrechtsordnung. Offene Probleme einer juristischen Entdeckung* (Berlin: Schweitzer, 1977).

pace with modern technologies,[17] it is hoped that the comprehensive treatment of the protection of the personal sphere in an independent book in the Chinese Civil Code, in conjunction with the remedial provisions in its Book of Tort Liability Law, can enrich the legislative modes of the entire family of civil codes and provide an alternative choice for legal projects in other jurisdictions.

In this chapter, we explain how the special Book of Personality Rights in the Civil Code responds to the rising consciousness of nonmaterial rights in Chinese civil society and then analyze the parallel challenges from three types of modern technologies to the protection of personality rights and critically assess the extent to which the protection of personality rights spelled out in the Civil Code can effectively address them. We conclude the chapter with several remarks on the future application of provisions on personality rights.

2.2 Growing Rights Consciousness and China's Personality Law

Personality rights in China, as in many other jurisdictions, have grown in a piecemeal fashion. It takes considerable time for the law to respond to new areas of human interest and to protect them as "rights," as the experience in both continental Europe and the United States shows.[18] Codifying personality rights law as a separate book in China's new Civil Code is primarily a response to the growing consciousness of rights in China's civil society. As economic development lifts millions out of poverty, more and more Chinese people are now enjoying a comfortable life, rather than a life of mere subsistence, and are becoming more assertive in pursuing their personal interests. The synthesis of social and economic rights has been a key foundation for the codification of the new code.

The Chinese people believe that not only should more such interests be recognized as rights but existing and established rights should also be expanded in their essence and scope, creating a new landscape that calls

[17] Giorgio Resta, "The new frontiers of personality rights and the problem of commodification: European and comparative perspectives" (2011) 26 *Tulane European & Civil Law Forum* 33–65; Lei, "Debating personality rights."

[18] Gert Brüggemeier, Aurelia Ciacchi, and Patrick O'Callaghan, *Personality Rights in European Tort Law* (Cambridge: Cambridge University Press, 2010), p. 3.

for a comprehensive statute, instead of the fragmented legal instruments that came before.[19]

2.2.1 Hierarchical Needs and the Demand for Emerging Rights

Personality rights, as they are known today, cover a wide range of rights, including a person's body, portrait, reputation, and privacy. These are recent ideas in China and are mostly the outcome of China's economic boom. A hungry nation might well care less about human dignity. Modern psychology shows that people's needs are hierarchical and that lower needs in this hierarchy generally have to be satisfied before people turn to "higher" needs. As Maslow put it,[20] "man lives by bread alone – when there is no bread." Similarly, according to an ancient Chinese saying, "When the granaries are full, [the people] will know propriety and moderation; when their clothing and food are adequate, they will know [the distinction between] honor and shame" (仓廪实则知礼节，衣食足则知荣辱).[21]

Socioeconomic and legal developments over the past four decades reflect more or less the same trajectory.[22] Economic development in China has lifted many people out of poverty and enabled them to turn to largely nonphysical higher needs in the hierarchy. New types of rights have arisen as people have started to have expectations for legal protection of previously unrecognized or under-recognized needs. As Warren and Brandeis put more than a century ago,[23]

> the intense intellectual and emotional life, and the heightening of sensations which came with the advance of civilization, made it clear to men that only a part of the pain, pleasure, and profit of life lay in physical things. Thoughts, emotions, and sensations demanded legal recognition.

[19] Chen Lei, "Codifying personality rights in China: Legislative innovation or scaremongering?" in Ken Oliphant, Zhang Pinghua, and Chen Lei (eds.), *The Legal Protection of Personality Rights: Chinese and European Perspectives* (Leiden: Brill/Nijhof, 2018), pp. 101–37, provides an introduction to the previous legal and statutory framework on personality rights in China.

[20] Abraham H. Maslow, "A theory of human motivation" (1943) 50 *Psychological Review* 370–96 at 374.

[21] This quote is from "Mu Min" ("On Shepherding the People"), a prose piece by Guan Zhong (d. 645 BCE), one of the best-known philosophers in the Confucianist school.

[22] Wang Liming, "The modernization of Chinese civil law over four decades" (2019) 14 *Frontiers of Law in China* (1) 39–72.

[23] Warren and Brandeis, "Right to privacy," 195.

The right to privacy epitomizes this trend. Unlike in common law countries, where the right to privacy has been a familiar idea since the noted article by Warren and Brandeis,[24] the concept of privacy seems rather strange to Chinese people. For thousands of years, China remained a rural society where social ties and interpersonal relationships were highly valued. People were so close to each other that even the number of eggs laid by the neighbor's hen was known to all. The idea of privacy in such a context is unimaginable.

This lack of attention to privacy in a largely rural China was carried into the People's Republic. A planned economy relying on state guidance replaced rural-based networks but placed a similar constraint on people's social ties, as individuals were seen as relatively closed units that bonded directly with the state. Privacy was distorted as an idea and was belittled and even resisted by the public because people largely equated privacy (隐私) with physical intimacy (阴私), two words that share a similar pronunciation (*yinsi*) with only a slight difference in tone. Even authoritative law dictionaries have defined cases of privacy as those involving content that is deemed offensive to public decency or involving sexual relations or other private matters. The derogatory connotation attached to privacy hindered its legal recognition as a right. It is not until the Reform and Opening-up that the idea of privacy as a legitimate claim began to gain acceptance. This comprehensive reform ushered in a market economy and industrialization, with more people moving into cities. Urbanization changed China fundamentally as people began to demand more private space.

With the rising desire for the right to privacy among the public, the law began to respond. The legal protection of privacy developed in four stages in China. When the General Principles of Civil Law was enacted in 1986 (the 1986 GPCL), the right to privacy was not recognized as an enumerated personality right. Unlike the right to life, health, and reputation, there was no direct provision addressing the right to privacy in the 1986 GPCL. However, privacy did not go unprotected in court. In the judicial interpretation (a de facto source of law though not directly binding on lower courts in China) issued by the Supreme People's Court on the 1986 GPCL, it was held that the violation of privacy could lead to damages if it adversely affected others' reputation.[25] In other

[24] Ibid.

[25] Supreme People's Court (最高人民法院) (1988), 最高人民法院印发 "关于贯彻执行'中华人民共和国民法通则' 若干问题的意见（试行）" 的通知 (Notice of the

words, the protection of privacy was achieved vicariously, by drawing an analogy with the right to reputation.

However, not all privacy infringements involve reputational losses. Thus, the Supreme People's Court issued another judicial interpretation in 2001, in which privacy was recognized for the first time as an independent *personal interest* to be protected by law.[26] This marked a major step in the legal protection of privacy. However, recognizing privacy as merely a personal interest rather than a legal right limits the rights of a victim. A victim can be compensated only when the infringement of his or her privacy is serious enough to constitute a violation of public interest and when the infringing party is malicious rather than merely at fault. With increasing public awareness of privacy rights, this approach needed to change.

In the 2009 Tort Liability Law, privacy was finally included as a *personality right*, alongside the right to life, health, body, name, portrait, reputation, and honor (NPCSC, 2009: Art. 2).[27] The 2017 General Principles of Civil Law (the 2017 GPCL) further acknowledges this (NPC, 2017: Art. 110). The enumeration of the right to privacy, being a response to the demand of the public, ushered in a new wave of privacy cases. As of February 5, 2020, a total of 89,482 court judgments including the keyword "privacy" were published on China Judgments Online, the official database for judgments from all levels of courtrooms. Only twenty-six were decided before 2009.

This large number of cases has laid a solid ground for the final stage in the legal protection of privacy. As courts across the country encountered more cases involving privacy, experiences began to accumulate. More detailed questions involving the right to privacy, such as its meaning, scope, categories, and the protection that each category deserves, are now being answered and such answers are being constantly challenged and refined. This explains why the more comprehensive Civil Code includes a whole chapter on the right to privacy. This shift from obscurity to recognition is proof that people are far more concerned about their privacy and demand greater protection of nonmaterial rights today.

Supreme People's Court on issuing opinions on several issues concerning the implementation of the general principles of the civil law of the People's Republic of China), Art. 140.

[26] Supreme People's Court (2001), 最高人民法院关于确定民事侵权精神损害赔 偿责任若干问题的解释 (Interpretation of the Supreme People's Court on problems regarding the ascertainment of compensation liability for emotional damages in civil torts), Art. 1.

[27] NPCSC (全国人民代表大会常务委员会) (2009), 中华人民共和国侵权责任法 (Tort liability law of China), Art. 2.

2.2.2 *Restrictive Commercial Exploitation of Personal Attributes*

The growing consciousness of the new category of rights is not the only trend that has unfolded with respect to personality rights. As Chinese people have become increasingly conscious of their rights, the idea of recognized categories is also being expanded. When the economic value of personal attributes becomes more apparent and well-received, a shift in the essence of personality rights renders the existing legal framework rather inadequate.

Original doctrines considered personality rights as inalienable. Kant,[28] for instance, refused to acknowledge a person's right to sell his or her body parts because to do so would mean degrading the human body for the sake of financial gain. Later, the rigid prohibition on the commercial exploitation of personal spheres was gradually thought of as inconsistent with an individual's autonomy to exercise his or her own private rights. The commoditization of certain personal aspects, particularly a person's name and portrait, has gained growing acceptance across different societies. In early cases such as *Shields* v. *Gross*,[29] the court denied a young model's petition to revoke her consent to the publication of a nude photograph of hers, though the snapshot was taken with her mother's authorization when she was just ten years old.

Nonetheless, a growing number of jurisdictions, in civil law countries in particular, tend to recognize a reduced binding force of a contract for the commercial exploitation of personal attributes if the performance of the contractual obligation is proved to be morally detrimental to the obligee.[30] The obligee is permitted to rescind such a contract provided that he or she indemnifies the obligor. The basic idea behind constraining contractual autonomy to transform personal attributes into pure commodities is to prioritize the inner world of a person and one's human dignity over his or her commercial engagement with outer society.[31]

Following this trend, the Book of Personality Rights in the Chinese Civil Code reflects the idea of reduced autonomy to exploit certain

[28] Immanuel Kant, "Duties toward the body in respect of sexual impulse" in Alan Soble (ed.), *The Philosophy of Sex: Contemporary Readings*. 4th ed. (Lanham, MD: Rowman & Littlefield, 2002), pp. 199–205.

[29] *Shields* v. *Gross*, 58 N. Y. 2d 338 (1983).

[30] Chantal Mak, *Fundamental Rights in European Contract Law. A Comparison of the Impact of Fundamental Rights on Contractual Relationships in Germany, the Netherlands, Italy and England* (Alphen aan den Rijn: Kluwer International, 2008).

[31] Resta, "New frontiers of personality rights"; Xue Jun, "薛军 '人的保护: 中国民法典编撰的价值基础" ("Protection of the person: A basic value in Chinese civil codification") (2006) 4 中国社会科学 117–28.

incorporeal personal attributes commercially. The traditionally defensive approach still holds sway, as the personality rights part lists the rights to life, body, and health in its second chapter, immediately after its general provisions. When the aggregate of personality rights expanded to include other personal spheres in relation to what Zhang Pinghua calls "derivative interests,"[32] the defensive model naturally came into play. The Chinese Civil Code prohibits unwarranted invasion by protecting individuals' right to control their personality.[33]

Nonetheless, new technologies and emerging business models have constantly reshaped the meaning of personality. The transformation of social and economic conditions owing to scientific and technological developments has gradually increased the practical significance of the instrumental exploitation of certain personal attributes to advance purely economic interests.[34] A person can, for instance, license his or her portrait in an endorsement deal. And a merchandiser can exploit the power of association and accumulate goodwill by suggesting that a celebrity favors his or her products. As Beverley-Smith et al. have observed,[35] even underexploited fame has "recognition value" and its commercial potential can be fully realized once advertisers identify the best way to use it. This commodification of personality is not limited to public figures, as digital economies render everyone's personal information an unprecedented asset.[36]

This new social and economic reality has significantly challenged the received wisdom of the defensive structure of personality rights protection. As Resta puts it, "whereas in the past the focus was mainly on the *protection* of the inviolate personality against invasions by third parties and on the recovery of *nonpecuniary* losses arising from the infringement of dignitary interests, the emphasis is now on the *exploitation* of the commercial value of personality and compensation for *profits* foregone

[32] Zhang Pinghua, "The structure of the interest in personality and the introduction of a statutory right of personality" in Ken Oliphant, Zhang Pinghua, and Chen Lei (eds.), *The Legal Protection of Personality Rights: Chinese and European Perspectives* (Leiden: Brill/Nijhoff, 2018) pp. 138–44.

[33] NPC (2020) Art. 991.

[34] Resta, "New frontiers of personality rights."

[35] Huw Beverley-Smith, Ansgar Ohly, and Agnès Lucas-Schloetter, *Privacy, Property and Personality: Civil Law Perspectives on Commercial Appropriation* (Cambridge: Cambridge University Press, 2005).

[36] Vera Bergelson, "It's personal but is it mine? Toward property rights in personal information" (2003) 37 *UC Davis Law Review* 436–38.

(or restitution of unlawfully earned profits) as a result of the unconsented use."[37] While the extra-contractual model can more or less deal with infringements on personality rights, the protection of personality in contractual relations is either unacceptably ignored or comes in a piecemeal fashion.

The Book of Personality Rights takes the complex nature of personality seriously and aims to close this loophole in traditional civil codes. While it primarily provides for control-based rules that prohibit infringement of all personality rights, attributes of certain personality rights with economic value are well recognized. For example, a natural person's right to name, as acknowledged by the personality rights part of the code, first and foremost includes the person's right to defend any infringement upon his or her name, including interference, theft, and counterfeiting, etc.[38] In addition to this inherently defensive right, the law also stipulates that the person can authorize others to use his or her name,[39] thus acknowledging the commercial exploitation of the right to name. This hybrid approach enables one's personality rights to include both moral and economic rights, and this can also be found in the right over a business name (NPC Art. 1013) and the right over a portrait or likeness (NPC 2020 Art. 1018).

To acknowledge the fact that some categories of personality rights are a mixture of defensive and proactive rights is significant. But the commodification of personal spheres is never absolute. Trading one's name or portraits will never be the same as trading cars or houses since personal attributes represent an integral part of the person's identity. Thus, the common law technique of labeling these attributes as one's property is often criticized for stretching the concept of property so far as to include interests that, on one hand, require legal protection and, on the other hand, do not possess all elements of full ownership.[40] Consequently, while certain personal attributes are transferable and licensable, the new Civil Code rules out a complete transfer of personality rights (NPC 2020 Arts. 992, 993). Furthermore, the difference in the object of licenses also dictates that personality licenses be revocable with "justiciable reason" (NPC 2020 Art. 1022). When disputes arise as to the scope and method of portrait licenses, the law allows an interpretation of

[37] Resta, "New frontiers of personality rights" (emphasis in the original).

[38] NPC (2020) Art. 1014.

[39] NPC (2020) Art. 1012.

[40] Beverley-Smith, Ohly, and Lucas-Schloetter, *Privacy, Property and Personality.*

the terms of portrait permission contracts in a manner that is favorable to the licensor (NPC 2020 Art. 1021). This is also proof that the law is skewed toward individuals, as commercialization must not be pursued at the expense of individual personality.

The fact that personal attributes can be traded also tests what some sociologists call "the moral limits of markets."[41] Some serious ethical concerns might arise. For instance, as human organs are in short supply, establishing a market for such scarce resources seems to make economic sense.[42] Yet, the sale of human organs is banned in most societies not only because of the moral concern of the objectification of the human body and the degrading of human dignity but also, more pragmatically, because market mechanisms are likely to involve problems of severe inequality. In a country with great economic discrepancies, the poor and disadvantaged tend to be exploited, both physically and mentally.[43] An inappropriate introduction of market mechanisms could cause public health disasters. In the early 1990s, thousands of low-income peasants in Henan in central China were infected with HIV/AIDS in illegal blood collection stations. Since then, tens of thousands more have faced the spread of the virus because of blood product consumption and sexual contact.[44] This case shows why there is little space for the market mechanism in the field of body parts transfer.

The Book of Personality Rights adopts this view. While acknowledging the economic value of human cells, tissues, organs, and remains and therefore allowing their donation, it explicitly bans any form of their sale (NPC 2020 Art. 1066). To ensure that the donation is decided upon carefully, the law requires a valid will or a donation agreement signed in writing by the donor (NPC 2020 Art. 1066). As for people who have not explicitly refused to donate before their death, the law entitles the spouse, adult children, and/or parents of the deceased to donate on behalf of the

[41] Debra Satz, *Why Some Things Should Not Be for Sale: The Moral Limits of Markets* (Oxford: Oxford University Press, 2010).

[42] Gary S. Becker and Julio J. Elias, "Introducing incentives in the market for live and cadaveric organ donations" (2007) 21 *Journal of Economic Perspectives* (3) 3–24; Kieran Healy, *Last Best Gifts: Altruism and the Market for Human Blood and Organs* (Chicago: University of Chicago Press, 2006).

[43] Rene Almeling, "Gender and the value of bodily goods: Commodification in egg and sperm donation" (2009) 72 *Law and Contemporary Problems* 37–58.

[44] China.org, "Despite progress, much to be done in Henan AIDS villages" China, June 30, 2004, www.china.org.cn/english/2004/Jun/99851.htm; Zhang Feng, "More HIV, AIDS cases expected in Henan," *China Daily*, June 6, 2004, www.chinadaily.com.cn/english/doc/2004-06/29/content_343934.htm.

deceased through a unanimous decision in writing (NPC 2020 Art. 1066). Nonetheless, the Book of Personality Rights is silent on donations by persons with limited civil capacity, which is strictly prohibited by a state regulation issued in 2007.[45] In the years after the issuance of the Regulation on Human Organ Transplantation, a few cases arose in which minors suffering from terminal illness voluntarily asked their parents to donate their organs after their death.[46] The silence in the Book of Personality Rights, arguably intentional, leaves room for further policy deliberation over donations by minors and the like, which may bring more hope to those in need of organ transplantation.

Surrogacy is another ethically controversial issue in the commercial exploitation of personality. It is not new to Chinese society. Even in ancient China, there were men who "borrowed women's bellies to produce offspring" (借腹生子) for the sake of extending their family line. Statistics show that, as of 2019, 10 to 15 percent of the couples in China suffer from fertility disorders, and about 20 percent of them need intervention in the form of reproductive technology to conceive.[47] Though China prohibits medical institutions and medical staff from providing surrogacy services, insider information on the massive underground surrogacy network and markets is shocking. It is estimated that there are over 400 surrogacy intermediaries in China, most of whom provide surrogacy services underground. Surrogacy fees can amount to 1.5 million yuan (about US$210,000). At the same time, the number of lawsuits concerning surrogacy has continued to rise. Chinese courts are frequently called upon to decide legal issues such as the validity of surrogacy contracts, parenthood of surrogate children, and the sole guardianship of surrogate children. Judicial opinions have varied from court to court, this partly because of the legislative vacuum on surrogacy outside of medical institutions.[48]

[45] State Council (国务院), "人体器官移植条例" ("The regulation on human organ transplantation") (2007), Art. 8 (English translation at http://en.pkulaw.cn/display.aspx?cgid=009cfa661624d1fcbdfb&lib=law).

[46] Wan Yunjie (万云洁) and Deng Mulin, "邓木林 '浅议父母捐献未成年子女器官的行为是否有效" ("On whether parents' donation of organs from minor children is valid") (February 12, 2015) 中国法院网, www.chinacourt.org/article/detail/2015/02/id/1555273.shtml.

[47] Wang Yang (王阳), "代孕黑色产业链调查" ("A survey of the black industry chain of surrogacy") (July 16, 2019) 法制日报, http://epaper.legaldaily.com.cn/fzrb/content/20190716/Articel04002GN.htm?spm=zm1012-001.0.0.1.UBL2UV.

[48] Chunyan Ding, "Surrogacy litigation in China and beyond" (2015) 2 *Journal of Law and the Biosciences* (1) 33–55.

Considering the strong demand for surrogacy services from a large number of Chinese couples and the presence of a massive surrogacy market in China, the legislature is unlikely to prohibit surrogacy altogether as it once planned to do years ago.[49] Nonetheless, it has been quite cautious about the regulation of surrogacy perhaps because of the ethical concern of the complete commoditization of surrogate mothers and babies. Several reports on the surrogacy markets in China and abroad suggest that more than a few surrogate mothers were turned into "reproduction machines in dark mills" and that surrogate babies became commodities that were sold to surrogate fathers by surrogacy agencies.[50] The insufficiency of institutional design to prevent the risk of degrading personhoods into material goods explains why the Book of Personality Rights continues to remain silent on surrogacy despite the many calls from academics and social media for legislating on surrogacy.[51] There is still a long road to walk before the NPC becomes confident about addressing surrogacy in the Civil Code. A pragmatic choice may be to address the legal issues surrounding surrogacy in special legislation or regulations in a piecemeal fashion.

2.2.3 Gender Equality and the Personal Right to Sexual Autonomy

Apart from the public demands that more rights should be protected and that such rights should be more inclusive, some more structural social changes are shaping public attitudes and further complicating the landscape of the legal protection of personality.

One such change involves gender. Before the modern era, China had more or less adhered to Confucianism, wherein everyone was expected to behave consistently with his or her status and identity in society. The idea that women should be obedient to their fathers when they are young, to

[49] On December 27, 2015, the Standing Committee of the NPC voted to amend the Population and Family Planning Law. Art. 35 of the Amendment (Draft) stated that "The sale of sperm, eggs, fertilized eggs and embryos is prohibited, and surrogacy in any form is prohibited." Eventually, this article was deleted because of strong opposition from academics and social media.

[50] Yang, "Survey of surrogacy."

[51] Li Dan, "李丹 '代孕法治化进程中的若干思考" ("Some thoughts on the road to the rule of law in surrogacy") (2017) 14 私法 (1) 314–31; Zhang Suhua (张素华) and Li Ya'nan, "李雅男 '代孕协议中 私法自治的边界 – 对代孕母人身权利的限制为中心" ("The border of private law autonomy in surrogacy agreements: Centering on restrictive clauses on the personal liberty of surrogate mothers") (2018) 2 私法 150–52.

their husbands when they are married, and to their sons when they are widowed dictated that women would be subordinate to men in Confucian China. This was attacked by Chinese intellectuals in the early twentieth century, as they considered the liberation of women an essential part of modernity for China.[52] The founding of the People's Republic of China also promoted women's emancipation, making gender equality a mainstream ideology and legal principle. Yet, gender equality has not been sufficiently achieved. Progressive economic development has led to widening social gaps. It later became clear that this "surging inequality in Chinese society is highly gendered."[53] Economically, gender disparity is found in employment, income, and unpaid care.[54] Culturally, women are discriminated against, as sons are preferred by rural families under the one child policy.[55]

Like in any other society, gender inequality cannot be addressed singlehandedly by law. Institutional and societal changes that empower women individually and collectively are necessary.[56] However, the law can play an essential role. The Book of Personality Rights, for example, tackles one of the most manifest forms of unfairness based on gender – sexual harassment. This is, to a large extent, a Chinese response to the global #MeToo movement. Notwithstanding censorship and a systemic bias against activism, Chinese women are joining the world in coming forward and being heard.[57] As more women level accusations of sexual

[52] Jieyu Liu, *Gender and Work in Urban China: Women Workers of the Unlucky Generation* (New York: Routledge, 2007), pp. 3–4.

[53] Qi Wang, "Introduction" in Qi Wang, Dongchao Min, and Bo Ærenlund Sørensen (eds.), *Revisiting Gender Inequality: Perspectives from the People's Republic of China* (New York: Palgrave Macmillan, 2016), pp. 1–20 at 2.

[54] Liu Bohong, Li Ling, and Yang Chunyu, "Gender (in)equality and China's economic transition" in Qi Wang, Min Dongchao, and Bo Ærenlund Sørensen (eds.), *Revisiting Gender Inequality: Perspectives from the People's Republic of China* (New York: Palgrave Macmillan, 2016), pp. 21–57.

[55] Li Huiying, "Son preference and the tradition of patriarchy in rural China: An empirical investigation of the sex ratio imbalance at birth" in Qi Wang, Min Dongchao, and Bo Ærenlund Sørensen (eds.), *Revisiting Gender Inequality: Perspectives from the People's Republic of China* (New York: Palgrave Macmillan, 2016), pp. 137–56.

[56] Zhongxuan Lin and Liu Yang "Individual and collective empowerment: Women's voices in the #MeToo movement in China" (2019) 25 *Asian Journal of Women's Studies* (1) 117–31.

[57] "The #MeToo movement arrives in the people's republic" *The Economist*, January 18, 2018, www.economist.com/china/2018/01/18/the-metoo-movement-arrives-in-the-peoples-republic; Lily Kuo, "#MeToo in China: Movement gathers pace amid wave of accusations" *Guardian*, July 31, 2018, www.theguardian.com/world/2018/jul/31/metoo-in-china-movement-gathers-pace-amid-wave-of-accusations.

harassment and misconduct against their former bosses, colleagues, and professors, it has been pointed out that the Chinese legal system seemed unacceptably inadequate to address such predatory behavior. Sexual harassment was not even defined by the law before this. The Supreme People's Court has only recently recognized it as a new cause of action for damages.[58] Feminist activists in China have resorted to social networking platforms such as Weibo and WeChat to advocate for anti–sexual harassment laws, on-campus prevention mechanisms, and helplines for victims.[59]

Partly in response, the Book of Personality Rights includes a lengthy article on sexual harassment, as sexual misconduct primarily violates one's right to bodily and psychological integrity.[60] Article 1010 NPC 2020 provides that a victim who suffers from any form of sexual harassment, be it verbal, in action, or by any other means, against their will, can apply under the law for the tortfeasor to bear civil liability. The article also imposes the duty on governments, enterprises, and schools to prevent sexual harassment. It stipulates that reasonable measures should be taken toward enabling reporting, investigating, and penalizing sexual misconduct owing to the exploitation of positions of power and relationships of subordination. This is primarily undertaken with the intent to address the imbalance in power relations that is often exploited in sexual harassment and violence cases.

The inclusion of this article promises to be a good starting point for the promotion of gender equality in Chinese society. However, this article is largely declaratory. It does not provide a clear definition of sexual harassment, probably because of the difficulty involved in generalizing a concept merely based on limited awareness of the types of such misconduct. It is up to the judiciary to interpret the concept in accordance with specific scenarios. One of the most debatable issues is whether sexual innuendo constitutes sexual harassment. Some courts have ruled in favor of the plaintiff because such misconduct is detrimental to the

[58] On December 12, 2018, the Supreme People's Court published a Notice by the Supreme People's Court of Adding Causes of Action in Civil Cases, where "dispute over tort liability in sexual harassment" was listed as an independent cause of action for the first time.

[59] Simina Mistreanu, "China's #MeToo activists have transformed a generation" *Foreign Policy*, January 10, 2019, https://foreignpolicy.com/2019/01/10/chinas-metoo-activists-have-transformed-a-generation/.

[60] Johann Neethling, "Personality rights: A comparative overview" (2005) 38 *Comparative and International Law Journal* 210–45.

mental health of the victim whereas other courts have rejected such complaints on the ground that such conduct had not materially violated the victim's sexual autonomy.[61] Another challenging issue concerns the standards of proof. Going by past judgments, the failure rate in this segment is high. A recent study of courtroom judgments suggests that up to 70 percent of the plaintiffs had failed to prove sexual harassment as they had no evidence but their own statements against the defendants. In a recent survey of 109 courtroom judgments concerning sexual harassment in China, disputes over the facts of sexual harassment arose in 16 judgments.[62] That said, the prevention of sexual harassment needs more tools in addition to the trajectory of civil liability, such as moral teaching and disciplinary education as required by the second paragraph of this article.

2.3 Technological Advances and Personality at Risk

Economic development enriches people's lives and encourages them to pursue needs beyond bare subsistence. A second and equally important consequence of this progress is the arrival of countless and dynamic technologies, with the power to transform and revolutionize modern life.[63] Technological advancements have always been a thorny problem for the protection of personality. As Warren and Brandeis put it in the late nineteenth century, "instantaneous photographs and newspaper enterprise have invaded the sacred precincts of private and domestic life; and numerous mechanical devices threaten to make good the prediction that 'what is whispered in the closet shall be proclaimed from the house-tops.'"[64] The latest scandalous event of the discovery of hidden cameras in hotel rooms again raises public concerns over privacy challenged by technologies.[65] While cameras themselves do not harm, the fact that such

61 Baidu, "百度 '性骚扰'独立案由施行一周年, 受害者打破沉默仍障碍重重" ("Obstacles to victims' breaking their silence remain one year after the adoption of 'sexual harassment' as an independent cause of action"), January 1, 2020, https://baijiahao.baidu.com/s?id=1654668638528750663&wfr=spider&for=pc.

62 Ibid.

63 Andrew Mcafee, Erik Brynjolfsson, Thomas H. Davenport, D. J. Patil, and Dominic Barton, "Big data: The management revolution" (2012) 90 *Harvard Business Review* 60–68; Andy Williamson, "Big data and the implications for government" (2014) 14 *Legal Information Management* 253–57.

64 Warren and Brandeis, "Right to privacy," 195.

65 Mandy Zuo, "Hidden hotel cameras lead to arrests in China" *South China Morning Post*, June 24, 2019.

neutral technologies can be exploited for immoral ends suffices to illustrate the vulnerability of personality. Risks that technologies have created to personality, technically, economically, and culturally, call for a comprehensive law in response.[66] The current Book of Personality Rights strives to address tech-related risks that generally involve the Internet, data, and biomedicine.

2.3.1 Internet-Based Risks to Personality Protection

For most people in modern China, the Internet is no longer an option but a must. The Internet is interwoven with important aspects of life. "In many ways the Internet has succeeded in remaking us inhabitants of a small village."[67] Such is the power of the Internet that its accessibility – or the lack of it – can affect people's standing socially, culturally, and financially.

Yet the Internet, with all its conveniences, can offend and intrude. Instantaneity not only brings people closer but is also capable of magnifying any damage to one's personality rights in a way that humankind has never seen before. One can become a victim of cyber bullying within hours or have his or her personal information collected through one click without even knowing it. One's rights to reputation, honor, portrait, and privacy have all become far more vulnerable in the internet era. While privacy issues related to the Internet generally concern data collection and breaches, a topic discussed below, other personality rights, such as the rights to name,[68] portrait, and reputation, can be easily infringed upon as well, perhaps even more easily. One empirical study shows that among the 204 internet-related Chinese district court cases on personality rights in 2017, 155 were concerned with the right to reputation and 64 with the right to portrait.[69]

66 Marta Minow, "The past, present, and future of legal education" *Harvard Law Today*, April 21, 2020, https://today.law.harvard.edu/minow-addresses-the-past-present-and-future-of-legal-education-video/.

67 Saul Levmore and Martha C. Nussbaum, "Introduction" in Saul Levmore and Martha C. Nussbaum (eds.), *The Offensive Internet: Speech, Privacy, and Reputation* (Cambridge, MA: Harvard University Press, 2010), pp. 1–12 at 1.

68 A typical mode of infringing upon one's right of name is cybersquatting. See Johannes H. Gatsik, "Cybersquatting: Identity theft in disguise" (2001) 35 *Suffolk University Law Review* 277–302. The Book of Personality Rights acknowledges the higher risks that well-known figures face and provides greater protection to their right of name (NPC [2020] Art. 1017).

69 Wei Daping, "魏大平 '网络人格侵权的法律保护路径探析 – 于204份判决书的实证分析" ("Analysis on the legal protection path of network personality infringement:

Take the right to reputation as an example. The Internet has undoubtedly brought tremendous challenges to the protection of one's reputation and honor in respect to the following three features. First, anonymity. While it is key to safeguarding free speech, it also serves as a catalyst for cyber mobs. Participating in online discussions while maintaining anonymity may help foster antisocial, malicious, and immoral behavior, which can easily ruin one's reputation.[70] Second, the fragmentation of information. Back in smaller, web-free communities, disreputable information was judged in the context of a person's whole life, as the audience knew the person relatively well. On the Internet, however, fragmented information is often taken out of context and used to judge people. This discrediting effect is becoming all the more worrisome. Third, permanence. This means that fragments of a person's information can be collected and stored forever and will be searchable in an instant. In essence, people are deprived of a second chance on the Internet. A tiny mistake is likely to permanently define a person. This "digital scarlet letter" prolongs the negative effect on one's reputation and exacerbates the damage.[71]

A good example in China that shows how anonymity, fragmentation, and permanence can combine to damage one's personality rights is commonly known as "human flesh search." In human flesh search, the aim is to identify individuals, and in the process people's acts are exposed online without their consent. This process then discloses more personally identifiable information of the victims, who are often the targets of ridicule, shaming, or punishment.[72] In the reportedly first case on human flesh search brought before a Chinese court, the victim, a cheating husband whose wife committed suicide after the exposure of his extramarital affairs, faced physical assault and was dismissed by his employer after internet users launched a human flesh search on him and disclosed his name, home address, and phone number.[73] In two other cases, a

Empirical analysis based on 204 judgments") (2019) 1 光华法学 *Guanghua Law Review* 182–97.

70 Diane Rowland, "Griping, bitching and speaking your mind: Defamation and free expression on the internet" (2006) 110 *Pennsylvania State Law Review* (2) 519–53.

71 Daniel J. Solove, *The Future of Reputation: Gossip, Rumor, and Privacy on the Internet* (New Haven, CT: Yale University Press, 2007), pp. 94–95.

72 Anne S. Y. Cheung, "Rethinking public privacy in the internet era: A study of virtual persecution by the internet crowd" (2009) 1 *Journal of Media and Law* (2) 191–217 at 191.

73 The district court held that extramarital affairs, however immoral, fall within the scope of privacy, a determination that was upheld by the intermediate court. See Wang Jia, "The right to privacy in the internet age: The Chinese perspective" in Ken Oliphant, Zhang

middle school teacher and a teenager committed suicide because of human flesh search invasions.[74]

It is because of this ease of wrecking one's reputation and creeping into one's privacy that the current Book of Personality Rights includes rules to deal with internet-based risks to personality rights. One noteworthy innovation is the device of interim injunctions. The 2009 Tort Liability Law already sets out a general liability for internet service providers.[75] The Book of Personality Rights follows this tradition by allowing victims of online defamation to require deletion or correction. It also takes a step forward to highlight, in its general provisions, the availability of the device of interim injunctions for victims of personal infringements (NPC 2020 Art. 997), the prototype of which appeared in China's Civil Procedure Law in 2012.[76] In an increasingly instantaneous and ubiquitous online environment, providing the victimized the device of an interim injunction to prevent further infringements before full trial and a permanent injunction may prove effective in defending one's personality rights against irreparable harm.

In 2013, a renowned scholar, Yang Jiang (杨绛), sued the International Auction Company of Zhongmao Shengjia (中贸圣佳国际拍卖有限公司) for an interim injunction against an auction.[77] The company wanted to auction the private letters of Mr. Qian Zhongshu, Ms. Yang's late husband, which contained information on their family life. Ms. Yang applied to the court to prohibit the company from auctioning the letters. The court decided in her favor under Article 100 of the Civil Procedure Law. Predictably, the reiteration of the interim injunction by a lengthy article in the Book of Personality Rights will encourage victims to take more effective action against personal infringements.

Pinghua, and Chen Lei (eds.), *The Legal Protection of Personality Rights: Chinese and European Perspectives* (Leiden: Brill/Nijhoff, 2018), pp. 178–80.

[74] RMZXB, "又一起! 女教师遭'人肉'后自杀, 网络暴力何时休?" ("One more case! Female teacher committed suicide after a 'human flesh' search for her. When will cyber violence stop?") 人民政协网, September 5, 2018, www.rmzxb.com.cn/c/2018-09-05/2161574.shtml; CNTV, "广东陆丰: '少女遭人肉搜索后自杀'事件追踪" ("Lufeng, Guangdong: reporting a young girl's suicide after a human flesh search for her"), December 19, 2013.

[75] NPCSC (2009) (Tort liability law of China), Art. 36.

[76] NPCSC (2017) 中华人民共和国民事诉讼法 (2017修正) (Civil procedure law of China, 2017 amendment), Art. 100 (English translation at www.pkulaw.com/en_law/d33df017c784876fbdfb.html?keyword=%E6%B0%91%E4%BA%8B%E8%AF%89%E8%AE%BC%E6%B3%95).

[77] Beijing Court 北京市高级人民法院 (2014) 民事判决书京高民终字第1152号 (Civil judgment no. 1152) Beijing High Court.

In the legal protection of personality rights in cyberspace, an individual's right to privacy or reputation should be balanced with others' right to free speech. A relevant question is whether public figures should enjoy the same level of legal protection of their privacy or reputation as ordinary people. The Book of Personality Rights makes genuine attempts to address such questions. It makes clear that news reporting and public opinion supervision are generally excluded from liability for reputational damage, while limitations exist to avoid overstretching free speech at the cost of others' reputation (NPC 2020 Art. 1025). The current law does not explicitly include a provision for the protection of public figures, but in explaining what constitutes the duty of reasonable review by journalists, it enumerates "the likelihood that victims' reputation would be disparaged" as one factor to be considered (NPC 2020 Art. 1026). This leaves room for courts to develop a detailed regime for the protection of public figures in the future.

2.3.2 Data-Based Risks to Personality Protection

Apart from the possible damage listed above related to the Internet, a conspicuous risk factor in today's digitized world is data. As the world undergoes a shift from Web 1.0 to Web 2.0, personal information continues to be collected in both unprecedented form and speed. Internet users are largely accustomed to free services that range from search engines to social networking sites, media platforms, and price comparison services. These services may be free monetarily, yet enterprises gain personal data in exchange overtly or covertly. Individuals and enterprises are mutually dependent in this new era of big data, forming a "symbiotic web." Actually, this data-based symbiosis is not limited to the online world. Loyalty cards and transport payment systems connect consumers and enterprises in an increasingly similar manner in cyberspace.[78]

In all these circumstances, people exchange their personal information for convenience. Yet the so far benign reality has the risk of turning dark. Its challenges are deeply felt, as major jurisdictions make efforts to legislate on data protection. Typical legislation concerning data protection include the European Union's General Data Protection Regulation and California's Consumer Privacy Act. Behind this kind of regulation lurks a shared worry about data-based risks, notably around how

[78] Paul Bernal, *Internet Privacy Rights: Rights to Protect Autonomy* (Cambridge: Cambridge University Press, 2014), pp. 53–81.

personal data may be exploited at the expense of privacy. In the Anglo-American tradition, legal discourses that have long been centered on "privacy" serve as the major academic vehicle for the conceptualization of dignitary interests and the closest analog to the continental concept of personality rights.[79] While privacy is traditionally understood as a defensive right to be left alone that prohibits unwanted intrusion or disclosure, the exploitation of personal information in the era of big data focuses primarily on the consent-based use of such information.[80] Simply put, the traditional understanding is centered on "privacy as secrecy," while in the latter the emphasis is on "privacy as control."[81]

This expansion leads Alan Westin to redefine privacy as "the claim of individuals, groups, or institutions to determine for themselves when, how, and to what extent information about them is communicated to others."[82] In a sense, the notion of privacy has been reoriented and has gained a social dimension. The traditional idea that privacy means the "individual against the world" is gradually shifting toward privacy being seen as trust. From this perspective, disclosure in the context of trust continues to remain private.[83] This also means that in a networked world, a privacy-careless person may disclose not only data about himself but about others as well. Data protection requires coordination and this has prompted Fairfield and Engel to argue that privacy is now a public good.[84] Yet as the World Economic Forum succinctly pointed out, "an information differential exists between institutions and individuals, creating a crisis of trust that results from uses of data being inconsistent with user expectations and preferences."[85]

[79] Daniel J. Solove, *Understanding Privacy* (Cambridge, MA: Harvard University Press, 2008); Stig Strömholm, "Right of privacy and rights of the personality: A comparative survey" International Commission of Jurists (May 1967), www.icj.org/wp-content/uploads/1967/06/right-to-privacy-working-paper-publication-1967-eng.pdf.

[80] Maurizio Borghi, Federico Ferretti, and Stavroula Karapapa, "Online data processing consent under EU law: A theoretical framework and empirical evidence from the UK" (2013) 21 *International Journal of Law and Information Technology* (2) 109–53.

[81] William L. Prosser, "Privacy" (1960) 48 *California Law Review* (3) 383–423; Alan Westin, *Privacy and Freedom* (New York: Atheneum, 1967).

[82] Westin, *Privacy and Freedom*, 7.

[83] Ari Ezra Waldman, "Privacy as trust: Sharing personal information in a networked world" (2015) 69 *University of Miami Law Review* (3) 559–630.

[84] Joshua A. T. Fairfield and Christoph Engel, "Privacy as a public good" (2015) 65 *Duke Law Journal* (3) 385–457.

[85] World Economic Forum (2014), "Rethinking Personal Data: Trust and Context in User-Centred Data Ecosystems" 1, www3.weforum.org/docs/WEF_RethinkingPersonalData_TrustandContext_Report_2014.pdf.

To some extent, China has witnessed this generational shift since the advent of Web 2.0. As outlined above, privacy underwent a gradual development as a personality right that culminated in the legal acknowledgment in the 2009 Tort Liability Law. However, only over a decade later, the protection of personal information was included explicitly, although only symbolically, in the 2017 GPCL.[86] Whether personal information should be protected primarily by the mechanism of entitlements to individuals under private law or regulatory regimes under public law remained controversial.[87] Nonetheless, the legislature eventually chose a multipronged approach to protect personal information. The current Book of Personality Rights in the Civil Code has followed the path of the GPCL and enriched private law entitlements to individuals to defend their personal information.

A separate chapter titled "Right to Privacy and Protection of Personal Information" (Chapter 6) systematically responds to data-based risks to personality. Article 1034 in this chapter defines personal information as "all kinds of information recorded electronically or in other form that can identify specific natural persons either by itself or when combined with other information, including the names, birth dates, ID numbers, biometric identification information, addresses, phone numbers, email addresses, health conditions, whereabouts, and so forth." This is consistent with the definition in the Cyber Security Law and offers a broad umbrella under which individuals can seek to protect all kinds of information that can be used to specify their personal identities. Around this umbrella are coordinating rules, including guiding principles for data processing (NPC 2020 Art. 1035) and the right of individuals to access their data and demand their correction or deletion (NPC 2020 Art. 1036–37). Those who have collected and stored data also have the legal duty to ensure their security and shall bear legal liability when such data are disclosed or divulged (NPC 2020 Art. 1038). This may not be the cure for all data-based risks in the ever-changing cyberspace, but it will be the first time that courts in China have principles and, more importantly, detailed rules under the Civil Code to rely on when judging individuals'

[86] NPC (2017) The General Principles of Civil Law Art. 111.

[87] Ding Xiaodong (丁晓东), "个人信息私法保护的困境与出路" ("The predicament of civil law protection of personal information and its solution") (2018) 法学研究 (6) 194–206; Cheng Xiao, "程啸 '民法典编纂视野下的个人信息保护" ("The protection of personal information from the perspective of the compilation of civil law") (2019) 4 中国法学 26–43.

claims for the protection of personal information against information collectors and processors.

The Book of Personality Rights also has established rules to strike a balance between the protection of personal information and the interests of information collectors and processors, as well as those of the general public. It provides for exceptional conditions to the prohibition on the illegal provision of personal information without consent, namely where information is processed in a way that makes it impossible to identify specific individuals and to restore the proceeded information to its original condition (NPC 2020 Art. 1038), allowing for some flexibility for information collectors. It also exempts collectors and processors from civil liabilities when the collection and processing of personal information of natural persons involves "other conduct reasonably carried out to preserve the public interest" (NPC 2020 Art. 1037), indicating that public interest outweighs the interest of specific natural persons in some circumstances. A good example is the collection and processing of travel information on confirmed or suspected patients with COVID-19 by the government for the purpose of epidemiological analysis and public health protection.

Despite the efforts mentioned above, the Book of Personality Law has left some questions unanswered. Following are three interconnected ones. First, what is the nature of the legally protected interest over personal information? Does it constitute a definitively enumerated type of civil right that, like the right to privacy, avails individuals self-determination over their personal information or merely a type of legally protected interest, the recognition of which is context dependent?[88] If it is merely a type of legally protected interest, then second, what is the relationship between "personal information" and "privacy"? Third, what is the scope of the legal interest over personal information? Aside from the right to access one's personal information, the right to copy one's personal information, and the right to correct errors in recording one's information, as already set forth in Article 1036, does the legal interest

[88] See Yang Lixin, "个人信息:法益抑或民事权利 – '民法总则' 第111 条规定的'个人信息'之解读" ("Personal information: Legal interest or civil rights? An interpretation of 'personal information' in Article 111 of the General Provisions of Civil Law") (2018) 33 法学论坛 34–55; Wang Liming (王利明), "论个人信息权的法律保护 – 个人信息权与隐私权的界分为中心" ("Legal protection of personal information: Centered on the line between personal information and privacy") (2013) 35 现代法学 62–72.

over personal information also avail individuals the rights to erasure and data portability and others?[89]

We believe that some confusion can be cleared up with the text available, while other questions are yet to be answered as social development unfolds. Unlike privacy, the subjects of which generally hope to keep personal information secret, individuals may use personal information in multiple contexts, and their expectations may vary depending on the context. In a job-seeking context, they want their LinkedIn profiles accessible to credible users. If a registrar makes mistakes while recording individuals' addresses, they want the mistakes corrected. When they no longer use an app, they want all their information stored on its servers deleted. When they move to another city, they want their social security information transferred to the new city.

The legal interest over personal information is hardly a definitive type of civil right but a broad umbrella under which individuals can safeguard multiple types of claims over their personal information, including the claim to access, copy, correct, and possibly erase and remove one's personal information. Each claim, once legally acknowledged, can constitute an independent type of civil right. The "legal interest over personal information" stipulated in Chapter 6 of the Book of Personality Rights acknowledges this combined nature. In an even broader sense, the right to privacy also falls under this umbrella, as it is no more than a legally acknowledged claim to keep certain personal information secret from others. The distinction between privacy claims and other personal information claims lies in individuals' expectations concerning their personal information. The former concerns passive restraint and the latter mainly involves active usage. This explains why Paragraph 3 under Article 1034 provides that "secret personal information is subject to both the

[89] The right to erasure, or the right to be forgotten, has been claimed in civil trials. For example, in *Ren Jiayu* (任甲玉) v. *Beijing Baidu Netcom Science and Technology Co., Ltd.* (北京百度网讯科技有限公司), the plaintiff claimed that Baidu had infringed upon his rights to name, reputation, and "to be forgotten," as included within the scope of the general personality right, by refusing to erase keywords for searches that related his name to an ill-reputed company for which he had worked for a short time in the past. For the "right to be forgotten" claim, without an enumerated "right to be forgotten" in Chinese law, the court of first trial examined the plaintiff's claim of legal interest in the case to see if it could be covered by the general personality right and denied that it could. The decision was upheld by the court of appeal (Beijing Court 北京市第一中级人民法院 (2015) 民事判决书京一中民终字第 09558号 (Civil judgment no. 09558) Beijing First Intermediate Court).

rules for personal information protection and the relevant provisions of privacy protection."

In response to whether the legal interest over personal information avails individuals the rights to erasure, data portability, and others, which was a widely debated question while drafting the Civil Code, the text in Chapter 6 suggests that the legislature has intentionally avoided the issue. In our view, the availability of these legal claims is still context dependent. As Bao Xiaoli and Xiong Bingwan have argued,[90] there is a "partnered" relationship between the individuals from whom personal information is generated and the collector or processor of such information, rendering self-determination an unfeasible and socially inefficient rule for the collection and processing of personal data.

2.3.3 Bioethical Risks to Personality Protection

While the Internet in general poses risks to the incorporeal personal spheres, ever-developing biotechnologies are bringing further challenges to corporeal personal attributes. Bioethical risks are arguably among the most controversial ones in the legal protection of personality, not least because they often involve hard ethical questions. Human embryos, surrogacy, organ transplantation, genetic engineering of embryos, and simulation by AI (artificial intelligence) entail fraught issues everywhere in the world. The sometimes intertwined relationship between biomedical and data risks complicates the situation further, as biological data such as fingerprints, faces, voices, and genomes are digitally collected, disseminated, and used, and are therefore subject to ever growing misuse and manipulation.[91]

Developments in biotech have immense implications for the law. For one thing, biomedical technologies in a way objectify human bodies, as modern technologies have blurred "the boundaries between nature and artifice, constraint and freedom" and controversial uses of body parts or tissues now abound in the private law area.[92] This process of objectification makes a person not only a legal subject but also a legal object at the

[90] Bao Xiaoli (包晓丽) and Xiong Bingwan (熊丙万), "通讯录数据中 的社会关系资本 – 据要素产权配置的研究范式" ("Social capitals in the data of contacts: A research paradigm for the distribution of data properties") (2020) 2 中国法律评论 (*China Law Review*) 146–68.

[91] Haidan Chen, Benny Chan, and Yann Joly, "Privacy and biobanking in China: A case of policy in transition" (2015) 43 *Journal of Law, Medicine & Ethics* (4) 726–42.

[92] Resta, "New frontiers of personality rights," 40.

same time, transcending the traditional subject/object dichotomy while also reinforcing the freedom of choice and self-determination. Objectifying such corporeal rights and interests inevitably leads to their commercialization. As Chapter 6, "Right to Privacy and Protection of Personal Information" points out, owing to ethical and equality concerns, they will never be fully commercialized. The distinctive measures taken by the current law for commercialization of corporeal/incorporeal rights is an example.

Yet biomedical risks can go far beyond the excessive commodification of personal attributes. Many medical advances in China rely on clinical trials on human bodies and scientific studies of human genes and embryos.[93] The inherent unpredictability of biotechnological risks also requires taking major precautions in clinical applications and trials and scientific studies. Otherwise, the result may be irreparable harm to individuals and possibly the general public.

Early cases brought before Chinese courts after the passage of the Tort Liability Law in 2009 were mainly centered on clinical trials of non-biological medical products, in which the medical institutions and staff neither fully respected the will of the testing participants nor fully informed the participants of all the risks involved.[94] Article 55 of the Tort Liability Law requires that

> during the diagnosis and treatments, the medical staff shall explain the illness condition and relevant medical measures to their patients. If any operation, special examination or special treatment is needed, the medical staff shall explain the medical risks, alternate medical treatment plans and other information to the patient in a timely manner, and obtain a written consent of the patient . . .. Where any medical staff members fails to fulfill the duties in the preceding paragraph and causes any harm to a patient, the medical institution shall assume the compensatory liability.

However, this fails to pay special attention to malpractice in clinical trials; at least, it does not specify whether medical staff should bear a higher level of duty of care in clinical trials than in ordinary clinical treatments. The ambiguity in this article has also led to divergent views in courtroom decisions on liability.[95]

[93] Man Hongjie (满洪杰), "医学人体试验中的侵权责任 – 比较法为视角" ("Tort liability and clinical trials: From the perspective of comparative law") (2012) 5 法学论坛 113–20.
[94] Ibid.
[95] Ibid.

More recently, the focus of the debate has shifted to cutting-edge biomedical technologies, as the necessity and appropriateness of gene editing is being significantly challenged. In late 2018, He Jiankui, a Chinese medical scientist, stunned the world by announcing that he had created the world's first genetically edited babies. Exploiting the most popular gene-editing tool, known as CRISPR-Cas9, his team edited the DNA of two embryos so that they would be less susceptible to HIV. The human embryos were later implanted into two women who gave birth to three babies.[96] The research has been condemned widely by scientists worldwide, raising questions of risk disclosure to and consent from the ones experiencing the procedure and of other unknown consequences. He Jiankui was later convicted of the illegal practice of medicine, practicing medicine without a certificate, and other serious violations of the law.[97] Though issues pertaining to ethical review did not figure in the criminal conviction, the court stated that the defendant had fabricated ethical review documents while carrying out embryo gene-editing.[98] According to Article 7 of Measures for Ethical Review of Biomedical Research Involving Humans (Measures for Ethical Review) issued in 2016 by the then National Health and Family Planning Commission, medical institutions conducting biomedical research involving humans shall establish ethics committees and take measures to ensure that the committees conduct ethics reviews.

Since 2003, when the China Food and Drug Administration enacted the Norms on Quality Management for the Clinical Trials of Drugs, China has been promoting two major measures in protecting patients who accept clinical trials. One aims to ensure that patients are well informed of the medical risks and legal consequences of clinical trials; the other aims to strengthen the ethics review process.[99] In addition to the Measures for Ethical Review issued in 2016, the State Council

96 Cyranoski D, Ledford H. Genome-edited baby claim provokes international outcry. *Nature*. 2018 Nov;563(7733) 607–8. doi: 10.1038/d41586-018-07545-0. PMID: 30482929.

97 Ian Sample, "Chinese scientist who edited babies' genes jailed for three years" *Guardian*, December 30, 2019, https://theguardian.com/world/2019/dec/30/gene-editing-chinese-scientist-he-jiankui-jailed-three-years.

98 Associated Press, "Scientist who claimed to make world's first gene-edited babies sentenced to 3 years" *USA Today*, December 30, 2019, www.usatoday.com/story/news/nation/2019/12/30/he-jiankui-chinese-scientist-gene-edited-babies-sentenced-3-years/2772994001/.

99 State Food and Drug Administration (国家食品药品监督管理总局) (2003), "药物临床试验质量管理规范" ("Norms on the quality management for the clinical trials of drugs"), Art. 8, 10, www.cnpharm.com/c/2020-06-03/733827.shtml.

promulgated the Regulation on the Prevention and Settlement of Medical Disputes in 2018 to maintain order and security in medical institutions. Article 11 of this state regulation reiterates the significance of the ethics review of clinical trials in medical institutions.[100] A year later, the Standing Committee of NPC adopted the Basic Healthcare and Health Promotion Law, which expanded the scope of the application of ethics review measures to include all medical research activities.[101]The Book of Personality Rights in the Civil Code has gone a step further, devoting two lengthy articles (NPC 2020 Arts. 1008, 1009) to systemically reconstructing the fragmented rules governing clinical trials and scientific studies at the national level. They provide a legal framework for the ethics of medical experiments in general and biomedical technologies related to human genomes and embryonic tissues as well, in order to prevent the moral hazards of life science and medical treatment. In conjunction with the rule of tort liability for malpractice in clinical applications in the Book of Tort Liability (NPC 2020 Art. 1219), the Civil Code has established a comprehensive system for the entire field of medical practices and disputes.

Article 1008 of the code covers not only the clinical trials of drugs and medical devices but also those of the medical methods of disease prevention and treatment. The application of gene editing for the sake of disease prevention and treatment, like the gene editing operation carried out by He Jiankui, falls within the scope of this article. The tried persons' consent in writing on the condition of detailed information on the purpose, usage, and possible risks involved in the medical research, as well as the approvals from the competent governmental departments and ethics committees, is clearly required before such clinical trials are conducted.

Article 1009 addresses medical and scientific research on human genes and embryos and the like. It provides that such activities shall observe laws, regulations, and other relevant state rules without jeopardizing human health and violating ethics and morality. This article is not declaratory but legally binding on the judiciary. In an era when cases of

[100] *China Daily*, "Preventing and handling medical disputes by rules" *China Daily*, September 10, 2018, http://global.chinadaily.com.cn/a/201809/10/WS5b95bd95a31033b4f465510c.html.

[101] NPCSC (2019) 中华人民共和国基本医疗卫生与健康促进法 (Basic healthcare and health promotion law) Art. 32, English translation at www.pkulaw.com/en_law/22a006a09f3565e4bdfb.html?flag=english.

animal cloning are not rare,[102] and discussions on human cloning have not stopped, it is foreseeable that both therapeutic and possible reproductive cloning concerning humans will be subject to definitive legal principles.[103] Where biomedical technologies revolutionize what it means to be human, these articles can arguably generate far-reaching effects in tackling the risks of biomedical technologies to personality protection.

Nonetheless, the Book of Personality Law's addressing of biomedical risks is still preliminary. Cases and experiences in Chinese society are not rich enough to spur a systematic response to all the various and sundry questions that have been raised. We reflect on two questions that are in need of answers today.

One centers on the scope of application. Whereas Article 1009 lays down the requirements for conducting "medical and scientific research relating to human genes and embryos," to what extent it operates as "relating to" needs an explanation. For example, is creating a chimeric virus considered medical and scientific research relating to human genes and embryos? During the COVID-19 pandemic, Dr. Shi Zhengli of the Wuhan Institute of Virology was questioned about a study she had participated in earlier, where a chimeric virus was made using a surface protein of SHC014 and the backbone of a SARS virus.[104] The study was questioned for virus engineering, which might pose a "non-natural risk."[105] There has been no scientific evidence proving such "non-natural

[102] Andy Coghaln, "Scientists have cloned monkeys and it could help treat cancer" *New Scientist*, January 24, 2018, www.newscientist.com/article/mg23731623-600-scientists-have-cloned-monkeys-and-it-could-help-treat-cancer/#ixzz6EedNgsvh.

[103] Current discussions on the legal restraints on human cloning in China are mainly from the perspective of constitutional and criminal law. See Meng Fanzhuang, 孟凡壮, '克隆人技术立法的宪法界限(*The Constitutional Limits on the Legislation of Human Cloning Technology*) (Shanghai:上海人民出版社, 2018); Liu Changqiu, "刘长秋, '刑法学视域下的克隆人及其立法" ("Human cloning and relative legislation: From the perspective of criminal law") (2010) 4 现代法学 97–104. International discussions rarely touch upon the Chinese context. See Mikyung Kim, "An overview of the regulation and patentability of human cloning and embryonic stem cell research in the United States and anti-cloning legislation in the South Korea" (2004) 21 *Santa Clara Computer & High Technology Law Journal* (4) 645–714; Judith Daar, *Reproductive Technologies and the Law* (Newark, NJ: LexisNexis, 2013).

[104] Vineet D. Menachery et al., "A SARS-like cluster of circulating bat coronaviruses shows potential for human emergence"(2015) 21 *Nature Medicine* (12) 1508–13.

[105] Declan Butler, "Engineered bat virus stirs debate over risky research" *Nature*, November 12, 2015, http://nature.com/news/engineered-bat-virus-stirs-debate-over-risky-research-1.18787.

risk" yet. However, given the ethical concerns that such research might raise, it may seem reasonable to interpret the law as covering such research activities in the future. Also, considering the context in which the article was added, it may also be interpreted as only applying to research "targeting" human genes and embryos.

Another question concerns the nature and "ownership" of biomedical "products." The nature and "ownership" of frozen embryos and correspondingly biobanks are two examples. In 2013, in *Shen Xinnan* (沈新南) *and Shao Yumei* (邵玉妹) v. *Liu Jinfa* (刘金法) *and Hu Xingxian* (胡杏仙), a couple in Jiangsu died in a car accident leaving behind four frozen embryos in a hospital. The parents of the husband filed a case against the parents of the wife to inherit the embryos. The court of first trial denied the claim on the ground that the embryos were not objects to be inherited,[106] while the court of appeal overturned the judgment, avoided mentioning "inheritance," and decided that the parents of both the husband and the wife should have the right of guardianship and disposal of the embryos.[107]

Disputes over the nature and "ownership" of frozen embryos continue. Professor Yang Lixin,[108] for example, argued that frozen embryos, as organs and tissues separated from the human body, should be recognized as "ethical objects" – special objects with attributes of a human being deserving particular protection, but not a third category beyond the subject/object dichotomy, which can be inherited. In contrast, Professor Ji Hailong recognized embryos as objects and the old couples' general right to inherit them.[109] Nonetheless, considering the ethical controversy over the old couples' high tendency to turn the embryos into human beings with assisted reproductive technology, Professor Ji argued that the old couple's claim that the embryos be given to them should be denied.

Regarding the issue of frozen embryos, whether the custodian should be free to dispose of frozen embryos just as is the case with frozen products should the depositor fail to renew the custody agreement, and whether this should be within the duties of biobanks, are questions yet to be discussed. Voices have spoken out on the comparative law experience,

[106] Yixing Court (宜兴市人民法院) (2013) 民事判决书宜民初字第2729号 (Civil judgment no. 2729) Yixing Municipal Court.

[107] Wuxi Court (无锡市中级人民法院) (2014) 民事判决书锡民终字第1235号 (Civil judgment no. 1235) Wuxi Intermediate Court.

[108] Yang Lixin (杨立新), "人的冷冻胚胎的法律属性及其继承问题" ("The legal nature of frozen human embryos and issues on their inheritance") (2014) 人民司法 (*People's Judicature*) (13) 25–30.

[109] Ji Hailong (纪海龙), "法教义学: 力量与弱点" ("Legal dogma: Strengths and weaknesses") (2015) 2 交大法学 90–104 at 90.

such as the five-year time limit for the third-party storage of frozen embryos in France (French Act 94-654, adopted on July 29, 1994), but such voices have not had much of an impact on legislation.

2.3.4 Personality Right: Methodology for an Ever-Evolving Landscape

In the face of ever-evolving technology, how far can the Book of Personality Rights reach? This is probably not determined by the enumeration of major types of personality rights. Rather, the general clause on personality rights in this Book of Personality Rights will play a crucial role in the long run. Enumerations cannot be all-encompassing owing to the limited circumstances legislators can apprehend while drafting the law, while, from time to time, evolving technologies may present new threats to significant personal spheres that have thus far not been enumerated in the Book of Personality Rights.

The general clause in the Book of Personality Rights stipulates that "In addition to the personality rights explicitly provided in the previous paragraph, natural persons enjoy other personality rights and interests arising from personal liberty and human dignity" (NPC 2020 Art. 990). This general clause reflects the inexhaustible nature of personality rights and acknowledges the emerging claims of personality interests that do fit into those enumerated types easily but are equally worthy of protection.

The articulation of "other personality rights" in this clause would require a comprehensive assessment of the social circumstances and impact of new claims for legal protection. Article 1026 illustrates this approach when enumerating factors considered to determine whether news reporters or watchdogs have met the "obligations for reasonable review":[110] "(1) credibility of the source of the content; (2) whether necessary investigation was conducted into the content that might clearly lead to controversy; (3) the time sensitivity of the content; (4) the relationship of the content with public order and good morals; (5) the likelihood that victims' reputation would be derogated; (6) the capacity and the cost for review." Here, the code requires that attention be paid to specific circumstances and interests of multiple stakeholders –the victim, the conductor, and the public. Whereas there is no definitive answer as to how to apply the general clause, similar approaches can be employed in the

[110] Except in situations including the failure to meet obligations to reasonably review inaccurate information provided by others, one does not bear civil liability by "affecting any other's reputation" merely because of one's conduct, such as carrying out news reporting or public opinion supervision (Item 2, Art. 1025).

sense that a comprehensive assessment of social circumstances and impacts is necessary and that the interests of all related stakeholders are balanced.

Moreover, the open, general clause may add to the probability that the Civil Code can make up for the shortcoming that China's Constitution cannot be directly invoked and enforced by courts in individual cases.[111] As we have argued throughout this chapter, while dealing with personality protection vis-à-vis private parties, the Book of Personality Rights has the merit of implementing Article 38 of the Constitution, which declares the inviolability of personal dignity.[112] While it is hard to tell how far such implementation might extend to the relationship between individuals and public authorities, an open general clause may be a major channel for such an extension.

For example, public authorities' disproportionate measures to coerce defaulting debtors to comply with effective court decisions can constitute an invasion of people's personality rights. Recently, some local courts have begun to post defaulters' information on their official Douyin (the Chinese version of TikTok) accounts or the news app Toutiao and display such information repeatedly among the defaulters' localities with the facilitation of big data.[113] This shaming measure has proven effective in uncovering hiding defaulters or coercing some of them to pay their debts.[114] But arguably, it is disproportionately detrimental to the defaulters' social reputation and should be replaced by other enforcement tools. While it is unlikely that overexposed defaulters may claim definitive enumerated rights under the Book of Personality Rights for practical remedies, an open general clause at least provides a possibility to make a claim before the court.

[111] Liu Kaixiang (刘凯湘), "人格权的宪法意义与民法表述" ("The constitutional properties of personality rights and their expression in civil law") (2012) 2 社会科学战线 (*Social Science Front*) 200–208; Zhang Xinbao (张新宝), "我国人格权立法: 体系、边界和保护" ("The legislation of personality right in China: System, boundaries and protection") (2012) 2 法商研究 3–7; Qianfan Zhang, "A constitution without constitutionalism? The paths of constitutional development in China" (2010) 8 *International Journal of Constitutional Law* (4) 950–76.

[112] Rémy Cabrillac, "Le Code civil chinois" (2020) *Recueil Dalloz* (24) 1375–79.

[113] Sohu, "搜狐 '厉害了! 利用抖音发布执行悬赏, 全国法院系统第一家!" ("Incredible! The first court to publicize 'wanted enforcees'") Sohu, June 8, 2018, www.sohu.com/a/234686240_100017684.

[114] You Yiwei (尤一炜), "精准推送线索悬赏令 法官九分钟破解执行难" ("Targeted push for wanted enforcees enables judges to find the enforcee in nine minutes") 南方都市报, November 13, 2019, http://epaper.oeeee.com/epaper/A/html/2019-11/13/content_47399.htm.

2.4 Concluding Thoughts

The adoption of a stand-alone book on personality rights in China's new Civil Code is not a mere technical matter. Instead, behind the technical change in the structures of conventional civil codes lies the growing consciousness of nonmaterial rights in Chinese civil society and the Chinese legislature's efforts to respond to them in a systemic manner. We hope that our investigation of the Book of Personality Law in the Chinese Civil Code can enrich Chinese studies that have primarily paid attention to the consciousness of both the right to subsistence and political rights.

The structural departure from conventional civil codes arguably provides a new approach to cope with the unprecedented quantitative and qualitative challenges to personality protection posed by technology explosion, inasmuch as a stand-alone part on personality rights may provide the opportunity to systemically address emerging claims in personal spheres against technological risks through high-level legislation.

Notwithstanding questions solved or likely to be solved by the Book of Personality Rights, its role in promoting personality protection in Chinese society should not be overestimated. The growth of rights consciousness and the evolution of technology are never-ending. The actual impact of the Book of Personality Rights is largely to be demonstrated in judgments following its adoption. In circumstances where the legislature remains silent, the courts inevitably have to decide whether certain claims of personality are worth protecting. For example, legal theorists have widely considered facial geometry and biometric information as an essential part of the personal sphere that are worth defending.[115] The collection of facial information, if leaked or hacked, may result in deep-fake videos and social discrimination. While the Book of Personality Rights has provisions addressing the right to privacy and personal information protection, it does not take an additional step, as

115 Issues arising out of facial recognition are not unique to China but are becoming matters of global concern. In the United Kingdom, a case was brought against police use of facial recognition (Adam Satariano, "Police use of facial recognition is accepted by British court" *New York Times*, September 4, 2019, www.nytimes.com/2019/09/04/business/facial-recognition-uk-court.html). Facebook and Google have also been sued for allegedly violating the Illinois Biometric Privacy Act by failing to get users' consent for collecting, storing, and using their biometric identifiers, including face geometry (see Ally Marotti, "After Facebook agrees to pay $550 million settlement to Illinois users, Google sued over same law" *Chicago Tribune*, February 11, 2020, www.chicagotribune.com/business/ct-biz-google-facial-recognition-lawsuit-20200211-3pzwk7qwznhfvgdv5lk2bdyqu4-story.html).

Shi Jiayou has proposed,[116] to label certain categories of personal information as "sensitive" in order to heighten their legal protection. It is questionable whether facial geometry can be effectively protected since facial recognition has become ubiquitous in China. In a recent case, a law professor from Zhejiang Sci-Tech University in eastern China filed a lawsuit against a wildlife safari for conducting facial recognition upon entry, claiming that the mandatory collection of visitors' facial data by the safari had violated its obligation to obtain his informed consent under China's Consumer Protection Law.[117] In the future, plaintiffs may invoke the Book of Personality Rights to challenge those who collect their facial information. As the Book of Personality Rights provides the same level of protection for personal biometric information as for other types of personal information, courts will play an essential role in deciding whether such a change in the cause of action from consumer protection law to civil law can establish a substantively strengthened personality protection regime or remain a matter of mere technical presentation.

[116] Shi Jiayou (石佳友), "人格权立法的进步与局限 – '民法典人 格权编草案(三审稿)'" ("Progress and limits on the legislation on personality rights: Remarks on the draft for the third reading of the Book of Personality Rights of the Civil Code") (2019) 13 清华法学 (5) 93–110.

[117] Shan Li, "Chinese professor files rare lawsuit over use of facial-recognition technology" *Wall Street Journal* (November 4, 2019).

3

Force Majeure or Change of Circumstances

An Enduring Dichotomy in Chinese Law?

LIU QIAO

Every legal system faces the challenge of balancing commercial certainty with fairness or justice when dealing with supervening events that impede contract performance. Chinese law handles the task through two distinct rules: the doctrine of *force majeure* and the doctrine of change of circumstances. Both are default rules attempting to allocate the risk of the relevant supervening event between the contracting parties where they fail to do so in their contract. Both have now become part of the Chinese Civil Code (CCC).[1] How have these two doctrines been applied by Chinese courts in practice? A quick search on the official China Judgment Online website turns up a striking revelation: in the past decade or so, a period in which both doctrines enjoyed formal legal status and online court judgments proliferated, for every contract case decided pursuant to the doctrine of change of circumstances, there were over ten contract cases decided pursuant to the doctrine of *force majeure*.[2] What might account for such disproportionality? What implications might it have for the interrelationship between the two doctrines? Might it, for example, suggest that there is something wrong with that relationship and that the two doctrines do not work well together? This chapter will first outline the key distinctions that create a dichotomy between the two doctrines (Section 3.1) and then examine how the interrelationship between the two doctrines has changed and might be further improved

[1] Civil Code of the People's Republic of China [中华人民共和国民法典] (adopted at the Third Session of the 13th National People's Congress on 28 May 28 2020, effective 1 January 2021) arts. 180 and 590 (definition of *force majeure* and exemption of liability), 563(1) (*force majeure* termination), 533 (change of circumstances).

[2] See http://wenshu.court.gov.cn. A search was conducted for all contract cases containing '*force majeure*/change of circumstances' as key words. In the year of 2020, for example, the numbers of *force majeure* cases and change of circumstances cases were respectively 32,047 and 2,524.

by reference to Chinese courts' approach to the SARS and the COVID-19 pandemics (Section 3.2), before arriving at some suggestions for possible future reformation of this area of Chinese law (Section 3.3).

3.1 The Existing Dichotomy

The doctrine of *force majeure* and the doctrine of change of circumstances have an opaque and troublesome relationship under Chinese law. This can be traced back to their different origins and paths of evolution. Briefly speaking, the doctrine of *force majeure* has long been recognised, in one form or another, by various 'laws' promulgated by the National People's Congress (NPC).[3] By contrast, the doctrine of change of circumstances is widely believed to have first emerged from judicial practice, in the form of an analogous application of the doctrine of *force majeure*.[4] In 1999, however, the NPC vetoed the inclusion of the doctrine of change of circumstances into the CCL, citing wide, unfettered judicial discretion as its main concern.[5] It was not until ten years later that the doctrine found its way into a SPC judicial interpretation.[6] Nevertheless, even after its elevation to a provision in the CCC,[7] the doctrine still suffers from lack of clarity in its interpretation and application. In particular, the division of work between the two doctrines remains a source of tension and confusion, and unnecessary overlapping and contradictions between them are

[3] E.g., Economic Contract Law of the People's Republic of China [中华人民共和国经济合同法] (adopted at the Fourth Session of the Fifth NPC on 13 December 1981, amended on 2 September 1993) arts. 26(2), 27, 30; General Principles of Civil Law of the People's Republic of China [中华人民共和国民法通则] (adopted at the Fourth session of the Sixth NPC, amended on 27 August 2009) arts. 107, 153; Contract Law of the People's Republic of China [中华人民共和国合同法] (adopted at the Second Session of the Ninth NPC on March 15, 1999 and effective as of 1 October 1999, hereafter CCL) arts. 94(1), 117, 118.

[4] *Wuhan Gas Company* v. *Chongqing Testing Instrument Factory* [武汉市煤气公司诉重庆检测仪表厂煤气装配线技术转让合同、煤气表散件购销合同纠纷案], Hubei High People's Court (HPC), in *Gazette of the Supreme People's Court [最高人民法院公报] (SPC Gazette)*, 1996, Issue 2, 63.

[5] Bing Ling, *Contract Law in China* (Sweet & Maxwell Asia, 2002) 293–94 [5.088].

[6] Interpretation II of the Supreme People's Court on Certain Issues concerning the Application of the Contract Law of the People's Republic of China [最高人民法院关于适用《中华人民共和国合同法》若干问题的解释（二）] (Fa Shi [2009] No. 5, adopted at the 1462nd meeting of the Judicial Committee of the SPC on 9 February 2009, effective as of 13 May 2009, repealed on 1 January 2021 [SPC Contract Interpretation II]) art. 26.

[7] CCC, art. 533.

not uncommon. This prompts one to make the following three enquiries about the interrelationship of the two doctrines.

3.1.1 Do They Address Different Events?

Force majeure is defined under Chinese law as an external event that must be at once 'unforeseeable, unavoidable, and insurmountable'.[8] Chinese courts have attached the label of *force majeure* to such events as the Severe Acute Respiratory Syndrome (SARS)[9] and the 12th of May Wenchuan earthquake.[10] Likewise, it has recently been declared by the Legal Work Committee of the NPC that the COVID-19 pandemic constitutes *force majeure*.[11] These categorical statements made by Chinese legal authorities demonstrate a general tendency to characterise an event as *force majeure* without assessing its actual or potential impact on the performance of the particular contract. The decision that a given event is 'unforeseeable, unavoidable and insurmountable' thus tends to be made in the abstract and at a macro level. That such a tendency should be resisted is well demonstrated by the *Tianjin Second Harbour* case, where the Tianjin HPC affirmed the first instance decision of the Tianjin Maritime Court, which designated storm 9711 as *force majeure*.[12] Of particular importance to the decision was the fact that the storm, although forecasted by the National Ocean Forecasting Station, had been joined by astronomical tides and rare ocean waves, whose presence or impact was 'unforeseeable' by either the port or the cargo owner (Zhongji). The storm was also adjudged 'unavoidable' and 'insurmountable' only in light of the limited manpower and mechanical equipment

[8] CCC, art. 180. Also, CCL, art. 117.

[9] Beijing No. 2 Intermediate People's Court (IPC, with Guangdong HPC), 'Dealing Properly with Cases of SARS Constituting a Force Majeure Event That Exempts Liability' ['正确处理'非典'疫情构成不可抗力免责事由案件'] (2003)(6) *Application of Law [法律适用]* 8 (SARS Report); Gao Hongbin, 'SARS Is Not Force *M*ajeure' ['SARS非不可抗力'] (2003)(7) *Application of Law* 11.

[10] Yang Lixin, 'The General Impact of Earthquake as a Cause of *Force Majeure* in Civil Law' ['地震作为民法不可抗力事由的一般影响'] (2008) 8(1) *Politics and Law [政治与法律]* 2.

[11] Zang Tiewei, 'Answers to Legal Questions of General Social Concern in the Prevention and Control of the Pandemic', 10 February 2020, Question 5, www.npc.gov.cn/npc/c30834/202002/23100ec6c65145eda26ad6dc288ff9c9.shtml.

[12] *Zhongji General Import & Export Co* v. *Tianjin Port No. 2 Port & Harbor Co Ltd* [中机通用进出口公司诉天津港第二港埠有限公司港口作业合同纠纷案), Tianjin HPC (1999) Gao Jing Ji Zhi No. 9. Civil Judgment, *SPC Gazette*, 2000, Issue 5, 176.

that the port commanded. Consequently, the port was held not liable for damage inflicted upon Zhongji's goods during the storm. This case shows that the above three criteria of a *force majeure* event do not represent some free-standing tests but are intrinsically interwoven with the particular parties and contract.

The above tendency to classify certain events as *force majeure* sometimes finds expression in an attempt to distinguish *force majeure* from a change of circumstances on the basis that the former is of a non-economic nature whereas the latter consists mainly of economic events.[13] This is an overly crude demarcation based solely upon unscrutinised historical experience. It leads to the fallacy that certain events such as natural disasters and government actions are categorically excluded from the ambit of the doctrine of change of circumstances.[14] Such an arbitral distinction has been resisted in some significant decisions handed down by the SPC. For example, a natural disaster such as an 'unprecedented low water level in the past 36 years' has been held to constitute a change of circumstances affecting a contract for excavating a sand mine.[15] Similarly, the release by a local government of a new merger and reorganisation plan might well constitute a change of circumstances affecting a contract for the transfer of interests in a coal mine.[16]

In fact, any attempt to artificially distinguish *force majeure* from a change of circumstances on the basis of the characters of the event has been dealt a fatal blow by art. 533 of the CCC, which removes the prior SPC requirement for a change of circumstances to be 'other than *force majeure*'.[17] However, that Article retains the requirement that a change of circumstances 'must not constitute a commercial risk'. The SPC offered the following authoritative interpretation of 'commercial risk':

[13] E.g., Liu Kaixiang and Zhang Haixia, 'On *Force Majeure*' ['论不可抗力'] (2000) 6 *Chinese Journal of Law [法学研究]* 117.

[14] Han Qiang, 'A Typological Study of the Doctrine of Change of Circumstances' ['情势变更原则的类型化研究'] (2010) 4(4) *Chinese Journal of Law* 62.

[15] *Chengdu Pengwei Industrial Co Ltd* v. *The People's Government of Yongxiu County, Jiangxi Province and Yongxiu County Poyang Lake Sand Mining Management Leading Group Office* [成都鹏伟实业有限公司与江西省永修县人民政府、永修县鄱阳湖采砂管理工作领导小组办公室采矿权纠纷案], SPC (2008) Min Er Zhan Zi No. 91 Civil Judgment, *SPC Gazette*, Vol. 2010, 348.

[16] *Ren Weijun* v. *Zhang Xiang* [任维俊、张翔采矿权转让合同纠纷案], SPC (2016) Zui Gao Fa Min Zhong No. 781 Civil Judgment (holding that the new plan had been unforeseeable by the parties).

[17] SPC Contract Interpretation II.

> Commercial risks refer to risks inherent in the conduct of commercial activities, such as changes in supply-demand and price fluctuations that have not as yet reached the level of abnormal changes. A change of circumstances is a risk which cannot be foreseen by the parties at the time of the contract and which is not inherent in the market system. When determining whether a major objective change constitutes a change of circumstances, a people's court should identify a change of circumstances and a commercial risk in individual cases by considering, together with the particular conditions of the market, such factors as whether the type of the risk is unforeseeable according to the general conception of the society, whether the degree of the risk far exceeds the reasonable expectation of ordinary people, whether the risk can be prevented and controlled, and whether the nature of the transaction falls within the scope of what is commonly held as 'high-risk, high-yield'.[18]

'Commercial risks' are, therefore, 'inherent', or more bluntly 'normal', risks. The concept is not intended to denote any 'non-commercial' nature of a change of circumstances. The passage quoted above also indicates the multifariousness of the concept. At least in part, it serves the same function as the foreseeability test. Indeed, it portends the same multifactorial test to be applied in identifying *any* qualified event, focussing on how the relevant risk should be borne and shared by the contracting parties. As such, there can be no dispute that the same event could constitute both *force majeure* and a change of circumstances, which are homogeneous in the sense that any qualified event must be 'unforeseeable, unavoidable and insurmountable'.[19] A categorical characterisation of certain events as *force majeure* has the effect of inflating its application, not only at the expense of the doctrine of change of circumstances but

[18] Guiding Opinions of the Supreme People's Court on Several Issues Concerning the Adjudication of Civil and Commercial Contract Dispute Cases under the Current Situation [最高人民法院关于当前形势下审理民商事合同纠纷案件若干问题的指导意见] (Fa Fa [2009] No. 40) art. 1(3).

[19] Wang Liming, 'Exploring Some Issues of the Regime of Change of Circumstances – Commenting on Article 323 of the Draft Civil Code Contracts (Second Review Draft)' ['情事变更制度若干问题探讨 – 评"民法典合同编（草案）"（二审稿）第３２３条'] (2019) 3 *Studies in Law and Business [法商研究]* 7–8; Cao Shouye, 'Understanding and Applying the SPC Interpretation II on Certain Issues concerning the Application of the Contract Law of the People's Republic of China' ['最高人民法院"关于适用<中华人民共和国合同法>若干问题的解释（二）" 之情势变更问题的理解与适用'] (2009) (8) *Application of Law* 45. Cf. the United Nations Convention on Contracts for the International Sale of Goods (CISG) art. 79(1); the UNCITRAL Digest of Case Law on the United Nations Convention on Contracts for the International Sale of Goods (2016), p. 375.

also in disregard of the differing 'contract impact' tests and legal consequences that they each espouse.

3.1.2 *What Different 'Contract Impact' Tests Are Applied?*

Both the doctrine of *force majeure* and the doctrine of change of circumstances have their own 'contract impact' tests, which measure the impact of a qualified event on the performance of the contract in question. In so far as an event is established as a 'sufficient' cause of the requisite impact,[20] different impact tests are applied. With respect to *force majeure*, there are two separate legal tests: for a *force majeure* to exempt a party wholly or partially from its liability for non-performance, the event must result in a situation that the party 'cannot perform' its side of the contract (the 'cannot perform' test);[21] for a party to terminate the contract, the event must render the purpose of the contract 'unfulfillable' (the 'contract purpose' test).[22] With respect to change of circumstances, the CCC has endorsed a single test for a court or arbitral tribunal to terminate or adapt the contract at a party's request: the event must render continuing performance of the contract 'manifestly unfair' to the requesting party (the 'manifest unfairness' test).[23] Consequently, the two doctrines are nowadays clearly distinguished first and foremost by virtue of the differing 'contract impact' tests they employ. In the low water level case above, the SPC held that it was the doctrine of change of circumstances that should be applied since the event, which reduced the amount of sand excavatable under the contract, did not lead to a

[20] *Jia-shan Jingxin Film Co Ltd* v. *Jia-shan Luo Shang Metal Products Co Ltd* [嘉善景鑫薄膜有限公司、嘉善骆商金属制品有限公司房屋买卖合同纠纷二审民事判决书], Jiaxing IPC (2018) Zhe 04 Min Zhong Zi No. 2840 Civil Judgment; *Chongqing Changhong Plastic Factory* v. *Chongqing Tianlong Real Estate Development Co Ltd* [重庆长虹塑料厂与重庆天龙房地产开发有限公司房屋拆迁安置补偿合同纠纷二审民事判决书], SPC (2016) Zui Gao Fa Min Zhong Zi No. 203 Civil Judgment. Such a causal requirement is seldom met in cases where the alleged impact takes the form of a failure to pay contractual sums: *Yao Sheng (Xiamen) Property Management Co Ltd* v. *Qingdao Haixie Trust Investment Co Ltd* [耀声（厦门）物业管理有限公司与青岛海协信托投资有限公司借款担保合同纠纷上诉案], SPC (2007) Min Er Zhong Zi No. 92 Civil Judgment.

[21] CCC, art. 590. Also, CCC, art. 832 (carrier's liability exempted); CCL, art. 117. The term 'cannot perform' reads '不能履行' in Chinese.

[22] CCC, art. 563. Also, CCL, art. 94(1). The original Chinese text for 'render the purpose of the contract unfulfillable' is '不能实现合同目的'.

[23] CCC, art. 533. The term 'manifestly unfair' reads '明显不公平' in Chinese. One major change the CCC made to the doctrine of change of circumstances as adopted in the SPC Contract Interpretation II is thus the removal of the 'contract purpose' test.

situation where either party 'could not perform' its contract or where the purpose of the contract became 'unfulfillable' but merely made continuous performance of the contract 'manifestly unfair'.[24]

As between the two tests enshrined under the doctrine of *force majeure*, the 'cannot perform' test has been in wider use. This test is open for two different interpretations. In a narrow sense, 'cannot perform' may be confined to inability or impossibility to perform. In a broad sense, 'cannot perform' may be understood as referring to a 'failure to perform'. Although the narrow sense has been adopted in some cases, it is too restrictive and not intended by the legislature. The broad sense seems preferable and, as will be seen, has gained the upper hand. By contrast, the 'contract purpose' test is by its nature a more limited application, as can be seen from its application in determining whether a 'fundamental breach' arises under Chinese law.[25] Likewise, in *force majeure* cases, it has been held that 'the purpose of the contract' is not divisible but refers to the main purpose of the whole contract.[26] Further, the mere fact that one of the parties fails to obtain the profits expected under the contract is also said to be insufficient to render the purpose of the contract unfulfillable.[27]

In comparison, the doctrine of change of circumstances is now fully occupied by the 'manifest unfairness' test, which seemingly possesses the elasticity to cover cases involving commercial impracticality, onerousness and reduced profitability. In practice, however, this test has been less frequently applied than the 'contract purpose' test. One explanation for this is the uncertainty generated by the very concept of 'manifest unfairness', which poses a considerable challenge to the judge resorting to that concept. A more important, one tends to say 'decisive', factor is the SPC's rather cautious requirement that a lower court must seek approval from

[24] *Chengdu Pengwei Industrial Co Ltd* v. *The People's Government of Yongxiu County, Jiangxi Province and Yongxiu County Poyang Lake Sand Mining Management Leading Group Office* [成都鹏伟实业有限公司与江西省永修县人民政府、永修县鄱阳湖采砂管理工作领导小组办公室采矿权纠纷案], SPC (2008) Min Er Zhan Zi No. 91 Civil Judgment, *SPC Gazette*, Vol. 2010, 348.

[25] CCC, art. 563(4). Also, CCL, art. 94(4). For such restrictive application, see *Xinjiang Yakun Commercial Trade Co Ltd* v. *Xinjiang Jinghe Kangrui Cotton Processing Co Ltd* [新疆亚坤商贸有限公司与新疆精河县康瑞棉花加工有限公司买卖合同纠纷案], SPC 9 December 2006 (2006) Min Er Zhong Zi No111 Civil Judgment, *SPC Gazette*, 2006, Vol. 11, 17.

[26] E.g., *Guo Yuefeng and Zhang Hongzhao* v. *Liu Yanwei* [郭跃峰、张红朝与刘艳伟股权转让纠纷申请再审民事裁定书], SPC (2013) Min Ti Zi No. 170 Civil Ruling.

[27] Han, 'A Typological Study', pp. 66–67.

an HPC, or the SPC when necessary, before applying the doctrine of change of circumstances.[28] This has accounted for a significantly higher proportion of SPC and HPC decisions in cases where the doctrine of change of circumstances is invoked.[29]

3.1.3 *How Do Their Legal Consequences Differ?*

The most obvious difference between the two doctrines in terms of their legal consequences is perhaps the availability of contract adaptation, which is unique to the doctrine of change of circumstances. If the SPC maintains its pre-CCC position, then contract adaptation will be prioritised over contract termination.[30] First, where a party requests contract adaptation, a court or arbitral tribunal may not order a termination/rescission of the contract; in contrast, an order of contract adaptation may be made where a party requests contract termination/rescission.[31] Second, it has been suggested that contract adaptation be adopted as the standard response to manifest unfairness and only where contract adaptation is impossible or inappropriate or where contract purpose becomes unfulfillable, should contract termination be ordered.[32] This favouritism towards contract adaptation reflects the principle of *favor contractus* in the European civilian tradition.[33]

[28] SPC Notice on the Correct Application of the Interpretation II to the Contract Law to Serve the Overall Work of the Party and the State [最高人民法院关于正确适用《中华人民共和国合同法》若干问题的解释(二)服务党和国家的工作大局的通知], Fa [2009] No. 165, 27 April 2009, pt. 2, para. 2.

[29] The figures in the search described at note 2 above show that roughly 0.3 per cent of change of circumstances cases were SPC decisions and 3.4 per cent were HPC decisions, compared to 0.1 per cent SPC decisions and 1.8 per cent HPC decisions in *force majeure* cases.

[30] Contrast: International Institute for the Unification of Private Law, Principles of International Commercial Contracts (2016, [UNIDROIT Principles 2016]), art. 6.2.3(4); Principles of European Contract Law, art. 6:111(3).

[31] CCL, art. 54; Opinion of the Supreme People's Court on Several Issues concerning the Implementation of the General Principles of the Civil Law of the People's Republic of China (Provisional) [最高人民法院关于贯彻执行＜中华人民共和国民法通则＞若干问题的意见（试行）], art. 73. Also: Cao, 'Understanding and Applying the SPC Interpretation II', p. 47.

[32] Han Shiyuan, 'Study on Certain Issues of Change of Circumstances' ['情事变更若干问题研究'] (2014) 3(3) *Peking University Law Journal* 668 et seq.

[33] Cf. J. P. Dawson, 'Judicial Revision of Frustrated Contracts: Germany' (1983) 63 *Boston University Law Review* 1039.

Contract adaptation should be, as a matter of principle, distinguished from exemption of liability triggered by *force majeure*. A liability exempted is a secondary obligation to (usually) pay damages arising from non-performance of a primary obligation. Hence, an exemption of liability does not affect the innocent party's right to demand performance, withhold its reciprocal performance or terminate the contract.[34] This distinction has, however, often been blurred in Chinese judicial practice. For example, in the *Shaanxi Zhongbei* case, the plaintiff contracted to buy some parts of a building with a total area of 27,000 square meters. Subsequently only 18,442 square meters were approved by the relevant planning authority for conveyance. The authority's decision was held to constitute *force majeure*. Nevertheless, the contract was enforced as if it had been adapted to a sale of 18,442 square meters of office area, with the vendor being ordered to return the price for the difference between the contracted and delivered areas and also to share a proportion of the loss of commercial value suffered by the purchaser.[35] The court failed to appreciate that the effect of the *force majeure* should be, and should only be, to excuse the vendor from the liability to pay damages for the short delivery. Instead, Chinese courts have vested in themselves a broad discretion to apportion losses between the parties based on the general principle of fairness, whether an external event gives rise to an exemption of liability, contract adaptation or contract termination.[36] Such a discretionary process tends to dismantle the proper confinement of liability exemption and hence to conflate it with other remedies such as contract adaptation.

[34] Huang Wei (ed.), *Interpretation on the Civil Code of the People's Republic of China* [中华人民共和国民法典释义] (Beijing: Law Press, 2020), vol. II, pp. 1142–43. Also CISG art. 79(1); UNIDROIT Principles 2016, art. 7.1.7; Stefan Vogenauer (ed.), *Commentary on the UNIDROIT Principles of International Commercial Contracts (PICC)* (Oxford: Oxford University Press, 2015), p. 866, nn. [3]–[4].

[35] *Shaanxi Zhongbei Real Estate Development Co Ltd* v. *Xi'an Tongfang Real Estate Development Co Ltd* [陕西中北房地产开发有限公司与西安市同方房地产开发有限公司土地使用权转让合同纠纷案], Shaanxi HPC (2007) Shaan Min Yi Zhong Zi No. 119 Civil Judgment.

[36] *Yumen City Xi Gui Renewable Resource Recovery Co Ltd* v. *Yumen Oil Field Branch of China National Petroleum Co* [玉门市喜贵再生资源回收有限责任公司、中国石油天然气股份有限公司玉门油田分公司合同纠纷再审审查与审判监督民事裁定书], SPC (2019) Zui Gao Fa Min Shen No. 3854 Civil Ruling; *Bai Junying* v. *Tumertzuo Banner People's Government* [白俊英、土默特左旗人民政府合同纠纷再审民事判决书], SPC (2016) Zui Gao Fa Min Zai No. 220 Civil Judgment.

Another difference between the two doctrines is the provision for contract renegotiation introduced by Article 533 of the CCC, which states that 'the party adversely affected may renegotiate with the other party'. Apparently, there is no obligation to engage in such renegotiation and no right to demand the other party to do so. A refusal to renegotiate or a failure to reach an agreement may not attract a pre-contractual liability in damages unless a party renegotiates 'under the pretext of' making a deal, deliberately conceals important facts or provides false information or conducts itself contrary to good faith.[37]

3.2 The Dichotomy at Work: COVID-19 and SARS Compared

The differences and interrelationship between the two doctrines are best assessed from their judicial application to the same event. The 2019 coronavirus disease, or COVID-19 as it is commonly known, is a global pandemic that has to date caused about 245 million confirmed cases and almost 5 million deaths worldwide, resulting in a mortality rate of 2 per cent.[38] Aside from the pandemic itself, measures adopted by national governments to combat the pandemic have caused great difficulties to social and business life and China is amongst the countries adopting the strictest of such measures. A similar pandemic of a more limited scale is the SARS, which took place in 2002–2003 and spread to 37 countries, causing more than 8,000 infections and 774 deaths, with a mortality rate of more than 10 per cent. The differing ways in which Chinese courts have handled these two pandemics shed light on the two doctrines.

3.2.1 Force Majeure *or Change of Circumstances?*

Should the SARS or COVID-19 pandemic or the corresponding measures be characterised as *force majeure* or a change of circumstances? An instructive answer may be found from the decision in *Zhang Lin* v. *South Cougar Catering Co Ltd and Zhenrui Hotel*,[39] widely proclaimed as 'the

[37] CCL, art. 42; CCC, art. 500. Also, UNIDROIT Principles 2016, art. 6.2.3 (1).

[38] World Health Organisation website: https://covid19.who.int/. China has a relatively high mortality rate of 4.5 per cent due largely to the fact that its cumulative number of cases is small and that many deaths were caused at the earlier stage of the pandemic.

[39] *People's Court Daily* [张林诉南美洲狮饮食有限责任公司、珍瑞大酒店案], 11 June 2003. Also discussed in Ma Qiang, 'The Establishment of the Change of Circumstances System and the Handling of SARS Cases' ['情事变更制度之确立与处理非典型肺炎疫情案件'] (2003) 3(13) *Judgment Studies* [判解研究] 99.

pioneering SARS case'. The parties signed a three-year lease of a hotel commencing from 1 January 2003. The contract stipulated that if the lessee (Zhang Lin) was unable to continue with the lease for business reasons, the lessee might terminate the contract in ninety days' notice, provided that 30 per cent of the annual lease fee (RMB 320,000) was paid as agreed damages. The outbreak of SARS led to a drastic decrease of overseas tourists and caused extreme difficulties to the operation of the hotel. Consequently, Zhang Lin sought to terminate the contract on the ground of *force majeure*, thus outflanking the contractual provision, and also to claim a refund of fees already paid under the lease (RMB 26,667). It was held by the Xuanwu District Court of Nanjing City that the SARS pandemic did not constitute a *force majeure* event since it had been relatively short-lived and had not in this case resulted in a situation where Zhang Lin 'could not perform the contract' or the purpose of the contract became unfulfillable. Rather, the doctrine of change of circumstances was regarded as a more suitable solution. However, since Zhang Lin refused to renegotiate the contract or accept the reduced fees proposed by the other party, the court had to order the contract to be terminated and Zhang Lin to shoulder responsibility for most of the resulting losses.

The *Zhang Lin* case raised a number of issues, including whether the contractual allocation of risk should not apply in preference to either the doctrine of *force majeure* or that of change of circumstances.[40] For the present purpose, however, an important feature of the decision is that it refrained from making any categorical characterisation of the SARS pandemic. Accordingly, the applicability of the two doctrines was made to depend separately on whether the facts of the case satisfied the 'contract impact' test they respectively endorsed. This approach is in sharp contrast to that adopted in the SARS Report, which categorically characterises the pandemic as *force majeure.*[41] The decision is consistent with the SPC's approach at the time: 'the principle of fairness' should apply where the SARS pandemic had a 'fundamental impact' on one of the contracting parties, whereas the doctrine of *force majeure* should apply where a party 'could not perform' its contract as a result of the

[40] For Chinese courts' position on such contract clauses in the context of COVID-19 cases, see Qiao Liu, 'COVID-19 in Civil or Commercial Disputes: First Responses from Chinese Courts' (2020) 8(2) *Chinese Journal of Comparative Law* 485, 490.

[41] SARS Report.

pandemic.[42] The approach in the *Zhang Lin* case is preferable to the above SPC approach not only because the latter completely overlooks the 'contract purpose' test but also because the latter's reference to 'the principle of fairness' is both vague and obsolete.[43]

In the context of the COVID-19 pandemic, a wider reception of the doctrine of change of circumstances can be observed from a majority of judicial documents issued by the SPC or HPCs.[44] It is increasingly recognised that the 'contract impact' test is key to the applicability of each of the two doctrines, which is to be determined on a case-by-case basis,[45] notwithstanding occasional statements to the effect that the pandemic invariably constitutes *force majeure*.[46]

3.2.2 The Changing Meaning and Role of the 'Cannot Perform' Test

One most remarkable change in Chinese courts' approach to COVID-19 cases compared to SARS cases relates to the 'cannot perform' test.

[42] Notice of the Supreme People's Court on the Implementation of the People's Courts' Judicial and Executive Work during the Period of Prevention and Control of Infectious Atypical Pneumonia [最高人民法院关于在防治传染性非典型肺炎期间依法做好人民法院相关审判、执行工作的通知] (issued and implemented on June 11, 2003, Fa [2003] No. 72, [SARS Notice]) art. 3(3).

[43] SPC Interpretation II, art. 26. Further, Liu, 'COVID-19 in Civil or Commercial Disputes', p. 487.

[44] E.g., SPC, Guiding Opinion I on Certain Issues Concerning the Lawful and Proper Adjudication of Civil Cases Involving the COVID-19 Pandemic [关于依法妥善审理涉新冠肺炎疫情民事案件若干问题的指导意见（一）] (16 April 2020, Fa Fa [2020] No. 12, [SPC COVID Opinion I]) arts. 2, 3; Sichuan HPC No. 1 Civil Tribunal, Minutes of Judges' Meeting Concerning Adjudication of Civil Cases Involving COVID-19 Pandemic [关于涉新冠肺炎疫情相关民事案件审理的法官会议纪要] Chuan Gao Fa Min Yi [2020] No. 1 (Sichuan HPC Minutes), Pt II; Zhejiang HPC No. 2 Civil Tribunal, Answers to Certain Questions Regarding Commercial Disputes Involving COVID-19 [关于审理涉新冠肺炎疫情相关商事纠纷的若干问题解答], Zhe Gao Fa Min Er [2020] No. 1 (Zhejiang HPC Answers), art. 2(4); Guangxi HPC No. 1 Civil Tribunal, Guiding Opinion on the Proper Adjudication of Civil Disputes Involving the COVID-19 Pandemic [关于妥善审理涉新冠肺炎疫情相关民事纠纷的指导意见] (Guangxi HPC Opinion), art. 2(7)-(8). Also, Liu, 'COVID-19 in Civil or Commercial Disputes', p. 487.

[45] The SPC Leaders' Team for the Implementation of the Civil Code (ed.), *Understanding and Applying the Contract Book of the Civil Code of the PRC* [中华人民共和国民法典合同编理解与适] (Beijing: People's Court Press, 2020), p. 827.

[46] E.g., 'The Head of the Research Office of the SPC Answers Reporters' Questions on the Introduction of Guiding Opinions on Several Issues Concerning the Proper Adjudication of Civil Cases Involving the New Coronary Pneumonia Epidemic According to Law (I)' ['最高人民法院研究室负责人就出台依法妥善审理涉新冠肺炎疫情民事案件若干问题的指导意见（一）答记者问'], 20 April 2020, Question 3, available at www.court.gov.cn/zixun-xiangqing-226251.html.

As seen above, that test is part of the doctrine of *force majeure* and is subject to two different interpretations. Its aim is to determine whether liability for non-performance is to be exempted. The passages below show that from the SARS pandemic to the COVID-19 pandemic, both the meaning and role of the 'cannot perform' test have undergone some transformation. This raises some acute issues as to the sustainability of the existing law.

The Dominance of a Narrowly Interpreted Test in SARS Cases

The SARS Report, which views the doctrine of *force majeure* as the only legal vehicle to tackle problems arising from the pandemic, adopts the 'cannot perform' test as the principal contract impact test. The report generally embraces a narrow interpretation of the test and hence requires an 'inability or impossibility to perform'; as a consequence, the test is effectively allowed to encroach upon some legitimate territory of the 'contract purpose' test.[47]

This can be seen from the way in which the report envisages the 'cannot perform' test applies to a number of specific contracts.[48] For instance, where a supplier was ordered by the local government to redirect all its manufacturing capacity to the production of face masks, the 'cannot perform' test was satisfied in that it became impossible for the supplier to manufacture other goods from its factory.[49] In contrast, no *force majeure* was found where a butchery remained in normal operation and beef could be transported to clients since the SARS pandemic did not lead to a cutting-off of the main roads.[50] The same narrow interpretation also seemed to be at work where SARS was said to affect only the 'macro-environment' and did not have 'any direct or necessary impact on' payment of money, such as under a loan contract.[51] Under a contract of personal service, where the employee is subject to quarantine

[47] SARS Report, p. 8.

[48] References at the time of the SARS pandemic to 'cannot perform at all' (根本不能履行) or 'unable to perform' (无法履行) suggests for a narrow interpretation: SARS Notice, art. 3(3).

[49] SARS Report, p. 8.

[50] *Hua Ken International Trade Co Ltd* v. *Shanxi Lunda Meat Industry Co Ltd* [华垦国际贸易有限公司与山西伦达肉类工业有限公司买卖合同纠纷上诉案], Shanxi HPC (2017) Jin Min Zhong No. 93 Civil Judgment.

[51] *Wang Ting et al* v. *The Business Department of the Agricultural Bank of China Guangdong Branch et al* [王挺等与中国农业银行广东省分行营业部等担保借款合同纠纷上诉案], Guangzhou IPC (2005) Sui Zhong Fa Min Er Zhong Zi No. 1150 Civil Judgment. Cf. SARS Report, 8.

measures, it is easy to see that he or she 'cannot perform', at least temporarily, the contract.[52] The same could happen under other service contracts. In the *Sanya Changyuan* case,[53] lock-down and local-recruitment-only measures adopted in Sanya City were held to have deprived a construction company of its main workforce and of its ability to complete the construction on time, hence amounting to *force majeure*. Consequently, the company was held not liable for interests accrued during the period of delay when those measures had been in force.

The above narrow interpretation of the 'cannot perform' test is too restrictive, unsupported by any legislative intent and unduly excludes cases where a party 'can', but decides not to, perform the contract. This error has been greatly exacerbated by an unwarranted expansion of the legal consequences attached to the test. The SARS Report thus explicitly states that where the test is satisfied, its legal effect is not confined to exemption of liability; instead, the court may 'adapt contract, postpone performance or allow partial performance' at the request of the party affected or 'order a straight termination'.[54] Under this scheme, contract termination or adaptation does not hinge on the 'contract purpose' test or the 'manifest unfairness' test but on a narrow interpretation of the 'cannot perform' test, which remains ill-defined and in flux.

The Revival of a Broadly Interpreted Test in COVID-19 Cases

The dominant role of the 'cannot perform' test in SARS cases has been fundamentally altered in COVID-19 cases. A wider reception of the doctrine of change of circumstances has brought about the recognition of contract adaptation as a preferred solution as compared to contract termination.[55] This recognition is based on an increasing appreciation of the role of the 'manifest unfairness' test in such cases as those featuring

52 SARS Report, pp. 8–9; SARS Notice, art. 3(1).

53 *Yin Wenmin* v. *Sanya Changyuan Property Development Co Ltd* [殷文敏与三亚长源物业发展有限公司商品房预售合同纠纷上诉案], Sanya IPC (2005) San Ya Min Yi Zhong Zi No. 79 Civil Judgment.

54 SARS Report, 9.

55 SPC COVID Opinion I, art. 3(2); SPC, Guiding Opinion II on Certain Issues Concerning the Lawful and Proper Adjudication of Civil Cases Involving the COVID-19 Pandemic [关于依法妥善审理涉新冠肺炎疫情民事案件若干问题的指导意见（二）] (15 May 2020, Fa Fa [2020] No. 17, [SPC COVID Opinion II]), arts. 2, 6, 7 and 14; SPC, Ministry of Justice, Ministry of Culture and Tourism, Notice on Lawful and Proper Handling of Disputes Related to Tourism Contracts Involving the Pandemic [关于依法妥善处理涉疫情旅游合同纠纷有关问题的通知] (13 July 2020, Fa [2020] No. 182), arts. 8 and 9. Also, Liu, 'COVID-19 in Civil or Commercial Disputes', pp. 489, 493.

rent reduction as the appropriate remedy where a lease contract was affected by the pandemic or government measures, which did not normally render the purpose of the contract unfulfillable but simply made it difficult for the lessee to run its business with regular profit margins.[56] Meanwhile, the 'contract purpose' test has been reinstated to its proper role as the clinching yardstick for the drastic measure of contract termination.[57] Therefore, if the impact of the pandemic or government measures on contract performance is simply that such contracts 'cannot be performed within the agreed time', without their purposes being rendered unfulfillable, then no termination should be granted.[58] Hence, the dominance by one single 'cannot performance' test in SARS cases is now replaced by a triad of tests each producing a corresponding distinctive legal consequence in COVID-19 cases. Under this new framework, the only legal consequence of satisfying the 'cannot perform' test is that the relevant party is exempted proportionately from its liability for non-performance.[59]

The above clarification of the separate roles of the three contract impact tests in COVID -19 cases comes hand in hand with the revival of a broad interpretation of the 'cannot perform' test. For example, a lessee or hirer 'cannot perform' its contract in the sense that 'rents/fees are not paid within the agreed period'.[60] A broad interpretation is also discernible from the provisions that *force majeure* shall exempt the liability of an employer who commits 'a failure to pay wages or social insurance in full and on time'[61] or a builder who 'fails to complete construction in accordance with the agreed time requirement'.[62] Unfortunately, this increased use of the broad interpretation has not obviated the narrow interpretation, which persists in some judicial

[56] *Zhang Haisheng and Nanchang Market Construction and Property Management Service Centre* [张海胜、南昌市市场建设物业管理服务中心物业服务合同纠纷二审民事判决书], Jiangxi HPC, 20 November 2020 (2020) Gan Min Zhong No. 813 Civil Judgment. Also, *Pa De Ke Ya Ku Pu Yaqup* v. *Abliz* [帕德克亚库甫与克力木江阿不力孜房屋租赁合同纠纷二审民事判决书], Xinjiang HPC, 31 May 2021 (2021) Xin 40 Min Zhong No. 634 Civil Judgment.

[57] Liu, 'COVID-19 in Civil or Commercial Disputes', pp. 489, 492.

[58] SPC COVID Opinion II, arts. 1, 4, 5 and 8; Sichuan HPC Minutes, Pt. V, art. 2.

[59] E.g., Sichuan HPC Minutes, Pt. II, sec (I), art. 4(2). Also, Liu, 'COVID-19 in Civil or Commercial Disputes', p. 491.

[60] SPC COVID Opinion II, art. 5.

[61] Sichuan HPC Minutes, Pt III, art. 11.

[62] SPC COVID Opinion II, art. 7.

documents addressing the COVID-19 pandemic.[63] Worse still, the 'cannot perform' test is still sometimes applied in determining whether the contract is terminable.[64] In fact, the failure to distinguish exemption of liability from other remedies in SARS cases has not been effectively redressed. A Chinese court exercising its discretion in apportioning losses may well overstep the limits of exemption of liability. Coupled with a broad interpretation of the 'cannot perform' test, such a stretch of the meaning of exemption of liability is liable to produce wider and greater resort to the doctrine of *force majeure*. If this situation is allowed to continue, the law is in danger of losing its vital capability to fashion a remedy proportionate to the impact of a supervening event on contract performance.

3.3 Concluding Remarks

The uneasy relationship between the doctrine of *force majeure* and the doctrine of change of circumstances under Chinese law may cause one to question the wisdom of adopting such a dichotomy. In practice, however, this dichotomy is watered down by Chinese courts' overwhelming and excessive reliance on the doctrine of *force majeure*. Aside from the SPC's stringent requirement for approval, such reliance has been fuelled by two vices that threaten to disintegrate the entire system governing impediment to contract performance.

First, the tendency to categorically characterise an event such as the SARS or COVID-19 pandemic as *force majeure* is an error to be avoided. It overlooks and dilutes the centrality of various contract impact tests, which are intrinsically tied, through the principle of proportionality, to their respective remedial consequences. With a reorientation towards such tests, greater scope will be given to the doctrine of change of circumstances, which provides the necessary flexibility to deal with complex events such as the COVID-19 pandemic.

Second, the 'cannot perform' test under the doctrine of *force majeure* has been widely misinterpreted, misapplied and overused. The COVID documents show that a broad interpretation, which equates 'cannot perform' with a 'failure to perform', should be adopted. Unfortunately, Chinese courts tend to understand 'exemption of liability' liberally,

[63] E.g., Sichuan HPC Minutes, Pt. V, art. 4; Guangxi HPC Opinion, art. 13; Zhejiang HPC Answers, arts. 2(2)–(3).

[64] E.g., Zhejiang HPC Answers, arts. 2(2)–(3).

fashioning any remedy they think fit for a 'failure to perform' caused by a *force majeure* event. This misunderstanding of 'exemption of liability', coupled with the above broad interpretation, has stretched the doctrine of *force majeure* significantly beyond its limits.

It may be that, as both the CISG and the UNIDROIT Principles demonstrate, the homogeneity of a qualifying event militates in favour of a unitary doctrine and the existing dichotomy between the two doctrines does more harm than good. As things stand, however, one has to acknowledge that the immediate task is to restore proper balance and stability to the system comprising essentially a triad of 'cannot perform', 'contract purpose' and 'manifest unfairness' tests. For this to materialise, these tests, as well as their remedial consequences, must operate in a mutually distinct yet coherent and coordinated manner. One point that requires more clarity from Chinese law, particularly Chinese courts, concerns what it means by exempting from liability for non-performance and what will happen afterwards. In this respect, it is time to rethink the current scheme, which leaves much to an elusive discretionary process.

4

Article 580 (2) of the Chinese Civil Code

Can Chinese Folk Medicine Cure Serious Illness?

HAN SHIYUAN

4.1 Introduction

Out of seven books of the Civil Code of the People's Republic of China (CCC), Book Three on Contracts occupies the largest space, which speaks to the importance of the area of contract law. In this book, the most controversial provision has to be Article 580 (2). It provides: '[w]-here one of the situations specified in the preceding paragraph exists so that the purpose of the contract cannot be achieved, the people's court or arbitration institution may terminate the contractual relationship of rights and obligations upon request by a party, but the default liability shall still be borne without being affected.'[1] This is a Chinese invention that is not based on foreign legal doctrines. Its purpose is said to relieve parties from a deadlock in contract performances. Nevertheless, the idea of 'deadlock in contractual performances' is not clear to either Western or Chinese lawyers. Following the German tradition, the non-breaching party has a legal right to demand performance and the breaching party does not have a right to termination. Yet, according to Article 580 (2), the breaching party may request a court or arbitration institution to terminate the contract according to the provision. The contract may be terminated by the court or arbitration institution, but the breaching party still bears its liability for breach. It is a judicial termination but totally different from that in a case of change of circumstances (hardship). In an earlier draft, there was a special rule that allowed the breaching party to sue for termination. This rule was abandoned due to strong

[1] With a reference to the English translation of Civil Code of the People's Republic of China on the website of the National People's Congress of the P. R. China, www.npc.gov.cn/englishnpc/c23934/202012/f627aa3a4651475db936899d69419d1e/files/47c16489e186437eab3244495cb47d66.pdf.

opposition. Still, it was ultimately slipped into the law in a different form. As controversial as it may be, it remains to be seen how the rule is interpreted in judicial practice.

This chapter will introduce the origin of this new judicial termination of contract in China (Section 4.2), discuss the debates over 'a breaching party's right to termination' (Section 4.3) in China and the progress made through the codification of civil law (Section 4.4). Then I will analyze some typical existing interpretations of Article 580, including legislative, judicial and some scholastic interpretations (Section 4.5). The chapter includes with my own interpretation of the provision (Section 4.6).

4.2 Deadlock in Contract Performance: A New Type of Judicial Termination

4.2.1 *The Origin of the Issue*

The question about whether a breaching party has a claim for contract termination was first raised in a case published in the popular Supreme People's Court (SPC) gazette, *Xinyu Corporation* v. *Feng Yumei* (*Xinyu* case).[2] Xinyu Corporation, the claimant, and Feng Yumei, the defendant, had concluded a store sale contract in October 1998. The defendant purchased from the claimant one of its stores in a multi-story department store building for the price of RMB 368,184 Yuan. These shops were divided units on the first three floors of a building owned by the claimant and had been sold to more than 150 owners including the defendant, while other floors (from the fourth to the sixth) of the building were still owned by the claimant. After the conclusion of the contract, the defendant paid the agreed prices in full. On 3 November 1998, the claimant delivered the shop to the defendant but failed to register the sale with the state. As a result, the transaction was not closed and the claimant was not willing to perform the contract because they rebranded the department store for a different line of business and none of the stores could still exist. The claimant sued to have the performance excused because of the change of circumstances. They asked the court to terminate the shop sale contract and to order the defendant to return the purchased shop to the claimant.

[2] Gazette of the Supreme People's Court of the People's Republic of China (中华人民共和国最高人民法院公报) (2006) 6, 37.

In the first instance trial, Nanjing Xuanwu District People's Court held that there was not a change of circumstance but the contract should be terminated because the purpose of the contract to profit could not be realized. Otherwise, the deadlock of performance 'not only injured the interests of both parties, but also caused enormous wastes of social wealth, which was detrimental to local economy'. Therefore, the Court adjudicated that the contract shall be terminated according to the principles of fairness and good faith (Articles 5 and 6 of the Contract Law 1999) and for the claimant to return payments of the contract, to pay damages and agreed payments to the defendant. The defendant appealed.

In the second instance trial (the appeal), Nanjing Intermediate People's Court upheld the trial court's decision to terminate the contract but increased the settlement amount awarded to the defendant. The Intermediate Court supplemented the reasoning of the first instance judgment by citing Article 110 of the Contract Law and treated the continuing performance of the contract as 'unreasonably burdensome or expensive'. It held, 'when the funds and material resources needed by the breaching party in continuing performing the contract exceed the interests to be gained by both parties through performing the contract, the breaching party shall be allowed to terminate the contract (应该允许违约方解除合同), and to replace continuing performance with damages'.

4.2.2 *Implications and Controversies*

The case has been published in the Gazette of the SPC, which means that it should be a model for future cases with similar facts in the lower courts.[3] From the abstract of the judgment, there are two main points: one is an interpretation of Article 110 of the Contract Law and the other is the specialty of a sale of partitioned shop from a sale of an independent shop. Article 110 is on performance of non-monetary obligation and similar to Article 7.2.2 of the UNIDROIT Principles of International Commercial Contracts (PICC). Therefore, Article 110 is only on the right to performance, it does not provide a normative ground for termination.

Therefore, the significance of this case is the fact that it created the right in the breaching party to terminate the contract. Article 110 is not the normal ground for the breaching party's termination, the judge in

[3] As an example following the SPC Gazette case, see Civil Judgment of Changsha Intermediate People's Court (长沙市中级人民法院民事判决书) (2014) Chang zhong min zai zhongzi No. 00288 (长中民再终字第00288号).

this case had actually played a lawmaker role by citing principles of fairness and good faith (Articles 5 and 6 of the Contract Law). And from this case on, there has arisen in China a saying: 'the breaching party's termination' (or 'the breaching party's right to termination').

'The breaching party shall be allowed to terminate the contract' is not so accurate, however, as it does not have a right of termination. And the termination in the case is not based on a party's exercising of its right to termination but is based, instead, on the judge's discretion; its substance is a kind of judicial termination.

Before the case, judicial termination was only admitted in change of circumstance cases in practice. So the *Xinyu* case is the leading case for this second type of judicial termination in China.

4.3 Debates over the Notion of 'Breaching Party's Right to Termination'

4.3.1 Arguments in Support of 'a Breaching Party's Right to Termination' Efficiency

It is efficient. The Contract Law does not expressly provide the breaching party any right to terminate the contract. This creates a deadlock: even though the plaintiff may refuse to continue its performance according to Article 110 of the Contract Law, they cannot terminate the contract. The judge filled the gap of the Contract Law by citing the general principles of fairness and good faith (Articles 5 and 6 of the Contract Law). The rationale is efficiency. As Sun Liangguo argued '[e]fficiency is the greatest justice in business transactions, even though people's courts in China normally embody it under the principles such as good faith or fairness'.[4]

The Abuse of Right to Demand Performance

Where it has been impracticable to perform the contract, the continuing existence of the contract would bring the breaching party negative results; however, the non-breaching party, who has a right to terminate the contract, refuses to do so. In this scenario, Cui Jianyuan argued

[4] Liangguo Sun (孙良国), 'The Breaching Party's Right to Terminate Contract and its Boundary' ('违约方的合同解除权及其界限') (2016) *Contemporary Law Review* (当代法学) 5.

that justice calls for a right in the breaching party to terminate the contract.[5]

Justice and Equity. The basic notion of equity also pointed to the creation of this special right to termination. Where performance is inappropriate because of personal character, or performance is unreasonably burdensome or expensive, or the party entitled to performance does not require performance within a reasonable time, and after a notice has been given to urge the non-breaching party to terminate and a reasonable time has passed, a right of termination then should be given to the breaching party, for the following reasons: (1) civil law is not a law of punishment but a law that makes whole when there is a loss. When the continued existence of a contract is meaningless to both parties, the contract should be terminated. Justice and equity require both parties to be liberated from the binding force of the contract so as to engage in new transactions. (2) The non-breaching party shall not have unlimited power to demand performance. Rather, they are only entitled to adequate and reasonable remedies. On the other hand, the non-breaching party's right to terminate, when exercised, shall be respected provided that it is not contrary to good faith.[6]

4.3.2 Arguments against 'a Breaching Party's Right to Termination'

Self-sufficiency of the Existing Law. (1) The *Xinyu* case is no doubt a difficult case, but this does not mean that it cannot be addressed within existing law. One possible approach is a judicial termination under the name of change of circumstance. Therefore, it is not necessary for the judges to 'make a law' under the name of fairness and good faith.[7] (2) Instead of acknowledging 'a breaching party's right to termination', it is possible under the existing law for the breaching party to discharge its contract by damages in lieu of

[5] Jianyuan Cui (崔建远), 'Legislative Proposal of the Improvement of the Contract Termination System' ('完善合同解除制度的立法建议') (2018) Wuhan University Journal (武汉大学学报) Sciences Edition 2.

[6] Ibid.

[7] Han Shiyuan (韩世远), 'Modernization of Contract Law: Why and How?' ('合同法的现代化：为何及如何?') (2019) Research on Rule of Law (法治研究) 6.

performance.[8] Where the non-breaching party's right to performance is excluded because of impossibility, and the non-breaching party has a duty of mitigation, then a 'deadlock of transaction' should not emerge, because what the obligor should bear are the damages in lieu of performance, and there is no need to create a breaching party's right to termination.[9]

Binding Force of Contract and Security of Transaction. The *Xinyu* case may be a case of individual justice realized by creative judicial rule-making. However, to maintain the safety of transaction, the general rule should still be *pacta sunt servanda*. Keeping in mind that there are still many repudiations and other non-performance provisions in practice that ought to bear the negative consequences provided by contract law, the legislature and judiciary should play a pilot role and uphold the binding force of contract.[10]

The Right to Demand Performance. Under Chinese contract law, unlike American common law,[11] as a starting point, a party (especially the breaching party) does not have freedom to break his contract and pay damages. *Meum est promittere, non dimittere* (It is mine to promise, not to discharge).[12] As in German law, Chinese contract law gives the non-breaching party a legal right to demand performance and treats enforced performance as a primary possible remedy for non-performance. This is considered a hallmark of German and German-inspired contract law. If the breaching party has been given a right to

[8] Rui Cai (蔡睿), 'To Absorb or to Abandon? Reconsider Breaching Party's Right to Termination' ('吸收还是摒弃：违约方合同解除权之反思') (2019) Modern Law Science (现代法学) 3.

[9] Liyan Hao (郝丽燕), 'Demystify Breaching Party's Right of Termination' ('走出违约方解除权的误区') (2020) Nanjing University Law Journal (南大法学) 3.

[10] Cai, 'Absorb or Abandon', 3.

[11] The basic position of American contract law is Holmes' classical saying: 'The only universal consequence of a legally binding promise is, that the law makes the promisor pay damages if the promised event does not come to pass. In every case it leaves him free from interference until the time for fulfilment has gone by, and therefore free to break his contract if he chooses.', Oliver Wendell Holmes Jr., *The Common Law* (Boston: Dover, 1991), p. 301.

[12] Yubo Zheng (郑玉波), *Legal Proverbs* (法谚), vol. 1 (Beijing: Law Press China, 2007), p. 111.

termination, then it defeats the inner logic of contract law.[13] Also, there are a few additional doctrinal difficulties raised by the *Xinyu* case. Firstly, the defendant did not raise any counterclaim. However, the settlement awards include damages and additional payments that would already overcompensate the defendant. It is questionable if the court could adjudicate on issues never raised by the litigants. Also, instead of recognizing a change of circumstance as claimed by the plaintiff, the judges introduced this second type of judicial termination. The relationship between the two parallel judiciary terminations needs further clarification from the Supreme People's Court so as to avoid possible overlap or contradiction.

4.4 The Legislative History of Article 580 (2)

Article 580(2) was a last-minute addition to the Civil Code. Previously, during the drafting process, it took two different forms before it turned into its current shape. In the August 2018 draft of the special part of the Civil Code, it first gave the breaching party a legal right to terminate the contract. In that draft, Article 353 (3) reads:

> If force majeure or other objective reasons makes it impossible to fulfill the purpose of contract, the party who has a right to termination does not terminate the contract, and thus it becomes obviously unfair to the other party, the other party may request the people's court or arbitration institution to terminate the contract, without affecting the assumption of the liability for breach of the contract.

Later, in the draft for the second discussion in December 2018, not exercising the right to terminate was defined as an abuse of right. Article 353 (3) provides:

> If force majeure or other objective reasons makes it impossible to fulfill the purpose of contract, the party who has a right to termination does not exercise that right, and thus constitutes an abuse of right and it becomes obviously unfair to the other party, the people's court or arbitration institution may terminate the contract at the request of the other party, without affecting the assumption of the liability for breach of contract.

The practical influence of this new doctrinal creation was soon picked up by the Supreme Court in its November 2019 Notice, by the Supreme People's Court on Issuing the Minutes of the National Courts' Civil and

[13] Han, 'Modernization of Contract Law', 6.

Commercial Trial Work Conference, also known as 'the Minutes 2019'. The Minutes 2019 is not a judicial interpretation, but it shows current judicial policies. Naturally, it drew a lot of attention and also played an important role in practice in China. In this document, the most eye-catching provision was Article 48, called 'the breaching party's claim for termination'.[14] The aim of this article is to solve a 'deadlock in contract performance'. In short, where the non-breaching party has a right to termination but does not exercise the right, the breaching party may sue for termination, so as to break the deadlock of performance. Since maintaining the contract is not useful to either party, the termination will be beneficial to both. If we accumulate this mutually beneficial effect, we will reach a societal beneficial result.

In a book written by the judges of the SPC on its Minutes 2019, it pointed out that Article 48 has a normative ground in law, namely Article 110 of the Chinese Contract Law. However, people may ask, is it really the legal authority on which Article 48 of the Minutes 2019 was based? Take the lease, for example, in which case the answer would be no. A typical lease dispute is a case in which the tenant vacated the premise without paying the rent before the lease reaches its end. The claimant landlord sues for the rent. The obligation of the tenant is only monetary. Therefore, Article 110 of the Contract Law, which dealt with enforced performance, is not applicable to the case.

Article 110 of the Contract Law resembles Article 7.2.2 (Performance of non-monetary obligation) of the PICC. As a remedy for breach, on the one hand, it gives the non-breaching party a right to require

[14] 48. [The breaching party's claim for termination] The breaching party does not have a right to terminate the contract unilaterally. However, during the performance of a long-term contract like a house lease contract, the parties may reach a deadlock as to the contract. If the breaching party is not absolutely permitted to file an action so as to terminate the contract, sometimes this may be unfavorable to both parties. In such a case, if the following conditions are met, and the breaching party files an action for the termination of the contract, the people's court shall grant support according to the law:

(1) the breaching party is not malicious while breaching the contract;
(2) it is unconscionable for the breaching party to continue to perform the contract; and
(3) the non-breaching party's refusal to terminate the contract contravenes the principle of good faith.

If the people's court adjudges the contract to be terminated, the liability for breach of contract to which the breaching party is subject shall not be reduced or waived because of the termination of the contract.

performance, on the other, it provides some exceptions to the right to require performance. However, it should be noted that this article focuses only on unilateral contracts. It does not deal with synallagmatic issues; this is not its aim and function to deal with the termination of a bilateral contract. The circumstances prescribed by Article 110 of the Contract Law aims only to draw reasonable boundaries of the right to require performance and implies that there will be a change of the obligation's form, that is, from a primary duty to a secondary one, if the obligor does not have an excuse in law (e.g., *force majeure*).

The December 2019 draft of the Civil Code Article 563 got rid of paragraph (3) of the earlier draft. The text remained the same in the May 2020 draft, right before the passage of the law. However, surprisingly, a new paragraph went into Article 580 without a chance to receive any scholarly input. It provides:

> Where one of the situations specified in the preceding paragraph exists so that the purpose of the contract cannot be fulfilled, the people's court or an arbitration institution may terminate the contractual relationship of rights and obligations upon request by a party, but the liability for breach shall not be affected.

Therefore, Article 580 of the Civil Code now reads:

> Art. 580 Where a party fails to perform the non-monetary obligations or his performance does not conform to the agreement, the other party may request for such performance unless:
>
> (1) the performance is impossible either *de jure* or *de facto*;
> (2) the object of the obligation is not suitable for a compulsory performance or the expenses for the performance are too high; or
> (3) the creditor fails to request for performance within a reasonable period of time.
>
> If any of the foregoing circumstances makes it impossible to achieve the purpose of contract, the people's court or arbitration institution may terminate the relation of contractual obligations and rights at the request of either party, without affecting the assumption of the liability for breach of the contract.

As we have seen, this breaching party's right to terminate, a twisted doctrine that cannot be explained, has been haunting Chinese law like a phantom since the *Xingyu* case, and finally in 2020, it is recognized officially by the Chinese Civil Code. Ironically, the breaching party's right to terminate is now placed in Article 580, which stipulates the non-breaching party's right to terminate.

4.5 Legislative, Judicial and Scholastic Interpretations of Article 580 (2)

4.5.1 A Legislative Interpretation

The Doctrinal Nature of the Right in Article 580 (2)

The main conceptual difficulty in explaining this particular right to terminate a contract is due to its doctrinal uncertainty. According to the official commentary published by the National People's Congress, this right to termination is a judicial termination (司法终止).

> Paragraph 2 is neither on party's right to termination (当事人的终止权) nor *Gestaltungsklagerecht* (形成诉权), but a judicial discretion to termination (司法的终止权). The people's court or an arbitration institution has such a discretion, taking the actual situation of an individual case into consideration and following the principles of good faith and fairness, to decide if a contract can be terminated.[15]

As we can see, there is no direct recognition of this right to terminate. Still, a few doctrinal clarifications are essential. First, it is a right to terminate a contract (终止) rather than a rescission (撤销);[16] also, it is not a legal right to terminate as in the circumstances provided in Article 563 of the Code. Rather, this right can only be vested through a judicial decision. Therefore, it is a judicial termination. Moreover, such a right belongs to 'either party' or 'debtor' instead of the 'breaching party'. This right to terminate a contract can only be triggered when justice and good faith require such a judicial action.

The commentary lists the following elements that determine if a contract needs to be terminated, namely: (a) whether there has been a partial performance; (b) whether the breach was malicious; (c) whether it was possible to perform; (d) whether the debtor will suffer great financial loss; whether a substitute performance may be easily obtained by the creditor; (f) whether the debtor has a claim of compensation from a third party or not; (g) whether the creditor's refusal of termination constitutes a sharp practice and becomes against good faith or not; (h) and whether without termination of the contract the relation of right and obligation between the parties will become obviously unbalanced or not and so on.[17]

15 Wei Huang (黄薇) (ed.), *Civil Code of PRC Book Contracts Commentary* (中华人民共和国民法典合同编释义) (Beijing: Law Press China, 2020), p. 274.

16 Vitiating factors such as fraud, duress and mistake need to be present at the time of contract for a contract to be rescinded.

17 Huang, *Civil Code of PRC Commentary*, p. 274.

4.5.2 *An Interpretation by SPC*

According to a commentary prepared by judges on the SPC, Article 580 (2) is a new formulation of 'the breaching party's claim for termination' based on Article 48 of the Minutes 2019, and its purpose is to solve the performance deadlock problem in practice and to improve the system of liabilities for breach in China.[18] This commentary tries to combine both Article 580 (2) and Article 48 of the 2019 Minutes.

The Nature of the Right in Article 580 (2)

Article 48 of the 2019 Minutes was also clear that the court does not recognize a unilateral right to terminate; rather, it can be granted only in exceptional circumstances. Unlike the above legislative interpretation, the SPC argues that nothing prohibits the breaching party's right to terminate (解除诉求权), which is a kind of *Gestaltungsklagerecht* (形成诉权) in nature. We can safely assume this is the view held by the SPC.

Prerequisites for Applying Article 580 (2)

Unlike the 'elements to be considered' listed in the legislative commentary, the SPC prefers a 'prerequisites – legal results' formula. By making a reference to Article 48 of the Minutes 2019, the breaching party establish the following three prerequisites, namely: (a) the breaching party was not malicious in breaching the contract; (b) it is grossly unfair for the breaching party to continue to perform the contract; (c) the non-breaching party's refusal to terminate the contract contravenes the principle of good faith.[19]

4.5.3 *Scholarly Interpretations*

Some leading scholars have also spoken. Professor Cui Jianyuan, a staunch advocate of 'a breaching party's right to termination', sees such a right as the ideal solution to break a contract impasse. According to Cui, it is a three-prong test: (a) regardless of whether the breaching party has a right of termination, it will be necessary for the breaching party to claim the termination of the contract, otherwise there is no way for a

[18] The Leading Group for Implementing the Civil Code of the SPC (ed.) (最高人民法院民法典贯彻实施工作领导小组), *Understanding and Application of the Civil Code of P. R. China – Book of Contracts* (中华人民共和国民法典合同编理解与适用), vol. 2 (Beijing: People's Court Press, 2020), p. 736.

[19] Ibid, pp. 741–42.

court to step in; and (b) judicial termination is essentially a legal right vested in the breaching party. When it is for a court or an arbitration institution to decide whether to terminate the contract, they do not have the discretion; rather, there are conditions that need to be met in order for the judicial termination. If such conditions are both necessary and sufficient at the same time, the two will become one. (c) The same logic applies also to voidable contract. The defrauded party or the coerced party has a right of rescission;[20] on the other hand, the law provides that the defrauded party or the coerced party can only request a people's court or an arbitral institution to rescind the contract: similar situation, similar logic. Therefore, there is no practical difference between the breaching party's right to terminate and the judicial power of termination.[21]

Professor Zhu Guangxin takes a completely opposite approach.[22] He reasoned that professor Cui's interpretation has departed from the plain meaning of paragraph 1 and paragraph 2 of Article 580 and could be subject to anybody's unscrupulous interpretation. Also, it is up to the creditor to exercise the right to termination and his choice is presumed to be rightful. If the law permits the breaching party to request termination where the non-breaching party has not chosen to exercise his right to termination, that jeopardizes the non-breaching party's choice not to use the right. Such a doctrine defeats the aims of the rules for breach of contract, which is to have the breaching party bear the negative consequence of his breach.

Emphasizing the meaning connection between paragraph 1 and paragraph 2 of Article 580, professor Zhu follows a totally different way of interpretation. The non-monetary obligation in Article 580 only has a narrow scope that concerns a right to specific performance. Accordingly, 'termination' (终止) in Article 580 (2) should be interpreted in the same way as in Articles 133 and 464, where it means the 'extinction' of a right, rather than creation or transfer of a right. Article 580 (2) deals only with dispute over the existence of the non-breaching party's right to performance. Article 565 (1) states: '[i]f the other party objects to such termination, either party may petition the people's court or an arbitration

[20] Articles 148–50 of the Chinese Civil Code.

[21] Jianyuan Cui (崔建远), 'On Breaking the Contract Impasse' ('关于合同僵局的破解之道') (2020) Oriental Law (东方法学) 4.

[22] Guangxin Zhu (朱广新) and Hongfei Xie (谢鸿飞) (eds.), Civil Code Commentary: Book of Contracts (General Part) (民法典评注：合同编通则), vol. 2 (Bejing: China Legal, 2020), p. 350.

institution to confirm the validity of the termination'. It should be the same with Article 580 (2), which means either party, when in doubt, may petition the people's court or an arbitration institution to confirm the extinction of the right to performance.[23]

4.6 My Own Interpretation

4.6.1 The Purpose of Article 580 (2)

The purpose of Article 580 (2) is to break the deadlock of performance of contract. The path to achieve the purpose is through a judicial termination. By the judicial termination, not only the breaching party's original obligation is discharged (or more accurately speaking, it transforms from its original obligation to a secondary obligation, e.g., damages), but the non-breaching party's counter obligation is also discharged.

For example, in the *Xinyu* case, there was a shop sale contract. The claimant had an obligation to deliver the shop and help to process the registration of ownership to the defendant. This is its obligation in a narrow sense (*Schuldverhaeltnis im engeren Sinn*). The claimant sued for a termination of the shop sale contract, as a relationship of obligations in a broad sense (*Schuldverhaeltnis im weiteren Sinn*).[24] The main purpose of Article 580 (2) is to provide help for the case like *Xinyu Company* v. *Feng Yumei*.

Above, professor Zhu's interpretation of Article 580 (2) limits *Zhongzhi* (终止, termination) in the paragraph to an extinction of the non-monitory obligation (i.e., obligation in a narrow sense) and treats the future destiny of the contract (i.e., obligation in a broad sense) as another thing that is not governed by the article.[25] However, professor Hongfei Xie, professor Zhu's co-editor, wrote that the *Zhongzhi* in Article 580 (2) means the same thing as *Jiechu* (解除, rescission) and called its corresponding right 'both parties' right of termination'.[26] As Rudolf von Jhering pointed out in his book *The Purpose of Law*, people should find out the purpose to be pursued in a legal provision while

[23] Ibid, pp. 348–52.

[24] See Wolfgang Fikentscher and Andreas Heinemann, *Schuldrecht*, 11th Ed. (Berlin: de Gruyter, 2017), p. 22.

[25] Zhu and Xie, *Civil Code Commentary*, p. 351.

[26] Hongfei Xie (谢鸿飞), 'The Rationale and General Ground of Statutory Rights of Termination in the Civil Code' ('"民法典"法定解除权的配置机理与统一基础') (2020) *Journal of Zhejiang Gongshang University* (浙江工商大学学报) 6.

interpreting it. It purpose shall be the top priority in its interpretation.[27] If we follow this logic, it should be clear that professor Zhu's interpretation is obviously different from the real purpose of the legislation regarding Article 580 (2) and therefore is unacceptable.

4.6.2 *The Nature of the Right and the Action according to Article 580 (2)*

According to Article 580 (2), either party may initiate an action or arbitration to plea a judicial termination of the contract. This means, from the contract parties' side, a right to initiate an action or arbitration. This is a right of action to form a legal relation (*Gestaltungsklagerecht*, 形成诉权), which is different from a right to form a legal relation (*Gestaltungsrecht*, 形成权).

As to the rationale of the design of the right of action to form a legal relation, it is briefly said that, in some special situations, in which important interests of legal relationship participants or the general public are placed under a win-loss situation, the law does not grant the right bearer the power to form a legal relation through his own expression of will (*Willenserklärung*). Conversely, he must exercise his right through litigation; the relation is formed through a winning judgment (*Gestaltungsurteil*). What a right bearer has, therefore, is not a right to form a legal relation but a right to sue to form a legal relation.[28] A classic example where there is a restriction against forming a legal relation on a sole party's will is divorce. Where it is not a mutually agreed divorce, the Chinese Civil Code requires the party who wishes to do so to commence divorce proceedings (Article 1079 (1)). Another example is change of circumstance (Article 533).

As to the nature of the action according to Article 580 (2), there are different opinions. One treats it as an action for a declaratory judgment (*Feststellungsklage*, 确认之诉); another treats it an action for a judgment dissolving a legal relationship (*Gestaltungsklage*, 形成之诉). In my opinion, the latter is correct. Take professor Zhu's view. Article 580 (2) means either party, who are not sure as to the existence of the obligee's right to performance, may petition to the people's court or an arbitration

[27] Huixing Liang (梁慧星), *Hermeneutics of Civil Law* (民法解释学) (Beijing: China University of Politics and Law Press, 1995), p. 226.

[28] See Hans Brox and Wolf-Dietrich Walker, *Allgemeiner Teil des BGB*, 32nd ed. (München: Vahlen, 2008), p. 250.

institution to confirm the extinction of the right to performance. However, this is against the purpose of Article 580 (2). Following the normative purpose of Article 580 (2), the court or arbitration institution has the authority not only to confirm the extinction of the right to performance but also to put an end to the contract. Therefore, the nature of the action here should be one for a judgment dissolving a legal relationship (*Gestaltungsklage*). In this action, the judge or arbitrator inevitably has the direct power to decide if the contract ought to be terminated. The termination therefore should be called a judicial termination.

4.6.3 *Some Reflections about Reasonable Limitations to a Judge's or Arbitrator's Discretion*

Is Article 580 (2) a Complete Legal Rule?

According to a popularly accepted legal theory, a complete legal rule (*vollstaendige Rechtssaeze*) is composed of two parts, namely pre-conditions (*Tatbestand*) and legal result (*Rechtsfolge*).[29] Accordingly, Article 580 (2) seems to be a complete legal rule. And the SPC's judicial commentary follows a 'pre-conditions – legal results' formula, taking the three pre-conditions of Article 48 of the Minutes 2019 as pre-conditions of Article 580 (2). Likely, judges will be of the opinion that, if the three pre-conditions are met, they must decide the contract to be terminated, as the legal result of law application of Article 580 (2). However, is Article 580 (2) really a complete legal rule?

In the first part of Article 580 (2), it mentions two requirements, namely 'one of the situations specified in the preceding paragraph exists' and 'the purpose of the contract cannot be achieved'. In the second part, it says the people's court or arbitration institution 'may' (可以) terminate the contractual relationship. This means the judge or arbitrator has the power or discretion to do so – it is not mandatory. Therefore, the 'legal result' is not a 'termination of contract', but the court or arbitration institution 'may' terminate the contract.

Why Should Such a Discretion Be Strictly Restricted?

The judicial termination based on Article 580 (2) should be strictly restricted. A reason may lie in the paradigm of three-tier regulations

[29] See Karl Larenz, *Methodenlehre der Rechtswissenschaft*, 6th ed. (Berlin: Springer, 1991), pp. 251–52; Reinhold Zippelius, *Juristische Methodenlehre*, 10th Ed. (München: C. H. Beck, 2006), p. 28.

followed by Chinese contract law. The paradigm may be described as following.

Firstly, where there is a *force majeure* causing the impossibility of performance, the obligor shall be exempt from liability according to Article 590 (1). Where it becomes impossible to achieve the purpose of the contract because of the *force majeure*, either party of the contract has a right of termination according to Article 563 (1). We can all agree that *force majeure* ensures the termination of the contract.

Secondly, where there is a change of circumstance (a hardship) after the conclusion of the contract, rendering the continuation of the performance of the contract unconscionable (economically unfair) for one party, the disadvantaged party is entitled to request renegotiations; if the renegotiation fails within a reasonable time, the disadvantaged party may request the people's court or an arbitration institution to modify or terminate the contract (Article 533 (1)). Here the termination is a kind of judicial termination.

Thirdly, where it is neither a *force majeure* nor a change of circumstance, it is a third tier, namely 'commercial risk', as it is called in Article 533 (1). In this layer, generally speaking, *pacta sunt servanda* prevails. According to the strict liability principle in breach of contract, as in Chinese contract law (Article 577), the obligor should be liable for the breach.

Since the *Xinyu* case, where the plaintiff initiated the action based on a change of circumstance, the judges of the case denied change of circumstance and still tried to find a way to terminate the contract even though it fits the third-tier scenario of commercial risk.

The justification for contract termination should decrease from the first-tier scenario to the third tier. In principle, when performance comes in at a high cost but when the risk of incurring a high cost still falls within a normal commercial risk, such a performance shall not be excused. Therefore, the judicial termination based on Article 580 (2) should be strictly restricted.

4.6.4 *Searching for More Detailed Criteria for Judicial Termination Based on Article 580 (2)*

One-Off and Long-Term Contracts

In the *Xinyu* case, there are still some unclear issues that beg for clarification. According to commercial practice, in such a scenario, there normally will be another contract called 'shopping mall management contract' between the buyer and the seller or its affiliate company that manages the property. The later contract governs the issues such as cash register, light, electricity, elevator, air-conditioner, security, sanitation and so on. This contract, intertwined with the shop sale contract, is a long-term contract. Was the termination just about the store sale contract or does it also concern a second contract regarding the property management at the mall? If that were the case, was the termination about a one-off transaction or a long term contract?

My view would be that the real obstacle is with the 'shopping mall management contract'. The reason is straightforward. The sale agreement was a one-off transaction that has been completed: the buyer had paid the price, and the seller had delivered the shop. What was left is simply the completion of the registration procedure. The argument that 'the expenses for the performance are too high' is not related to the continuing performance of the shop sale contract but to the 'shopping mall management contract'. Because the two contracts are intertwined, if the 'shopping mall management contract' is terminated, the commercial purpose of the shop sale contract would be difficult to achieve. Therefore, it will lead to the question of whether we should terminate the two intertwined contracts.[30]

The one question we should ask is what is really wrong with this issue in Chinese law. The case reveals a lack of good rules in contract termination, especially as to the termination of a long-term contract. In order to have better rules, the legislature added a new provision on the breaching party suing for termination in the drafts of Civil Code, which attracted harsh criticism. During the course of inquiring opinions organized by the legislature, at the request of the legislature, I was tasked to come up with a substitute provision. After a close study of relevant doctrines in German law and Japanese law, I made a proposal recommending that the legislature borrow the rule from German Civil Code (BGB) § 314 and add an additional provision on termination of a long-term contract for a compelling reason.[31] However, this substitute draft was not adopted by the Civil Code. Now, as to termination of a long-term contract, there is only one general provision (Article 563 (2)) for ordinary termination,

[30] Han Shiyuan (韩世远), 'Termination of a Long-term Contract: The Breaching Party's Right to Termination or a Compelling Reason?' ('继续性合同的解除：违约方解除抑或重大事由解除?') (2020) *Peking University Law Journal* (中外法学) 1.

[31] Ibid.

dealing with a contract for an indefinite period. There is no corresponding provision on extraordinary termination of a long-term contract.

If the idea for the Civil Code to provide a provision on termination of a long-term contract for a compelling reason was a 'prescription' borrowed from German law, then Article 580 (2) of the CCC, which covers both one-off transactions and long-term contracts, is a unique Chinese solution, just like Chinese folk medicine. However, can the Chinese folk medicine cure serious illness?

Article 580 (2) of the CCC and German BGB § 314 may share one common element – the judicial discretion[32]. In order for Art. 580 (2) to work, judges and arbitrators should be provided with some concrete standards. In the legislative commentary, there are some elements that ought to be considered by judges and arbitrators before they apply the rule. We also need to ascertain scenarios in which the provision is not applicable.

Self-Induced Deadlock of Performance

Where the deadlock of performance is intentionally caused by the breaching party, my view is that judges or arbitrators shall not be permitted to grant the breaching party's request for termination. This argument has some solid backing in foreign laws. One example is BGB § 323 (6), '[t]ermination is excluded if the obligee is solely or very predominantly responsible for the circumstance that would entitle him to terminate the contract or if the circumstance for which the obligor is not responsible occurs at a time when the obligee is in default of acceptance'. Another example is the Japanese Civil Code (revised in 2017) Article 543: 'Where the non-performance of the obligation is due to a cause that the obligee is responsible for, the obligee shall not terminate the contract according to the provisions of the preceding two Articles.' Not only in the above civil law traditions, but also in common law, a party who has been at fault will generally not be entitled to invoke the doctrine of frustration. A modern example that demonstrates self-induced frustration is *J Lauritzen AS* v. *Wijsmuller BV (The 'Super Servant Two')*.[33] If the above doctrines are indicative of a trend, it is consistent with a simple legal

[32] Chinese law allows arbitrators to exercise the same judicial power as judges in both contract rescission and contract termination.

[33] [1990] 1 Lloyd's Rep 1, Court of Appeal; see also Ewan McKendrick, *Contract Law: Text, Cases, and Materials*, 6th ed. (Oxford: Oxford University Press, 2014), p. 713.

proverb: *Nullus commodum capere potest de injuria sua propria* (No one can take advantage of his own wrong).

Self-induced deadlock of performance shall preclude a party from requesting a judicial termination, this is also in accordance with the first precondition of Article 48 of Minutes 2019; namely, the breaching party is not malicious while it breaches the contract. Following this requirement, maybe the *Xinyu* case should be judged in a different way. Two facts are pertinent here. One is that the claimant Xinyu Company's shareholding structure went through two major changes, and the new shareholders decided to change the existing business directions. Therefore, the plaintiff took back the stores that were already sold. Feng Yumei was the last hold-out. The other is that on 27 March 2003, ignoring the objection from the defendant, the plaintiff demolished the glass curtain walls and some pipeline facilities of Feng Yumei's store. In view of these two facts, the case is clearly about an intentional breach that led to a self-induced deadlock of performance.

A Possible Case for Article 580 (2)

Clearly, the *Xinyu* case is not the right case for Article 580 (2). What kind of cases can it be applied to?

Since Article 580 deals only with the right to performance of a non-monetary obligation, Article 580 (2) shall not apply to the deadlock of performance of a monetary obligation. If the English case *Taylor* v. *Cardwell*[34] would happen in China, it may be a case for Article 580 (2). In this case, the plaintiff and defendant had entered into a contract by which the defendant agreed to let the plaintiff have the use of The Surrey Gardens and Music Hall on four days, for the purpose of giving a series of four grand concerts; and the plaintiff agreed to take the Gardens and Hall on those days and pay money for each day. After the making of the agreement, and before the first day on which a concert was to be given, the Hall was destroyed by fire. The destruction was without the fault of either party. What would the results of the case be if it were under Chinese law?

If Chinese law were the applicable law and the fire was held a *force majeure*, either party has a right of termination according to Article 563 (1) of the CCC. Normally, there is no need to initiate an action for judicial termination according to Article 580 (2). However, if the fire was not

[34] (1863) 3 B & S 826, Queen's Bench; see also McKendrick, *Contract Law*, p. 698.

caused by a *force majeure* but a third party (e.g., a neighbour negligently burnt his own house), it would still be impossible for the defendant as the lessor of the Music Hall to deliver the leased premise; and it would also be impossible for the purpose of the contract to be fulfilled. According to Article 563 (1)(4), the plaintiff could obtain a right of termination. Where the plaintiff did not terminate the contract, but only sued for specific performance, or for damages or agreed payments for the breach, then the defendant may at least raise a counterclaim for termination of the contract. The benefit for doing so is that a ruling in favour of this counterclaim would indicate both the termination of contract and the timing of the termination. This would be important for the long-term contracts like a lease.

4.7 Conclusion

Since the *Xinyu* case was published in the Gazette of the Supreme People's Court in 2006, this peculiar expression, 'a breaching party's right to termination', emerged in China. An incoherent doctrine, it reveals some problems about the rules on termination under the Chinese Contract Law 1999. The main issue here is that the law is inadequate in dealing with long-term contracts.

CCC Article 563 (2) is a step forward. However, as revealed by the *Xinyu* case, the real crux is a termination of a long-term contract for a definite period. In this aspect, the CCC still has left some gaps (especially as to extraordinary termination of a long-term contract). Article 580 (2) may provide some help but only with cases that involve performance of non-monetary obligation. For those involving performance of monetary obligation, there is still a gap to be filled.

Unlike rules in any other jurisdictions, Article 580 (2) is a unique creature. It is Chinese folk medicine that deals with a serious issue: the deadlock of performance. It may provide help for some cases, but its efficacy is limited.

Judicial termination of contract according to Article 580 (2) should be done very cautiously. The justification for termination, from *force majeure* to change of circumstance and to commercial risk, decreases in sequence.

5

Contractual Consent in the New Chinese Civil Code

CATHERINE VALCKE

5.1 Introduction

As per the Chinese codifier's self-proclaimed aspirations, the provisions on contract found in the new PRC Civil Code (2021) combine a number of distinct Western influences.[1] If so, parsing out and tracking these Western influences within the various provisions should prove a valuable exercise for the purpose of understanding them better. That is what I propose to do here, focusing on codal texts devoted to issues on which Western legal systems tend to diverge – for alignment with any given Western legal system clearly is most meaningful where other such systems take a different route. As such, the present chapter hopefully will interest comparative lawyers and contract lawyers alike, in China and beyond.

I argued elsewhere[2] that conceptions of contractual consent can be formalized into three models (or Weberian "ideal-types"),[3] roughly reflecting what seems to emerge from, respectively, the French, German and English law on the issue. Focusing first on the *content* of contractual

[1] Bing Ling, "The New Contract Law in the Chinese Civil Code" (2020) 8(3) *Chinese Journal of Comparative Law* 558, 561.

[2] Catherine Valcke, "Consent in Contract," in Jan Smits, Jaakko Husa, Catherine Valcke and Madalena Narciso (eds.), *The Elgar Encyclopedia of Comparative Law* (2nd ed., Cheltenham: Edward Elgar, forthcoming). The proposed, tripartite typology should not be taken to suggest that French, German and English contract law have nothing in common. Comparative lawyers in fact have successfully established exactly the opposite: "Western private laws are similar in nature even when the technical rules are different." (Hao Jiang, "Freedom of Contract Under State Supervision" (2016) 7[3] *George Mason Journal of International Law* 202, 202, citing extensive work to that effect by James Gordley and others.) The question of the relative extent to which French, German and English laws align and diverge however is beyond the scope of the present chapter.

[3] See likewise, Mirjan Damaška, *The Faces of Justice and State Authority: A Comparative Approach to the Legal Process* (New Haven: Yale University Press, 1986).

consent, I there suggested that French and German law, on the one hand, tend to conceptualize that consent narrowly, in terms of actual intention – "what the parties can reasonably be taken to have *in fact* consented to" – while English law, on the other hand, tends to conceptualize it more broadly, normatively as well as factually – "what the parties reasonably *ought* to have consented to." Thereafter focusing on the *standpoint* from which to identify such actual and normative contractual contents, I maintained that French law tends to privilege the standpoint of the party making the promise – "what in fact went on in the promisor's mind" – whereas German law prefers that of the party receiving the promise – "what the promisee could reasonably assume in fact went on in the promisor's mind." The rest of the argument was then devoted to showing that these respectively narrow (French), somewhat narrow (German) and broader (English) conceptions of contractual consent account for the different ways and extents to which contractual content came to be supplemented with normative content extraneous to the contract, in the form of rule of law–like relief for mistakes and unforeseen changes of circumstances, good faith and abuse of rights doctrines, intervention with unfair contracts and sanctions for breach, as well as with inversely broader or narrower conceptions of delictual liability.

Insofar as those three models seem at all plausible, they likely can prove most useful here for the purpose of identifying the particular conception(s) of contractual consent grounding the contract and contract-related provisions found in the General Part and the Book on Contracts of the PRC CC.[4] To that end, we will survey in turn the provisions bearing on, in particular, contract formation, contract interpretation, mistake as to present or future facts, good faith and abuse of rights, contractual fairness in the context of standard form contracts and some aspects of contract remedies. For, in any legal system, the rules on these issues arguably are those speaking the loudest to the nature of contractual consent. One and the same question will be asked with respect to each of these areas of contract law, namely, which of the three

[4] Doctrinal and judicial commentary discussing these provisions are ignored for present purposes, which arguably is justified with regard to such deliberate and carefully crafted legal language as code provisions, intended to apply over as long a future as the past from which they emerge. In addition, as code provisions, these texts can be seen as embodying or at least accounting for scholarly and judicial views accumulated to date, as they indeed aim to crystallize or reject, confirm or correct and redirect, pre-existing Chinese private law. See Ling, "The New Contract Law," pp. 558–65.

models of contractual consent described above emerge(s) most saliently from the rules at play.

5.2 Contract Formation

While the PRC CC boasts a structure similar to that of the German BGB – a General Part followed by the various Parts governing property, contracts, family, etc. –, it will come as no surprise that the German influence might reach beyond mere structure. Already with respect to the formation of contracts, one observes that the rules on the timing and effectiveness of offers, acceptances and offer revocations in correspondence contexts align with those found in the BGB. Acceptance, like offer revocation, is effective on reception by the addressee rather than on despatch by the sender (arts. 137, 477, 481 PRC CC), as they are in German law (art. 130 BGB).[5] Chinese law hence at first sight seems to share the German focus on protecting the interests of the "reasonable addressee."[6]

However, as Kant explained[7] and despite suggestions to the contrary[8], such rules do not say much, if at all, about the law's conceptual foundations, as they are mere rules of coordination, akin to those mandating driving on the right or the left side of the road, hence rules whose actual content matters little, despite the clear necessity that they be understood and followed in the same way by all. Indeed, one could certainly imagine a system like the French, focused on the promisor's actual intention, that would nonetheless endorse a reception theory of acceptance on the ground that, in order for an acceptance to be given legal recognition, it must embody a very firm intention, one so firm as to be expressed

[5] "Reception" under the PRC CC, however, corresponds to the moment the addressee "learns" of the contents of the expression of intent whereas in German law, it arguably corresponds to the moment the addressee is in a position to learn about its contents.

[6] Peter Benson, *Justice in Transactions: A Theory of Contract Law* (Cambridge, MA: The Belknap Press of Harvard University Press, 2019), pp. 112–13: "In fact, the most widely accepted formulations of the objective test do exactly this: they hold that both the existence and the content of a party's manifestation of assent are decided by *how that party's manifestation of assent are decided by how that party's words or conduct appear to a reasonable person in the position of the other party, taking into account the surrounding circumstances and context of their transaction*, including any facts or underlying assumptions that are known by or reasonably available to both."

[7] Dominique Ferrand, *Droit privé allemand* (Paris: Éditions Dalloz-Sirey, 1997), §186.

[8] Wayne Barnes, "The French Subjective Theory of Contract: Separating Rhetoric from Reality" (2008) 83 *Tulane Law Review* 359, 368.

through irrevocable means, and this entirely independently of any concern for what the offeror might or might not know. From the standpoint of analyzing contractual consent, therefore, one should refrain from reading too much into the particular rules on timing of offer and acceptance that have been favoured at any given time in any given system. In fact, French law has traditionally endorsed the despatch theory of acceptance, but recently moved to the reception theory,[9] and English law just happens to have borrowed the despatch theory from French law long before the French reversal and to have stuck with it[10] – all of which ultimately serves to confirm, if anything, the conceptual arbitrariness of these rules.

More revealing, however, are, first, the doctrinal and judicial explanations typically offered in support of these various (ultimately arbitrary) positions and, second, the particular treatment of offer revocation. The despatch theory of acceptance has long been justified by French scholars on the ground that the moral principle of the autonomy of the will requires no more than that an actual contractual intention *form* in the mind of the offeree, with the result that to demand that that intention also be *communicated* to the offeror would be tantamount to "adding a new and arbitrary element to contractual intention and the contract as such."[11] (Note that the interest of the addressee is entirely absent from that analysis.) Along the same lines, offers in principle are freely revocable prior to acceptance because the offeror at that time has yet to "promise" anything proper, and revoking such unilateral juristic acts as offers accordingly cannot, as such, be viewed as "wrongful" (or "sinful").[12] Moreover, an offer is to be considered revoked upon mere proof of the offeror's change of heart (such as the same offer being made

[9] Art. 1121 Fr. CC (2016).

[10] *Charlebois* v. *Baril* [1928] SCR 8. See also J. M. Perillo, "Robert J. Pothier's Influence on the Common Law of Contract" (2005) 11 *Texas Wesleyan Law Review* 627.

[11] G. Marty and P. Raynaud, *Droit civil* (1962), vol. 2 (Les Obligations), §§ 111, 380, cited in Barnes, "The French Subjective Theory of Contract," pp. 379–80 [my translation]. To the same effect, see H. and L. Mazeaud, *Leçons de droit civil* (2nd ed., 1962), vol. 2, §§ 146, 120; A. Colin and H. Capitant, *Cours élémentaire de droit civil français* (4th ed., 1924).

[12] An offer accordingly dies with the person of the offeror: art. 1117 Fr. CC (2016). For a number of policy reasons, the Fr. CC (2016) now prohibits premature withdrawals of offers with terms (art. 1116), but the obligation thus created indeed is legal, not contractual. See Gaël Chantepie and Mathias Latina, *Le nouveau droit des obligations: Commentaire théorique et pratique dans l'ordre du Code civil* (2nd ed., Paris: Éditions Dalloz, 2018), pp. 174–75.

to a third party), even uncommunicated to the offeree,[13] for such proof suffices to establish that, from that moment on, there simply no longer is an actual intention to contract on the part of at least one of the parties. Where a term is attached to the offer, the offer's premature withdrawal in contrast has traditionally been viewed as indeed "wrongful" but in the extra-contractual sense of the offeror having faultily misled the offeree into thinking the offer would be maintained for the stated time, thus leading to delictual rather than contractual liability.[14]

In English law, offers with or without a term can be freely revoked prior to acceptance and/or the expiration of the term, as the case may be, on the reasoning that, under the above-described objective conception, there can be no obligation without a bargain.[15] Thus, even offers with a term fail to bind the offeror to keep the offer open for the stated term unless the offeree has bargained for that benefit, that is, unless that benefit itself was the object of a contract between the parties – thus confirming that any such obligation cannot but be contractual in nature.[16]

In German law, finally, such unilateral juristic acts as offers are generally binding, presumably on the ground that they are relied upon by others, the reasonable addressee's reliance being, again, privileged over the moral dimension of promises or the economic dimension of bargains. As a result, whereas the wrongful withdrawal of an offer is, in French and English law alike, feasible albeit possibly generative of an obligation to repair the damages suffered as a result, such withdrawals simply are deemed altogether ineffective in German law, with the result that, however much the offeror may try to revoke the offer, the contract will form when the acceptance meets the (deemed still present) offer.[17]

In this respect, the PRC CC clearly aligns with the German position just described. Indeed, its art. 476 prohibits the revocation of offers, not

[13] Hugh Beale et al. (eds.), *Cases, Materials and Text on Contract Law* (Oxford: Hart, 2002), p. 199.

[14] The obligation to keep the offer open for the stated term, or in the absence of such term, a "reasonable" term is now codified at art. 1116 of the Fr. CC (2016).

[15] *Dickinson* v. *Dodds* [1876] 2 ChD 463 (CA).

[16] Of course, insofar as it could be established that the offer's premature withdrawal was fraudulent or tantamount to a negligent misrepresentation, a tort claim might lie, as it might in French law.

[17] Beale et al., *Cases, Materials and Text on Contract Law*, p. 199. Accordingly, contrary to the situation in French law, upon the offeror's death, the offer does not expire automatically but passes to the offeror's successors: arts. 130(2), 153 BGB.

only where (1) it has been presented as irrevocable for a certain period of time but also, and most tellingly, where (2) "the offeree has reasons to believe that the offer is irrevocable and has made reasonable preparation to perform the contract," thus clearly privileging the standpoint and interests of the reasonable addressee. That the offeree might or might not have "bargained" for the benefit of considering the offer for a particular period of time is neither here nor there, moreover, as consideration is not a requirement of a valid contract in Chinese law: it appears nowhere among the various such requirements discussed at arts. 469ff PRC CC, and art. 543 PRC CC confirms that unilateral modifications of contracts can be effected through sheer agreement of the parties to that effect. Finally, as per the German law on the issue,[18] whereas as between the parties, contracts take effect upon the moment of consent (art. 215 PRC CC), their effect on the property rights that they target is, out of protection for third-party reliance, postponed until registration (art. 224 PRC CC).

5.2.1 *Contract Interpretation*

The way different legal systems go about interpreting contracts clearly is immediately revealing as to their respective conceptions of contractual consent. Here again, the contrast is starkest between French and English law, with German law sitting quite close to, yet still some distance from, French law, and Chinese law appearing to align with German law.

French law is known for having traditionally favoured the parties' actual over their declared intention.[19] At least in principle, therefore, the declaration of intention is seen as serving little more than an evidentiary function: one would think that the declared intention reflects the actual one, but when it turns out not to, the latter prevails. That is hardly

[18] Arts. 929–32 BGB. See, more generally, the German distinction between juristic acts creative of obligations (*Verpflichtungsgeschäft*) and juristic acts of disposition (*Verfügungsgeschäft*): Ferrand, *Droit privé allemand*, pp. 226–29.

[19] Barnes, *The French Subjective Theory of Contract*, p. 379. See art. 1188 Fr. CC (2016): "A contract is to be interpreted according to the common intention of the parties rather than stopping at the literal meaning of its terms. Where this intention cannot be discerned, a contract is to be interpreted in the sense which a reasonable person placed in the same situation would give it" (as translated in John Cartwright, Bénédicte Fauvarque-Cosson and Simon Whittaker, "The Law of Contract, the General Regime of Obligations, and Proof of Obligations: The New Provisions of the Code Civil Created by Ordonnance n° 2016-131 of 10 February 2016," translated into English).

surprising: as explained, if the parties are ultimately being held accountable from a moral standpoint, only their actual thoughts ought to matter.

In English law, in stark contrast, as per Lord Denning's famous words, "[i]n contracts you do not look into the actual intent in a man's mind. You look at what he said and did. A contract is formed when there is, to all outward appearances, a contract."[20] As explained above, moreover, the relevant "outward" perspective at play here is not that of both parties, nor even that of one of them, but rather the perspective of what seems (normatively) "reasonable" in the circumstances.[21] Applied in the context of written contracts, that objective conception of contractual consent fully accounts, I would argue, for such English staples as the parol evidence rule, the doctrine of *non est factum* and the rules on rectification. By barring evidence of party interaction that is peripheral to the written contract, the parol evidence rule confirms that the parties' contractual obligations are to be determined through quasi-exclusive reference to what the parties themselves have designated as their declared intention for the purpose of that particular transaction.[22] Insofar as one party's endorsement of the written contract may have resulted from some sort of foul play, however, justice requires that corrective measures such as *non est factum* and rectification be available on an exceptional basis. The long-standing presence of all three of these rules in English law hence ultimately serves to confirm the firmness of the objective conception under that law.[23] In contrast, French and German law know of no such rules, as these indeed would be out of place where contractual consent is conceptualized subjectively.[24]

German law diverges from both French and English law, insofar as it dictates that different perspectives be adopted for recipient-aimed and non-recipient–aimed juristic acts. While this may at first seem surprising, such differential treatment in fact is fully coherent with the German concern for protecting the interests of the reasonable addressee.

[20] *Storer* v. *Manchester City Council* [1974] 3 All ER 825 (C.A.), 1408.

[21] *Parker* v. *The South Eastern Railway Co* [1877] 2 CPD 416 (CA), as per *Bramwell J.*; *Thornton* v. *Shoe Lane Parking Ltd.* [1971] 2 QB 163 (CA).

[22] *Gallen* v. *Allstate* [1984] BCJ No 1621 (QL).

[23] Lord Sumption, "A Question of Taste: The Supreme Court and the Interpretation of Contracts," Harris Society Annual Lecture, Oxford, May 2017.

[24] The parol evidence and rectification rules simply have no French equivalent, and *non est factum* is unnecessary given the central role played by the doctrine of mistake. See *Québec (Agence du Revenu)* v. *Services Environnementaux AES inc*, 2013 SCC 65; *Jean Coutu Group (PJC) Inc* v. *Canada (Attorney General)*, 2016 SCC 55.

Art. 133 BGB indeed provides that, in interpreting recipient-aimed juristic acts (contracts), one seeks to determine the declarant's will *as it appears to the reasonable addressee*, specified by art. 157 BGB as being the objective, good faith addressee aware of the larger context, whereas in interpreting non-recipient–aimed acts, as there simply *is no* reasonable addressee whose standpoint can be adopted, the interpreter instead seeks to uncover the declarant's actual, internal will.[25] (Note that in neither case is the interpretation to focus on the literal meaning of the declaration, as it arguably might in English law.) With respect to recipient-aimed juristic acts, moreover, where the addressee is shown not to be "worthy" of protection, as when he or she in fact knows or ought to have known that the declaration does not match its author's real intention, the latter is exceptionally made to prevail.[26]

The PRC CC's counterpart text (art. 142) admittedly diverges from the German insofar as it declares the literal meaning a valid interpretive starting point, whereas art. 133 BGB refers to it only to steer interpreters away from it. The Chinese and German texts nonetheless end up coming together, as the PRC CC thereafter clarifies that said literal meaning is to be considered along with "the relevant articles, nature and purpose of the act, usual practices, and the principle of good faith." More significantly, however, the same recipient-aimed/non-recipient–aimed distinction structuring the German text also is central to the Chinese, as art. 142 PRC CC dictates that, with respect to the latter acts, "the real intention of the actor shall be sought rather than the literal meaning of the words used," such real intention likewise being informed by "the relevant articles, nature and purpose of the act, usual practices, and the principle of good faith." Yet, however clear the PRC CC's alignment with the German law may seem at this point, art. 143 immediately thereafter conditions the validity of juristic acts on the expressed intention being "genuine," which condition in fact smacks of the French conception.

5.2.2 *Mistake as to Present and Future Facts*

Like French and German law, and unlike English law, Chinese law seems clearly destined to recognizing "rule of law"–type relief for mistake

[25] See Florian Faust, *Bürgerliches Gesetzbuch Allgemeiner Teil* (7th ed., Baden-Baden: Nomos Verlagsgesellschaft, 2020), p. 34, para. 9 (discussing art. 133 BGB).

[26] Ferrand, *Droit privé allemand*, pp. 221–22. That situation is similar to that in *Dickinson* v. *Dodds*, which arguably militates in favour of reading the court's judgment in that case as one rendered in Equity.

("substantial misunderstanding" art. 148 PRC CC), as well as for unforeseen changes of circumstances other than resulting from a "force majeure,"[27] that is, relief of a kind that cannot be said to derive from the contract itself – thus confirming its endorsement of the French and German conceptions of contractual consent as actual consent. Though the French, German and Chinese texts are phrased slightly differently, all three do converge on the general idea that where performance of the contract has become impossible or unduly onerous due to a substantial mistake as to present facts or a major change of circumstances unforeseeable at the time of contracting, the risk of which the contract does not allocate to one of the parties, the contract can be modified or else altogether terminated by the court, should the parties' own renegotiations to that end fail.[28]

It could be pointed out that, at least at first sight, English law seems to stand for the very same proposition.[29] Yet it is well known that relief on the ground of mistake is far easier to obtain in French or German law than in English law.[30] How can that be? I would suggest that it indeed has to do with the fact that French and German judges are far less inclined than their English counterparts to read the contract as allocating the risk of the mistake at issue to one of the parties. That is, precisely because English judges are not looking for an *actual* allocation of the risk of mistake in the contract, merely one that can be reasonably implied from the fact that one of the parties was better positioned to fend off that risk, they will end up finding such an allocation far more often than the French or German judges. Despite an apparent convergence on principle,

[27] Relief for force majeure is the rule in French law (art. 1218 Fr. CC (2016), unlike in German law, where it falls to the debtor to prove that he was not responsible for the event leading to the impossibility of performance (art. 287 BGB). In English law, it tends to be defined as precisely the kind of risk that the debtor was not meant to shoulder: in English law, the doctrine of frustration is the closest equivalent to the French concept of force majeure. In the seminal case of *Davis Contractors Ltd* v. *Fareham UDC* [1956] AC 696, Lord Radcliffe stated that "frustration occurs whenever the law recognizes that without default of either party a contractual obligation has become incapable of being performed because the circumstances in which performance is called for would render it a thing radically different from that which was undertaken by the contract."

[28] Compare arts. 1132–36, 1195 Fr. CC (2016), arts. 119–20, 313 BGB and arts. 146–47, 533 PRC CC.

[29] See *Great Peace Shipping Ltd* v. *Tsavliris (International) Ltd* [2002] EWCA Civ 1407.

[30] Barry Nicholas, "Introduction to the French Law of Contract," in Donald Harris and Denis Tallon (eds.), *Contract Law Today: Anglo-French Comparisons* (Oxford: Clarendon Press, 1989), ch. 1.

therefore, French, German and Chinese law, on the one hand, and English law, on the other hand, remain far apart on that point.

As between French and German law, however, Chinese law here seems, for once, to come closer to the French, at least when considering the codal texts alone. Like classical French texts, arts. 146–47 of the PRC CC do not make relief for mistake conditional upon the source of the mistake or upon whether the importance attached by the mistaken party to the mistaken quality was known to the non-mistaken party, as a strong concern for the non-mistaken party's contractual reliance would dictate that it be done.[31] French law has long shown concern for the non-mistaken party's reliance, but it has done so by supplementing the contractual, mistake analysis proper with a delictual inquiry into whether the mistake might have resulted from the mistaken party's own fault or involved some kind of deception of the non-mistaken party. For, the very open-ended nature of delictual liability in French law allows for precisely such kinds of moves[32] – as might perhaps likewise do the Chinese texts.

Arts. 120 and 176 PRC CC do appear to provide for a very open-ended form of delictual liability, akin to the French, one that is unconstrained by some kind of *numerus clausus* of duties, as is the case in German law. Insofar as this might indeed be the case, it arguably would help explain why concern for the non-mistaken party's reliance is unaccounted for in the Chinese texts on mistake as such. German law's strong concern to protect non-mistaken parties' reliance caused it to make relief for mistake come with automatic compensation of the non-mistaken party's reliance interest (*Vertrauensschaden*) by the mistaken party, regardless of any kind of fault or information requirement.[33] Again, though, such provision was there deemed necessary only insofar as German law could not account for such concern through its comparatively more constrained delictual liability regime. Insofar as Chinese law might share the French's broader conception of delictual liability, it may just be spared having to account for non-mistaken party reliance within the contractual analysis of mistake proper. In sum, whereas the relatively

[31] See art. 1110 Fr. CC (1804).

[32] These elements have now been brought to the fore in arts. 1132 and 1133 Fr. C.C. (2016).

[33] Art. 122 BGB. Section 122 thus establishes a form of liability without fault on the part of the mistaken party, one that is triggered solely through his claiming rescission, with the one caveat that the obligation to compensate does not arise "if the injured party knew the ground of the . . . rescission or did not know it due to negligence (should have known it)" (art. 122 (2) BGB).

narrow, German conception of delict resulted in concern for non-mistaken party reliance being moved front and center into the contractual analysis in German law, the reverse, relative broadness of the French conception resulted in that same concern there being instead addressed only as a qualitatively distinct, and analytically secondary, (delictual) step – which move might, again, perhaps be that which emerges from the Chinese text as well.

5.2.3 *Good Faith and Abuse of Rights*

That difference between French and German delictual law, which tracks that between French and German conceptions of contractual consent, also arguably explains the different French and German conceptions of good faith. A pillar of German private law,[34] the duty of good faith also is important in French law, though not nearly to the same extent, arguably for the very reason that much of the work that is done via that doctrine in German law in fact is accomplished through delicts in French law. More exactly, although French judges and scholars make ample references to good faith, at least in name, that notion for them is, on a conceptual level, quasi-indistinguishable from delictual fault: breaching good faith is just one way to commit a fault, under French law, the sanction for which indeed is delictual compensation in damages for the harm resulting. (The notion of "abuse of rights" moreover helps little in this respect, as it only specifies that good faith is to be had in the exercise, not just the determination of the contents, of the rights and obligations.)[35] In German law, in contrast, the duty of good faith partakes of contractual consent, insofar as it serves to define, as already explained, the "reasonableness" of the "reasonable addressee." More generally, a breach of art. 242 BGB (the *Treu und Glauben* clause) does usually yield a contractual rather than delictual claim, resolved through contractual damages.[36]

[34] Ferrand, *Droit privé allemand*, paras. 288ff.

[35] The notion of "abuse of rights" appears nowhere in the new Fr. CC (2016) and is mentioned in tandem with good faith in the Civil Code of Quebec: see arts. 6, 7, 1372, 1375 C.C.Q. In German law, it is part and parcel of the good faith requirement of art. 242 BGB.

[36] Even *culpa in contrahendo* – fault in the negotiation process leading up to a contract – is treated as at least quasi-contractual. Breach of art. 826 ("intentional immoral damage"), however, leads to delictual liability. The other "general clause," the *gute Sitten* clause of art. 138 BGB, which is often used in tandem with art. 242 BGB, appears in the general part. But art. 138 BGB is typically thought of as governing more precisely targeted

It is, however, important to keep in mind that the German notion of "reasonableness" here at play remains fundamentally distinct from the English, normative conception of contractual "objectivity": the intention that can reasonably be attributed to the contracting parties is not the same as that which such parties, as reasonable people, should have had. The first inception of "reasonable" remains factual, whereas the second treads on normative territory. That is, it is entirely possible *reasonably* to ascribe to the parties an intention that they, as reasonable people, *ought not* have had. Thus, while the German conception of consent, as it includes some notion of reasonableness, indeed is thicker than the French, both it and the French remain closer together as against the English, given that they both stand firmly ensconced on the factual rather than normative side of things.

Consistently with their possible alignment with the French conception of delictual fault, the PRC CC provisions would also appear to line up with the French conception of good faith. The kindred requirements of adherence to fairness, good faith and honesty, and non-violation of public order and good morals are found at the very outset of the Chinese code, at arts. 6, 7 and 8, thus presumably applicable to all private law contexts, with good faith as to the exercise of rights being underscored at art. 131, and its particular application in the contractual context, being detailed at art. 500. The duty of good faith hence seems to be highly open-textured, ultimately subsuming all else, much like delictual liability might be viewed as subsuming contractual liability in French law[37] and like might also be the case at Chinese law: the general – delictual? – principle of art. 120 PRC CC (perhaps redundantly reiterated at art. 176 PRC CC), according to which the victim of an "infringement of civil rights and interests . . . is entitled to request the infringer assume the [non-descript] liability for such infringement," immediately follows the assertion that "[a] contract entered into in accordance with the law is legally binding on the parties concerned" (art. 119 PCR CC). The sequence and immediacy of these two articles arguably can be read as

situations involving a public policy dimension. See Christian Armbrüster, "Kommentiert die §§ 116–124, §§134–138 BGB und das ProstG," in *Münchener Kommentar zum BGB* (8th ed., Munich: Verlag C. H. Beck, 2018), § 242, para. 128.

[37] While the issue has been the object of much debate in both classical and contemporary French law, breach of contract clearly more constitutes a delictual fault under the Quebec Civil Code. See arts. 1457–58 C.c.Q. (1991).

indicating that breach of contract is treated as giving rise to just one kind of the more general, delictual form of liability.

The most salient offspring of the doctrine of good faith in both French and German law may be the contracting parties' duty to inform one another on aspects of the contract that each of them knows about and has reason to suspect that the other also would want to know about (*devoir d'information, Aufklärungspflicht*), which English law has steadfastly rejected.[38] In the famous case of *Smith* v. *Hughes*,[39] involving a sale of oats by sample, the English Court of Appeal indeed explicitly denied that the seller of new oats, which, as the seller was well aware, the buyer needed to be old, had a duty to alert the buyer to his mistake. Seeing that the parties were not mistaken about the terms and/or nature of their contract as a sale by sample, the Court reasoned that their rights and obligations were to be determined by reference to that contract alone, with the result that the seller was (normatively) entitled to disregard anything not dictated by it, in particular what might have (actually) gone on in his and the other party's minds at the time of contracting. Had the mistake related to a term and/or nature of the contract, the Court noted, the seller in contrast would not have been entitled to ignore it and accordingly would have been estopped from asserting his understanding of the contract in court.[40] In such cases relief will be had, as the dispute then goes to the content of the contract if any, but it will come from Equity rather than Law, Equity being, it will be recalled, the "civilian organ" of English law, historically implanted with a view to appease those intent on overhauling the entire system towards a continental model.[41]

Interestingly, while the PRC CC, consistently with the subjective conception of consent, as indicated endorses a general duty of good faith, it does not explicitly mention any kind of "duty to inform." Such explicit mention admittedly also is absent from the BGB, as it was from the

[38] The longevity of recent feeble overtures towards the idea remains to be seen: *MSC Mediterranean Shipping Company SA* v. *Cottonex Anstalt* [2016] EWCA Civ 789; *Mid Essex Hospital Services NHS Trust* v. *Compass Group UK and Ireland Ltd* [2013] EWCA Civ 200; *Yam Seng Pte Ltd* v. *International Trade Corporation Ltd* [2013] EWHC 111 (Q.B.); *Interfoto Picture Library Ltd* v. *Stiletto Visual Programmes* [1989] QB 433. In Canada, see *Bhasin* v. *Hrynew*, 2014 SCC 71; *C.M. Callow Inc.* v. *Zollinger* [2020] SCC 45; *National Bank* v. *Soucisse et al* [1981] 2 SCR 339; *Houle* v. *Canadian National Bank* [1990] 3 SCR 122, 74 DLR (4th) 577; *Bank of Montréal* v. *Bail Ltée* [1992] 2 SCR 554, 93 DLR (4th) 490.

[39] [1871] L.R. 6 Q.B. 597.

[40] Ibid., 606.

[41] Ibid.

French Code of 1804, the matter then being considered adequately governed by case law and doctrinal commentary alone. The new French Code of 2016 formally recognizes the duty to inform, however, devoting no less than six paragraphs to unpacking its various parameters.[42] The question thus arises as to why the Chinese codifier, presumably presented with the very same drafting choices as was its French counterpart, went the opposite way. As this issue is most divisive between civil law and common law systems, one cannot help but think that the absence of explicit mention of a duty to inform in the PRC CC might be indicative of quiet support for the common law position, if not with respect to good faith in general, at least with respect to the more pointed duty to inform. Chinese scholarly commentaries and judicial decisions on the question will clearly need to be consulted in order to determine whether this is in fact the case.

5.2.4 *Standard Form Contracts*

In at least one common law jurisdiction, the objective conception of contractual consent was found sufficiently malleable to allow for prohibiting the use of onerous clauses contained in standard form contracts. In *Tilden Rent-A-Car* v. *Clendenning*,[43] the Court of Appeal for Ontario indeed refused to enforce such a clause on the ground that it had been "apparent to the employee of Tilden Rent-A-Car that Mr. Clendenning had not in fact read the document in its entirety before signing it."[44] As misleading information about the contents of the car rental contract had moreover been given by the employee prior to Clendenning's signature, which contract was internally contradictory and in fact never meant to be read, and as speediness served the plaintiff's business interests, the Court concluded that, in such circumstances, the plaintiff could not possibly be seen as having "entered into the contract in the belief that Mr. Clendenning was assenting to all [its] terms."[45]

I would suggest that the Court's reasoning here harks back to German, not English, contractual consent, as it focuses on "reasonableness" rather than "objectivity" proper. In fact, the Court itself acknowledges that its ruling departs from the classic English view on the matter crystallized in

[42] Art. 1112-1 Fr CC (2016).
[43] [1978] O.J. No 3260 (Q.L.), 83 DLR (3d) 400.
[44] Ibid, para. 17.
[45] Ibid.

L'Estrange v. *F Graucob Ltd*,[46] according to which the objective theory of contract would entail that one's signing a contract calling for a signature constitutes quasi-irrefragable proof of that person's contractual consent, thereby relieving the other of having to enquire into whether such apparent consent in reality was reflective of actual assent with respect to any given part of the contract's contents,[47] even when accounting for the full "matrix of facts" that necessarily feeds into the interpretation of any kind of linguistic statement.[48] In my view, a better reading of the Court's judgment – one more coherent with the English conception of contract as bargain – accordingly would be as one rendered in Equity, wherein the problematic clause remains very much part of the contract (which it would not, under a strict consent analysis at Law) yet is such that Tilden would be "estopped" from relying on it in court. And the Court does in fact stop short of suggesting that said clause be altogether read out of the contract, instead repeatedly floating precisely such estoppel-like language throughout the judgment. For the English view of contract as bargain, wherein all terms are to be viewed as forming a package, makes it very difficult for English courts to cherry-pick certain contract terms over others, whether with a view to adding them to, or excluding them from, the contract.

In contrast, the concern to identifying merely the promises that were made in fact, which concern is shared by French and German law alike (albeit from different, promisor and the promisee's respective, standpoints), entails no obstacles to judges overtly fiddling with the contract so as to carve out objectionable parts or add missing ones that they (rather than the parties) deem necessary. It therefore is hardly surprising that the French and the German civil codes would both explicitly dictate that "abusive" clauses found in standard form contracts simply be "reputed non-written"[49] or "not part of the contract."[50] And the PRC CC hence appears to join them both in mandating, at art. 497 (2) and (3), that "[a] standard clause *is void* [where] . . . the party providing the standard clause unreasonably exempts or alleviates himself from the liability, imposes heavier liability on the other party, or restricts the main rights

[46] [1934] 2 K.B. 394.

[47] See, likewise, *McCutcheon* v. *David Macbrayne Ltd.* [1964] 1 WLR 125 (HL).

[48] *Investors Compensation Scheme Ltd* v. *West Bromwich Building Society* [1998] 1 WLR 896.

[49] Art. 1171 Fr.CC (2016).

[50] Art. 307 BGB.

of the other party; or ... deprives the other party of his main rights."[51] Here again, the alignment with continental law, be it French of German, seems incontrovertible.

5.2.5 *Remedies*

One PRC CC provision that is particularly intriguing from a comparative standpoint is art. 470 (VII), according to which "liabilities for breach of contract" generally fall within what is to be agreed upon by the parties themselves. For that provision may, at least at first sight, seem to tap into contemporary English law, whereas all other parts of the Chinese code considered to this point as we saw sit more closely to French and/or German law.

In the famous case of *Transfield Shipping Inc* v. *Mercator Shipping Inc (The Achilleas)*,[52] the English House of Lords put an end to decades of uncertainty by resolving that the damages payable to the non-breaching party for consequential losses are not so much those that the parties could have contemplated at contract formation as likely to flow from such a breach *as a matter of fact*, as those for which they could reasonably be held liable *as a matter of law*, given the objective nature, contents and circumstances of their bargain with one another.[53] In so doing, the Lords clarified "the fundamental point of principle in the law of contractual damages: is the rule that a party may recover losses which were foreseeable ... an external rule of law imposed upon the parties to every contract in default of express provisions to the contrary, or is it a *prima facie* assumption about what the parties may be taken to have intended ...?"[54] Their response in favour of the latter arguably clearly established that, in English law, rulings concerning remedies, just like those concerning contractual interpretation or the contracting process more generally, may ultimately be derivable from the parties' own bargain – "rules of interpretation" rather than "rules of law."

The alignment of Chinese with English law here is apparent only, however. For deeper analysis reveals that, while the PRC CC does aim to attribute to the parties the task of determining the resolution of breach situations, it does so by dictating that they *actually* include provisions to

[51] Italics added.
[52] [2008] UKHL 48.
[53] Ibid., para. 8.
[54] Ibid., para. 9.

that effect in their contract, which in no way modifies the underlying conception of contractual consent. That is to say, while in both Chinese and English law the parties may end up determining the remedies for breach of their contract, in Chinese law they will do so only insofar as they *actually*, subjectively turned their minds to the issue, whereas in English law they will be *deemed* to have done so if that is consistent with their objective bargain. If anything, then, art. 470 (VII) PRC CC only serves to confirm that the Chinese codifiers meant to endorse the continental conception of contractual consent as actual such consent. That moreover is further reiterated by art. 584 PRC CC, which lists foreseeability in-fact as the criterion for determining which of the losses suffered by the non-breaching party are compensable by the breaching party.

5.3 Conclusion

The aim of this chapter was to identify and analyze some of the Western influences that played into the PRC CC provisions on contracts. To that end, we set various such provisions against three models developed elsewhere, which present French contractual consent as most narrow, for focused on the promising party's actual intention; German contractual consent as somewhat narrow, for its focus on the reasonable addressee's perception of the promisor's actual intention; and English contractual consent as broadest, for including a normative alongside a factual dimension. Looking to the Chinese treatment of various contract issues that seem most telling as to the underlying view of contractual consent – contract formation, contract interpretation, mistake as to present or future facts, good faith and abuse of rights, contractual fairness in the context of standard form contracts and some aspects of contract remedies – it was determined that the Chinese code provisions on contract on the whole clearly motion to a continental rather than English model, the only exception perhaps being with respect to the duty to inform, which the Chinese code refrains from explicitly endorsing. As between the French and the German models, moreover, the PRC CC seems to align more consistently with the latter, it coming closest to the French only with respect to mistake as to present facts and certain aspects of good faith. At least, this is so insofar as the Chinese conception of delictual liability can be analogized to the French, which remains to be seen.

6

The Security Interests in Chinese Law

Some Nuances

LEI CHEN

6.1 Introduction: Historical Development

When the Civil Code was promulgated in 2020, one area of property law that experienced the most significant change was security interests. Whether real or personal, security interests play a pivotal role in fostering credit in economic activities and facilitating homeownership. Conceptually, security rights burden a borrower's property in favour of a lender to ensure the satisfaction of a lender's claim should the borrower default or become insolvent. Civil and common law jurisdictions have each developed a relatively sophisticated set of rules governing security interests. Historically, under Chinese law, there were no rules governing security interests in China from 1949 to 1986. Under the General Principles of Civil Law (GPCL) enacted in 1986, only four types of security interests were recognised and regulated albeit in a sketchy manner: personal guarantee, mortgage, deposit, and lien.[1] From 1949 to 1988, there were no individual land rights and no private land ownership in China. This explains why there was no mention of pledges whatsoever and little mention of mortgages in the GPCL.[2] In 1988, China amended its Constitution to allow the creation and transfer of privately held land-use rights. The recognition of land-use rights generated a real

[1] Each of the four types of security interests was regulated in one article, i.e., Article 89 of the GPCL 1986.

[2] The Supreme People's Court formulated the 'Opinions on Several Issues Concerning the Implementation of the GPCL (for trial implementation)' (hereinafter referred to as the Opinions on the GPCL). Article 89 of the 'General Principles of Civil Law' is further explained with twelve provisions. It can be said that the GPCL together with the SPC Opinions on the GPCL were the first-generation security interest rules in the People's Republic of China.

estate construction boom and unprecedented commercial dealings in the real estate industry.[3] In 1994, the State Council further adopted a sweeping nationwide Housing Reform Policy to privatise and commercialise the housing market.

China, a late but rapid bloomer in the private property market, enacted the Chinese Security Law (hereafter Security Law) in 1995,[4] governing real security interests and personal guarantees before the Property Law in 2007. The Security Law provides a fundamental legal framework governing personal guarantees and real security to deal with real estate financing problems and facilitate the housing privatisation policy. Due to the rapid developments in the real property market practice following the legislation and a still-primitive understanding of property law, several apparent defects can be found in the Security Law. For example, it has been stipulated that the mortgage contract over immovable property is invalid if it is not registered.[5] In fact, there is no distinction between the effectiveness of the mortgage contract and the effectiveness of the real security right of the mortgage.[6] Therefore, the Security Law lagged far behind fast-changing economic and social conditions.

Nevertheless, the Security Law continued to apply even though it was insufficient to address some practical concerns. It is for this reason that in December 2000, the Supreme People's Court (SPC) issued the 'Interpretation on Several Issues Concerning the Application of the Security Law' (Judicial Interpretation of the Security Law), with a total of 134 articles.[7] The Judicial Interpretation of the Security Law purported to provide nuanced rules where there were some perceived gaps.

When the Property Law was enacted in 2007, it incorporated a chapter on real security, including mortgage, pledge, and lien laws. Before the Property Law, many departmental rules and administrative regulations had been issued concerning emerging problems related to security interests.[8]

[3] Lei Chen, 'The evolution of the property system in China: Between the socialist heritage and liberal market', in H. Fu, J. Gillespie, P. Nicholson and W. Partlett (eds.), *Socialist Law in Socialist East Asia* (Cambridge: Cambridge University Press, 2018), 385–405.

[4] Enacted on 30 June 1995, became effective on 1 October 1995.

[5] Article 41 of the Security law.

[6] Liu Guixiang, 'Several Key Issues in Security Interest under the Civil Code' (2021) 1 *Journal of Law Application* 9.

[7] Issued by the SPC, became effective on 13 December 2000.

[8] Lei Chen, '100 years of Chinese property law: Looking back and thinking forward', in L. Chen, C. H. van Rhee (eds.), *Towards a Chinese Civil Code* (Leiden: Brill Nijhoff, 2012), https://doi.org/10.1163/9789004204881_006.

There is a plethora of judicial and administrative regulations and instruments, including the SPC Judicial Interpretation, Circular of the State Administration of Foreign Exchange on Transmitting and Executing the Judicial Interpretation of the SPC Application of Judicial Interpretations to Guarantee Dispute Cases and the Determination of Guarantee Liability Forms, and the Land Registration Measures and the Real Estate Property Registration Measures, both enacted in 2008. It is worth noting that in the case of any discrepancy between the Security Law and the Property Law, the Property Law prevails.[9]

While most of the legal provisions under the Security Law were kept unchanged or retained with only minor changes or extended to the Property Law, some new rules were introduced to override the previous legal position under the Security Law.[10] In judicial practice, it is worth noting that since the enactment of Property Law, some landmark cases, including guiding cases, constitute the legal basis in the judicial decision making.

Some post-2007 Property Law judicial opinions have shaped the content and contour of the security interests provisions in the Civil Code. Under the Civil Code, a singular term, "security institution" (担保制度), has straddled the laws of contract, (e.g., guaranty contract, financial leasing contract, factoring contract), and property (mortgage, pledge, and lien). The Civil Code has consolidated many rules that were scattered around and substantiated some new ones. For instance, the rules for the transfer of chattel mortgages have been rewritten.[11] The rules concerning assignment security, retention of ownership, financial leases, and factoring contract have been mapped out.[12] What is worth noting is that given the buoyant market practice, the Civil Code balances legal certainty under the *numerus clausus* principle and party autonomy through the principle of freedom of contract. While the Property Book addresses mortgage, pledge, and lien specifically, it also allows the parties to contractually derogate from the statutory list to create a collateral contract. The second sentence of Article 388 of the Civil Code provides

9 Chinese Property Law 2007 Article 178.

10 Such as the rules on priority order in realising real security and personal security and right of recourse against other security providers, see Lei Chen, 'Private Property with Chinese Characteristics: A Critical Analysis of the Chinese Law on Property of 2007' (2010) 18.5 *European Review of Private Law* 983–1004; for more details, please see Sections 6.3.1 and 6.3.2.

11 Articles 404 and 416 of the Chinese Civil Code 2020 (Chinese Civil Code).

12 Articles 388, 642, 735, and 761 of the Chinese Civil Code.

that 'a collateral contract refers to a contract of charge, a pledge contract, or other kinds of contracts with security functions'. It has become clear that the Civil Code adopts an open-ended conception of collateral contracts rather than a closed catalogue as incentivised by the notion of freedom of contract and free market practices. This practice affirms the saying that 'fancies are for contract, not for property, to meet the market expectations'.[13]

Given the sheer volume of legal disputes concerning the security interest, it is imperative to understand how the security interest rules have evolved in China. More to the point, what are the notable rule changes under the new Civil Code? Can the new changes be understood as pro-creditor or pro-security provider? In tandem with the security interests provisions in the Civil Code, the SPC issued the Judicial Interpretation on the application of the Civil Code concerning the Institution of Security (the SPC Interpretation on Security).[14] The SPC Security Interest Rules sets out detailed rules governing personal guarantees, mortgages, liens, pledges, factoring, finance leasing, and retention of title. It is an integral part of the Chinese legal framework governing security interests, which aims to provide practical guidance and facilitate the uniform application of the PRC Civil Code by the PRC courts.

This chapter provides a snapshot of the recent developments in Chinese security interest law. Several questions will be explored. Firstly, were there any needs for changes? Secondly, what are the recent changes? Thirdly, have these changes achieved the purpose? I will offer some critical reflections of the law in terms of clarity, simplicity, convenience, and fairness. Not only are the relevant background and statutory framework of the security interests explained, but its theoretical structure and several practical issues will also be discussed. For instance, where a loan has been secured by both a personal guarantee and a mortgage, in the absence of any agreement, will the creditor have a free choice on which one to enforce first? Another question to be addressed is raised in situations where more than two securities had secured a loan (including a personal guarantee and mortgages) on a joint and several liability basis;

[13] Bernard Rudden, 'Economic theory v property law: The numerus clausus problem', in J. Eekelaar and J. Bell (eds.), *Oxford Essays in Jurisprudence* (Oxford: Oxford University Press, 1987), 243.

[14] Judicial Interpretations on the application of the Civil Code concerning Security System (Effective 1 January 2021)

in the absence of any agreement, can a security provider indemnify from the others after it fulfilled its security obligation in case of the debtor's insolvency?

6.2 Legal Nature of the Security Interests: Accessoriness and Flexibility

For historical reasons, Chinese Security Law is conveniently allocated within civil law.[15] The accessoriness principle, which may be traced back to Roman law, has established itself as a persistent rule of personal and real security in China.[16] Consequently, Chinese Law characterises a security interest as (1) an accessory right contingent on having a principal obligation, (2) an indivisible right, and (3) a preferential right.

First, a security interest is an accessory, meaning it does not stand on its own and it is contingent on the secured principal obligation.[17] The Civil Code explicitly provides the fundamental principle that there must be an obligation the security interest secures.[18] The accessory principle indicates that a security right is linked to or dependent on a principal obligation.[19] Since a security interest is an accessory, it cannot exist independently of a valid principal obligation.[20] Under Chinese law, where the creditor's right in the main contract is reassigned, the assignee will acquire the pre-existing secured rights.[21] It is contractually

[15] Lei Chen, 'The Historical Development of the Civil Law Tradition in China: A Private Law Perspective' (2010) 78.1–2 *Tijdschrift voor Rechtsgeschiedenis/Revue d'Histoire du Droit/The Legal History Review* 159–181.

[16] Lei Chen, 'A Structural Analysis of Chinese Mortgage Law', in *Essays in Honour of CG van der Merwe* (s.l.: Lexisnexis, 2011) 395–412.

[17] Cornelius G. Van der Merwe, *International Encyclopedia of Comparative Law: Property and Trust. Security in Immovables* (Tuebingen: Mohr Siebeck, 2014) 27–29.

[18] Articles 388, 682 of the Chinese Civil Code.

[19] Article 50 of the Chinese Security Law.

[20] Article 2 of the SPC Interpretation on the Security Interest Rules 2021 provides: 'If the parties agree in the guarantee contract that the effectiveness of the guarantee contract is independent of the main contract, or agree that the guarantor shall bear the guarantee responsibility for the legal consequences of the invalidity of the main contract, the agreement on the independence of the guarantee shall be invalid. If the main contract is valid, the invalidity of the agreement on the independence of the guarantee does not affect the validity of the guarantee contract; if the main contract is invalid, the people's court shall determine that the guarantee contract is invalid, unless otherwise provided by law.'

[21] Article 547 of the Civil Code provides that where the obligee assigns its creditor's right, the assignee shall acquire the collateral rights related to the principal rights, unless the collateral rights exclusively belong to the obligee. The acquisition of the collateral rights

dependent on the obligations it secures. This means that the secured interest such as a mortgage will be transferred automatically even when the transfer failed to be registered.

Moreover, the security interest automatically ends once the secured debt is discharged.[22] Chinese Law adopts the accessory principle with certain exceptions.[23] In China, the principal obligation is often a monetary obligation, but it may be possible for a non-monetary obligation to be secured. For example, a tort claim or a claim based on unjust enrichment may also be secured on the condition that such a non-contractual obligation can be made for a definite amount of money.[24] The same mortgage may secure more than one principal obligation.[25] Consequently, the accessory nature of the security interest implies that the amount of the security cannot exceed that of the secured claim. The security interest cannot be terminated unless the secured claim is extinguished as a result.[26]

Second, a security interest is indivisible. When a part of the underlying principal obligation is discharged, the security continues to exist on the mortgaged property but only for the outstanding amount of the debt. Although neither the Property Law nor the Security Law explicitly provides for this feature, the Judicial Interpretation stipulates that the mortgagee can execute the security for the entire mortgaged property before full payment of the principal obligation.[27] Article 389 of the Civil Code provides that the scope of secured debts covered by a security interest includes the principal debt and its interest, (agreed) damages, as well as expenses for keeping the collateral in good custody and for

shall not be affected by the failure to proceed the registration of transfer or to transfer the occupation.

22 Article 393 of the Chinese Civil Code.

23 For example, where there is an independent guarantee in writing undertaken by a bank or a non-banking financial institution, the guarantee contract is independent of the principal obligation. An independent guarantee means that the above-mentioned financial institutions as the issuer to the beneficiary for the payment of a certain amount or an amount within the maximum guaranteed amount at the request of the beneficiary when submitting documents is in conformity with the guarantee. See para. 2 of Article 2 of the SPC Interpretation on Security Interest Rules.

24 Cui Jianyuan, *Real Property Law* (Beijing: Renmin University of China Press, 2009), 467–68 (Chinese version); see comparative survey of A. Steven, 'The Effect of Security Rights *inter partes*', in U. Drobnig, H. Snijders, and E.-J. Zippro (eds.), *Divergences of Property Law, an Obstacle to the Internal Market?* (München: Sellier, 2006), 50.

25 E.g., the maximum amount mortgage.

26 Art 172(1) Property Law, Article 393 of the Civil Code.

27 Article 71 of the SPC Interpretation of Security Law.

enforcing the security interest, except when agreed otherwise by the parties.[28]

Third, a claim based on a security interest is a preferential right compared to that of unsecured lenders to pay the debt. For example, when the mortgaged-backed preferential claim is higher than the proceeds of the sale of the mortgaged property, little or nothing will be left for the unsecured lenders.[29] Arising from this rule, the Civil Code further provides that where the subject matter of a security interest is destroyed, lost, or expropriated during the period of security, the security interest holder is entitled to have the priority of debt repayment to the extent of the acquired insurance money, damages, or compensation.[30] Where the secured debt is not due, the rights holder may elect to escrow the insurance money, damages, or compensation.[31]

Nonetheless, the accessory principle has been relaxed given several exceptions in the Civil Code. First, the extent of guarantee liability is not affected if the principal contract has been modified to increase the principal obligation.[32] Without written consent from the guarantor, where the creditor and the debtor agree to alter the content of the principal obligation contract, the guarantor still bears guaranty liability for the modified obligation where the principal obligation is reduced.[33] Where the principal obligation is increased, the guarantor does not bear guaranty liability for the increased portion.[34] In the absence of written consent from the guarantor, where the creditor and the debtor vary the time for performance under the principal obligation contract, the guaranty period is unaffected by such variation.

Secondly, can the security interest be transferred separately from the principal debt when the principal debt is assigned to a new creditor? If Chinese law adheres to the accessory principle, a mortgage right cannot be separated from the secured claim and be transferred separately. However, while upholding the accessory principle, the Civil Code provides some leeway for party autonomy. Article 407 of the Civil Code stipulates that

[28] Article 389 of the Civil Code.
[29] Article 394 of the Civil Code.
[30] Article 390 of the Civil Code.
[31] Ibid.
[32] Article 695 of the Civil Code.
[33] Ibid.
[34] Ibid.

> the mortgage cannot be transferred separately from the principal debt or be used to secure another debt. Where the main debt is assigned to another person, the mortgage securing such debt is also transferred, except if otherwise provided by law or agreed by the parties.[35]

The proviso in paragraph 2 of this article means that the clause on the transfer of mortgage rights along with the debt is not a mandatory rule. Parties can come to a different arrangement by agreement. Also, the parties can exclude its application through agreement. Suppose the parties agree that the mortgage rights will not be transferred with the principal debt; in that case, the court shall not consider the agreement invalid on the grounds of violating the provisions on the principle of accessoriness.

The Civil Code does not address the situation where the parties agree that the original debt can be replaced with an entirely new debt. In this case, should the novated claim be secured by the original mortgage by retaining its priority ranking? Does Chinese Law ease the rigidity of accessoriness in assigning secured debt? Article 16 of the SPC Interpretation on Security deals explicitly with this by providing that the security provider of the old debt does not assume the security responsibility under such circumstances.[36] When borrowing a new loan to repay the old debt, the old loan is extinguished due to debt repayment, and so is the guarantee provided for the old loan. This rule makes sense because of its accessoriness nature. However, where the security provider of the new loan is the same as that of the old one, the court shall support the creditor's claim requesting the security provider of the new loan to assume the liability.[37] Where the security provider of the new loan is different from the old loan, or if the old loan is unsecured and the new loan is secured, as a matter of principle, the court will not support the creditor's claim. But the creditor may prove that when providing the security to the new loan, the security provider knew or ought to have known that the new loan is used to repay the old loan; in this case, a creditor's claim may be sustained by the court.[38]

Where the security provider of the old loan agrees to continue to provide security for the new loan and the registration of the security has not yet been extinguished, while for the same secured property

[35] Article 407 of the Civil Code.

[36] Article 16 para. 1 SPC Interpretation on Security .

[37] Ibid.

[38] Ibid.

security had also been established in the favour of other creditors before the conclusion of the new loan, under Chinese law, the other creditors cannot claim that their secured property rights take precedence over the new loan creditors.[39] The court will uphold the surviving security on the new loan as if it were to secure the old loan.

This rule eases the rigidity of accessoriness by allowing party autonomy. When borrowing the new loan to repay the old ones, the old loan security provider is not liable for the security for the new loan as the old loan has been extinguished, except that it continues to provide guarantees for the new loan. When the new loan has not been executed, and the old loan has not been paid off, the security interest for the old loan has not been wiped out. If the parties subsequently sign a new loan contract, it is equivalent to the extension of the old loan. Therefore, the creditor of the new loan still has the right to stand in priority over other creditors when realising the security.

Third, another exception to the accessoriness principle is the maximum amount mortgage, which secures a future debt. Here, the maximum amount of a mortgage securing future debts has to be shown on the mortgage deed, and the amount must correspond to the amount entered in the land registry.[40] If this amount is less than the total value of the mortgaged property, there can be subsequent mortgages to bring their total amount up to the full value of the mortgaged property.[41] Consequently, the maximum mortgage amount is not transferred with a secure claim. Where the creditor assigns some of the debts secured by the maximum amount mortgage to another person before the definition of all the debts, the maximum amount mortgage shall not be transferred at the same time, except if otherwise agreed to by the parties.[42] In other words, a maximum amount mortgage is not an accessory to its principal obligation unless the parties agree so.

Fourth, the secured interest holder can also abandon the security right or vary its ranking order. Paragraph 1 of Article 409 of the Civil Code stipulates that the mortgage creditor may waive the charge or the order of priority concerning the mortgage.[43] The parties may alter the ranking order of priority, the amount of the secured debt, and so forth by

39 Article 16 para. 2 SPC Interpretation on Security .
40 Article 47 of the SPC Interpretation on Security.
41 Article 420 of the Civil Code.
42 Article 421 of the Civil Code.
43 Article 409 of the Civil Code.

agreement. However, such alteration shall not make another mortgage creditor worse off without its written consent. Here, the accessories do not have to be attached to the original mortgage creditor's right. In a way, accessories are a statutory default rule but subject to contractual deviation under party autonomy.

6.3 Some Noteworthy Rules under the Civil Code

6.3.1 *Realising Real Security and Personal Security on Equal Footing*

Before the Civil Code, if a personal guarantee and real security secured a credit, a pressing issue was whether there is a realisation order among the security providers. Specifically, can the parties agree on the priority order of the security interests to satisfy the creditor's right? In the absence of such an agreement on the realisation order among the parties, must the real security be exhausted before resorting to the assets of the personal guarantor? Are there different rules where the contract debtor or a third party provides the real security? Should the third party have recourse against the guarantor after having borne security liabilities when the creditor successfully claimed the third party's security interest?

Before the Civil Code, the mainstream position was a 'realising real security first' approach. This means that when the contract debtor defaults, the creditor must exhaust the real security before resorting to the assets of the personal guarantor.[44] This rule was protective of the personal guarantor. The advantage was facilitating the guarantee undertaking as its liability was kept to a low probability given that the real security had to be realised before approaching the personal guarantor's assets. The disadvantage was that, first, the creditor was not provided with an option to choose the order of preference because the law dictated the sequence. Second, where real security is provided for the same contract, the personal guarantee was rendered less meaningful. The guarantee liability could only be invoked without real security or if the real security could not satisfy the debt. Third, related to the above, a company or an individual would assume a personal guarantee easily, particularly when they knew that the main contract was provided with real security. To address these concerns, the SPC Interpretation on

[44] Article 28 para. 1 of the Guarantee Law 1995: If the same creditor's rights has both guarantee and real security, the guarantor assumes guarantee responsibilities over the creditor's right other than guaranteed by real security.

Guarantee Law issued in 2000 changed the position by stipulating that where there is a mixture of personal guarantee and real security for the same contract, the creditor has discretion in choosing between the guarantor and the real security provider to bear the liability.[45] However, as with the Guarantee Law 1995, it was silent on the situation where the parties reached an agreement on the realisation order of the security interests. Hence, a loophole arose as to the validity of the parties' agreement that differs from the legislative provision.

When the Property Law was enacted, this loophole seemed to be closed by a refined rule. Article 176 provides that where a contract is provided with real security and personal security, the creditor shall realise the security specified in the parties' contractual stipulations if the debtor fails to perform the due debt. Where such stipulation does not exist or is equivocal, the creditor shall enforce the real security first if the debtor provided a real security. The creditor may elect first to enforce the real security or the personal security if a third party provides the real security. After having borne security liabilities, the third party has the right to recover from the debtor.[46]

First, Article 176 of the Property Law respects party autonomy by upholding the contractual stipulations made by the parties. Second, it distinguishes the contract debtor's real security from a third party's real security. With regard to the former, the debtor's real security must be realised first before enforcing against the third party's guarantor. As to the latter, the personal guarantee and a third party's real security are put on equal footing at the creditor's choice when there is a breach. In other words, the personal guarantee provided by a third party cannot be invoked where the contract creditor did not enforce the real security provided by another party first.

The Civil Code adopts the equal footing approach by retaining Article 176 of the Property Law in Article 392.[47] This is commendable, given that the balanced approach promotes certainty while preserving contractual freedom. As a result, the Chinese courts uphold that the creditor shall realise the security according to the parties' contractual stipulations.[48]

[45] Article 38(1) of the SPC Interpretation on Guarantee Law 2000.

[46] Article 176 of the Property Law.

[47] Article 392 of the Civil Code almost copies out the wording of Article 176 of the Property Law.

[48] *Zhong Xiang and Guangzhou Yuexiu Small Loan Co., Ltd*, Guangzhou Intermediate People's Court of Guangdong Province Civil Judgment (2017) Yue 01 Min Zhong No. 17661.

Where there is a contractual stipulation, or the stipulation is unclear, the creditor has a free choice on the sequence when both personal guarantee and real security are provided.[49]

Nonetheless, Article 393 of the Civil Code only provides that the third party has the right to recover from the debtor after having borne security liabilities. It does not address whether the third party real security provider has a right of recourse against the personal guarantor and if so, under what conditions? This is a pressing question about ascertaining the extent of the co-security providers. In the old legal regime under the Guarantee Law 1995, if a creditor waived the real security that was supposed to be enforced first, the guarantor will be exempt from the guarantor rights over the rights that the creditor gave up.[50] Under the Civil Code, where any selected co-security provider bears liability for the whole debt, can the selected co-security provider have a right of recourse against other security providers in the absence of any agreement?

6.3.2 *Right of Recourse among the Joint Security Providers in the Absence of an Agreement*

This issue refers to a situation where there are several proprietary security providers and personal security providers. How to design a rule governing the mutual rights and obligations of internal recourse among themselves? Recourse against the debtor is a separate issue, which will not be dealt with in this chapter. Since the implementation of the Security Law 1995, for more than twenty years, Article 19 of the SPC Interpretation of the Security Law has provided only a somewhat inadequate provision mentioning joint and several joint guarantees.[51] In the Civil Code and the SPC Interpretation of Security System, there are only some provisions addressing the issue where 'the same debt has more than two security providers', 'the secured creditor's rights are both secured by

[49] *China Minsheng Bank Co., Ltd. Taiyuan Branch and Shanxi Huairen Zhongneng Luzigou Coal Industry Co., Ltd., Shanxi Huairen Nanyao Jintong Sand and Stone Coal Industry Co., Ltd.*, Beijing Fourth Intermediate People's Court Civil Judgment (2017) Jing 04 No. 6.

[50] Article 28 para. 2 of the Security Law 1995.

[51] Article 19 of the Chinese Civil Code: 'Where two or more guarantors secure the same debt simultaneously or respectively, but guarantors and creditor have not agreed on guarantee shares, such guarantee shall be deemed as joint guarantee. Where the joint guarantors defend against creditor with their internal agreement of guarantee shares, such defense shall not be supported by the people's court.'

both real and personal security'.[52] Apart from the expressions of 'security provided by two or more third parties' and 'agreement to undertake joint and several joint security', the Civil Code does not further define joint security.[53]

In this chapter, joint security means the situation where two or more third parties provide security for the same claim. Joint security is divided into two main types according to whether the more than two collaterals are of the same nature, that is, joint security of the same kind and mixed joint security. The same kind of joint security includes a joint guarantee, a joint mortgage, a joint pledge, etc. As the title suggests, mixed joint security includes a combination of personal guarantee and real security over the same claim. Joint security can further be divided into joint and several security and joint security with defined shares due to the difference that the creditor can claim the share of security liability from the security provider.

Where there are more than two security providers after a security provider was selected to undertake the security liability, can the selected security provider seek recourse against the other joint security providers for indemnity if the debtor fails to pay back? Since the Security Law was promulgated in 1995, legislative and judicial rules have changed over time, attempting to address this question.

(1) Between 1995 and 2007, The Security Law and the SPC Interpretation on the Security Law essentially allowed the right of recourse among the joint security providers under certain circumstances. In the cases of joint and several guarantees,[54] mixed joint security,[55] and joint mortgages,[56] the security provider who had undertaken the guarantee responsibility had the right to request other security providers to pay off their share. If there is no agreement on the share in the joint security, the joint security providers shall share equally.
(2) The Property Law 2007 was unclear in that it did not address this issue specifically. Unlike the Security Law, the Property Law does not stipulate whether the security provider can recover compensation

52 Article 392 of the Civil Code; Article 13 of the SPC Interpretation on Security.
53 Article 392 of the Civil Code; Article 13 of the SPC Interpretation on Security.
54 Article 12 of the Security Law 1995.
55 Article 20 (2) of the SPC Interpretation of the Security Law 2000.
56 Article 75 (3) of the SPC Interpretation of the Security Law 2000.

from others in joint mortgages. Regarding mixed joint guarantees, Article 176 of the Property Law only stipulates that the third party providing the security shall have the right to recover from the debtor after assuming the responsibility. It does not stipulate whether it can recover from other security providers. While the Security Law continued to be effective when the Property Law was enacted, Article 178 of the Property Law provides that if the Security Law is inconsistent with the provisions of Property Law, Property Law shall apply. As a result, diverging judicial outcomes arose. To tackle this, the SPC issued a Judicial Announcement in 2019 that disallows the joint security provider's right of recourse in case of mixed security.

(3) Since 2021, the Civil Code, following the Property Law, does not explicitly state the right of recourse among the joint security providers. However, Article 13 of the SPC Interpretation on the Security System allows the security provider, who has borne liability, to exercise the right of recourse against other third-party security providers subject to one of the following specified conditions:[57]
   (i) where there is an agreement among the guarantors on the proportional liability and the right of recourse;
   (ii) where there is an agreement among the security providers on the joint and several liabilities or the right of mutual recourse but it does not specify the proportions;
   (iii) where there is no agreement on the right of recourse, but all security providers signed the same contract with signatures or company chops.

As shown above, neither Article 176 of the Property Law nor Article 392 of the Civil Code directly created the right of recourse. But the Chinese courts seem to recognise such a right of internal recourse. The SPC held in *Gu Zhengkang* v. *Shiyan Ronghua Dongfeng Automobile Ltd* that

> Article 176 of the Property Law only stipulates that the third party who provides the guarantee in the mixed security has the right to recover from the debtor after taking the guarantee responsibility, but it does not specify whether the guarantors can be recovered. Article 38 of the Interpretation of the Guarantee Law affirms that the guarantors enjoy the right of recovery in mixed security. Where there is no provision in the Property Law but there is an explicit provision in the Interpretation of the

[57] Article 13 of the SPC Security Interests Rules.

> Guarantee Law, both the first instance court and the appellate court applied the Interpretation of the Guarantee Law and found that it was not inappropriate for the mortgagor to have the right of recourse against the guarantor after assuming the guarantee responsibility. The guarantor avers that the mortgagor does not have the right of recourse, and this court does not support it.[58]

In addition to the reasoning on the legislative application in support of the right of recourse by the SPC, the Tianjin High People's Court furnished a cogent analysis in *Tianjin Huaqing Trading Co., Ltd. and Tianjin Hengjing Recycled Alloy Materials Co., Ltd., Zhejiang Zhihu Investment Management Co., Ltd.* from the perspective of the principle of fairness.[59] It was held that

> if the guarantor and the real security provider do not agree on how to share the guaranty responsibility, the ex-post balance of their rights and obligations should be realised by applying the principle of fairness. After the guarantor assumes the guaranty responsibility, it steps into the position of the secured creditor. Other security providers are exempted from their responsibility, and they, in a way, have obtained actual legal benefits. If the sharing of security liability is not supported, that causes unfairness. Finally, suppose mutual recovery between security providers is prohibited. In that case, it will encourage creditors to collude with a certain guarantor and maliciously choose other guarantors to assume responsibility, thereby exempting them from the abusive selection.[60]

Nonetheless, it appears that the test adopted by the SPC is not based on whether it is joint and several security or joint security with defined shares. Rather, the underlying rationale seems to be based on a common intention test. That is to say, whether the parties have demonstrated a common intention expressly to share the security liability in proportion or there is an inferred common intention due to the contract. There is no such right of recourse in the absence of a common intention, whether express or inferred. This common intention test is commendable as it upholds party autonomy.

However, there are two unsolved issues with this approach. First, where all the security providers sign the same contract, but their security

[58] Retrial Civil Judgment *of Gu Zhengkang and Shiyan Ronghua Dongfeng Automobile Franchise Co., Ltd.*, Supreme People's Court (2017) Supreme Fa Min Zai No. 137.

[59] *Tianjin Huaqing Trading Co., Ltd. and Tianjin Hengjing Recycled Alloy Materials Co., Ltd., Zhejiang Zhihu Investment Management Co., Ltd.*, Tianjin Higher People's Court Civil Judgment (2017) Jin Min Chu No. 121.

[60] Ibid.

liabilities do not secure the whole debt, it would be problematic to recognise the right of recourse against each other. For example, A and B undertake to each secure 40 per cent of the debt, and C bears the remaining 20 per cent. It would be artificial if not counterproductive to permit a right of recourse in such a circumstance. The prerequisite for the recourse is that the security provider assumes more than its share of liability. If A undertakes his liability for 40 per cent, a right of recourse will not arise even when they sign on the same document. If A undertakes his liability for 50 per cent, can A take recourse against B and C to claim back the exceeding 10 per cent liability? The answer is negative because the respective share of security liability has been clearly defined as agreed. Therefore, invoking a right of recourse solely based on the joint signature on the same contract may be inadequate. An additional element is needed– all the security providers undertake joint and several security liabilities.

Secondly, if the rationale is to infer a common intention from having parties sign the same contract, are there any other conducts that could ascertain such a common intention? For example, how about when the security providers entered into multiple guarantee contracts separately at the same time, or the security providers entered into the guarantee contracts at a different time. Still, they know who the other security providers are when the guarantee contract is concluded.

Despite the gaps identified above, the SPC appears to uphold party autonomy by disallowing the right of mutual recourse between the mixed joint security providers while only recognising and enforcing the mutual recourse by agreement. In addition to agreeing on mutual recourse rights or agreeing to form joint and several joint guarantees, signing the same contract can also be considered an expression of mutual recovery between the parties.

6.3.3 *Ascertaining the Validity of a Company's Undertaking of a Security Interest*

In recent years, there has arisen the thorny issue besetting the Chinese courts and arbitration tribunals of how to ascertain a company's security liability under an unauthorised contract. For example, it remains to be seen whether the Chinese courts will uniformly regard the unauthorised agreements as invalid and unenforceable where a managing director/legal representative of a company concludes a security undertaking agreement with a third party without going through the corporate resolution required by Article 16 of the PRC Company Law.

This legal question straddles contract, property, and company law. Chinese courts have been torn when there is no explicit statutory guidance. Many relevant factors could be taken into account, such as the relationship between the security agreement and the main contract, whether the security provider is a listed company, whether the debtor is a shareholder or actual controller of the guarantor, whether the creditor is a shareholder or related party of the guarantor, whether the security provider or the secured party has acted in good faith in concluding the security agreement, and more vexingly, whether the absence of corporate resolution can be regarded as an apparent authority in Chinese contract law. As a result, judicial decisions are inconsistent. The judicial outcome has been leaning towards favouring the secured party at the expense of the security provider companies. According to a recent empirical study, it was revealed that out of 226 decisions involving unauthorised security agreements handed down by the provisional high people's court level, 79.3 per cent of the decisions were ruled in favour of being enforceable. Even among the 20.7 per cent of cases where the security agreement was held unenforceable, more than a quarter of the decisions held the security provider company partially liable for the liability.[61] In a way, this would lead to legal arbitrage by incentivising the managing director or the company's legal representative to engage in such misconduct.

The PRC Civil Code and the SPC Interpretation on Security clarified the circumstances where corporate resolutions are required to be passed by a company providing a guarantee or security. In case of an unauthorised security agreement, if the counterparty acted in good faith, the security agreement is valid and enforceable; if the counterparty acted not in good faith, the agreement is unenforceable. According to the legal test, good faith is to be assumed

> If the counterparty does not know and should not have known that the legal representative exceeds the authority when concluding the guarantee contract. The counterparty has evidence to prove that a reasonable review of the company's resolution has been conducted. The people's court shall determine that it constitutes good faith unless the company has evidence

[61] Charles Zhen Qu, 'Corporate Law Issue, Civil Law Solutions: Resolving Disputes Arising from Unauthorized Corporate Security Contracts in People's Republic of China High Courts' (2020) 1.1 *Corporate and Business Law Journal* 12.

to prove that the counterparty knew or should have known that the resolution was forged or altered.[62]

The legal implications are clear. Firstly, the counterparty bears the burden of proof to show that it has conducted a reasonable review to satisfy the good faith requirement. Secondly, the counterparty must take active steps to conduct a reasonable review of the corporate resolutions. While the SPC Interpretation does not define the meaning of 'reasonable review', it is expected that the threshold of a reasonable review is higher than the formality check, which was contained in the early trial guidance document issued by the SPC.[63]

In addition, the SPC provides a somewhat restrictive list of exceptions to where a corporate resolution should be provided. As a general rule, the provision of guarantee or security should be authorised by corporate resolutions unless one of the following exceptions applies:

1, issuance of a letter of credit by financial institutions or granting of a guarantee and security by licensed guarantee companies (担保公司);

2, granting of a guarantee or security by a non-listed company for the operation of wholly-owned subsidiaries; and

3, consent by signing the guarantee or security document by the shareholders of a non-listed company, constituting not less than two-thirds of shareholder voting rights.[64]

Finally, where a listed company or a publicly disclosed subsidiary of a listed company provides security by signing an agreement, the listed company must make a public announcement in connection with the passing of corporate resolutions for granting a guarantee or security. This is commendable because the legal representative's room for signing an unauthorised security agreement is therefore severely curtailed. Also, transparency by disclosure is required in some department rules for a listed company.[65] The listed company should publicly disclose any security undertakings, and it is reasonable to expect the counterparty to provide such proof to hold a listed company liable.

[62] Article 7 of the SPC Interpretation on Security.

[63] Notice by the Supreme People's Court of Issuing the Minutes of the National Courts' Civil and Commercial Trial Work Conference (九民纪要) in 2019 (the SPC's 2019 Notice).

[64] Article 8 of the SPC Interpretation on Security.

[65] Article 6 of the Listed Company Information Disclosure Regulatory Measures.

The SPC has taken a nuanced approach to fill the gap in light of the above. However, the security provider still bears the liability of an invalid security contract when the main contract is valid. A security contract is invalid for several reasons, such as where the property interest intended to be secured is not legally allowed to be a mortgage,[66] or the property to be mortgaged is subject to title dispute,[67] or where the board of a company did not approve it to be the security provider. In any event, when a security contact is held to be invalid, does it mean the security provider is free from liability whatsoever? Chinese Law adopts a refined typology hinged upon the test of fault.

To be specific, Article 17 of the SPC Interpretation on Security provides that where the main contract is valid, but the guarantee contract provided by a third party is invalid, the people's court shall determine the security liability according to different situations:

(1) Where both the creditor and the security provider are at fault, the security provider's liability for compensation shall not exceed one-half of the debtor's unpaid portion.
(2) If the security provider is at fault and the creditor is not at fault, the security provider shall be liable for the part unpaid by the debtor.
(3) If the creditor is at fault and the security provider is not at fault, the security provider shall not be liable for compensation.

It is worth noting that the SPC Interpretation does not explicitly recite the test of fault, and it seems that a common sense approach is adopted to allocate the liability under such circumstances. What is particularly remarkable under Chinese Law is that where the principal contract is invalid, the security contract provided by the third party should be invalid arising from the accessory principle. The security provider will not be liable for compensation if it is not at fault; if the security provider is at fault, the liability for compensation will be capped at one-third of the part that the debtor cannot pay.[68]

6.3.4 *Termination of Security Interest*

Chinese Law adheres to the accessory principle, albeit with some deviations as elucidated above. Therefore, the security interest is extinguished

[66] Article 399 of the Chinese Civil Code.
[67] Ibid.
[68] Article 17 (2) of the SPC Interpretation on Security.

on discharge of the secured claim by payment or otherwise. In addition, a security interest may be extinguished by waiver or release of the mortgage and other ways. The Civil Code provides a rather sketchy list of situations where the security interest can be extinguished, namely where

(1) the main debt is extinguished;
(2) the security interest is realised;
(3) the creditor waives the security interest; or
(4) any other circumstances of the termination of security interest provided by law.[69]

The extinction of a secured obligation (main debt) is not always sufficient to terminate the mortgage. Cancellation of a mortgage needs to be registered in the land registration office.[70] When the mortgage over a building is created, it is required to be registered, and the mortgage is created upon registration.[71] However, it is surprising that no provision governs the registration of the mortgage cancellation in the Civil Code. This may cause some potential disputes over the timing of termination of the security interest.

The waiver or release of the mortgage leads to its termination.[72] However, the terminology employed in the Civil Code is 放弃, in English 'abandon'. It is unclear from this provision whether a bilateral agreement is apposite for abandonment, the secured creditor may unilaterally waive the mortgage, or both unilateral waiver and bilateral agreement are permissible. Another related question is whether the abandonment can be exercised tacitly or only expressly. For example, where a mortgage creditor consents to the transfer of the mortgaged property free from the mortgage, would this amount to abandonment? Does the abandonment require a change in the land registration? The Civil Code remains silent on these issues.

The list above does not cover situations where the mortgaged property is destructed or where the title of the mortgage debtor is expropriated beyond his control, or where the mortgage creditor becomes the owner of the mortgaged property. The SPC plays a gap-filling role by mapping out some detailed rules.

[69] Article 393 of the Chinese Civil Code.
[70] Lei Chen, 'Land Registration, Property Rights and Institutional Performance in China: Progress Achieved and Challenges Ahead' (2014) 44 *Hong Kong Law Journal* 841.
[71] Article 402 of the Chinese Civil Code.
[72] Article 409 of the Chinese Civil Code.

Where the mortgaged property is damaged, lost, or expropriated, if the mortgagee requests that the insurance compensation, expropriation compensation, or damages be paid in priority according to the order of the original mortgage, the people's court shall support it.[73] Suppose compensation was paid to the mortgagor, and the mortgagee requests the party liable for compensation to pay directly to the mortgagee. In that case, the court shall not support it except where the party responsible for compensation still pays the mortgagor after the mortgagee has served a payment. In other words, under Chinese Law, the created mortgage is not terminated upon expropriation or destruction. Suppose the mortgaged property is lost or expropriated before the registration for reasons not attributable to the mortgagor itself. Still, the compensation has been paid to the mortgagor when the creditor requests the mortgagor to assume mortgage liability. In that case, the court shall support this request.[74] This surviving mortgage rule is necessarily premised on attribution to the party liable for compensation. This is understandable because the mortgage affects the real right and not the building per se. The continued existence of the mortgage is closely related to a continuation of the mortgage debtor's interest in the building. This rule is protective of the mortgage creditor. However, The SPC Interpretation does not address whether the mortgage is terminated where the expropriation compensation is uncompensated. In case of under-compensation or delayed compensation, will this affect the scope of security liability agreed in the original mortgage? It remains to be seen in future case law.

Although the Property Law does not address the issue where the mortgage creditor becomes the owner of the mortgaged property. Under the Chinese contract law principle, this amounts to a merge[75] and results in the contract termination. But even if the mortgage is extinguished according to contract rules, the question remains unanswered whether the mortgage creditor who has acquired the mortgaged property is still entitled to enforce the mortgage against subsequent mortgage creditors.

6.4 Conclusion

The Civil Code has made significant improvements regarding security interests by straightening pre-existing laws. Remarkably, the SPC has

[73] Article 42 (1) SPC Interpretation on Security.
[74] Ibid., Article 46 (2).
[75] Article 557 of the Chinese Civil Code.

pronounced many detailed legal tests in a Judicial Interpretation on the Institution of Security in the era of the Civil Code. The new rules are fine-tuned to balance the interests among the debtor, the creditor, and the security provider. In a similar vein, the new rules seem to tinker with the accessory principle, which has long been held dear in Chinese law.

It appears that rigid adherence to the accessoriness principle is not worthwhile. For this reason, there is a movement away from the accessoriness principle in the Civil Code. For example, a maximum amount mortgage[76] and floating charge[77] have gained ground in China. Moreover, the current legal framework governing security interests gears towards private ordering. It allows the parties to create non-standard security (atypical security) by contract, which renders the security effective. Nevertheless, these are only in a nascent development stage and still require further legal clarifications from the judiciary.

However, some provisions are still vague with more details to be furnished, such as the conflicts between the standard security made public through registration and non-standard security only through private contract without publicity, rules on the internal recourse among the security providers, and termination of security interests. Expectedly, many detailed legal tests/rules need to be mapped out by the courts through judicial decisions.

[76] Article 420 of the Chinese Civil Code.
[77] Article 396 of the Chinese Civil Code.

7

Chinese Tort Law in the Era of the Civil Code

DING CHUNYAN

7.1 Introduction

China's Civil Code (民法典), promulgated by the National People's Congress on May 28, 2020, took effect on January 1, 2021 and has since replaced the previous relevant legal principles embodied in various sources of civil law. Its seventh Book on Tort Liability (侵权责任) codifies the new version of Chinese tort law and has replaced the Tort Liability Law[1] made by the Standing Committee of the National People's Congress in 2009. On the one hand, the Book on Tort Liability follows to a large extent its predecessor in terms of the structure and content; on the other hand, it has introduced some substantive revisions. This chapter focuses on Chinese tort law in the era of the Civil Code. It first examines three major revisions that the Civil Code brings to Chinese tort law, including redefining the concept of "tort liability," expanding the application of punitive damages, and refining the rules of cybertort liability. It then analyzes features of Chinese tort law codified in the Civil Code, specifically regarding the compensation system, the imputation system, and the multi-tier liability system. It finally discusses the approaches to developing Chinese tort law in the era of the Civil Code.

7.2 Major Revisions of the Book on Tort Liability of the Civil Code

7.2.1 Redefining the Concept of "Tort Liability"

The Book on Tort Liability (TLB) has ninety-five provisions contained in ten chapters. Although it shares similarities with the Tort Liability Law (TLL) in terms of the title, scale, and structure, it has brought some substantive revisions to the Chinese tort law. The first change is made

[1] The Tort Liability Law (侵权责任法) was promulgated by the Standing Committee of the National People's Congress on December 26, 2009, effective July 1, 2010, invalidated January 1, 2021.

with regard to the meaning of the concept of "tort liability." Article 15 of the TLL provided eight types of tort liability. They are cession of infringement, removal of nuisance, elimination of danger, return of property, restoration to the original condition, compensation for damages, apology, and elimination of adverse effects and restoration of reputation. By contrast, the TLB excludes four of them – return of property, restoration to the original condition, elimination of adverse effects and restoration of reputation, as well as apology, which nevertheless now appear in Article 179 of the Civil Code as specific types of "civil liability" (民事责任). In other words, the TLB redefines "tort liability" by limiting it to (1) compensation for damages[2] and (2) cession of infringement, removal of nuisance, and elimination of danger when a tort endangers personal or property safety of others.[3]

This change can also be recognized in the relevant provisions of other Books of the Civil Code. For example, four provisions (Articles 235 to 238) of Chapter III (titled "Protection of Real Rights") of the Book on Real Rights have stated five legal remedies for infringements of real rights. They are return of property, removal of nuisance, elimination of danger, restoration to the original condition (including repair, redoing, and replacement of a damaged object), and compensation for damages. Article 238 of the Civil Code, in particular, deliberately uses the wording "civil liability" rather than "tort liability" to refer to the legal remedies other than compensation for damages where real rights are infringed and the rights holder suffers damages as a result.[4] Similarly, Articles 994 and 995 in the Book on Personality Rights of the Civil Code also use the wording "civil liability" rather than "tort liability" when addressing the legal consequences of infringements of personality rights.

As some scholars have explained, the redefinition of "tort liability" as noted above was premised on the following concerns: return of property, cession of infringement, removal of nuisance, elimination of danger, restoration to the original condition, and elimination of adverse effects and restoration of reputation are claims deriving from "absolute rights"

[2] See Chapter II of TLB.

[3] See Article 1167 of the Civil Code, which provides that where a tortious act endangers another person's personal or property safety, the aggrieved person has the right to request the tortfeasor to assume tort liability such as cessation of the infringement, removal of the nuisance, or elimination of the danger.

[4] Wang Liming, "Several Controversial Issues in the Drafting the Civil Code" ("民法典编纂中的若干争论问题") (2020) 4 *Journal of Shanghai Political Science and Law College* (上海政法学院学报) 14–28 at 22.

(e.g., real rights and personality rights), which are actionable per se, not subject to the fault principle and the statute of limitation, and may serve as *ex ante* remedies to prevent infringements of absolute rights.[5] By contrast, compensation for damages is a claim based on a tortious obligation (侵权之债). It is owed by the tortfeasor to the victim, requires actual damages, and is subject to the statute of limitation and the fault principle (in general). It always serves as *ex post* remedy.[6] As such, "tort liability" should be limited to "compensation for damages" and exclude other types of legal remedies that derive from absolute rights.

It seems that this redefinition was intended to justify having a separate Book on Personality Rights in the Civil Code, which was heatedly debated during the drafting process.[7] Scholars opposing this idea argued that a separate Book on Personality Rights would cause an unnecessary overlap with the TLB.[8] In my opinion, the redefinition of "tort liability" is not only a significant departure from the long-standing understanding of this concept since the General Principles of Civil Law[9] but also has the following drawbacks: firstly, the above explanations about the differences between the claims deriving from absolute rights and the claim for compensation based on a tortious obligation is not fully accurate. "Restoration to the original condition" and "elimination of adverse effects and restoration of reputation" are the same as compensation for damages in terms of the nature of legal remedy; monetary remedy is seen as the second-best option when the former remedies are unavailable.[10] Hence, "restoration to the original condition" and "elimination of adverse effects and restoration of reputation" are also based on a tortious obligation rather than absolute rights. In addition, the above explanations about the difference between the two sets of claims cannot logically

[5] Wang Liming, "On the Separation of the Claims Deriving from Personality Rights and the Claim for Compensation for Damages" ("论人格权请求权与侵权损害赔偿请求权的分离") (2019) 1 *China Legal Science* (中国法学) 224–43 at 228–30.

[6] Ibid.

[7] Ibid.; Liang Huixing, "Major Debates in the Drafting the Civil Code" ("民法典编纂中的重大争论") (2018) 3 *Journal of Guangsu Political Science and Law College* (甘肃政法学院学报) 1–19 at 12–19.

[8] Liang, "Major Debates," 16.

[9] The General Principles of Civil Law (民法通则) was promulgated by the National People's Congress on April 12, 1987, effective January 1, 1987, amended August 27, 2009, invalidated January 1, 2021.

[10] Cui Jianyuan, "Defining the Claim for Restoration to the Original Condition and Return of Property" ("关于恢复原状请求权和返还财产的辨析") (2020) 1 *Contemporary Law Review* (当代法学) 63–74 at 67.

explain why cession of infringement, removal of nuisance, and elimination of danger are retained as part of tort liability under the TLB[11] while return of property is excluded therein although all of these claims are deriving from absolute rights. Indeed, the previous understanding of "tort liability" in TLL has caused no confusion over the differences between these two sets of claims and generated no practical problems in tort litigation. Moreover, "apology," which has been traditionally seen as a type of tort liability in Chinese law, is excluded from the TLB but retained as one type of civil liability in the Book on General Provisions[12] and one available legal remedy for infringements of personality rights in the Book on Personality Rights.[13] Does this structural arrangement mean that the Civil Code disallows the victim of a tort – other than the infringement of personality rights – to seek the remedy of apology? If the answer is negative (as the TLB indicates), it will cause a clash between the law in the books and the law in action[14] and deprive many tort victims of this remedy that has conventionally played an important role in appeasement as well as deterrence in Chinese tort law.[15] Besides, the fact that the TLB excludes return of property, restoration to the original condition, elimination of adverse effects and restoration of reputation and apology from the scope of "tort liability" will cause unnecessary inconvenience to the tort victims submitting personality or property rights infringements given that many of them are laymen and often do not have access to lawyers.

As Article 120 of the Civil Code provides, in the case of infringements of civil rights or interests (i.e., tort), the victims are entitled to request the tortfeasor to assume the "tort liability." Literally, all civil liabilities arising from infringements of civil law rights or interests (民事权益, including real rights and personality rights) should be "tort liability." Moreover, "tort liability" has been understood neither as the same as nor as being

[11] Article 1167 of the Civil Code.

[12] Article 179 of the Civil Code.

[13] Article 995 of the Civil Code.

[14] For example, apology is claimed and supported by the courts in environmental tort lawsuits, public interest civil litigation in practice, see Que Zhanwen, "Applications and Limitations of Apology in Public Interest Civil Litigation" ("赔礼道歉在民事公益诉讼中的适用及其限制") (2019) 7 *Tribune of Political Science and Law* (政法论坛) 119–28 at 120.

[15] Deng Kezhu, "On Apology in Environmental Civil Public Interest Litigation" ("论环境民事公益诉讼中的赔礼道歉") (2021) 1 *Journal of Liaoning Normal University (Social Science Edition)* (辽宁师范大学学报（社会科学版）) 34–41 at 35.

limited to a tortious obligation since the General Principles of Civil Code; it covers a wider scope of liabilities beyond compensation for torts and includes liabilities that derive from absolute rights (e.g., cession of infringement, removal of nuisance, elimination of danger, return of property, apology). Therefore, I view the redefinition of "tort liability" as a flaw in the Civil Code. It causes confusion and inconvenience and is likely to be ignored by the judges and legal practitioners, who will continue adopting the previous understanding of "tort liability" in practice.

7.2.2 Expanding the Application of Punitive Damages

The TLB enables tort victims to claim punitive damages in three situations: (1) the intentional infringement of intellectual property rights that involves serious circumstances;[16] (2) the manufacturer or seller knowingly manufacturing or selling defective products or failing to take remedial measures (e.g., stopping sales, providing warnings, recalling defective products) that causes death or serious personal injury;[17] and (3) the intentional pollution of the environment or harm of the ecological system in violation of the statute that causes serious consequences.[18] Compared to the TLL, the TLB has two substantive revisions regarding punitive damages: first, although the TLL has already provided that punitive damages can be claimed against a manufacturer or seller who knowingly produces or sells defective products thus causing others' death or serious personal injury, the TLB further makes a manufacturer or seller who has failed to take remedial measures subject to punitive damages. In addition, the TLB, for the first time, makes punitive damages available in another two specific torts: intellectual property tort and environmental tort.

To add one caveat, punitive damages may be claimed in other circumstances of tort because Article 179(2) of the Civil Code recognizes the availability of punitive damages if provided by other laws. For example, Article 55(2) of the Law on the Protection of Consumer Rights and Interests[19] requires a business operator who knows about a defect in goods or services but continues to supply such goods or services to the

[16] Article 1185 of the Civil Code.
[17] Article 1207 of the Civil Code.
[18] Article 1232 of the Civil Code.
[19] The Law on the Protection of Consumer Rights and Interests (消费者权益保护法) was promulgated by the Standing Committee of the National People's Congress on October 31, 1993, effective January 1, 1994, amended August 27, 2009 and October 25, 2013.

consumer, thus causing death or serious personal injury to the consumer or others, to pay punitive damages of no more than double the amount of compensatory damages. In addition, Article 148(2) of the Food Safety Law[20] provides that where a manufacturer produces food that fails to meet the food safety standards and a business operator knowingly deals such food, thus causing damages to the consumers, the consumers are entitled to claim, in addition to compensatory damages, an increased compensation in an amount of ten times of the food price or three times of the losses that he has suffered (the minimum amount of punitive damages is 1,000 yuan), except in cases of a defect in the label or instruction of the food that neither makes the food unsafe nor misleads the consumer.

The expanded scope of application for punitive damages by the TLB has two important implications: firstly, it reflects China's governing policy of strengthening product safety, intellectual property protection, and environmental protection by promoting private enforcement through tort litigation. The recovery of punitive damages creates a great incentive for tort victims (as private regulators) to sue the tortfeasor who not only intentionally infringed the victim's civil law rights but also violated the relevant public regulations. For example, Article 1232 of the Civil Code requires violation of statutory provisions as a prerequisite in claiming punitive damages in environmental tort. Because of the incentive for claiming punitive damages, more private regulators are likely to engage in private enforcement through tort litigation, which will help to mitigate the inadequacy of public enforcement in the fields of food and drug governance, intellectual property governance, and environmental governance.[21] Due to the same policy, the TLB has also supplemented two provisions that specify the coverage of pecuniary damages that the relevant public authority and environmental organizations are entitled to claim in environmental public interest litigation.[22] Secondly, given the expanded application scope of punitive damages under the TLB and their deterrent effects, Chinese tort law is expected to play a more significant role in terms of prevention than before.

[20] The Food Safety Law (食品安全法) was promulgated by the Standing Committee of the National People's Congress on February 28, 2009, effective June 1, 2009, amended April 24, 2015, December 29, 2018, April 29, 2021.

[21] Alex Wong, "The Search for Substantive Legitimacy: Environmental Law and Bureaucracy in China" (2013) 37 *Harvard Environmental Law Review* 365–440 at 367.

[22] Articles 1234 and 1235 of the Civil Code.

Moreover, the new provisions on punitive damages under the TLB adopt rather vague and flexible wording (such as "serious circumstances" and "serious consequences") and set no limitation or cap on the amount of punitive damages in intellectual property tort and environment tort. This inevitably grants great discretion to the judiciary in awarding punitive damages and allows judges to make use of punitive damages to deter potential tortfeasors from infringing intellectual property rights and harming environmental interests.

7.2.3 Refining the Rules of Cybertort Liability

In response to the increasing internet-related torts, the TLB has refined the rules of liability for cybertorts in the following three aspects: firstly, the number of the provisions on cybertorts has increased from one provision (Article 36 of the TLL) to four provisions under the TLB (Articles 1194 to 1197 of the Civil Code). The first subsection of Article 36 of the TLL has been incorporated in Article 1194 of the Civil Code; the previous third subsection has become Article 1197 of the Civil Code; and the second subsection has developed into two provisions in the TLB: Article 1195 and Article 1196. Moreover, the TLB has imposed two-tier tort liability on Internet Service Providers (ISPs). The first-tier liability is established by Article 1194 of the Civil Code, which provides that ISPs should bear primary tort liability for the direct infringement of civil law rights and interests through the Internet unless otherwise provided by the law. The second-tier liability is established by Article 1197 of the Civil Code, which provides that ISPs should bear secondary joint and several liability for their failure to take necessary measures when ISPs know or ought to have known the internet service user has infringed civil law rights and interests of others through using their internet service. In other words, ISPs have a duty to take necessary measures when they have actual knowledge or should have known about their service user's infringements. The expressions of "ought to have known" and "necessary" show that such secondary liability of ISPs is fault-based and not strict liability.

Furthermore, the TLB has introduced a three-stage rule for handling a cybertort dispute: (1) the rights holder should issue a notification to the ISP; (2) the ISP forwards the notification to the alleged infringing internet service user; and (3) the alleged infringing internet service user may submit a non-infringement declaration (i.e., counter-notification) to the ISP. Specifically, Article 1195 of the Civil Code requires the rights holder to include the following information in the notification: (1) the preliminary evidence establishing the tort; (2) the real identity information of the rights holder; and (3) the request for the ISP's necessary measures such as deletion, block, and disconnection. The rights holder should bear tort liability to the alleged infringing internet service user and the ISP for the harm caused by any erroneous notification. The same provision also requires the ISP, after receiving the rights holder's notification, to take necessary measures in a timely manner based on the preliminary evidence establishing the tort and the type of internet service concerned, otherwise the ISP should bear joint and several liability together with the alleged infringing internet service user for the "increased part" of harm. Moreover, Article 1196 of the Civil Code requires the alleged infringing internet service user to include the following two items in the non-infringement declaration: (1) the preliminary evidence of non-infringement and (2) the real identity information of the alleged infringing internet service user. Similarly, after receiving the non-infringement declaration, the ISP should forward the declaration to the rights holder and inform the latter of the right to file a complaint to the relevant authority or file a lawsuit with the court. If the ISP does not receive a notification that the rights holder has filed a complaint or a lawsuit within a reasonable period of time after forwarding the declaration, it should terminate measures taken in a timely manner.

Therefore, the TLB has set up a general liability framework for cybertorts, along with four sets of judicial interpretation of the Supreme People's Court (SPC) in relation to specific types of cybertort: the Provisions on Issues concerning the Application of Law in Adjudicating Civil Disputes involving Infringements of the Right of Dissemination on Information Networks,[23] the Provisions on Issues concerning the Application of Law in Adjudicating Civil Disputes over Infringements of Personal Rights and Interests through Information Networks,[24] the Guiding Opinions on the Adjudication of Intellectual

[23] The Provisions on Issues concerning the Application of Law in Adjudicating Civil Disputes involving Infringements of the Right of Dissemination on Information Networks (关于审理侵害信息网络传播权民事纠纷案件适用法律若干问题的规定) were promulgated by the SPC on December 17, 2012, effective January 1, 2013, amended December 29, 2020.

[24] The Provisions on Issues concerning the Application of Law in Adjudicating Civil Disputes over Infringements of Personal Rights and Interests through Information Networks (关于审理利用信息网络侵害人身权益民事纠纷案件适用法律若干问题

Property Civil Cases Involving E-Commerce Platforms,[25] and the Reply on Issues concerning the Application of Law to Disputes over Internet-related Intellectual Property Right Infringements.[26] These judicial interpretations have provided helpful detailed rules to assist the judges in determining practically important issues, including but not limited to whether the ISP has taken necessary measures "in a timely manner," whether the ISP "ought to have known" an infringement, or how to decide "the degree of the ISP's fault" in individual cases.

However, the TLB has created three controversial legal issues regarding cybertort liability that will arouse debates. The first controversy is concerned with the nature of the three-stage rule for handling a cybertort dispute set out in Articles 1195 and 1196 of the Civil Code. Some labeled it as "the safe harbor provision,"[27] which originated from American copyright statutes (e.g., the Digital Millennium Copyright Act) that intended to provide the ISP immunity protection from liability provided that the notification-take down requirement is met.[28] Others have argued that the three-stage rule differs from the safe harbor provision because it does not aim to protect the ISP from liability when it has taken certain actions (such as deleting or disabling access to the infringing information) upon receiving the rights holder's notification.[29] I agree that the three-stage rule set out in Articles 1195 and 1196 of the Civil Code is not exactly the same as the safe harbor provision in terms of the content and purpose of the rule, because Article 1195 requires the ISP to take necessary measures "based on the preliminary evidence

的规定) was promulgated by the SPC on August 21, 2014, effective October 10, 2014, amended December 29, 2020.

25 The Guiding Opinions on the Adjudication of Intellectual Property Civil Cases Involving E-Commerce Platforms (关于审理涉电子商务平台知识产权民事案件的指导意见) were promulgated by the SPC on September 10, 2020, effective on the same day.

26 The Reply on Issues concerning the Application of Law to Disputes over Internet-related Intellectual Property Right Infringements (关于涉网络知识产权侵权纠纷几个法律适用问题的批复) was promulgated by the SPC on September 12, 2020, effective September 14, 2020.

27 Yang Lixin, "The Status and Duty of ISP regarding Cybertort under the Safe Harbours Provision" ("网络服务提供商在网络侵权避风港规则中的地位和义务") (2020) 5 *Journal of Fujian Normal University (Philosophy and Social Science Edition)* (福建师范大学学报（哲学社会科学版）) 139–72 at 140.

28 Salil K. Mehra and Marketa Trimble, "Secondary Liability, ISP Immunity, and Incumbent Entrenchment" (2014) 62 *American Journal of Comparative Law Supplement* 685–705 at 687.

29 Xie Jun, "Study of Cybertort Provisions of the Civil Code" ("民法典网络侵权条款研究") (2020) 4 *Comparative Law Study* (比较法学) 131–44 at 133–34.

establishing the tort and the type of Internet service concerned" in a timely manner, which imposes a reasonable duty of care on the ISP upon receiving a notification from the rights holder (rather than absolutely preventing the ISP from tort liability once it meets certain conditions, such as deleting the infringing online information). The issue of whether the ISP has discharged such duty of reasonable care depends on specific circumstances of individual cases. If the ISP has fulfilled the duty, it should not need to bear tort liability to the rights holder.

The second controversy is about the ISP's liability to the alleged infringing internet service user.[30] In light of Articles 1195 and 1196, the lawmakers of the Civil Code intended to balance the competing interests of the rights holders and internet service users. This is evidenced by the following: Article 1195 confirms the tort liability of the rights holder for erroneous notification as well as the ISP's duty to terminate the measures taken in a timely manner when it has not received a notification that the rights holder has filed a complaint or a lawsuit within a reasonable period of time after forwarding the declaration. However, the TLB is silent on the issue of whether the ISP should bear tort liability when it has taken excessive measures after receiving the right holder's notification, or it has failed to forward the non-infringement declaration of the alleged infringing internet service user to the rights holder, or it has failed to timely terminate the measures taken as required by Article 1196.

Thirdly, the TLB has not clarified whether the ISP should examine the authenticity of the claim and evidence stated in the notification of the rights holder as well as the non-infringement declaration of the alleged infringing internet service user and, if the answer is positive, whether this will affect the ISP's duty respectively owed to the rights holder and the alleged infringing internet service user. This issue essentially depends on the role of the ISP: is it merely a passive messenger or a private regulator of an internet service platform and a private adjudicator of cyber disputes? Therefore, these controversial legal issues regarding cybertort liability that the TLB has generated should be further discussed and

[30] Research Group of the No. 1 Intermediate Court of Shanghai, "Determination on the Liability for Failing to Forward the Non-infringement Declaration by the E-Commerce Platform Operator in the First Case as Such in the Country" ("关于首例电子商务平台经营者未实施'反通知'程序的责任认定") (2021) 7 *Law Application* (法律适用) 112–21 at 116–20.

appropriately solved despite the establishment of a general liability framework for cybertorts under the TLB.

7.3 Major Features of Chinese Tort Law in the Era of the Civil Code

7.3.1 The Compensation System under Chinese Tort Law

The compensation system under the TLB encompasses three types of damages – pecuniary damages, non-pecuniary damages, and punitive damages. Firstly, Chapter II of the TLB titled "compensation for damages" provides a set of provisions on pecuniary damages in the case of infringements of personal rights and interests[31] and property rights.[32] It is worth noting that Article 1182 of the Civil Code provides the method for assessing pecuniary damages caused by infringements of personal rights and interests. It allows the victim to claim pecuniary damages either based on the loss sustained by the victim or on the account of profits gained by the tortfeasor. In other words, the victim may choose a favorable method to claim pecuniary damages resulting from the infringement of personal rights and interests, which was disallowed by the equivalent Article 20 of the TLL. Secondly, Article 1183 of the Civil Code confirms the availability of non-pecuniary damages in two situations: (1) the infringement of personal rights and interests that causes serious mental suffering and (2) the infringement of a special object of personal significance of a natural person by intent or gross negligence that causes serious mental suffering. The second situation was newly added to the TLB although a similar legal rule has existed for years in Article 4 of the SPC's Judicial Interpretation on Issues concerning the Determination of Compensation Liability for Mental Suffering Damages in Torts.[33] Moreover, Article 996 of the Civil Code provides that a victim, who chooses to file a lawsuit based on breach of contract in a concurrent liability case, retains the right to claim non-pecuniary damages under tort law when the breaching party infringes a personality right of the victim who has thus sustained serious mental suffering. This is as an exception

[31] Articles 1179, 1181, and 1182 of the Civil Code.

[32] Article 1184 of the Civil Code.

[33] The Judicial Interpretation on Issues concerning the Determination of Compensation Liability for Mental Suffering Damages in Torts (关于确定民事侵权精神损害赔偿责任若干问题的解释) was promulgated by the SPC on March 8, 2001, effective March 10, 2001, amended December 29, 2020.

to Article 186 of the Civil Code, which requires the victim must select either breach of contract or tort as a cause of action to lodge a claim in a concurrent liability case. In addition, punitive damages, as noted above, have been expansively applied in product liability cases, intellectual property torts, and environmental torts under the TLB.

Both non-pecuniary damages and punitive damages were originally absent in the General Principles of Civil Law. They were respectively introduced through judicial interpretation of the SPC and special laws made by the National People's Congress and its Standing Committee.[34] In line with the TLL, the TLB has consolidated and developed these two heads of damages and then formally established a complete compensation system under Chinese tort law. However, as the TLB only provides general provisions, detailed legal principles about the assessment of pecuniary damages in personal injury and wrongful death cases and the assessment of non-pecuniary damages are provided in the SPC's Interpretation on Issues concerning the Application of Law for the Adjudication of Cases on Compensation for Personal Injury[35] and the SPC's Interpretation on Issues concerning the Determination of Compensation Liability for Mental Suffering Damages in Torts. These two sets of judicial interpretation constitute an important part of the compensation system under Chinese tort law. Furthermore, the TLB also authorizes the judges to exercise great discretion in deciding judicial awards of compensation for pecuniary damages mainly in two circumstances: firstly, Article 1182 of the Civil Code grants the court an authority to determine the amount of pecuniary damages in the circumstances where it is difficult to determine the amount of the losses sustained by the victim or the account of profits gained by the tortfeasor as a result of the infringement of personal rights and interests. Secondly, Article 1184 of the Civil Code widely authorizes the court to adopt "other reasonable methods" as the alternative to the market price rule when assessing pecuniary damages in the case of infringements of property rights.

[34] Specifically, the Judicial Interpretation on Issues concerning the Determination of Compensation Liability for Mental Suffering Damages in Torts, and the Law on the Protection of Consumer Rights and Interests.

[35] The Interpretation on Issues concerning the Application of Law for the Adjudication of Cases on Compensation for Personal Injury (关于审理人身损害赔偿案件适用法律若干问题的解释) was promulgated by the SPC on December 26, 2003, effective May 1, 2004, amended December 29, 2020 and April 24, 2022.

7.3.2 The Imputation System under Chinese Tort Law

Article 1165(1) of the Civil Code reiterates the fault principle as the general imputation principle for giving rise to tort liability. Just to name a few, fault is required for the ISP's secondary liability for cybertort directly committed by the internet service user (Article 1197); the operator's, administrator's, or the organizer's liability for breaching the duty of maintaining safety (Article 1198); the school's or other education institution's liability for personal injury sustained by the student with limited legal capacity to act during the course of their study or life therein (Article 1200); and general liability for medical negligence (Article 1218). It is worth noting that although Article 1165(2) establishes the presumed fault principle, it does not change the fault principle in itself but only reverses the burden of proof to the alleged tortfeasor regarding the issue of fault. Table 7.1 shows all examples of specific torts based on presumed fault liability under the TLB. Moreover, Article 1166 of the Civil Code provides that the law may require the actor to bear tort liability regardless of whether or not the actor is at fault, which is strict liability as an exception to the fault principle. Specifically, the TLB includes twenty-four provisions that establish special torts based on strict liability (Table 7.2).

Table 7.1 *Torts based on presumed fault liability under the TLB*

Torts based on presumed fault liability	Examples
School's liability for the injury to minors without legal capacity to act	Art. 1199
Medical institution's liability for medical negligence	Art. 1222
Owner and administrator's liability for harm caused by ultra-hazardous materials in illegal possession of a third party	Art. 1242
Administrator's liability to the trespasser on ultra-hazardous premises	Art. 1243
Liability of the zoo regarding injuries caused by animals	Art. 1248
Owner, administrator, and user's liability for falling parts of a building or structure	Art. 1253
Liability of a person who piles up the stack for stack collapse	Art. 1255
Public road manager's liability for road obstruction	Art. 1256
Tree owner and manager's liability for harm caused by falling tree, branch or fruit	Art. 1257
Constructor's liability for harm caused by the construction work of underground facility; administrator's liability for harm caused by manhole or underground facility	Art. 1258

Table 7.2 *Torts based on strict liability under the TLB*

Torts based on strict liability	Examples
Guardian's liability for harm caused by minors	Arts. 1188(1), 1189
Employer's vicarious liability for tort committed by employees	Art. 1191(1)
Service recipient's vicarious liability for tort committed by the service provider	Art. 1192(1)
Manufacturer and seller's vicarious liability for defective product	Arts. 1203, 1204
Liability of an entity with whom a motor vehicle is associated for a traffic accident caused by the vehicle user	Art. 1211
Liability of the transferer of an illegally assembled or below the standard motor vehicle for a traffic accident caused by the transferee	Art. 1214
Liability of the thief, robber, or snatcher of a vehicle for a traffic accident caused by the vehicle user	Art. 1215
Manufacturer, seller, drug marketing license holder, and medical institution's vicarious liability for defective drug and medical device, and substandard blood	Art. 1223
Environmental tort	Arts. 1229, 1233
Liability for ultra-hazardous operations	Arts .1236–1242
Animal liability	Arts .1245, 1247, 1249, 1250
Liability for harm caused by a collapsed building or structure	Art. 1252

Fault based liability and strict liability, however, are only a partial picture of the imputation system under the TLB. In addition to strict liability as the first type of non-fault-based liability, the TLB has another two types of non-fault-based liability, both of which are unique to Chinese tort law. The first of these is "equitable liability" (公平责任), as provided by Article 1186 of the Civil Code, which reads as follows: "where neither the victim nor the actor is at fault for the occurrence of the damages, the losses shall be shared by both parties in accordance with the provisions of the law." The equitable liability principle was originally introduced to Chinese tort law by Article 132 of the General Principles of Civil Law, then adopted by Article 24 of the TLL, and further incorporated by Article 1186 of the Civil Code. However, there is a substantive difference between the TLB and the previous two laws in terms of equitable liability – the TLB requires the losses should be shared by both parties "in accordance with the provisions of the law," instead of "based on the actual circumstances" as provided in the previous two laws. Where there is a special law that addresses how to apportion the damages when both parties are free of fault, it is obvious that such special law will be followed, regardless of Article 1186 of the Civil Code.[36] For example, Article 76 of the Road Traffic Safety Law[37] provides that in a road traffic accident occurring between a motor vehicle and a non-motor vehicle or a pedestrian, the motor vehicle driver shall bear liability for compensation limited to a maximum of 10 percent of the total damages sustained by the victim when both parties are not at fault for the occurrence of the damages. However, when there is no special law that provides a rule on the distribution of damages between the innocent parties, do the judges have authority to decide the apportionment issue based on the actual circumstances of the case? Will the judges ignore such differences between the laws and continue to exercise discretion to apportion the damages between the parties in the case of equitable liability? The ambiguity that Article 1186 of the Civil Code has generated needs to be solved in due course.

The other type of non-fault-based liability under the TLB is "liability for reimbursement" (补偿责任). It can be further divided into three categories: the first category is labeled "the beneficiary's liability for reimbursement." For example, Article 182 of the Civil Code is concerned with the defense of "avoiding a peril in emergency" (紧急避险); its second subsection provides that where the peril is caused by natural forces, the person who causes harm to others when seeking to avoid the peril bears no civil liability (due to the defense of avoiding a peril in emergency) but may make appropriate reimbursement to the victim. Another example is Article 183 of the Civil Code that deals with the defense of necessity, which provides that where a party is injured for protecting the civil rights and interests of another person, the tortfeasor shall bear civil liability, and the beneficiary may make appropriate

[36] Liang Huixin, "Ten Issues regarding the Interpretation and Application of the Civil Code" ("民法典解释与适用中的十个问题") (2021) 1 *Journal of Wenzhou University (Social Science Edition)* (温州大学学报（社会科学版）) 1–13 at 11.

[37] The Road Traffic Safety Law (道路交通安全法) was promulgated by the Standing Committee of the National People's Congress on October 28, 2003, effective May 1, 2004, amended December 29, 2007, April 22, 2011, and April 29, 2021.

reimbursement to the injured person; in the absence of a tortfeasor, or if the tortfeasor flees or is incapable of assuming civil liability, upon request of the injured person, the beneficiary shall make appropriate reimbursement. The third example is Article 1192(2) of the Civil Code, which provides that the service provider who suffers damage caused by a third party during the course of providing the service is entitled to request the service recipient to make reimbursement in addition to a claim for tort liability against the third-party tortfeasor. All three provisions show that although the beneficiary is not liable for tort, he has obtained certain benefits from the victim's damage and therefore is required by law to make appropriate reimbursement when the latter needs relief.

The second category of liability for reimbursement is Article 1190(1) of the Civil Code, which provides that a person with full legal capacity to act who is not at fault for causing damage to a victim due to temporary loss of consciousness or loss of control shall not bear tort liability but shall make appropriate compensation to the victim according to his financial ability. The legal rationale for this category of liability for reimbursement lies in a causal link between the victim's damage and the actor's conduct although the actor is not liable for tort given the absence of fault, thus this may be labeled "causation-based liability for reimbursement."

The third category is concerned with the notorious cases of "throwing an object from a high-rise building" (高空抛物). According to Article 1254(1) of the Civil Code, where it is difficult for the victim to identify the specific tortfeasor upon investigation, any user of the building who may have caused the damage shall make reimbursement unless he can prove otherwise and has the right to have recourse from the tortfeasor if found later. The liability for reimbursement set out in this provision makes all users of the building collectively insure against the risk of throwing an object from a high-rise building when the victim has difficulty to identify the tortfeasor. Therefore, this category may be labeled "quasi-insurance liability for reimbursement."

To sum up, Table 7.3 presents a complete imputation system under Chinese tort law. In particular, the last two categories of non-fault-based liability (i.e., equitable liability and liability for reimbursement) under the TLB have interesting implications. First, they have demonstrated the notion of equity underlying Chinese tort law. Where an actor has no fault and should not bear tort liability for the damage sustained by the victim, Chinese tort law, based on the rationale of equity, holds an actor who either obtains benefit from the harm or has a causal link with the

Table 7.3 *The imputation system under the TLB*

Imputation principles	Subcategories	
Fault-based liability	Fault liability	
	Presumed fault liability	
Non-fault-based liability	Strict liability	
	Equitable liability	
	Liability for reimbursement	Beneficiary's liability for reimbursement
		Causation-based liability for reimbursement
		Quasi-insurance liability for reimbursement

harm to bear liability for reimbursement to the victim in need. However, the wording "make appropriate reimbursement" used by the TLB shows that the amount of reimbursement should be significantly less than that of compensation where the actor is liable in tort for damages. Moreover, the judges have an authority to decide an appropriate level or amount of reimbursement according to the circumstances of the case, such as the financial ability of an actor, the victim's need for reimbursement, etc. Secondly, the last two categories of non-fault-based liability under the TLB have shown that with undeveloped insurance systems in the country, Chinese tort law places a strong emphasis on distributive justice where the victim suffers innocent harm or cannot get compensation because the tortfeasor is not found or unable to pay compensation. Article 1254(1) of the Civil Code is a typical example because it is intended to distribute among all users of a high-rise building the losses of the victim when the tortfeasor who has thrown an object from the building is not identifiable even after an investigation.

7.3.3 The Multi-Tier Liability System under Chinese Tort Law

The TLB has established a multi-tier tort liability system. Table 7.4 below illustrates all five tiers of liability. Primarily, the primary liability is normally imposed on the primary tortfeasor either based on fault (e.g., Article 1198(1)), presumed fault (e.g., Article 1199), or strict liability (Article 1120).

Table 7.4 *The multi-tier liability system under the TLB*

Multi-tier liability	Examples
Primary liability	Arts. 1194, 1198(1), 1199, 1120 etc.
Joint and several liability	Arts. 1168, 1169(1), 1170, 1171, 1195(2), 1197, 1203, 1204, 1211, 1214, 1215, 1223, 1233, 1241, 1242, 1250, 1252
Several liability (corresponding liability)	Arts. 1169(2), 1172, 1189, 1191(2), 1193, 1256
Supplementary liability	Arts. 1198(2), 1201
Contributory liability	Arts. 1173, 1192(1), 1239, 1240, 1245, 1246

In addition to the cases of typical joint torts (Article 1168), accessory torts (by inciting and assisting an act) (Article 1169(1)), joint dangerous acts (Article 1170), and quasi-joint torts (Article 1171), the TLB has provided joint and several liability for a wide range of torts either based on fault (e.g., Article 1195(2) and Article 1197), presumed fault (e.g., Article 1241 and Article 1242), or strict liability (e.g., Articles 1211, 1214, 1215, 1223, 1233, 1250, and 1252).

Thirdly, the TLB has imposed several (but not joint) liability when there are multiple tortfeasors involved in a case, each of whom bears several liability for part of the harm sustained by the victim. For example, Article 1189 of the Civil Code requires the guardian to bear strict liability and a person who is delegated to exercise the supervision duty by the guardian to bear negligence-based liability for the victim's harm caused by a minor without or with limited legal capacity to act. Another example is Article 1191(2) of the Civil Code, which requires the borrowing employer to bear vicarious liability for the tort committed by the employee and the lending employer to bear negligence-based liability toward the victim.

Furthermore, as a Chinese characteristic rule, the TLB has provided supplementary liability with respect to some torts. The party who bears such a liability can only be held liable to the victim when the primary tortfeasor cannot adequately compensate the victim; moreover, such a party, having paid the compensation, has a claim against the primary tortfeasor. For example, according to Article 1198(2) of the Civil Code, the negligent operator, administrator, or the organizer bears supplementary liability to the victim who has suffered damage on the former's premises directly caused by a third-party tortfeasor. Similarly, Article 1201 imposes supplementary liability on the negligent educational institution for a student's harm directly caused by a third-party tortfeasor.

Finally, the TLB requires the victims to bear contributory liability according to their comparative fault. Article 1173 of the Civil Code requires the victim who is also at fault for the occurrence or aggravation of the damage sustained by himself to share the damage accordingly with the tortfeasor. It is a general principle of comparative fault; the term "fault" on the part of victim that leads to the occurrence of the damage normally refers to negligence (but not intent) because Article 1174 of the Civil Code excludes the actor's tort liability for any harm that is caused intentionally by the victim. Specifically, Article 1192(1) of the Civil Code can be seen as an application of the general principle of comparative fault because it allocates the liability between the service provider and the service recipient based on the fault on each side for the damage that the service provider suffers during the course of the service. However, Article 1246 of the Civil Code provides an exception to the general principle of comparative fault as it allows the animal keeper or custodian's fault-based liability to be reduced only when the victim has intentionally caused the damage (which is also an exception to Article 1174). Moreover, in terms of strict liability set out in Articles 1239, 1240, and 1245 of the Civil Code, the TLB requires the victim to bear contributory liability only when the damage is caused by his gross negligence. In other words, mere negligence on the part of the victim will not help the tortfeasor reduce its liability in those strict liability torts.

Therefore, the multi-tier liability system represents a complicated framework of tort liability under Chinese tort law. First, the second-tier "joint and several liability" covers different scenarios where the law requires the multiple tortfeasors to jointly bear tort liability to the victim for different reasons. Typical joint tort (Article 1168), accessory tort (Article1169(1)), joint dangerous act (Article 1170), and quasi-joint tort (Article 1171) are the four traditional scenarios that give rise to joint and several liability in tort law. However, the TLB has also established policy-driven joint and several liability in relation to specific torts (as illustrated in Table 7.4). For example, Article 1195(2) and Article 1197 of the Civil Code require the negligent ISP and the infringing internet service user to jointly bear tort liability to the victim in cybertort; Article 1203 and Article 1204 require the manufacturer and the seller to jointly bear product liability for defective products; such a liability can be either attributable to the manufacturer, the seller, the transporter, or the warehouse. Articles 1211, 1214, and 1215 require the entity with whom a motor vehicle is associated; the transferer of an illegally assembled or a below-the-standard motor vehicle; and the thief, robber, or snatcher of a vehicle to bear joint and several liability with the negligent vehicle user. Hence, the establishment of joint and several liability in the specific torts must be understood and applied in the light of the relevant policy objectives that they aim to achieve.

Secondly, the third-tier "several liability" also contributes to the complexity of the tort liability framework under Chinese tort law. The victim cannot claim full compensation for the damages that he has sustained and his claim for compensation is limited to the liability that the tortfeasor bears. Because the TLB has adopted the vague wording "corresponding liability" regarding several liability, the judges have much discretion to decide how to allocate tort liability between multiple tortfeasors by considering the nature and extent of each one's several liability. This will create considerable room for disagreement in tort litigation. Moreover, the fourth-tier "supplementary liability" is unique to the Chinese tort law because the tortfeasor who bears supplementary liability serves as statutory guarantee for the primary tortfeasor. Compared to joint and several liability, supplementary liability is not in favor of the victim because a supplementary tortfeasor in these circumstances can argue that the victim must have exhausted the assets of the primary tortfeasor before claiming compensation from him. Moreover, in practice, judges may further limit the supplementary liability of the tortfeasor to a certain percentage of the total damages sustained by the victim, thus putting the victim in a more unfavorable legal position.[38]

Finally, I treat contributory liability on the part of the victim as part of the tort liability framework under Chinese tort law because it substantially affects the extent of tort liability of the tortfeasor. From the language of Article 1173 of the Civil Code, contributory liability may be imposed on the victim no matter whether the tortfeasor is subject to the fault-based liability or not. However, the TLB has generated the following unsettled issues that await clarification: first, can the party who bears non-fault-based "liability for reimbursement" use contributory

[38] For example, in *Wen Qiong* v. *Li Hongbin, Li Guanlin, Miaomingshi Dianbaqu Diyitan Youle Zhongxin and Miaomingshi Dianbaiqu Binhai Lvyou Fuwu Youxian Gongsi* (2020) 粤09民终70号, the plaintiff was injured due to Li Hongbin's negligent driving a beach motorcycle borrowed by Li Guanlin from the third defendant on the premises managed by the fourth defendant. The court held that the fourth defendant should bear supplementary liability for its breach of the duty of maintaining safety and limited its supplementary liability to 30 percent of the total damages suffered by the plaintiff.

negligence as a defense to reduce the liability? Moreover, since only Articles 1239, 1240, and 1245 of the Civil Code require "gross negligence" on the part of the victim in relation to torts based on strict liability, does it mean that the tortfeasor in other torts based on strict liability under the TLB is entitled to claim contributory liability when the victim was merely negligent? Also, should Article 1174 of the Civil Code be applied by analogy when the victim's damage is aggregated due to his own intentional act? These pending issues also contribute to the complexity of the tort liability framework under Chinese tort law.[39]

7.4 Approaches to Developing Chinese Tort Law in the Era of the Civil Code

7.4.1 Judicial Interpretations of the SPC

Judicial Interpretations as a source of law have played an active and significant role in developing Chinese tort law since the General Principles of Civil Law, either by introducing new tort legal principles to fill the gap of the laws made by the national legislature[40] or by providing detailed interpretations on the ambiguous or unsettled legal issues in response to the practical demand for clarification.[41] It has been a common practice that the SPC would issue judicial interpretation soon after the promulgation of a new law was made by the national legislature.[42] In relation to the TLB, the SPC has made thirteen sets of judicial interpretation since the promulgation of the Civil Code in May 2020. Among them, six are amendments to the previous judicial interpretations in order to accommodate the relevant rules revised by the TLB and another seven are brand new (Table 7.5 below). Those with

[39] It is noteworthy that Article 1217 of the Civil Code adds a new rule that a moto vehicle driver's liability for compensation should be mitigated in noncommercial carpooling cases, unless the driver causes the damage intentionally or by gross negligence. This provision also reduces the tortfeasor's liability due to the nature of the activity (i.e., noncommercial carpooling) but not due to comparative fault on the part of the victim.

[40] Such as the Judicial Interpretation on Issues concerning the Determination of Compensation Liability for Mental Suffering Damages in Torts.

[41] Such as, the Interpretation on Issues concerning the Application of Law in Determining Liability for Medical Injury Cases (关于审理医疗损害责任纠纷案件适用法律若干问题的解释), which was promulgated by the SPC on December 13, 2017 (effective December 14, 2017, amended December 29, 2020).

[42] Ding Chunyan, "Judicial Activism of Provincial Courts in China: Medical Negligence Law as a Case Study" (2019) 7(3) *Chinese Journal of Comparative Law* 505–36 at 506.

Table 7.5 *The SPC's judicial interpretations regarding the TLB (May 2020 to December 2021)*

SPC's judicial interpretations regarding the TLB	Issuing/amending date
Guiding Opinions on the Adjudication of Intellectual Property Civil Cases Involving E-Commerce Platforms	September 10, 2020
Reply on Issues concerning the Application of Law to Disputes over Internet-related Intellectual Property Right Infringements	September 12, 2020
Opinions on Legally Imposing Heavier Punishments for Infringements of Intellectual Property Rights	September 14, 2020
Judicial Interpretation on Issues concerning the Determination of Compensation Liability for Mental Suffering Damages in Torts	Issued March 8, 2001, amended December 29, 2020
Reply on Issues of Whether the Victim of Product Liability Cases Can Sue the Brand Owner of the Product in Civil Proceeding	Issued July 4, 2002, amended December 29, 2020
Interpretation on Issues concerning the Application of Law for the Adjudication of Cases on Compensation for Personal Injury	Issued December 26, 2003, amended December 29, 2020
Provisions on Issues concerning the Application of Law in Adjudicating Civil Disputes Involving Infringements of the Right of Dissemination on Information Networks	Issued November 26, 2012, amended December 29, 2020
Provisions on Several Issues concerning the Application of Law in Adjudicating Civil Disputes over Infringements of Personal Rights and Interests through Information Networks	Issued August 21, 2014, amended December 29, 2020
Interpretation on Issues concerning the Application of Law in Adjudicating Disputes on Environmental Tort Liability	Issued 09/02/2015, amended 29/12/2020
Interpretation concerning the Application of Punitive Damages in the Adjudicating Civil Cases Involving Infringements of Intellectual Property Rights	02/03/2021
Reply on Issue concerning the Defendant's Claim for Compensation of Reasonable Expenses Based on the Plaintiff's Abuse of Right in the Cases of Intellectual Property Right Infringements	03/06/2021
Provisions on Issues concerning the Application of Law in the Adjudication of Civil Cases Relating to Processing of Personal Information by Using the Facial Recognition Technology	27/07/2021
Interpretation on the Application of Punitive Damages in the Adjudication of Ecological Environmental Tort Cases	01/12/2022

"Interpretation" (解释), "Provisions" (规定), or "Opinions" (意见) in the title are the SPC's formal judicial interpretations that include written provisions similar to statutes made by the legislature, while those with "Reply" (批复) in the title are the SPC's official reply to specific legal questions that lower courts submitted for clarification and guidance.

These judicial Interpretations constitute an important and useful source of law of Chinese tort law. For example, Article 1185 of the Civil Code simply provides that punitive damages are available where intellectual property rights are intentionally infringed under serious circumstances. The SPC then issued the Interpretation concerning the Application of Punitive Damages in the Adjudicating Civil Cases Involving Infringements of Intellectual Property Rights on March 2, 2021,[43] which includes seven provisions that covers the meaning of intent and relevant factors for ascertaining the intent of the actor, the relevant factors for determining "serious circumstances," and the approaches to deciding the amount of punitive damages. This judicial interpretation has largely mitigated the problem of the general and vague language of Article 1185 and provided helpful legal guidelines for judges and legal practitioners in dealing with punitive damages in intellectual property tort cases.

However, judicial interpretations of the SPC normally focus on a specific tort or a specific legal issue. Moreover, the SPC has its policy priority in setting up the agenda to make judicial interpretations. For example, the newly made judicial interpretations regarding the TLB shows that the SPC has given a special priority to tort cases involving internet-related infringements of intellectual property rights since the promulgation of the Civil Code (Table 7.5).

7.4.2 Soft Case Law

Although Chinese law is primarily a civil law jurisdiction, cases made by the higher level courts are persuasive in judicial practice. There are three types of cases that are supposed to have practical significance in China: the SPC's guiding cases (指导案例), gazette cases (公报案例), and typical cases (典型案例). However, these selected cases are limited in terms of

[43] The Interpretation concerning the Application of Punitive Damages in the Adjudicating Civil Cases Involving Infringements of Intellectual Property Rights (关于审理侵害知识产权民事案件适用惩罚性赔偿的解释) was promulgated by the SPC on March 2, 2021, effective March 3, 2021.

the number and coverage of legal issues. For example, as of 6 December 2021, the SPC has only issued 20 guiding cases, 70 gazette cases, and 97 typical cases of tort disputes (excluding the cases of intellectual property right infringements) since the 1980's.[44] Given more than two million tort lawsuits annually occurring in the country since 2013,[45] these selected cases account for a very small portion of real tort cases.

Chinese tort law adopts an open-ended model. Article 120 of the Civil Code provides that a person is entitled to claim tort liability against the tortfeasor when the latter infringes the civil rights and interests of the former. This provision echoes Article 1164 of the Civil Code, which defines the application scope of the TLB: that is, to regulate all civil relationships arising from the infringement of the civil rights and interests of others. Theoretically, tort liability may arise from any infringement of the civil rights and interests protected by the Civil Code. The specific civil rights and interests are illustrated in Chapter Five (titled "Civil Law Rights") in the Book on General Part of the Civil Code, which sets out a variety of civil law rights as well as civil interests. Specifically, civil rights include personality rights, right to personal data, personal rights based on the marital or familial relationship, real rights, obligation rights, intellectual property rights, succession rights, shareholder rights, and other investor rights. Civil interests include those associated with physical freedom, human dignity, data, and virtual assets. Moreover, Article 126 of the Civil Code is a catch-all provision that covers all other civil rights and interests as provided by the law. Because the scope of civil rights and interests as defined is elastic and open-ended, the scope of tort liability becomes open-ended as well.

The open-ended nature of the scope of tort protection makes the case law a necessary component in the development of Chinese tort law. Take the infringement of obligation rights as an example. It is true that obligatory rights are civil rights codified in the Civil Code. Nevertheless, the issue of whether an infringement of an obligatory right by a third-party amounts to a tort and thus gives rise to tort liability must be answered through a careful study of relevant cases. In the case *Su Yongli* v. *Yunnan Gaosheng Lianhe Touzi Youxian Gongsi*,[46] the High Court of Beijing held that a third party owes a duty not to knowingly harm a lawful and certain obligatory right. It further reasoned that

[44] The data are from the Case Database of PKU Law (www.pkulaw.com/case/).

[45] National Bureau of Statistics, *China Statistics Yearbook* (Beijing: China Statistics Press, 2014–2017). The data are from the Yearbook Database of CNKI (www.cnki.net).

[46] The case docket number: (2017) 京民初24号.

Article 2 of the TLL (the equivalent to Article 1164 of the Civil Code) does not exclude obligatory rights from the scope of civil rights and interests protected by law; a third party should bear tort liability for the harm caused to property rights and interests (财产权益) linked to an obligatory right when such a right is lawful and certain, and the third party has acted in a manner that is contrary to the public policy and acted to the detriment of the victim knowingly that doing so would cause harm. Soon, the SPC also confirmed the tort liability for the intentional infringement upon obligation rights. In the case *Zhongguo Changcheng Zichan Guanli Gufen Youxian Gongsi Jilinsheng Fengongsi v Jilinshi Zhongxiao Qiye Xinyong Danbao Jituan Youxian Gongsi*,[47] the SPC held that the TLL protected the civil subject's lawful personal and property rights and interests; a lawful and valid obligatory right fell within the creditor's lawful property rights and interests; therefore, it should be protected by law, and nobody should infringe upon it without justification. However, because obligatory rights are relative rights and unknown to the outsiders due to a lack of publicity, the court ought to be cautious in holding a third party liable in tort for infringement of an obligation right, which should only be the last resort. When a third party knew or ought to have known the existence of an obligatory right, yet intentionally harmed such a right either through violation of the relevant law, regulation or enactment that aims to protect the creditor, or contrary to public policy, he should be liable for compensating the creditor for the harm unrecoverable from the liable contracting party. Therefore, the judiciary has deliberately narrowed the scope of tort liability by supplementing an additional requirement that obligatory rights must be intentionally harmed in a manner either violating the law intended to protect the victim or contrary to public policy, thus adjusting the open-ended model of Chinese tort law in practice.

Similarly, due to the open-ended model of Chinese tort law, soft case law will also be instructive to answer the issue of whether pure economic interests fall within the scope of civil interests protected by the Civil Code and whether the intentionally or negligently inflicted economic losses are recoverable or the issue of whether other personality interests associated with personal liberty and human dignity (such as reproductive liberty) are recovered in Chinese tort law. Hence, to have a comprehensive understanding of Chinese tort law, tort legal principles developed and embodied by the soft case law should not be overlooked.

[47] The case docket number: (2017) 最高法民终181号.

Moreover, as noted in the above discussion, the TLB has generated many unsettled doctrinal issues that urge clarification or solution. For example, Article 1176 of the Civil Code has introduced the defense of "voluntary assumption of risk" into Chinese tort law. Accordingly, a tortfeasor is not liable for his negligence in causing the harm during a recreational or sports activity when the victim voluntarily participates in the activity that comes with certain inherent risks. He will, however, be liable if the harm was caused by his intentional act or gross negligence. However, this provision also produces a new issue of whether the defense of voluntary assumption of risk provided therein can be claimed by analogy by the tortfeasor in a tort not occurring in a recreational or sports activity (such as accepting a ride from a drunk driver). Another example is that the TLB is silent on the illegality as defense, which may arise in real cases. For example, should a driver be allowed to claim damages suffered in a traffic accident when he was in possession of small quantities of cannabis at that time or when he was driving a getaway car after a burglary? Therefore, I suggest that Chinese tort law be developed through soft case law in the era of the Civil Code. At least significant legal principles developed through cases should be consolidated and formally integrated into the SPC's judicial interpretations.

7.5 Conclusion

The Book on Tort Liability of the Civil Code has provided a basic legal framework of Chinese tort law and established a compensation system, an imputation system, and a multi-tier liability system in line with the Chinese characteristics. It has also refined some legal principles regarding cybertorts, motor vehicle traffic accidents, and environmental torts. However, Chinese tort law as codified in the Civil Code is far from satisfactory because the Book on Tort Liability contains quite a number of unsettled legal issues that await clarification or solution. Both judicial interpretations and soft case law will play an important role in addressing these unsettled issues, thus developing Chinese tort law in the era of the Civil Code. Moreover, due to the open-ended scope of tort liability and the flexibility of judicial interpretation and soft case law, Chinese tort law has the potential to effectively respond to emerging tort issues or new types of torts under the influence of social changes and advanced technologies, such as breach of privacy relating to the use of web crawler technology, infringements of virtual assets, etc. We can reasonably foresee a dynamic evolvement of Chinese tort law for the years to come.

8

Causation in the Chinese Civil Code

A Comparative Law Appraisal

MARTA INFANTINO AND WEIWEI WANG

8.1 Introduction

Our contribution focuses on the treatment of causation in the newly adopted Chinese Civil Code (CCC), reviewing it in light of recent developments in both Chinese and continental European legal scholarship and case law. After some remarks on the role that legislation can play in governing the assessment of causation (Section 8.2), we will examine from a comparative perspective the location and breadth of provisions on causation in the CCC (Sections 8.3 and 8.4), as well as the contents of some specific rules, such as those on the victim's contribution to the harm suffered (Section 8.5) and on multiple tortfeasors (Sections 8.6–8.7). As highlighted in the Conclusions (Section 8.8), what the CCC says, and, perhaps more importantly, what it does not say, on causation is not only largely concordant with continental European legislative and interpretive choices but also shows a deep awareness of the relentless dynamics underlying tort law discourses and practices.

Before getting there, a few caveats are needed with respect to the terms of our comparative exercise. In regard to the CCC, our analysis is mostly centred on rules contained in Book VII ('Tort Liability') of the Code, the contents of which are largely similar to those of the Chinese Tort Liability Law of 2009 (TLL). Chinese texts were consulted in their original language by one of the authors and in English translation by the other author.[1] Since the core of our analysis lies in the CCC, we selected the continental European legal systems as the relevant locus of comparison.[2]

1 The transliteration and translation in English of Chinese names, titles and law reviews were done by Weiwei Wang.

2 The term 'Europe' will be used in this chapter for continental European countries.

This choice is grounded in the circumstances that European countries share with China, including their roots in the civil law tradition and a common faith in a top-down approach to legislation.

8.2 Causation and Codification

Comparative law research on causation in tort law has long made clear that, in all jurisdictions belonging to the civil law tradition, legislators play a very small role in the making of causation rules.

In countries with codified law, the black-letter words of the civil codes usually set out the general architecture of the private law system. Yet, these codes give very limited guidance about what causation is and how it should be assessed.[3] While it is undeniable that, from the French Civil Code to the latest European codifications, there has been a trend towards increasing statutory attention to problems of causation;[4] the expansion in the number of statutory rules has not changed the fact that, in the realm of causation, legislative provisions are the lodestar neither of legal theory nor of legal practice. On the contrary, it is doctrinal debates and judicial opinions that, although in different forms across countries, make up the pillars of causation reasoning, providing answers to causal questions.[5]

This of course does not mean that legislation has no say in the way in which a legal system approaches causation issues. The few rules that codes devote to causation help to effectively channel scholarly reflections and judicial practices. Moreover, there is undoubtedly a correlation between the general requirements of a country's tort law and the space and the role reserved in that country for causation analysis. As shown by many studies in jurisdictions where the general provisions for negligence liability rely solely on the elements of fault, damage and causation, the latter element ends up working as a filter for claims that elsewhere would

[3] For an overview of the mentioned trend, see Marta Infantino, 'Causation Theories and Causation Rules', in M. Bussani and A. J. Sebok (eds.), *Comparative Tort Law. Global Perspectives*, 2nd ed. (Cheltenham: Edward Elgar, 2021), p. 264 at 271–73; Anthony M Honoré, 'Causation and Remoteness', in *International Encyclopedia of Comparative Law* (Tübingen: Mohr Siebeck, 1971), vol. XI, ch. 7, 11, note 91.

[4] Infantino, 'Causation Theories and Causation Rules', pp. 287–88.

[5] For a tentative list of causal questions, see Marta Infantino and Eleni Zervogianni, 'The Place and Space of Causation', in M. Infantino and E. Zervogianni (eds.), *Causation in European Tort Law* (Cambridge: Cambridge University Press, 2017), pp. 3, 12.

be evaluated through the lens of other requirements of liability for negligence, such as duty of care and wrongfulness.[6]

Yet, there is also little doubt that the way in which causation is understood and employed by scholars and courts depends on a variety of factors that may or may not be enshrined in legislation. Such factors may include the aims pursued by the tort law system, the breadth given to non-tort law remedies (e.g., contract law and compensation schemes), the degree of creativity and policy-making that judges are entrusted with, the comparative models by which a given system is influenced, the deeply rooted assumptions about for what one should blame others and what one should accept as inherent risks in life and so on and so forth.[7]

All the above does not mean that any attempt to govern causation assessments by legislation is futile; it rather serves as a reminder that, in this field more than in others, legislation – even in codified jurisdictions – is not the central place where tort law rules and remedies are defined and administered. As we will see, it seems that the drafters of the CCC were fully aware of this. Let us see why, starting from drawing a map of causation rules in the CCC.

8.3 The Place for Causation

Following the approach of the TLL, Book VII of the CCC provides eight general rules about causation, dealing with multiple tortfeasors (arts. 1168–1172), with the victim's comparative and contributory fault (arts. 1173–1174) and with third parties' acts (art. 1175). Other specific causation rules, mostly about multiple tortfeasors, are then contained in the ensuing chapters of the same Book VI on particular liability regimes.[8] These rules are completed by a few provisions of Chapter VIII ('Civil Liability') of Book I, focusing on multiple debtors and force majeure (arts. 177–178 and 180). Additional rules on multiple debtors (arts.

[6] Cf. Cees van Dam, *European Tort Law*, 2nd ed. (Oxford: Oxford University Press, 2013), p. 309; on the same lines, see Christian von Bar, *The Common European Law of Torts* (Oxford: Oxford University Press, 2000), vol. II, pp. 436 f.; see also, for some refinements, Marta Infantino and Eleni Zervogianni, 'Unravelling Causation in European Tort Laws. Three Commonplaces through the Lens of Comparative Law' (2019) 83 *Rabels Zeitschrift* 647–73.

[7] Infantino and Zervogianni, 'Unravelling Causation in European Tort Laws', 665–72.

[8] For a list of these rules, see Section 8.6. A special mention here goes to art. 1230 CCC, which, in case of environmental harm, establishes a presumption of causation that defendants should rebut in order to avoid liability.

519–520), hardship and force majeure (arts. 533 and 590), compensation of foreseeable losses (arts. 583–584) and creditor's comparative negligence in both causing and failing to mitigate his losses (arts. 591–592) are contained in Book III on contracts.

The issue of topography of causation rules is relevant because causation is a requirement for both contractual and tort liability. This means that a preliminary problem that all code drafters have to face is where they should best place causation in the Code: in the section devoted to contract law, in the section on tort law or in the general part (if any)? Which rules should be placed where? From what we just saw, the CCC adopts a mixed approach. A few general rules on causation are in Book I, some specific provisions are located in Book III on Contracts, while issues that are more specific to tort law are in Book VII.

Rather than being exotic, this mixed solution is very common, at least among the European codifications.[9] In Europe, a few codes place causation rules under the heading of contractual or tort liability only,[10] while others deal with causation in a section devoted to obligations or liability in general.[11] Yet the majority of European codifications adopt a mixed approach, treating causation in more than one section – most often discussing how to assess causation and the victim's contribution to the harm under the heading of obligations in general and then dictating special rules on multiple tortfeasors under the tort law section. For instance, in the German BGB of 1900, § 254 BGB on victim's contributory fault is included in Division I ('Subject Matter of Obligations') of the Book II on the 'Law of Obligations', while §§ 830 and 840 on multiple tortfeasors are in the Title 27 ('Torts') of Division VIII ('Particular Types of Obligations') of the same book. The main rules of causation in the Italian Civil Code of 1942 – arts. 1223, 1225 and 1227 – are located in Title I ('Obligations in General') of Book IV ('The Law of Obligations'),

[9] The text of European rules on causation are collected in Ken Oliphant and Barbara C. Steininger (eds.), *European Tort Law. Basic Texts*, 2nd ed. (Vienna: Jan Sramek Verlag, 2018); Infantino and Zervogianni, 'Causation in European Tort Law', pp. xxvii–xlx.

[10] In the French Civil Code (CC) of 1804, causation rules are mostly to be found under the section devoted to 'breach of contract': see arts. 1231–1233 (former 1150) and 1231–1234 (former 1151). In other codifications, causation rules are mostly dealt with in the section devoted to tort law: see arts. 51 and 53 Bulgarian Law on Obligations and Contracts (LOC) of 1950; arts. 926–927 Greek CC of 1946; arts. 6.279, 6.280 and 6.282 Lithuanian CC of 2000.

[11] For instance, §§ 1301–1304 of the Austrian ABGB of 1811 are in a chapter on 'The Law of Compensation and Satisfaction', common to contractual and tortious liability.

but they should be coordinated with art. 2055 on multiple tortfeasors, which is in Title IX ('Torts') of the same book.[12]

Against such a comparative picture, it seems that the CCC is aligned with many of the existing European codifications. The CCC deals with complex obligations with multiple debtors in general in Book I; it then devotes some provisions on multiple debtors in Book III and adds many special rules in Book VII – a choice that is understandable since the thorniest issues about multiple debtors arise in the context of tortious obligations. Force majeure is discussed in Book I, given that impossibility is a defence to both contractual and tortious liability, and again in Book III, while it is not addressed in Book VII. By contrast, the victim's comparative negligence, which is also an issue that often arises in cases of contractual liability, is dealt with in the Books III and VII on Contracts and Torts but not included in Book I. As it happens in continental European codifications, the task of fleshing out the relationships between these general and special provisions and of determining their precise scope of application is left to the interpretations of scholars and courts.

8.4 The Space for Causation

Apart from deciding where to place rules about causation, another fundamental question for lawmakers concerns the issues that ought to be covered by the Civil Code.

We already mentioned that European codifications are rather concise on the point of causation and attempt neither to provide guidance as to how causation should be intended nor to address the whole possible range of causation problems. The only qualification is that the reluctance to provide a legal discipline for causation has diminished through time. While regulation of causation in older codes is quite minimal, newer texts tend to offer a higher number of provisions covering a variety of possible problems of causal assessment.[13]

The CCC fully fits into this trend. On the one hand, like European codes and like its predecessor, the TLL, the CCC refrains from defining what causation is and from entering into the debate about the criteria against which it should be assessed – a debate that in recent decades was

[12] Along the same lines, cf., the place of causation rules in the Dutch BW of 1992 (arts. 6:98, 6:99, 6:106), the Polish CC of 1964 (arts. 361 and 441), the Portuguese CC of 1966 (arts. 490, 497, 563, 570) and the Romanian CC of 2009 (arts. 1351, 1352, 1369–1371).

[13] Marta Infantino, 'Causation Theories and Causation Rules', pp. 287–88.

particularly heated in Chinese legal scholarship, especially between supporters of the so-called necessity theory and supporters of the so-called adequacy theory, and eventually ended up with the victory of the latter.[14]

On the other hand, following the path taken by some of the most recent European codifications, as well as by the TLL,[15] Book VII of the CCC contains special rules on multiple tortfeasors (arts. 1168–1172), on the victim's negligent and malicious contribution (arts. 1173–1174) and on third parties' intervening acts (art. 1175). In particular, the Code establishes joint and several liability in cases of multiple authors of the harm (art. 1168), of aiding and abetting (art. 1169), of indeterminate defendants (that is, cases where the plaintiff is able to prove that his injury was tortiously caused by one or more persons within the group of potentially tortious actors but is unable to identify which particular person(s) caused it: art. 1170) and of cumulative causation (that is, cases in which the harm is caused by concurrent events, each of them sufficient to cause the harm: art. 1171). Liability, by contrast, is several in cases in which many tortfeasors contribute to producing different portions of the final harm, provided that the extent of their contribution can be clearly determined (art. 1172). The CCC also establishes that, in cases in which the victim played a role in causing the injury, his negligence should be taken into account as a factor limiting the defendant's liability (art. 1173), while his malicious contribution fully exempts the defendant from

[14] Ming Fang (方明), 'On the Restructuring of Causation Theories in Chinese Tort Law' ('论我国侵权法因果关系理论的构建') (2011) 11 *Shangdong Social Science* (*山东社会科学*) 68–71 (supporting the adequacy theory); Kexiang Zhao (赵克祥), 'The Comparison of the Concepts of Causation in Philosophy and Tort – From the Perspective of Philosophy' ('侵权法上因果关系概念辨析 – 哲学视角为出发点') (2008) 5 *Journal of Kunming University of Science & Technology (Social Science)* (*昆明理工大学学报(社会科学版)*) 32–37 (discussing the limitations of the necessity theory); Yumin Zhang and Yisong Li (张玉敏, 李益松), 'Reflections on the Causation Theories in Chinese Tort Law' ('侵权法上因果关系理论的反思') (2005) 6 *Journal of Yunnan University (law edition)* (*云南大学学报(法学版)*) 1–8 (discussing different causation theories and supporting the adequacy theory); Zhibing Zhou (周植赟), 'Critical Evaluation and Restructuring of Causation Theories in China' ('我国侵权法因果关系理论的批判与重构') (2003) 1 *Journal of Ocean University of China (Social Science)* (*中国海洋大学学报(社会科学版)*) 82–85 (defending the introduction of adequacy theory into Chinese tort law).

[15] See arts. 8–14 TLL. For a comparative analysis of the rules brought by the TLL, see Ken Oliphant, 'Uncertain Causes: The Chinese Tort Liability Law in Comparative Perspective', in L. Chen and C. H. (Remco) van Rhee (eds.), *Towards a Chinese Civil Code: Comparative and Historical Perspectives* (Leiden: Martinus Nijhoff, 2012), pp. 395–408; Helmut Koziol and Yan Zhu, 'Backgrounds and Key Contents of the New Chinese Tort Liability Law' (2010) 1 *Journal of European Tort Law* 328 at 341–42.

liability (art. 1174), as it does a third party's act amounting to a *nova causa interveniens* (art. 1175).

The final picture is one in which no general guideline is given as to the core foundation of causation; the CCC says nothing about the tests against which causation should be affirmed and about the factors that should help in defining which consequences can be attributed to the defendant and which cannot (and who bears the burden of proof and what is the applicable standard of proof). There are instead a few rules dealing with recurring or difficult problems of multiple contributions to the harm, some of which will be investigated later on. What should be stressed now is that the CCC purportedly leaves several issues unaddressed. Among such instances, one might think, for example, of the extent of liability of malicious defendants, of cases of multiple non-sufficient causes (that is, cases in which the harm is caused by concurrent events, each of which is not per se sufficient to cause the harm), of cases in which a natural factor not amounting to force majeure contributes to the production of the injury and of cases in which the final harm is rendered extraordinarily more severe than expected due to a pre-existing concealed disposition of the victim.

Such a legislative restraint, with regard both to the CCC and the TLL, was criticized by many commentators, who noted that the Chinese legislators missed the opportunity 'to clarify the many uncertainties which are discussed in nearly all legal systems'.[16] We respectfully disagree with this conclusion.

If there is a lesson to be learned by causation in European codified tort law (as we saw above in Section 8.2), it is that the task of elaborating tests and factors for assessing causation and of devising special causal rules – such as those applying to malicious defendants, multiple non-sufficient

[16] Koziol and Zhu, 'Backgrounds and Key Contents of the New Chinese Tort Liability Law', 341. On the same lines, see also Pinghua Zhang (张平华), 'An Analysis of Liability of Multiple Tortfeasors in the Civil Code' ('"民法典" 多数人侵权体系及相关法律适用问题') (2020) 5 *Southeast Academic Research* (东南学术) 37–46; Lixin Yang (杨立新), 'Research on the Convergence of Tort Liabilities' ('论侵权责任并合') (2017) 34(2) *Studies in Law and Business* (法商研究) 101–12, at 101; Zhongyuan Li (李中原), 'Appraisal and Distribution Model for the Liability of Multiple Tortfeasors on the Basis of Comparative Fault' ('论与有过失前提下多数人侵权责任的评估和分担模式') (2016) 33(1) *Studies in Law and Business* (法商研究) 82–94, at 82; Rongxia Zhang (张荣霞), 'Reflection on "Jointly" in Case of Multiple Authors of Harm" ('共同侵权之"共同性" 反思') (2016) 11 *Academic Exchange* (学术交流) 73–78; Oliphant, 'Uncertain Causes', 396; Mo Zhang, 'Tort Liability and Torts Law: The New Frontier of Chinese Legal Horizon' (2011) 10 *Richmond Journal of Global Law & Business* 415 at 437.

causes, contribution of natural factors and victims' fragility – is always taken up by scholars and judges. Causation is a flexible requirement, whose assessment can be made only against the background of the issues that, under the circumstances of each kind of situation, end up being the most relevant to the liability claim – be they the nature and extent of the losses claimed by the plaintiff, the magnitude of the risk posed by the defendant's activity, the number of potential and actual victims and tortfeasors, the availability of alternative remedies and/or of insurance coverage, the functions that judges assign to tort law and to themselves, as well as policy reasons of various kind.[17] Needless to say, scholars and courts perform this role in dissimilar ways across different jurisdictions, adopting styles that might be more or less openly policy-oriented and paying diverse degrees of respect for each other and for the black-letter law. But what remains valid is that many, if not most, of the basic ingredients of the causation recipe are not determined by statutory provisions.

In fact, the legislative restraint of the CCC as to causation in general is to be praised because it allows flexibility in causal judgments. At the same time, the silence of the Code on the notion of causation in general and the criteria to be employed to assess does not leave courts without guidance, since Book VII pays attention to specific causal problems that are more frequent or harder to solve. We will now go into more detail on some of them – namely, the role of the victim's predispositions (Section 8.5) and issues involving multiple tortfeasors (Sections 8.6 and 8.7).

8.5 The Victim's Contribution to the Harm

According to arts. 1173 and 1174 of the CCC, the victim's contribution to the harm might operate as a full or partial defence to liability, depending on whether the victim acted negligently or maliciously. The CCC thus embraces a general principle that, whether codified or not,[18] is widely shared by continental European (contract and) tort laws. In particular, under art. 1174 CCC (former art. 27 TLL) the defendant's liability is

[17] Infantino and Zervogianni, 'Unravelling Causation in European Tort Laws', 661–62.

[18] The majority of European codifications provide an express rule in this regard, but the principle is accepted even in jurisdictions in which it is not codified: Marta Infantino and Eleni Zervogianni, 'Summary and Survey of the Results', in Infantino and Zervogianni (eds.), *Causation in European Tort Law*, pp. 587, 654–57.

excluded 'for any damage intentionally caused by the victim'.[19] Under art. 1173 CCC (former art. 26 TLL), the defendant's liability may be mitigated when the victim 'is also at fault for the occurrence or aggravation of the same damage to himself'. A similar rule applies to the creditor's own fault in contractual liability (art. 592 CCC).

In this regard, it is interesting to note what the CCC does not regulate. For instance, art. 1174 CCC avoids specifying what is meant by 'any damage intentionally caused by the victim', leaving it unclear as to which forms of plaintiff's intentional misconduct the provision refers. The literal meaning of the provision seems to always exclude liability when the victim knowingly contributed to producing the final harm. Yet, Chinese literature regarding art. 27 TLL makes it clear that the notion of the victim's intention is to be interpreted restrictively, referring only to cases in which the plaintiff deliberately harmed himself.[20] This means that courts are open to appreciate the victim's 'intentional' act against the circumstances of the case, which is not different from what happens in continental European legal systems.[21]

As to art. 1173 CCC, it says nothing about what happens in the quite frequent cases in which the victim's own predispositions (that is, victim's physical or psychological features, such as a concealed condition, latent disease or susceptibility to disease), combined with the defendant's act, give rise to an extraordinarily serious personal injury that the latter could not have reasonably anticipated. Yet, the so-called eggshell skull rule, which prohibits consideration of the victim's pre-existing predispositions as a factor reducing defendant's liability, is well-known in the Chinese legal system. The Chinese Supreme People's Court officially adopted this position in 2014, when it included the decision *Rong* v. *Wang &*

[19] The victim's intentional act is further mentioned as a defence available to the defendant by several other provisions: cf. arts. 1237–1240 and 1245 CCC.

[20] See Mo Zhang, 'Tort Liability and Torts Law', 460 (with regard to the TLL). On the complex meaning of 'intention' in Chinese tort law, see Hao Jiang, 'Chinese Tort law: Tradition, Transplants, and Some Difficulties', in Bussani and Sebok (eds.), *Comparative Tort Law*, pp. 397, 415–16; Mo Zhang, 'Tort Liability and Torts Law', 434–37, 460–61.

[21] In continental Europe, the principle that the victim bears the loss she intentionally caused is (generally uncodified and yet) widely agreed. The principle is however flexibly understood and applied; it does not preclude recovery, for instance, in cases in which the tortfeasor, who had a duty to take care of the self-harming victim, failed to do so or acted maliciously, knowing that his behaviour would stimulate the self-damaging reaction of the victim: Marta Infantino, *La causalità nella responsabilità extracontrattuale. Studio di diritto comparato* (Bern: Stämpfli, 2012), pp. 132–33, 227; Honoré, 'Causation and Remoteness', p. 131.

Yongcheng Insurance Company in the series No. 24 of its Guiding Cases.[22] In this case, the defendant, a car driver, ran over the plaintiff, an old woman who was crossing the street on the crosswalk lines. The first instance court admitted the expert opinion that assessed the victim's osteoporosis as a causative factor at 25 per cent of her harm. On the basis of this evidence, the court reduced the victim's award for damages by 25 per cent. Upon the claimant's appeal, the Intermediate People's Court of Wuxi Municipality clarified that the victim's old age and her predispositions to osteoporosis could not be taken into account as a factor mitigating the liability of the defendant, also considering that the latter was in breach of traffic rules, while the plaintiff was not.

It should however be noted that, outside the realm of traffic accidents, the principle seems to have little application. Following the publication of *Rong* v. *Wang & Yongcheng Insurance Company*, many Chinese courts have refused to see the decision as a proclamation of the applicability of the 'eggshell skull' rule in all tort law litigation and have rather opted, in non-traffic cases, for treating the victim's predispositions as a causal factor that might reduce the defendant's liability.[23] This approach seems

[22] Wuxi Binhu Dist. People's Court, *Rong Baoying* v. *Wang Yang & Yongcheng Property Ins. Ltd., Jiangyin Branch*, 8 February 2013, at http://cgc.law.stanford.edu/guiding-cases/guiding-case-24/ (in English). Besides the power of adopting quasi-legislative guidance opinions that interpret and clarify the law for lower courts (under art. 127 of the 1982 Chinese Constitution and art. 32 of the Organic Law of the People's Courts of the People's Republic of China), the People's Supreme Court also regularly selects exemplary local decisions and publishes them in order for all local courts nationwide to follow: see Jinting Deng, 'The Guiding Case System in Mainland China' (2015) 10 *Frontiers of Law in China* 1; Ding Qi, *The Power of the Supreme People's Court: Reconceptualizing Judicial Power in Contemporary China* (London: Routledge, 2020).

[23] See Tong'an District Court (Xiamen), *Du Moumou* v. *Chen Moumou et al.* (selected by the Supreme People's Court on 25 July 2014 as one of the four model cases), at www.lawinfochina.com/display.aspx?id=17631&lib=law&EncodingName=gb2312 (in both English and Chinese) (a eighty-eight-year-old man was knocked down by the minor defendant on the streets nearby his residence home. The plaintiff broke his bones, was hospitalized and died six months later because of an infection caused by the fractures; according to the District Court, the victim's predisposition was a factor that contributed to his death for 50 per cent); Hefei Intermediate Court (Anhui), He Min Yi Zhong Zi, No. 00571 Civil Decision (2014) (the plaintiff, while working for the defendant, was stung by a bee and died; the court found that the plaintiff's physical sensitivity contributed for 25 per cent to cause his death); Hezhou Intermediate Court (Guangxi autonomous zone), He Min Yi Zhong Zi, No. 138 Civil Decision (2014) (while a couple was quarrelling with the victim, the latter fell to the ground abruptly; despite hospitalization, the victim died. The court found that the couple's tortious conduct triggered the victim's death but held that the latter was mainly caused by the victim's own predispositions). See also Peng Sun (孙鹏), 'Reconsideration and Deconstruction of the Egg-shell Skull Rule' ('"蛋壳脑袋"规

to have been confirmed by the Supreme People's Court, which in October 2020 included the decision *Liu Minglian, Guo Lili and Guo Shuangshuang* v. *Sun Wei & Lanting Property Management Co. Ltd* in the series No. 142 of its Guiding Cases.[24] In the case, the victim was a sixty-seven-year-old man who was caught pickpocketing two eggs in a supermarket. He suddenly died during the ensuing quarrel with the supermarket employees. The wrongful death action brought by the relatives of the victim against the supermarket was dismissed by the first instance court, which found that the resort to self-help by the supermarket's employees was legitimate and had no causal effect on the victim's death. The decision was confirmed on appeal by the intermediate court of Nantong city and then included by the Chinese Supreme People's Court in the series No. 142 of its Guiding Cases. Such a restrictive approach towards the universal application of the egg-shell skull rule has been applauded by the majority of legal scholars. However, legal scholars have also invited the Supreme People's Court to identify the situations in which the victim's predispositions might play no role and to provide Chinese judges with plausible standards for deciding cases involving aggravated harm due to the victim's predispositions.[25]

In continental Europe, none of the existing codes have an express rule on fragile victims. Nevertheless, scholars and courts generally agree that the defendant has to 'take the victim as he finds him' – in other words, he shall be held liable even though the plaintiff's weakness made the injury greater than would have normally been the case. The rationale underlying this conclusion is that one cannot expect the fragile victim either to refrain from any social activity, to always wear special protections to

则之反思与解构') (2017) 1 *China Legal Science* (中国法学) 268–87 at 270; Yinpo Xu (徐银波), 'Tort liability for Causing Harm to Victims of Particular Predispositions: On the Basis of No. 24 Guding Case Series of the Supreme People's Court' ('侵害特殊体质者的赔偿责任承担—从最高人民法院指导案例24号谈起') (2017) 6 *Law Science* (法学) 64–78 at 65–66; Xiaowei Yu, 'Causal Uncertainty in Chinese Medical Malpractice Law – When Theories Meet Facts' (2016) 9 *Tsinghua China Law Review* 23–62 at 48–50.

[24] Xinyang Pingqiao District People's Court, *Lui Minglian GuoLili and Guo Shuangshuang* v. *Sun Wei & Lanting Property Mangement Co. Ltd., Xinyang branch*, 30 December 2019, at www.court.gov.cn/fabu-xiangqing-263591.html (in Chinese).

[25] Sun, 'Reconsideration and Deconstruction of the Egg-shell Skull Rule', 282–87; Xu, 'Tort Liability for Causing Harm to Victims of Particular Predispositions', 64–67. There are also authors who support the general use of the egg-shell skull rule: see, for example, Xiao Cheng (程啸), 'The Victim's Special Constitution and the Mitigation of Tort Liability – A Commentary on the Guiding Case No. 24 of the Supreme People's Court' ('受害人特殊体质与损害赔偿责任的减轻 – 最高人民法院第24号指导案例评析') (2018) 1 *Chinese Journal of Law* (法学研究) 67–86, at 82–86.

protect himself from the risk of accidents or to inform potential defendants of his special morbidity. Moreover, it is stated that the discrepancy between the defendant's negligence and the extraordinary consequences it generated is, in these cases, less significant than the imbalance between the victim's innocence and the gravity of these consequences the latter suffered.[26]

What should be stressed, however, is that, in continental European legal thought and practice, the rule and its rationale are to be appreciated in the context of each case. European courts are reluctant to apply the principle that 'the tortfeasor shall take the victim as he finds him', for instance, when the victim cannot demonstrate with certainty that the extraordinary magnitude of the loss is due to his concealed fragility or when the defendant proves that he was slightly negligent or that the accident simply anticipated the exceptional consequences that the victim, sooner or later, would have suffered anyway because of his exceptional conditions.[27]

In other words, absent statutory provisions indicating otherwise, continental European courts acknowledge that the defendant should answer for all of the consequences stemming from his conduct, even if they are due to the concealed morbidity of the victim. Yet, similarly to what happens in China, European courts are ready to abandon such a rule when there are reasons justifying a different outcome.

8.6 Multiple Tortfeasors: General Rules

Besides the victim's own actions, accidents are often the result of the combination of the behaviour of multiple persons. In Chapter I ('General Rules') of Book VII, as many as five provisions of the CCC (arts. 1168–1172, largely corresponding to arts. 9–12 of the TLL) are devoted to multiple tortfeasors. In particular, art. 1168 states the general rule of joint and several liability, which is extended by the following articles to cases of aiding and abetting, indeterminate defendants and cumulative causation (respectively, arts. 1169–1171).[28] Liability is, by contrast,

26 On all the above, see the scholarly references and cases cited by Infantino and Zervogianni, 'Summary and Survey of the Results', 657–60; Ulrich Magnus and Miquel Martín-Casals, 'Comparative Conclusions', in U. Magnus and M. Martín-Casals (eds.), *Unification of Tort Law: Contributory Negligence* (The Hague; London: Kluwer, 2004), pp. 290–91.

27 Infantino and Zervogianni, 'Summary and Survey of the Results', 659.

28 Joint and several liability is also the rule in contract law: see arts. 519–520 CCC.

several when many tortfeasors contribute to producing the final harm, but the contribution of each of them can be easily determined (art. 1172). One should add to this list art. 1175 CCC (former art. 28 of the TLL), which clarifies that, when a third party's act operates as an autonomous cause of the damage, the defendant may not be held liable.

Further, a number of provisions in the ensuing Chapters of Book VII, on special liability regimes, deal with cases in which multiple persons might be sued as defendants for the same harm, not because they all contributed to cause the damage, but rather because one or more did it, while the others answer for what happened under either vicarious or strict liability.[29] In all of these instances, one or more persons are the concrete authors of the harm, and the others are involved insofar as they legally respond for such harms under the same or a different heading of liability. These cases should be distinguished from two further groups of cases where multiple persons are involved but joint and several liability is not established. In 'unreal' joint and several liability cases, the CCC allows the plaintiff to sue either the tortfeasor or another person; in case that other person makes the victim whole, he then has a right of full recourse against the original tortfeasor.[30] Still, in other cases, a person

[29] See, for instance, arts. 1197 (former art. 36(2) TLL), 1211, 1214 (former art. 51 TLL), 1215 (former art. 52 TLL), 1241 and 1242 (former arts. 74 and 75 TLL), 1252 (former art. 85 TLL) of the CCC. One should further add to the list art. 1254(1) CCC (former art. 87 TLL), which provides that, in cases in which an object falling from a building causes damage to a person and yet it cannot be determined from which apartment the object fell, 'any user of the building who may have caused the damage shall make compensation'. Differently from former art. 87 TLL, art. 1254(2) and (3) CCC provide that the manager of the building is liable for the damage caused by the fallen object if he did not adopt adequate safety measures and that the police has a duty to promptly investigate the accident. In this way, art. 1254 overcomes many limitations that affected art. 87 TLL: see Kai Feng (冯恺), 'A Systematic Interpretation of the Liability of Throwing Objects from Buildings in the Civil Code of PRC: Limitations and Solutions' ('民法典高空抛物致害责任规则的体系性解读：局限与克服') (2021) 1 *Journal of Comparative Law* (*比较法研究*) 76–89; Xinbao Zhang (张新宝) and Xintian Zhang (张馨天), 'From Article 87 of the Tort Law to Article 1254 of the Civil Code: The Improvement of the Tort Law for Harm Caused by Throwing (Falling) Objects from Buildings' ('从"侵权责任法"第87条到"民法典"第1254条："高空抛（坠）物"致人损害责任规则的进步') (2020) 6 *Journal of Comparative Law* (*比较法研究*) 91–104; Liming Wang (王利明), 'Complimenting the Rule for Harm Caused by Throwing Objects from Height' ('论高楼抛物致人损害责任的完善') (2020) 1 *Law Science Magazine* (*法学杂志*) 1–9; Xianfeng Cao (曹险峰), 'The Tort Liability Rule for Throwing Objects from Height' ('侵权法之法理与高空抛物规则') (2020) 1 *Law and Social Development* (*法制与社会发展*) 48–61.

[30] See arts. 1203 (former art. 43 TLL), 1223 (former art. 59 TLL), 1233 (former art. 68 TLL), 1250 (former art. 83 TLL) of the CCC.

who did not concretely bring about the harm and yet had some sort of duty to avoid its occurrence assumes 'corresponding' liability in case a third party causes harm to the victim; but, the person who bears 'corresponding' liability answers for his own fault and does not become a solidary debtor with the author of the harm.[31]

This complex picture prompts several considerations; we will start in this section by making some observations with regard to the general rules and then briefly move in the next section to special cases of multiple defendants.

As to arts. 1168–1172 of the CCC, their ensemble, including provisions on causal over-determination and of indeterminate defendants, seems to be inspired by a pro-plaintiff attitude and to favour joint and several liability rather than several or proportional liability (although it should be noted that, whenever it is possible to distinguish individual contributions, Chinese courts often opt for several or proportional liability awards).[32]

These rules are generally aligned with those emerging from continental European tort law, whether codified or not. In the European continent too, in cases in which the harm can be attributed to the behaviour of more than one person (other than the victim), tortfeasors' liability is joint and several, unless the contribution of each of them can be precisely determined, in which case responsibility is several.[33] Similarly, although only a few continental European countries explicitly provide for joint and several liability of those who aid or instigate others to commit a wrongful act,[34] all European countries recognize that joint and several liability

[31] See, for instance, arts. 1189, 1191 (former art. 34 TLL), 1198 (former art. 37 TLL), 1201 (former art. 40 TLL), 1209 (former art. 49 TLL), 1256 of the CCC.

[32] Cf. Zhang Pinghua, 'An Analysis of Liability of Multiple Tortfeasors in the Civil Code', 37–46; Lixin Yang, 'Research on the Convergence of Tort Liabilities', 101.

[33] Cf. § 1302 ABGB; art. 53 Bulgarian LOC; § 2915 Czech CC of 2012; § 137 Estonian Law of Obligations Act (hereinafter LAC) of 2002; § 840 BGB; art. 926 Greek CC; art. 2055 Italian CC; arts. 6:99 and 6:102 BW; art. 6.279 Lithuanian CC; art. 441 Polish CC; arts. 490 and 497 Portuguese CC; art. 1382 Romanian CC; art. 186 Slovenian Code of Obligations (hereinafter CO) of 2001. The same rule also applies in jurisdictions in which the principle is not codified: see Mauro Bussani and Marta Infantino, '西方侵权法中的多数人侵权：一种比较法的视角' ('Multiple Tortfeasors in Western Tort Law: A Comparative Outline') (2014) 35 *Journal of Soochow University* 80–93.

[34] See § 1302 ABGB; § 2915(2) Czech CC; § 830(2) BGB; art. 1781 Latvian CC of 1997; art. 422 Polish CC; art. 490 Portuguese CC; art. 1369 Romanian CC; art. 186(2) Slovenian CO. Other codifications rather specify that intentional tortfeasors are responsible for any direct damage caused, albeit unforeseeable: see art. 1231–1234 French CC; art. 82 Bulgarian LOC; art. 1225 Italian CC; art. 1107(2) Spanish CC of 1889.

should apply to cases of psychological causation, that is, to cases in which one person commits the wrong under the inducement of another.[35] When the harm is brought by an unidentifiable member of a group of people, there is little doubt that all of the people who participated in the enterprise that resulted in the harm should be jointly and severally liable, no matter which one of them actually caused it[36] – although in some countries there is a discernible trend in favour of establishing proportional liability (that is, liability only for the extent to which it is likely that each defendant caused the harm).[37] Even though few legal systems have expressly codified rules on cumulative causation,[38] there is general consensus that, when different persons put the victim at risk with the result that, had not the victim been harmed by one of them, it would have been harmed by another one, they should all be liable.[39]

Yet, the continental European practice also shows that – in line with what we described above, in Section 8.5, with regard to the victim's contribution to the harm – all the above rules are applied with some degree of flexibility.

For instance, while joint and several liability for all of the authors of the harm is the rule, it may happen that, considering each defendant's behaviour and position vis-à-vis each victim's, their respective degrees of fault, the proximity in time and the extent of the involvement of each

[35] See Mauro Bussani, 'Intention et lien de causalité dans le droit comparé de la responsabilité civile (la fable très peu convenue de la malice qui accroche)', in *De tous horizons. Mélanges Xavier Blanc-Jouvan* (Paris: Société de législation comparée, 2005), pp. 459–60.

[36] The rule is codified in several codes: see § 1302 ABGB; § 2915(1) Czech CC; § 138 Estonian LAC; §§ 830(1) and 840(1) BGB; arts. 6:99 and 6:166 BW; art. 926 Greek CC; art. 1370 Romanian CC; art. 186 Slovenian CO. But see also the references quoted by Bussani and Infantino, 'Multiple Tortfeasors in Western Tort Law', 86–89; Infantino, *La causalità nella responsabilità extracontrattuale*, pp. 157–64.

[37] The trend is discernible not only in the case law of countries, such as Austria and the Netherlands, where judges openly apply rules of proportional liability (see Bernhard A. Koch, 'Proportional Liability for Causal Uncertainty: How It Works on the Basis of a 200-Year-Old Code', in M. Martîn-Casals and D. M. Papayannis (eds.), *Uncertain Causation in Tort* (Cambridge: Cambridge University Press, 2016), pp. 67–86; Anne L. M. Keirse, 'Going Dutch: How to Address Cases of Causal Uncertainty', in I. Gilead, M. D. Green and B. A. Koch (eds.), *Proportional Liability: Analytical and Comparative Perspectives* (Berlin-Boston: de Gruyter, 2013), pp. 227–48), but also in the most recent codifications: see, for instance, § 138(3) Estonian LAC.

[38] On cumulative causation, see, for instance, § 2915(2) Czech CC.

[39] See the references in Marta Infantino and Eleni Zervogianni, 'Comparative Remarks', in Infantino and Zervogianni (eds.), *Causation in European Tort Law* (Cambridge: Cambridge University Press, 2016), pp. 270–71.

defendant, as well as the number of people involved, European courts might deny any liability for defendants who failed to prevent others from bringing about the harm, especially if the latter acted intentionally.[40]

Notwithstanding the fact that collective liability is the accepted rule in the case of indeterminate defendants, one should keep in mind that the rule is applied by courts only when the circumstances and considerations surrounding the case warrant that the plaintiff not be left uncompensated despite his loss – because, for example, the victim suffered a substantial property damage or a highly disabling, if not fatal, injury, the number of potential tortfeasors is limited and the accident occurred while the latter were engaging in a dangerous activity. When elements such as these are missing, reasons to impose collective liability cease to be compelling, and the plaintiff's impossibility in identifying with precision who actually caused his damage may have his claim rejected.[41]

Similarly, in cases of cumulative causation, the ordinary outcome of joint and several liability might be overturned, and one of the defendants might fully or partially escape liability, depending on who brought about the pre-emptive and the pre-empted cause, on whether both causes would have resulted in the same damage or in different ones, on the timing with which the pre-emptive and the pre-empted cause respectively took and would have taken effect, on the numbers of actual and potential causal sequences involved and so on and so forth.[42]

Vis-à-vis the continental European experience, the current phrasing of arts. 1168–1172 of the CCC should be praised. The provisions just mentioned have the merit of providing clear guidelines regarding how courts should establish liability in simple and in difficult cases, combining predictability with fairness, and leaving room for flexibility when needed. As such, these rules represent a commendable compromise between the desire of regulating tort law by legislation and the awareness that tort law is too wide and varied in reality to be fully captured by the black-letter rules.

Different considerations apply to special rules of the CCC on multiple tortfeasors.

[40] Bussani and Infantino, 'Multiple Tortfeasors in Western Tort Law', 89–91; Infantino, *La causalità nella responsabilità extracontrattuale*, pp. 128–38, 226–32.

[41] See the cases quoted in Infantino, *La causalità nella responsabilità extracontrattuale*, pp. 161–64.

[42] See the cases and the scholarly references quoted by Infantino, *La causalità nella responsabilità extracontrattuale*, pp. 150–57, 242–47.

8.7 Multiple Tortfeasors: Special Regimes

As we described above, in addition to arts. 1168–1172 and 1175, a number of provisions in Chapters III–X of Book VII on special regimes deal with cases of multiple tortfeasors. Some of these rules establish joint and several liability on multiple persons; others create instances of 'unreal' joint and several liability, in which the plaintiff is allowed to choose whether to sue the tortfeasor or a different subject, but the latter has a right of full recourse against the tortfeasor; still other provisions impose 'corresponding' liability on persons who breached a duty to prevent harm caused to the plaintiff by third parties but do not make them jointly and severally liable with the actual harm doer.[43]

This collection of rules is very complex and distinct from the style of drafting embraced by continental European codes. The majority of continental European codifications do not try to regulate the inner relationships between multiple liable persons under every heading of liability but rather defer to general rules on multiple tortfeasors for determinations on these relationships. General rules usually provide that, in case of joint and several liability, the inner shares of defendants' liability should be determined in light of each defendant's respective degree of fault – thus allowing those who are vicariously or strictly liable in case of damage caused by others to have a right of full recourse against the concrete authors of the injury.[44] Solving the issue once and for all through a general rule might leave greater discretion to courts but at the same time enhance the legibility and the inner consistency of the whole system.

By contrast, the approach adopted by the CCC is much more detailed and pointillistic. Rules on multiple tortfeasors cover a variety of different scenarios and make them subject to different treatments, depending on the relationships between the persons involved, the liability regime they are subject to and the ways in which their roles encroach. One might wonder to what extent such rules are to be interpreted as applications of

[43] See notes 29–31.

[44] See § 1313 ABGB; arts. 53–54 Bulgarian LOC; § 137 Estonian LAC; arts. 926–927 Greek CC; art. 2055(2) Italian CC; art. 6.280 Lithuanian CC; art. 441(2) Polish CC; art. 497(2) Portuguese CC; art. 1383 Romanian CC; art. 188 Slovenian CO. A few codes set out clearly that, in cases of vicarious liability, the person who is responsible for the act of another has a right of full recourse against the subject who concretely brought the damage in and for the acts of whom the former has to respond: cf. art. 54 Bulgarian LOC; § 840(2) BGB; art. 1384 Romanian CC.

the same general principles or rather as exceptions to them, and what is their relationship with the rules on multiple tortfeasors contained in Chapter I of Book VII. This matters because the rules enshrined in the CCC might be applied by analogy to situations different from those textually envisaged by the Code. The scenarios not covered by the CCC and yet likely to occur are manifold; it remains to be seen whether or not the provisions in the CCC will be interpreted extensively.

8.8 Conclusions

The treatment of causation in the CCC is largely in line with the legislative approaches to causal problems adopted in continental European codifications. As in Europe, the CCC treats causation both as a general principle of civil liability and as a specific tort requirement. As in Europe, the CCC refrains from defining what causation is and from stepping into the debate regarding under which theories and standards it should be assessed. As many recent continental European codes do, specific provisions are devoted to the victim's contribution to the damage and to the thorniest issues of multiple tortfeasors. As in Europe, however, many problems – such as the role of victims' predispositions – are expressly left unaddressed.

This of course does not imply that the CCC does not take an original stance on the subject matter. For instance, the CCC explicitly states many rules (such as the one on the exonerating effect of the plaintiff's intentional act) that in European codes have been determined by scholars and courts. It also provides a detailed regulation of multiple tortfeasors cases and of their relationships vis-à-vis themselves and the victim that remains far away from its civil law homologues.

What the above also shows is that the overall choices made by the drafters of the CCC as to the place and space of causation, and as to the balance between precision and flexibility, detail and simplicity, are highly understandable and plausible. Both general and specific provisions are carefully written and exceptionally designed. What the Code says, as well as what it does not say, strikes a well-balanced compromise between clear statutory guidance and substantial flexibility to maneuver in light of the specific circumstances of each case. We are eager to see how the CCC will work in practice.

9

The Aims of Tort Law across China and the West

MAURO BUSSANI*

9.1 Introduction

It has not been long since scholarly attention has been extended to tort law and its aims: it dates back to no more than two generations in China[1] and about five in the West.[2] In China, the ideas underpinning civil liability catered to the rising culture of individual rights triggered by the late 1970s' reforms; in the West, it was the statistic growth of lawsuits and decided cases during the second industrial revolution that pushed jurists to muse deeply and largely upon the role and the functions of tort law.[3] Yet, in

* I wish to thank Dr. Hao Jiang for his beneficial comments on the draft and Dr. Wang Weiwei for his valuable insights as well as for his translation into English of Chinese language wherever necessary.

1 As to the Chinese "discovery" of Tort Law – with the appearance of a set of dedicated rules in the 1986 general Principles of Civil Law – one can see Weiwei Wang, "Tort Law in China," in F. Fiorentini and M. Infantino (eds.), *Mentoring Comparative Lawyers: Methods, Times, and Places* (Cham: Springer, 2020), pp. 76 f.; Hao Jiang, "Chinese Tort Law: Tradition, Transplants and Some Sifficulties," in M. Bussani and A. J. Sebok (eds.), *Comparative Tort Law Global Perspectives*, 2nd ed. (Cheltenham: Edward Elgar, 2021), pp. 397, 408 f.

2 See Nils Jansen, "The Development of Legal Doctrine in Europe: Extracontractual Liability for Fault," in Nils Jansen (ed.), *The Development and Making of Legal Doctrine* (Cambridge: Cambridge University Press, 2010), pp. 1 ff.; Robert L. Rabin, "The Historical Development of the Fault Principle: A Reinterpretation" (1981) 15 *Georgia Law Review* 925, 945, 948; G. Edward White, *Tort Law in America*, 2nd ed. (Oxford: Oxford University Press, 2003), pp. 3 f., 16 f.; Leon Green, "Tort Law Public Law in Disguise" (1959/1960) 38 *Texas Law Review* 1, 257; as well as John C. P. Goldberg, "Twentieth Century Tort Law Theory" (2003) 91 *Georgetown Law Journal* 513, 524.

3 In order to urge practitioners, judges, and scholars to peruse the functions of a legal field and the ways worth pursuing to achieve those goals, a preliminary condition is a critical mass of disputes and a widespread knowledge about the nature of the disputes and the inner technicalities supporting their solutions. The multiplication of the accidents deemed worthy of a trial and the parallel development of the insurance industry contributed to satisfy this condition. As to China, see Cheng Xiao (程啸), "Forty-Year Chinese Tort Law" ("中国侵权法四十年") (2019) 2 *Review of Legal Studies* (法学评论) 28, 28–32, 40–41; Zhang Jun yan (张俊岩), "The Risk Society and Plural Ways of Relief for Infringement

every legal system, the problem of the aims to be assigned to tort law still is at the forefront of the debate and remains one of the core issues in the field.[4] This contribution is not a reminder of the importance of this topic; rather, it is meant to show how these debates are largely indifferent not only to history, geography, and statistics but also to the inner functioning of tort law in its official and unofficial disguises. This indifference should be overcome in cultural terms, and all the more so when at issue is an effort to understand Chinese Civil Code, a fundamental piece of the private law structure in a leading jurisdiction such as China. Chinese Tort Liability Law, the predecessor of the Tort Law Book of the Chinese Civil Code, extraordinarily listed promotion of social harmony and stability as one of the goals of tort law in its first Article. Most people would not think that such a stated aim, or any aims of tort law, has any significance beyond a mere declaratory statement. This chapter will set out to prove otherwise.

From this perspective, I will start by reviewing the intellectual history that shaped the horizon of the issue and exposing them to a series of critical remarks surfacing the existence of different accounts of the same

Damages" ("风险社会与侵权损害救济多元化") (2011) 2 *The Jurist* (法学家) 91, 91–102. As to the West, at the turn of the twentieth century, the emergence in the United States of a public debate on the aims of tort law was also due to the intellectual activism of some courts and scholars, which drove a vision of both tort law as a powerful tool of social engineering and of judges and academics as capable of promoting policy choices concurring or competing with those taken by legislators. In Europe, the birth of a thriving debate on tort law took place later than on the other side of the ocean and was due to different factors: besides a gradual differentiation in the social extraction of legal actors, it was especially the growing attention for the issues related to social welfare, and to the value of the individual well-being for the society at large, that over time prompted scholars first, and then judges, to bring tort law at the center of the legal stage. What is still radically different across the continents is what forges the legal culture and the expectations society nourishes as against the law and the legal actors. In the United States and in China (see Benjamin L. Liebman, "Watchdog or Demagogue? The Media in the Chinese Legal System" [2005] 105 *Columbia Law Review* 1, 65–157) tort law cases and scholarly discussions trickle down into the public debate where they find an intellectual and mediatic arena ready to receive and scrutinize the legal solutions and their implications. In Europe, the same cases and discussions most often remain clustered in the professional circuits inhabited by jurists only – judges, practitioners, and scholars (at the most, PhD candidates).

4 Ye Jinqiang (叶金强), "On the Basic Definition of Tort Law" ("论侵权法的基本定位") (2015) 5 *Modern Law Science* (现代法学) 63–73; Wang Zejian (王泽鉴), "The Functions of Tort Law: Compensation, Prevention, and Punishment" ("损害赔偿法之目的：损害填补、损害预防、损害制裁") (2005) 123 *The Taiwan Law Review* (月旦法学杂志) 207–19.

phenomena. I will then stress the lack of awareness about the empirical dimension of tort law, which is crucial in order to put any vision of the aims of tort law within its own proper context. Further, I will emphasize the variety of factors that, in and out of the tort law adjudication process, may affect whichever abstract theory on the aims of tort law one is willing to emphasize. Conclusions will follow with a note dealing specifically with the Book on Tort Liability in the Chinese Civil Code.

9.2 Along the Time Dimension

From both a synchronic and a diachronic perspective, one may easily find out that tort law is bent to serve a plurality of aims that can be differently prioritized according to the time, the place, and the prevailing ideology.

While in the rest of this chapter I will try to keep together the analysis of Western and Chinese legal experiences, in this section I will focus on the Western side of the picture, the only one for which historical data are at my disposal.

In the second half of the nineteenth century, Western industrialization, and the parallel and connected increase of accidents, was on the rise. At that time the thin flow of injuries occasionally caused by animals, servants, craftsmen and farmers had already become a stream that had been carrying with it the hardship of the interaction between men and machines.[5] Whereas – as the mainstream narrative goes – fault liability in common law systems surfaced through the maze of the causes of action; on the European continent, the traditional fault principle, imbued as it was with moral and subjective connotations, began with the objective standard of care the society expects any fellow countryman to meet under the given circumstances.[6] Thus, on the one hand, the principle of "no

[5] On this point, see Rabin, "Historical Development of the Fault Principle," in Miquel Martín-Casals (ed.), *The Development of Liability in Relation to Technological Change* (Cambridge: Cambridge University Press, 2010), pp. 945, 948; John Bell and David Ibbetson, *European Legal Development. The Case of Tort* (Cambridge: Cambridge University Press, 2012).

[6] On US common law, see Oliver W. Holmes, *The Common Law* (Boston: Little, Brown & Co., 1881), pp. 112–13; Lawrence M. Friedman, *A History of American Law* (New York: Simon & Schuster, 1973), pp. 261 f., 409 f.; Morton J. Horwitz, *The Transformation of American Law (1780–1860)* (Cambridge, MA: Harvard University Press, 1977), pp. 67–108; and Morton J. Horwitz, *The Transformation of American Law (1870–1960)* (Oxford: Oxford University Press, 1992; reprint 1994), pp. 13 f. (but one should consider

liability without fault" comes to mean "no liability without objective fault." On the other hand, the duty requirement and the standard of objective fault are called upon to mediate between the need of physical safety and that of productive activities, putting tort law infrastructure at the service of the laissez-faire economy postulates. In principle, therefore, the loss should lie where it falls and a (physical) injury may be compensated if, and only if, it is caused by the breach of an existing duty and/or by an objectively negligent behavior – the assessment of which is left in the hands of the judicial coteries of the time.[7]

So far we have seen the mainstream narrative. A few remarks are in order, though. Firstly, it is an overreaching statement to view the main goals of torts as an instrument to assist capital accumulation and meet the needs of the rising bourgeoisie class at the detriment of the victims of industrialization.[8] Beyond that radar screen, one finds disputes where the parties were not bringing to the fore individual safety versus business

also White, "Tort Law in America," pp. 3 f., 16 f.). On the partially different path taken by English law, see David Ibbetson, "The Tort of Negligence in England," in N. Jansen (ed.), *The Development and Making of Legal Doctrine* (Cambridge: Cambridge University Press, 2010), pp. 46, 49 ff., 57 ff. As to the continental legal experiences, see N. Jansen (ed.), *The Development and Making of Legal Doctrine* (Cambridge: Cambridge University Press, 2010), pp. 29–30, and therein the essays by Jean-Louis Halpérin (73 ff.), Nils Jansen (96 ff.), Michele Graziadei (126 ff.), Antoine Hol (164 ff.), Miquel Martîn-Casals and Albert Ruda (183 ff.), Kjell Å Modéer (212 ff.).

7 Bell and Ibbetson, "European Legal Development," pp. 59–66, 161–62, 173 ff.; Rabin, "Historical Development of the Fault Principle," pp. 959–60; Cesare Salvi, *Capitalismo e diritto civile. Itinerari giuridici dal Code civil ai Trattati europei* (Bologna: Il Mulino, 2015), p. 59. One should note that some early industrialized countries, such as England and the United States, did (and still largely do: see John C. P. Goldberg and Benjamin C. Zipursky, "The Moral of MacPherson" (1998) 146 *University of Pennsylvania Law Review* 1733, 1821–33) without a general clause on fault liability à la continental law. The task of narrowing down the scope of liability was actually fulfilled by the traditional model of typical causes of action. As to English law, see F. Harry Lawson and Basil S. Markesinis, *Tortious Liability for Unintentional Harm in the Common Law and the Civil Law* (Cambridge: Cambridge University Press, 1982), vol. I, pp. 142 ff.; in the United States, for the view following which (a wavering model of) fault liability came to replace what in practical terms was a general rule of no liability, see White, "Tort Law in America," pp. 13–15; Rabin, "Historical Development of the Fault Principle"; Gregory C. Keating, "Recovering Rylands: An Essay for Robert Rabin" (2012) 61 *DePaul Law Review* at 543, 547, 549; and Mark A. Geistfeld, "Social Value as a Policy-Based Limitation of the Ordinary Duty to Exercise Reasonable Care" (2009) 44 *Wake Forest Law Review* 899.

8 See also Duncan Kennedy, "Distributive and Paternalist Motives in Contract and Tort Law, with Special Reference to Compulsory Terms and Unequal Bargaining Power" (1982) 41 *Maryland Law Review* 563, 579: "I do not think one could show that the economy was any less 'interdependent,' commodities any less 'complex,' or people any more 'individualistic' in the early than in the late nineteenth or mid-twentieth century."

interests.[9] Further, one cannot disregard the fact that continental Europe, especially during the last three decades of the nineteenth century, saw the rise of the voice of the unions advocating for less unjust working conditions and also of the socialist ideas contrasting against the pillars of bourgeois individualism.[10] These phenomena drew the attention of scholars and judges and trickled down in the academic literature and judicial rulings where one can even find the idea surfacing (closely tied to a view of tort law as a distributive justice tool or as a substitute for the lack of a developed social insurance and security schemes)[11] that the entrepreneurs are the cheapest cost avoiders and, consequently, in principle they should be held strictly liable for the harms caused by their actions.[12] In the same decades, special statutes were enacted across Europe to establish strict liability for a variety of business activities[13] and to impose upon entrepreneurs compulsory participation in social insurance mechanisms designed in particular to address the mounting problem of workplace accidents.[14]

Moreover, there is no doubt that in the twentieth century the call for implementing a laissez-faire ideology also in the tort law realm (thereby

[9] See, for example, as to the common law strict liabilities traditionally protecting property rights (especially over immovables), Rabin, "Historical Development of the Fault Principle"; Keating, "Recovering Rylands," 584, 586, and therein further references; as to the then relatively large field of traffic accidents, see Bell and Ibbetson, "European Legal Development," pp. 111–38; Giovanni Cazzetta, *Responsabilità aquiliana e frammentazione del diritto comune civilistico (1865–1914)* (Milan: Giuffrè, 1991), pp. 327–40.

[10] Bassano Gabba, *Trenta anni di legislazione sociale* (Turin: Bocca, 1901); Gioele Solari, *Socialismo e diritto privato. Influenze delle dottrine socialiste sul diritto privato* (Milan: Giuffrè, 1980; reprint 1906); Christine Sypnovich, "The Left and the Wrongs: Marxism, Law and Torts," in M. Lobban and J. Moses (eds.), *The Impact of Ideas on Legal Development* (Cambridge: Cambridge University Press, 2012), pp. 150 ff.; see also Duncan Kennedy, "Three Globalizations of Law and Legal Thought: 1850–2000," in D. M. Trubek and A. A. Santos (eds.), *The New Law and Economic Development: A Critical Appraisal* (Cambridge: Cambridge University Press, 2006), p. 19, spec. 42 f.

[11] See in these terms, discussing the current situation in China, Liu Jinrui and Cui Jianyuan, "The Compensatory Function of Tort Liability Law," in H. Koziol (ed.), *The Aims of Tort Law. Chinese and European Perspectives* (Wien: Jan Sramek Verlag, 2017), pp. 13, 17.

[12] Michael Lobban and Julia Moses, "Introduction," in M. Lobban and J. Moses (eds.), *The Impact of Ideas on Legal Development* (Cambridge: Cambridge University Press, 2012) pp. 1, 11 ff.; José Harris, "The 'Welfare State' in Legal and Social Philosophy: Origins and Controversies," in M. Lobban and J. Moses (eds.), *The Impact of Ideas on Legal Development* (Cambridge: Cambridge University Press, 2012), pp. 75 ff. See also authors and works quoted in note 6.

[13] See Bell and Ibbetson, "European Legal Development," pp. 118 f., 173 ff., 178.

[14] See, e.g., the studies collected in Ulrich Magnus (ed.), *The Impact of Social Security Law on Tort Law* (New York: Springer, 2003).

shrinking as much as possible the scope of liability) has never gone away in the Western world. Yet, while in the common law jurisdictions we have been witnessing an incremental expansion of the scope of the tort of negligence,[15] continental Europe saw an increasing responsiveness of the judiciary (and of the legal profession as a whole) to the need of enlarging the range of interest worth protecting through contract and tort liability rules[16] and of widening the scope of strict liability and of legal devices intended to shift the cost of the injury upon the one who is better equipped to bear it.[17] All this led the continent to what has been called a change of perspective from the defendant to the plaintiff[18] and, in both Western legal worlds, to a parallel increase (some name it an "explosion")[19] of tort law litigation.[20]

9.3 Demanding Measurements

As we have seen, not everything is black or white, not even in tort law history. Understanding the overall context and its dynamics is simply necessary for any accurate analysis of this legal field (too). Across jurisdictions, the debate on the aims of tort law usually relies, instead, on

[15] Rabin, "Historical Development of the Fault Principle," pp. 959–60; Tony Weir, "The Staggering March of Negligence," in P. Cane and J. Stapleton (eds.), *The Law of Obligations: Essays in Celebration of John Fleming* (Oxford: Oxford University Press, 1988), pp. 102 ff.

[16] On this point, see, e.g., Salvi, *Capitalismo e diritto civile*, p. 93; Geneviève Viney, *Le déclin de la responsabilité individuelle* (Paris: LGDJ, 1965), pp. 7 ff.; Christian von Bar, *The Common European Law of Torts* (Oxford: Oxford University Press, 1998), vol. I, pp. 45 ff; Jansen, "Development of Legal Doctrine in Europe," pp. 15 ff.; and note 3.

[17] Bell and Ibbetson, "European Legal Development," pp. 153 ff.; Salvi, *Capitalismo e diritto civile*, pp. 59–60.

[18] George Ripert, *Le régime democratique et le droit civil moderne* (Paris: Libr. générale de droit et de jurisprudence, 1936), p. 331 ("Le droit moderne ne regarde plus du côté de l'auteur de l'acte, mais du côté de la victime"); later on, Stefano Rodotà, "Modelli e funzioni della responsabilità civile" (1984) *Rivista critica del diritto privato* 596 f.

[19] E.g., Jaap Spier, "Uncertainties and the State of the Art: A Legal Nightmare" (2011) 14 *Journal of Risk Research* 501.

[20] See, e.g., André Tunc, *La responsabilité civile*, 2nd ed. (Paris: Economica, 1981), pp. 2 f.; Francesco D. Busnelli and Salvatore Patti, *Danno e responsabilità civile*, 3rd ed. (Turin: Giappichelli, 2013), pp. 147–85; Basil S. Markesinis, "Litigation Mania in England, Germany, and the USA: Are We So Very Different?" (1990) 49 *Cambridge Law Journal* 233; George L. Priest, "The Modern Transformation of Civil Law" (2006) 54 *Buffalo Law Review* 957, 974; John G. Fleming, *The American Tort Process* (Oxford: Oxford University Press, 1991), p. 2.

all-encompassing catchphrases, such as compensation, deterrence, and punishment.

How can we assess the actual value and persuasiveness of these views in the overall contexts and dynamics that drive tort law in each society? We would need a sophisticated factual analysis perusing the conformity of the law in action to the theoretical postulates. Yet, what is missing in any of the above perspectives – be they focused on compensation, deterrence, or punishment – is precisely a close and strong connection to the ground data that shapes the day-by-day functioning of tort law.

In order to understand how the various aims of tort law are pursued in practice, many questions will need to be asked and answered. What is the ratio of tort law trials to the number of accidents? What is the ratio of damages to the GDP, to public expenditure for the justice system, and to the number of lawyers? How did the cost of access to justice filter the number and nature of the lawsuits? How many plaintiffs and defendants are women, older people, psychically or physically impaired persons, business entities, professionals, blue- and white-collar workers? Who are the successful plaintiffs and the successful defendants? What is the average income of plaintiffs and of defendants? What is the ratio of coverage of social insurance and of first- and third-party liability insurance across the cohorts of plaintiffs and defendants? What are the tort law claims that are successful? How many awards of damages are there? What is their size and for what kind of harm? What is the difference, if any, in prices of goods and services before and after liability has been established against product manufacturers and service providers? And the list could go on.

In some countries, some of these questions are specifically addressed but not always put in perspective with the debate on the aims of tort law.[21] In most countries, those data are simply missing.

Still on the empirical side of the legal picture, another series of remarks is worth our attention. Some efforts have been made to reconcile the appropriate goal of tort law with the quantitative dimension of the analysis in the context of law and economics. Law and economics scholars advocate that whenever wrongful behaviors create a private loss,

[21] See, e.g., Michael Faure, "Economic Optimization of Tort Law," in H. Koziol (ed.), *The Aims of Tort Law* (Wien: Jan Sramek Verlag, 2017), pp. 79, 94–96, 99–100; Ben C. J. van Velthoven, "Empirics of Tort," in Michael Faure (ed.), *Tort Law and Economics* (Cheltenham: Edward Elgar, 2009), p. 453.

the magnitude of which differs from the resulting social loss, the victim should not necessarily be compensated. Only the portion of the private loss (if any) that amounts to a social cost should be subject to liability.[22] But what is a "social loss"?[23]

It is often said that any damage may amount to a social loss inasmuch as it corresponds to a loss of the total wealth of the society as a whole.[24] Now, to narrow down a wide debate, the latter argument might prove true in cases of physical harm, where there usually is a correlation (not always direct or clear) between an action and the extent of the private and social cost of the harm. But this is not always the result of tortious conduct. As it has been pointed out,[25] for example, when an unlawful behavior interrupts the production process of a manufacturing firm, the firm's lost profits are not necessarily social costs, given the possible presence of other firms who could enter the market or expand its production making up the foregone output of the incumbent firm with the supply of perfect substitutes at comparable or even lesser cost. Others observe that, if an incumbent monopolistic firm loses part of its market share to a competitor selling the same product at a lower price as a result of a tort committed by the latter, the alleged tort, while

[22] See Steven Shavell, *Economic Analysis of Accident Law* (Cambridge, MA: Harvard University Press, 1987), pp. 135–40; Jennifer Arlen, "Tort Damages," in B. Bouckaert and G. De Geest (eds.), *Encyclopedia of Law and Economics* (Cheltenham: Edward Elgar, 2000), vol. II, pp. 682 f.

[23] In general, on the intricacies of the notion of social loss, see, e.g., Yu Yan and Michael Faure, "Recovery of Pure Economic Loss in China: Current Situation, Problems, and Future Prospect" (2020) 11 *Journal of European Tort Law* 286, 308–13; Mauro Bussani, Vernon V. Palmer, and Francesco Parisi, "Liability for Pure Financial Loss in Europe: An Economic Restatement" (2003) 51 *American Journal of Comparative Law* 113, 132–34.

[24] See William Bishop, "Economic Loss in Tort" (1982) 2 *Oxford Journal of Legal Studies* 1–29; Shavell, "Economic Analysis of Accident Law"; Arlen, "Tort Damages"; Guo Mingrui and Bi Xiaoxiao, "The Main Function of Tort Liability Law of the People's Republic of China: To Prevent, to Deter and to Punish Tortious Conduct," in H. Koziol (ed.), *The Aims of Tort Law* (Wien: Jan Sramek Verlag, 2017), pp. 43, 44. Cf. Mario J. Rizzo, "A Theory of Economic Loss in the Law of Torts" (1982) 11 *Journal of Legal Studies* 281. One should take stock, however, of the direct impact that any harm may have on the GDP via the services and goods that may be produced to make up for it. See some references in Mauro Bussani, *L'illecito civile* (Naples: Edizioni scientifiche italiane, 2020), pp. 152–54.

[25] See Shavell, "Economic Analysis of Accident Law."

occasioning the victim's lost profits, may actually be at the origin of a social welfare gain.[26]

Other examples could follow from this "empirical" perspective. But, while the validity of its conceptual framework remains generally undisputed, the question we asked earlier is still awaiting an answer: How can we seriously identify and measure a social loss? Except for some theoretical models, we do not have a clear and accurate picture of what a social loss actually amounts to, given the great variety of circumstances that the real life of torts supplies to our analysis. Therefore, without that clear and accurate picture, most of the arguments assigning the aim of punishing, or compensating, or deterring the occurrence of a "social loss" are largely doomed to remain a rhetorical exercise – at its best an intriguing academic debate.

9.4 On and Off the Grid of Official Law

The foregoing is not all. The mainstream analyses are usually oblivious also to another crucial phenomenon – the pre- and extrajudicial dynamics of tort law.

As an abundance of literature both in China and the West has pointed out, not all potential claims become lawsuits.[27] People may be unaware that their claims may give rise to a legal remedy, people may think that their claims are *de minimis*, or that it is not socially acceptable for them to pursue their interests further. For instance, victims with ongoing social or economic relationships with their wrongdoers might not be at ease with the idea of vindicating their rights publicly against their counterparts. People may also be suspicious of the fairness of the judicial system, or they may lack the resources necessary to fight back.[28] Some, however,

[26] See, e.g., *supra* note 22. Arlen, "Tort Damages."

[27] See Su Li (苏力), *Read the Order* (*阅读秩序*) (Shandong: Shandong Educational Press (山东教育出版社), 1999), p. 111; Wang, "Tort Law in China," pp. 83–87. In the West, the "Urtext" of these analyses, mainly focused on tort law, are the articles of William L. F. Felstiner, Richard L. Abel, and Austin Sarat, "The Emergence and Transformation of Disputes: Naming, Blaming, Claiming . . ." (1980–1981) 15 *Law & Society Review* 631–54, esp. 633–37, 641; and of Richard E. Miller and Austin Sarat, "Grievances, Claims, and Disputes: Assessing the Adversary Culture" (1980–1981) 15 *Law & Society Review* 525, 543–45. Among later studies, see Mauro Bussani and Marta Infantino, "Tort Law and Legal Cultures" (2015) 63 *American Journal of Comparative Law* 77–108.

[28] As to China, Xin He, Lungang Wang, and Yang Su, "Above the Roof, Beneath the Law: Perceived Justice behind Disruptive Tactics of Migrant Wage Claimants in China" (2013) 47 *Law &Society Review* 703, 718–27 (reporting migrant workers' suspicion of the

do complain, typically to the human agency they think is responsible for the losses they incurred. Many of these complaints are satisfied in whole or in part because the concerned human agency straightforwardly assumes responsibility for what happened, issues an apology, and/or voluntarily pays compensation or restores the situation existing prior to the wrong – either personally or through the insurer. In all these scenarios, the matter may be resolved without ever reaching the courthouse. But if the complaints are not redressed, they become legal disputes that go into the hands of lawyers. Among the disputes that reach these actors, some of them are abandoned, and some end up in a courtroom – in fact, as is well known, many filed cases result in settlements and only a small fraction of them reach the trial stage, eventually becoming decided cases.[29]

fairness of the judicial system); Michael Ng and Xuanming Pan, "Nonprofessional Access to Justice in Rural China: A History of Atypical Legal Development and Legal Service Provision" (2017) 17 *The China Review* 59, 77–79 (reporting China's regional disparities in legal resources and legal development). In the Western literature, Roderick A. MacDonald, "Access to Civil Justice," in P. Cane and H. M. Kritzer (eds.), *Oxford Handbook of Empirical Legal Research* (Oxford: Oxford University Press, 2012), pp. 492, 510–15; Austin Sarat, "Access to Justice" (1981) 94 *Harvard Law Review* 1911, 1916–17; see also Gideon Parchomovsky and Alex Stein, "The Relational Contingency of Rights" (2012) 98 *Virginia Law Review* 1313, 1352–55.

29 See also David Engel, "The Oven Bird's Song: Insiders, Outsiders, and Personal Injuries in an American Community," in Mary Nell Trautner (ed.), *Insiders, Outsiders, Injuries, and Law: Revisiting "The Oven Bird's Song"* (Cambridge: Cambridge University Press, 2018), pp. 8 f.; Barbara Yngvesson, "Emulating Sherlock Holmes: The Dog That Didn't Bark, the Victim Who Didn't Sue, and Other Contradictions of the 'Hyper-Litigious' Society,'" in Mary Nell Trautner (ed.), *Insiders, Outsiders, Injuries, and Law: Revisiting "The Oven Bird's Song"* (Cambridge: Cambridge University Press, 2018), pp. 38 f. As to China, see Carl F. Minzner, "China's Turn Against Law" (2011) 59 *American Journal of Comparative Law* 935, 943–48 (reporting that Chinese authorities promote mediation as the key to solve all disputes). One can add that in China, civil cases that are settled by Chinese courts usually result in mediation agreements. These agreements have the same legal value as court decisions and orders. However, unlike the latter two, mediation agreements become effective immediately after the parties sign them (Article 97 of Chinese civil procedure law of 2017) while court decisions and orders would take fifteen days and ten days to become effective after the parties receive them, respectively (Article 164 of Chinese civil procedure law). Once mediation agreements, court decisions, and orders become effective, the parties cannot appeal them anymore. However, with regard to mediation agreements (excluding meditation agreements for divorce), if a party can prove that the agreement violates the principle of free consent or a relevant law, he/she can request a new trial, which is known as "a trial supervision proceeding" (Articles 200, 201 and 202 of Chinese civil procedure law). See, e.g., Feng Yujun and Peng Xiaolong, "China's Dispute-Resolution Mechanisms and Innovation in the Transformation Era" (2015) 3 *China Legal Science* 3, 14.

Such a picture prompts several considerations,[30] but for the purpose of this chapter, it makes clear that many claims falling under the umbrella of state law (and of its circuits of adjudication) ultimately remain outside of it. As we have seen, reasons are manifold, but the point still is that a great number of (official law-grounded) potential claims are caught by unofficial mechanisms of conflict avoidance and dispute settlements and are administered daily outside of courts, that is, outside the reach of State apparatuses.[31] All of these also urge one to take stock of how the set of rules, doctrines, and procedures produced by official legal actors may only provide the starting point of any research about the disputes arising in a society,[32] about the tort law in force, and about its aims.[33]

[30] See, e.g., Bussani and Infantino, "Tort Law and Legal Cultures," 89–90.

[31] Insurance companies alone absorb a substantial fraction of potential tort law controversies, providing routinized and widely available procedures for dealing with compensation problems (see, among many others, Parchomovsky and Stein, "The Relational Contingency of Rights," 1352–55; Richard Lewis, "Insurance and the Tort System" (2005) 25 *Legal Studies* 85, 88; Michael J. Saks, "Do We Really Know Anything about the Behavior of the Tort Litigation System – And Why Not?" (1992) 140 *University of Pennsylvania Law Review* 1147, 1213 f., 1222 f. But many cases do not even reach insurance companies. Even when insurance coverage is available, claims may not mature, or disputes may be abandoned or settled (before they enter into any formal level of complaint) according to unofficial rules and mechanisms on how to redress injuries. See the works cited in note 28; and as to China, Ke Li, "Relational Embeddedness and Socially Motivated Case Screening in the Practice of Law in Rural China" (2016) 50 *Law & Society Review* 920, 921–22, 941–43 (at 922 the author underscores "the importance of the context-specific norms and ethics in shaping legal services at the grassroots level" with specific reference to local norms and practices in rural China, which include "*mianzi* (face), *renqing* (human emotions), *lishang wanglai* (reciprocity), and *huzhu* (mutual assistance).")

[32] See Su Li (苏力), *Read the Order* (阅读秩序) (Shandong: Shandong Educational Press (山东教育出版社), 1999), p. 111. See also Susan Falk Moore, "Law and Social Change: The Semi-Autonomous Social Field as an Appropriate Subject of Study" (1973) 7 *Law & Society Review* 719, 729 ("many of the pressures to conform to 'the law' probably emanate from the several social milieu in which an individual participates. The potentiality of state action is often far less immediate than other pressures and inducements") and at 743 ("The law (in the sense of state enforceable law) is only one of a number of factors that affect the decisions people make, the actions they take and the relationships they have. Consequently, important aspects of the connection between law and social change emerge only if law is inspected in the context of ordinary social life").

[33] "[L]aw belongs to society before it belongs to the state. The modern era had reduced the law by making it a province of the state and it [is] now the time to return it to society's embrace": Paolo Grossi, *A History of European Law* (Malden: Wiley, 2010), p. 141. Should we take unofficial law seriously, we could also question whether we have to start with teaching unofficial law(s) in our schools. We could do it including the topic in some "Law & . . ." course, or we could expose our students to the different dimensions of private law in ad hoc courses focused on the nature, inner dynamics, and actual

This holds true in the West as well as in China. In the latter's legal system too, statutory rules do not paint the whole picture.[34] Despite the mainstream view that Westernization equals modernization, internationalization, and a bright economic future, in the 1990s, scholars started realizing that complete Westernization is not always compatible with the customs and conventions in the Chinese society.[35] Zhu Suli is representative of these scholars. According to Zhu, the Westernized law as official law is not well accepted by many local communities and does not reach the rural areas of the country where different sets of rules based on customs are at work.[36] Such rules are not official laws and yet, according to Zhu, are laws with legitimacy and are widely accepted by the villagers. More importantly, official law and legal institutions provide "an undersupply of remedies" and their "product" does not fit the needs of the people.[37] Zhu used the plot from a well-known movie, *The Story of Qiuju* (秋菊打官司), to make the argument that Westernization with a complete disregard of China's own legal tradition lacks reasonableness and that China should rely on its own indigenous resources in law-making.[38] In the movie, the wife of a villager persistently sought official channels to sue the head of the village for kicking her husband in the genitals in response to an offensive comment about the village head not being able to have a son.[39] All that she asked was that the village head issue an apology and acknowledge that what he did was wrong. In her mind, the village head had the right to kick her husband but just not in the genitals.[40] Zhu concluded that such a request had no legal basis in the eyes of lawyers who have received formal Western legal training and yet it was a reasonable claim.[41] According to the author's line of thought, the

functioning of non-State legal sets. Both ways we would provide students with a reservoir of knowledge that – it may be – is not going to swell their wallet (in the short run) but may certainly enrich their critical approach to the law and its multiple dimensions, as well as allow them to approach global legal phenomena with a less Western-centric naïve attitude.

[34] Hao Jiang, "Chinese Tort Law," p. 397.

[35] 朱苏力(Zhu Suli), *法治及其本土资源 (Rule of Law and the Indigenous Resources)* (Peking: Peking University Press (北京大学出版社), 2014), 3rd ed,.

[36] See ibid., 33–34.

[37] See ibid., 34–35.

[38] See ibid., 25–40.

[39] See ibid., 25–26.

[40] See ibid.

[41] See ibid., 30–31.

remedies provided by the Westernized law are insufficient to address the problem. Unless Western law provides a functional equivalent to the customs that Chinese people hold dear to, such imported laws will never replace the customs.[42]

Above all, the foregoing reminds us once again of how any discussion on the aims of tort law should be carried out by taking into consideration the overall picture (including unofficial tort law, as well as local customs or even long-standing ideologies) and not only the pieces of case law or of legislation supporting this or that scholarly or judicial perspective.[43] Otherwise, we simply bind ourselves to the impossibility of fully understanding and scrutinizing the functioning of tort law as well as its role and aims, within and outside its own realm.

9.5 Fate and Liability

Further, even if we limit our analysis to what is debated by lawyers and adjudicated in the courts, we should be aware that tort law technicalities may work in different directions, and these directions, in their turn, may depend on a variety of factors. Illustrations could be countless.[44] Due to the limited space, I will give only a few (albeit telling) examples.

Two bikers, A and B, travel the same road a few minutes one after the other. Both get absent-minded at the very same moment when they pass by a house on the brink of the street. A regains his attention to the road again without anything happening to anyone. When B passes by the house, his absent-mindedness causes an accident. When a child runs out of the gate of the house, B has no time to avoid the child, who is run over

[42] See ibid., 38–39.

[43] See also Mauro Bussani, "Strangers in the Law. Lawyers' Law and the Other Legal Dimensions" (2019) 40 *Cardozo Law Review* 3125.

[44] See, e.g., Marc A. Franklin, "Replacing the Negligence Lottery: Compensation and Selective Reimbursement" (1967) 53 *Virginia Law Review* 774; Jeffrey O'Connell, *The Lawsuit Lottery: Only the Lawyers Win* (New York: Free Press, 1979); Patrick S. Atiyah, *The Damages Lottery* (Oxford: Hart, 1997). In my view, however, any reference to the tort adjudication process in terms of "lottery" does not represent per se a devastating (let alone a definitive) critique. Rather, it sounds like a reminder that an accurate and bias-free analysis is ever needed for any legal field, which, like (official) tort law, filters the actual relevance of rights and duties through the judicial apparatus, its cost of access, its technicalities, and its inner functioning.

by the bike and has his finger broken. It may be that the judge will find the child's fault concurring with that of B; but even so, B will waste time and money in a dispute that A will never be part of. What distinction can one find between the two cases if not the good/bad luck of the two bikers? What function does tort law pursue in adjudicating B's case and leaving A scot-free: punishing bad luck, compensating at least partially the child, giving the right incentive to prevent absent-mindedness, or rewarding good luck?[45]

Not so dissimilar are the issues arising from the very same facts – that is, A and B again, two bikers, travel the same street a few minutes apart and get absent-minded for a short while. This time, however, B runs over the CEO of a bank group, while A injures a tramp. Both are right-handed victims that have their right arms broken. The same degree of fault for the two bikers, the same injury caused by them, but B is certainly exposed to a much higher claim for compensation than A.[46]

Is it acceptable that the different destiny of A and B is determined only by the wealth of the victim?[47] And again, what function is tort law pursuing in adjudicating the two cases: punishing bad luck, compensating the market price of the broken arm, giving the right incentive to prevent absent-mindedness, or rewarding good luck?

Similar puzzling questions about the aims of tort law arise also if one of the two bikers is covered by a third-party liability insurance and the other is not, or if – turning away from the above example – the victim is

[45] See, e.g., Thomas Nagel, *Mortal Questions* (Cambridge: Cambridge University Press, 1979), p. 29.

[46] See Parchomovsky and Stein, "The Relational Contingency of Rights," 1352–55; Jules L. Coleman, *Risks and Wrongs* (Oxford: Oxford University Press, 1992), p. 304.

[47] Coleman, *Risks and Wrongs*. The Chinese Supreme Court's interpretation regarding issues arising in the adjudication of personal injury cases (2003) urged judges to shape the award considering the victim's *Hukou* (i.e., the households' register), which distinguishes between rural and urban average annual income standards, as provided by the statistical agency of the province where the court is situated in. See Wang, "Tort Law in China," pp. 87–89. "The heavy criticism received by the Interpretation led, in 2022, the Supreme Court to abandon the previous orientation and to stand for unifying personal injury compensation standards across urban and rural areas in the same province. See the Supreme People's Court's Decision on Amending 'the Supreme People's Court's Interpretation on Several Issues Concerning the Application of the Law in the Trial of Personal Injury Compensation Cases', (最高人民法院关于修改〈最高人民法院关于审理人身损害赔偿案件适用法律若干问题的解释〉的决定), May 1, 2022."

unable to identify the wrongdoer; or does not have the financial resources to defend his/her right in court; or when judges award damages that are burdensome for a middle-income defendant, irrelevant for a wealthy individual, or unbearable for a destitute one; or whenever judges award only nominal damages to "compensate" an injury to one's own dignity, which often is the only valuable asset belonging to the plaintiff.[48]

9.6 The Pursuit of Harmony and Stability

Needless to say, to all the questions and issues I sketched so far there is not a single answer or solution, nor is there an answer or solution to be considered "just" no matter where and when. The foregoing remarks, along with the critique of one-sided narratives and of the absence of a critical mass of data, on which to base any accurate analysis, were simply meant to contribute to drive the debate on the aims of tort law in a direction close to the overall contexts and respectful of the variety of issues that shape the daily life of tort law.

I have a final note, however, and it specifically concerns the Chinese codification process.

The Chinese tort law of 2009 pointed at the promotion of social harmony and stability as its primary goal.[49] I regret that this statement disappeared from the new code. I do think that the protection of social harmony and stability is one of the main goals of state law in any legal system, Western or otherwise. This is certainly true also for state-posited tort law – besides and beyond any other of its possible goals (be they compensation, punishment, or deterrence).[50] As it has been said, tort law "is itself a kind of political duty that the state owes its citizens."[51] The machinery, but also the communicative and symbolic value of the adjudication process, does contribute to preserve the social harmony

[48] See Bussani, "L'illecito civile," pp. 285–87; Mauro Bussani, "Le passé et les inconnus: quelle protection pour la vie privée?," in E. M. Belser, P. Pichonnaz, and H. Stöckli (eds.), *Le droit sans frontières. Mélanges pour Franz Werro* (Bern: Stämpfli, 2022), pp. 117, 122–24.

[49] "侵权责任法" 第一条 [Tort Liability Law of People's Republic of China (2010) Art. 1]

[50] See also Ken Oliphant, "Promoting Social Harmony and Stability as an Aim of Tort Law," in H. Koziol (ed.), *The Aims of Tort Law* (Wien: Jan Sramek Verlag, 2017), pp. 139 ff.; Glanville Williams, "The Aims of the Law of Tort" (1951) *Current Legal Problems* 137, 138–44.

[51] John C. P. Goldberg and Benjamin Zipursky, "Civil Recourse Defended" (2013) 88 *Indiana Law Journal* 569, 572.

preventing citizens – including the victims of an injury – from feeling left behind by the legal system. To put it in other terms, citizens and victims of injuries need to know that in the public space there is someone able to defend her/his rights against anyone and this is precisely what, in turn, is needed to preserve social harmony and stability.

Some commentators argue that the cultural roots of the (missing) reference to harmony and stability as one of the primary goals of tort law survive in the "liability in equity" rule – a rule that initially appeared in the 1986 General Principles of Civil Law and now is set forth in Article 1186 of the Chinese Civil Code.[52] The argument runs as follows: outside the scope of application of strict liability rules, whenever a harm is caused by the defendant but neither the victim nor the defendant is at fault, "losses shall be shared by both parties according to law" (Article 1186 Chinese Civil Code). Moreover, the defendant here can be liable for the partial loss only if he/she has the financial means. Such a rule runs counter to the principle of corrective justice that supposedly unifies the Western tort law but is in line with the distributive justice principle China has traditionally embraced as a matter of social policy.[53] The allocation of the loss is based on a comparison between the financial statuses of the victim and the alleged tortfeasor, that is, it is directly related to their respective ability to shoulder the loss. From this perspective, "liability in equity" would appear as a "regime that reflects traditional Chinese values and supplements the fault liability regime."[54]

It is still to be seen how and when the "liability in equity" rule will be implemented in the light of the new Code. What is certain is that assigning to tort law such broad aims as to promote harmony and stability, or to pursue distributive justice, always entails the "risk" of enhancing the judicial power of implementing social and economic policies. Nevertheless, this is something judges do in many parts of the world, and – with the exception of the common law planet – they usually do it in disguise, hiding the policies underpinning the rulings behind the veil of the cause of action technicalities. Therefore, keeping explicitly and officially social harmony as the main goal of tort law would simply oblige

[52] Hao Jiang, "The Three Myths of Tort Law in the Chinese Civil Code" (2021) 7 *Italian Law Journal* 713, 723–27, where one can find also the normative roots of the provision.

[53] Ibid., 723.

[54] Ibid. Others highlight the socialist moral foundation of the rule: Wang L., Zhou Y., and Gao S., *Textbook on the Tort Liability Law of China* (Beijing Shi: People's Court Press, 2010), pp. 167–69.

the judiciary to act transparently and give clear reasons for their rulings in compliance with that aim. On the other hand, supposing the existence or the fear of an overflowing judicial power – called upon to implement such a broad social and economic policy -, one can note that to contain this risk in legally and socially acceptable terms should be a task of the political system, and of the legal system as a whole, and certainly not one to be carried out by tort law all alone.

10

Classifying the Passive Appreciation of Separate Property during Marriage in the Chinese Civil Code

A Legal and Economic Analysis

JIAN HE

10.1 Introduction

10.1.1 The Classification of Passive Appreciation as a 'Boundary Issue'

In the family law literature, it is generally taken for granted that each spouse's wages, salaries and other *labour income* during marriage shall be classified as marital property or community property[1] and thereby shared by both spouses, especially in a divorce. Accordingly, the marriage is regarded as a community of (marital) labour as far as the property matters between the spouses are concerned. In most jurisdictions, the sharing of labour income is also a widely recognized rule of a statutory matrimonial regime. By contrast, there is no comparable consensus as to the classification of each spouse's *asset income* (in the broad sense)[2] during marriage.

To illustrate, suppose A bought a house and obtained a mortgage several days before his marriage. The house was registered under his own name. The total purchase price was 100,000 dollars, including a down payment (30,000 dollars) and a loan (70,000 dollars). The house will be used as a family home. A and his wife paid the mortgage every month out of their salaries during the marriage. After ten years' marriage, they got divorced. The total mortgage payment made during the

[1] Technically, marital property and community property are different terms, but both of them serve as a legal tool for the spouses to share certain assets acquired during marriage. This chapter uses the two terms interchangeably.

[2] This chapter uses the term 'income' in the broad sense, which includes both income in the narrow sense, as an independent influx, e.g., rents, bonus and appreciation (increase in value of a thing).

marriage was 55,000 dollars (including principal and interest). The remaining principal balance is 43,000 dollars (while the remaining interest balance is 12,000 dollars). At the time of divorce, the mortgage house was worth 300,000 dollars, with an increase in value of 200,000 dollars during the marriage. How much, if any, of the marital property increase in value should be shared by the spouses?

This question arises in almost every modern society. However, the answer varies from jurisdiction to jurisdiction. In the United States, for example, there are at least *seven* different rules from different states on this issue, all allowing both spouses to share that 200,000 dollars proportionally.[3] In Switzerland, where similar approach is taken, there is only one uniform rule on the proportional sharing.[4] In Germany, in contrast, the law literally would allow an equal sharing of the 200,000 dollars between the spouses; later, as the case law develops, only the 200,000 dollars minus the inflation would be shared.[5]

This chapter explores the classification of a special genre of asset income – *passive appreciation* or *natural increase* of one spouse's separate property during marriage, such as the 200,000 dollars' increase in value in the illustration above.

Asset income arises from different factors. It may go back directly to labour or asset contribution, as in the case of constructing or renovating a house. It may result purely from the market (or inflation). The increase in value in the latter case, typically an increase in housing price, is called natural increase or passive appreciation. The appreciation is passive or natural, because it is not caused by active human behaviours, such as contribution of labour or asset, but by natural or passive factors, such as the market.

By definition, passive appreciation is a very special type of income, as it is absolutely unrelated to a spouse's income; neither can it be supported by the general recognized idea that each spouse's labour income during marriage shall be shared. In this context, the classification of passive appreciation during marriage constitutes a *boundary issue* for any statutory matrimonial regime. It is an important and probably the most important part of the whole big question: apart from the labour income, to what extent shall the asset income during marriage also be shared by

[3] See J. Thomas Oldham, *Divorce, Separation, and the Distribution of Property* (New York: Law Journal Press, 2006), § 7.05.

[4] See §§ 206, 209 of the Swiss Civil Code; BGE 88 II 142; BGE 96 II 305.

[5] See §§ 1373–1378 of the German Civil Code; BGH, NJW 1974, 137.

both spouses? And why? The solution of the appreciation issue helps us to clarify not only the issue itself but also the spirit or the *ratio legis* of a statutory matrimonial regime.

10.1.2 Background: Three Features of Chinese Family Law on Property Matters

Before analyzing the appreciation issue specifically, a brief introduction of Chinese family law on property matters in general is necessary. There are at least three crucial features that a foreign observer shall not ignore.

First, regarding the sources of law, Chinese family law comprises not only statutes promulgated by the highest legislature (i.e., the National People's Congress or its Standing Committee) but also *judicial interpretations* issued by the highest court, the Supreme People's Court (SPC). This is also a common feature of the Chinese law in general.

Currently, the most important Chinese family 'law' is the fifth Book of the Civil Code of the People's Republic of China (the Civil Code),[6] the Book of 'Marriage and Family'. Its predecessor is the 1950 Marriage Law. As the first 'statute' in the history of the People's Republic of China, this law went through two revisions, in 1980[7] and in 2001 respectively, before it was codified into the Civil Code. It is worth emphasizing that the codification is primarily a compilation of existing rules, not a creation of new rules. As to Chinese family law in particular, many existing rules in the Marriage Law were basically retained in the Civil Code. So is it for the associated judicial interpretations. Before 2021, there were mainly three judicial interpretations on the Marriage Law; after 2021, they are all integrated into a new judicial interpretation.[8] Most pre-existing rules are retained, and only a few are modified or abandoned.

[6] Promulgated on 28 May 2020, effective on 1 January 2021. For the English translation of the Civil Code used in this chapter, see Lei Chen (convener), Jiangqiu Ge, Jian He, Qiao Liu, Zhicheng Wu and Bingwan Xiong, *The Civil Code of the People's Republic of China: English Translation* (Leiden; Boston: Brill/Nijhoff, 2021). There is an official English translation of the Civil Code available on the NPC's website, www.npc.gov.cn/englishnpc/c23934/202012/f627aa3a4651475db936899d69419d1e/files/47c16489e186437eab3244495cb47d66.pdf.

[7] The Marriage Law (1950) was replaced by the Marriage Law (1980).

[8] See Interpretation I of the SPC on Several Issues in the Application of the Marriage Law (Supreme Court Interpretation No. 30, 2001); Interpretation II of the SPC on Several Issues in the Application of the Marriage Law (Supreme Court Interpretation No. 19, 2003); Interpretation III of the SPC on Several Issues in the Application of the Marriage Law (Supreme Court Interpretation No. 18, 2011) (Interpretation I, II and III of Marriage

Secondly, the historical starting point of Chinese family law is unique. Under the 1950 Marriage Law, all the assets acquired before or during marriage shall be shared by both spouses in a divorce, with the only exception that the wife's premarital asset still belongs to her.[9] Given this starting point, the two revisions afterwards tend to restrict the scope of asset sharing. The revision in 1980 excluded the sharing of premarital assets and classified all the assets acquired during marriage as 'community property'.[10] The revision in 2001 confirmed this tendency and recognized more scenarios for separate property.[11] Although the 'tendency' is clear, its purpose and its justification are unclear. That partly explains why the classification of passive appreciation became a problem for Chinese family law. This problem still exists today because the classification rules on community property and separate property in the Marriage Law were merely absorbed into the Civil Code, with only a few technical changes.[12]

Thirdly, the statutory matrimonial regime in China operates normally outside Marriage Law and is applied through other family law institutions on property matters, including child support, alimony and marital tort.[13] This functional overlap is realized primarily through the special rule of community property distribution. As art. 1087(1) of the Civil Code provides, absent any agreement between the spouses, the community property shall be divided 'in light of the specific circumstances of the assets as well as in the interests of the children, the woman and the party without fault'.

Law, respectively); Interpretation I of the SPC on the Application of Book of Marriage and Family of the Chinese Civil Code (Supreme Court Interpretation No. 22, 2020) (Interpretation I on Marriage and Family).

9 See art. 23 of the Marriage Law (1950).

10 See art. 13 of the Marriage Law (1980). It is one of the most controversial issues whether the Chinese statutory matrimonial regime adopts a community property system or a marital property system. In a community property system, any specific asset as community property will be co-owned by both spouses automatically, even if it is acquired by one spouse based on a contract with a third party. That is a deviation from the general rule on property transfers, where a registration or a delivery is required in most cases. In contrast, in a marital property system, the marital property is still subject to the general rule on property transfers. In other words, the marital property system does not affect the property allocation between the spouses automatically; it only yields certain personal obligations within the relationship of spouses, especially at the time of a divorce.

11 See arts. 17, 18 of the Marriage Law (2001 revision).

12 See arts. 1162, 1163 of the Civil Code.

13 See arts. 1085, 1090, 1091 of the Civil Code respectively.

10.1.3 *The Structure*

The following sections of this chapter are constructed as follows. Section 10.2 depicts and analyzes different approaches of classifying passive appreciation of separate property during marriage under the existing Chinese law. Section 10.3 focuses on the popular yet unsuccessful arguments for the currently mainstream proportional approach. Section 10.4 suggests a new doctrinal construction of the proportional approach, the theory of joint investment, and attempts to justify it with a fairness argument, as well as a *hypothetical intention argument*, that as a default rule, the family law on the appreciation issue shall mimic what most spouses would have wanted. Further, Section 10.5 points out the defects of the hypothetical intention argument in Section 10.4 and revises it to advocate the affirmative approach, that all the passive appreciation of separate property during marriage shall be classified as community property and equally shared by both spouses. Section 10.6 concludes.

10.2 Different Approaches in Classifying Passive Appreciation

There are basically three approaches to classifying passive appreciation of each spouse's separate property during marriage, namely the 'affirmative' approach, the 'negative' approach and the proportional approach. Under Chinese law, all three exist, leading to doctrinal inconsistencies.

10.2.1 *The 'Negative' Approach: Passive Appreciation Generally as Separate Property*

The negative approach refers to the rule that any appreciation not attributable to the contribution of each spouse's labour shall be classified as separate property and therefore may not be shared by the spouses. This approach is generally applicable, as art. 5 of Judicial Interpretation III of Marriage Law prescribes:

> income of each spouse's separate property during marriage, except for its fruits or *natural increase*, shall be classified as community property. (emphasis added)

The negative approach has its roots in the aforesaid distinction between active appreciation and passive appreciation. Active appreciation comes from the contribution from marital labour, in contrast to appreciation from assets within the community property. In contrast, passive appreciation (of separate property) arises merely from the market rather than the labour contribution; therefore, it may not be shared by both spouses.

The distinction between active appreciation and passive appreciation in Chinese family law was heavily influenced by American family law.[14] In 1999, this distinction was first introduced to China by professor Yinlan Xia, a leading family law scholar and for many years the president of the Chinese Marriage and Family Law Association.[15] Soon, this distinction was accepted by at least two provincial high courts.[16] One of them adopted the term 'natural increase', which has the same meaning as passive appreciation.[17] In an influential commentary on the Judicial Interpretation II of Marriage Law published by the SPC, the aforesaid distinction in American family law was also mentioned in detail.[18] Finally, this distinction found its way into the judicial interpretation in 2011 and was adopted by the Civil Code.[19]

10.2.2 The Affirmative Approach: Especially in the Case of Investment Income

The affirmative approach recognizes appreciation of separate property as community property. It refers to the rule that even the appreciation of separate property during marriage is not attributable to the contribution of each spouse's labour, it shall be classified as community property.

[14] In American family law, passive appreciation is also known as natural increase, inherent value etc., see Marry M. Wenig, 'Increase in Value of Separate Property during Marriage: Examination and Proposals' (1989) 23 *Family Law Quarterly* 309.

[15] See Yinlan Xia, *The Contemporary Rules of Marriage and Family in the United States* (美国现代婚姻家庭制度) (Beijing: China University of Political Science and Law Press, 1999), p. 244.

[16] For a detailed review, see Jian He, 'The Effect of "Theories" on the Judicial Practices: A Review on the Judicial Distribution of the Fruits of Separate Property during Marriage' ('理论"在司法实践中的影响 – 关于夫妻个人财产婚后孳息归属的司法实践为中心') (2014) 3 *Law and Social Development* (法制与社会发展) 134–35.

[17] See art. 1(4) of Interpretation I of Shanghai High Court on the Interpretation II of the SPC on Several Issues in the Application of the Marriage Law (Senate I of Shanghai High Court, No. 24, 2004).

[18] See Songyou Huang (ed.), *Understanding and Applying the Judicial Interpretation II of Marriage Law* (最高人民法院婚姻法司法解释(二)的理解与适用) (Beijing: China Legal Publishing House, 2004), pp. 117–18.

[19] See art. 5 of Interpretation III of Marriage Law; art. 26 of Interpretation I on Marriage and Family.

Currently, this approach is only recognized in a few cases under Chinese law.

The most representative one is a case of investment income. Since 2003, it has been an established rule that investment income of each spouse's separate property during marriage is considered community property.[20] However, this rule is not consistent with the idea of community of labour. Any investment income results arise not only from the labour contribution (e.g., doing research and making investment decisions) but also from luck and market fluctuation. If we believe in the community of labour, only the part of appreciation that reflects the value of the labour contribution should be classified (proportionally) as community property, while the rest of appreciation attributable to luck or market fluctuation will still be classified as separate property.

Actually, the aforesaid tension between the classification of investment income and the idea of community labour was not ignored when the SPC first considered this issue in drafting the related judicial interpretation in 2003. The SPC considered at least the following two options: (1) investment that comes from separate property during marriage shall be purely separate property; and (2) the passive appreciation that concerns the investment income shall be separate property, except when the other spouse substantially contributes to the investment. In the end, these alternatives were not adopted. The reason is simple: investment income should not be treated differently from production income and income from business operations; and the latter two types of income are community property, as expressly prescribed by art. 17 of the Marriage Law.[21]

10.2.3 The Proportional Approach: The Case of Appreciation of a Mortgage House

The proportional approach refers to the rule that passive appreciation of separate property during marriage shall be proportionally classified as community property according to certain criteria. This approach is primarily enforced where the mortgage of one spouse's premarital house was partly or fully paid with assets from community property.

As prescribed by art. 10 of Interpretation III of Marriage Law, where one spouse made the down payment using his or her separate

[20] See art. 11(1)(ii) of Interpretation II of Marriage Law; art. 1062 (1)(ii) of the Civil Code.

[21] See Huang, 'Understanding Interpretation II', p. 109.

property and financed it with a mortgage before the marriage, yet paid the mortgage during marriage with community property, the court 'may' classify the mortgage house as the separate property of the spouse who made the purchase, as long as the house was registered solely under their name (hereinafter 'the owner spouse'). The other spouse not owning the house (hereinafter 'the non-owner spouse') is entitled to reimbursement for 'the loan paid jointly by both parties during marriage' (i.e., with the community property of either spouse) and 'the corresponding appreciation' of the mortgage house during marriage. After the promulgation of the Civil Code, this rule remains unchanged.[22]

The proportional approach does not bode well with the idea of community of labour, either. According to the latter, the appreciation of a mortgage house, usually attributable to the market, shall be classified as passive appreciation and may not be shared by the spouses. However, the proportional approach allows a (proportional) sharing between the spouses. This deviation from the general classification of passive appreciation can be partly traced back to the fact that the proportional approach was developed ad hoc for the case of distributing appreciation of a mortgage house, while its relationship with the rule on passive appreciation was not considered at all.[23] The experience, rather than the logic, dominates the development of the proportional approach.

10.2.4 The Tension between the Three Different Approaches

Both the *affirmative* approach and the *proportional* approach differ from the *negative* approach and thereby deviate from the idea of marriage as a community of labour. The tension cannot be simply eliminated by asserting that the former two approaches are simply rare exceptions of the *negative* approach. To the contrary, it is technically possible that either of the two approaches can be extended by analogy to other cases and thereby challenge the position of the *negative* approach as a general rule.

Given this inherent tension, it is worth exploring the potential arguments for a deviation from the idea of community of labour. The

[22] See art. 78 of Interpretation I on Marriage and Family.

[23] See Xiaoming Xi (ed.), *Understanding and Applying the SPC's Judicial Interpretation III of Marriage Law* (最高人民法院婚姻法司法解释(三)理解与适用) (Beijing: People's Court Press, 2011), pp. 161–65.

following sections will first focus on the arguments for the proportional approach and then arguments for the affirmative approach.

10.3 The Unsuccessful Arguments for the Proportional Approach

Before examining potential arguments for the proportional approach, it should be noted that the general rules in civil law might not support such a remedy. Where one spouse uses the community property for the benefit of its premarital mortgaged house, like paying its mortgage, neither the law of unjust enrichment nor the law of contract (based on an implied loan agreement between the spouses) would support a reimbursement beyond the actual payment made with the community property. The sharing of the home appreciation is impossible by nature. The appreciation itself is not an independent property or right. It is only part of a home that belongs to the owner, just as ownership. In this context, we now seek potential arguments in the family law for distributing the passive appreciation of a mortgaged house between the spouses.

10.3.1 Compensation for Lost Opportunity?

An important argument for passive appreciation given by the SPC is that increases in real estate prices 'increase the opportunity cost of the spouse not owning the house', causing the non-owner spouse to lose 'the best opportunity to buy a house when entering into a marriage'[24] and the 'right to benefit from owning one's own property'.[25] Therefore, the non-owner spouse shall be compensated for this loss of opportunity in the form of sharing the corresponding house appreciation.[26]

This argument is apparently inspired by the idea to compensate reliance damages in contract law, but it is fraught with logical defects.

First, important requirements for compensating reliance damages were ignored in the argument. In China, most couples would buy one and usually only one (marital) house when entering into a marriage.

[24] See Xi, 'Understanding Interpretation III', p. 163.

[25] See Xiaofang Wu, 'Hard Issues in the Contemporary Marriage and Family Law Practice' ('当前婚姻家庭案件的疑难问题探析') (2010) 1 *People's Judicature* (人民司法) 58.

[26] For a similar approach in American family law, see *Anthony* v. *Anthony*, 514 A.2d 91, 94–95 (Pa. Super. 1986) (based on the idea of compensation for the loss of opportunity, the court ruled that the spouses share equally the appreciation of the house during marriage and thereby loss of the opportunity to buy a house); Peter Sevareid, 'Increase in Value of Separate Property in Pennsylvania' (1995) 68 *Temple Law Review* 563–65.

Therefore, it would be appropriate to conclude that 'entering into a marriage' causes the non-owner spouse's loss of opportunity in buying a solely owned house. However, entering into a marriage contract itself cannot support a liability for reliance damages. Breach of contract or fault is also required. That is, for the liability of compensating the loss of opportunity, the owner spouse should at least be at fault for the divorce. Obviously, the presence of fault will change the equation entirely and does not bode well with the proportional approach. Moreover, where the non-owner spouse actually owns one extra house or more before or during the marriage, there is no loss of opportunity.

In addition, the idea of compensating reliance damages would result in a different rule from what the proportional approach is alleged to be. The amount of reliance damages in failing to buy a solely owned house is determined by many factors, including duration of marriage, funds actually available etc. In other words, it does not merely depend on the non-owner spouse's actual capital contribution in the form of paying the mortgage during marriage and therefore is not necessarily equal to the corresponding appreciation calculated based on such payments actually made.

10.3.2 Offset for Inflation?

The second potential argument for the proportional approach concerns damages to community property that are caused by inflation. For example, in an American case in 1980, it was held that the restitution of the principal (i.e., the payment made for the mortgage loan during the marriage) would be appropriate during ordinary economic periods. But, when inflation was as high as 19–20 per cent, the restitution of the principal would not be a 'true restitution' given the diminished purchasing power. Therefore, although the mortgaged house is a separate property of the owner spouse, both spouses shall be allowed to share the house appreciation, as a community property, during the marriage in proportion to the respective capital contribution.[27]

This argument treats the proportional sharing of passive appreciation as an alternative to the statutory interests available for a monetary restitution claim. However, its defect lies in the fact that the inflation rate is not usually equal to the rate of increase in housing value. Where

[27] *McCoy* v. *Ware*, 25 Wn. App. 648, 651 (1980) (Roe, J., concurring). This opinion was later affirmed by relevant precedents. See *In re Marriage of Elam*, 97 Wn. 2d 811, 817 (1982).

the disparity is gross between the two rates, as was the case in the past decades for China, this equation will be questionable.

10.3.3 Restitution of Active Appreciation?

The third potential argument sees the proportional approach not as a distribution of passive appreciation but as a restitution of active appreciation. That is the majority view in the Chinese scholarly literature. Some scholars, for example, hold the simple view that the appreciation of a mortgaged house during marriage is 'inseparable from the other spouse's contribution'[28] or that it is 'not attributable to the inflation, but the efforts and contribution of the other spouse'.[29] This is obviously unconvincing.

The relatively persuasive analysis focuses on the fact that the continuous payment of the mortgage during the marriage helps the spouses prevent foreclosure, so that they may enjoy the home appreciation. In this context, such appreciation is 'the result of the spouses' joint efforts' or 'the result of the natural increase and both spouses' joint contributions'.[30] But that does not make sense either. By definition, the appreciation or the increase in home value must be deemed passive appreciation, because it is purely attributable to the market, not to the labour or capital contribution. Paying the mortgage during the marriage itself does not contribute to the appreciation, but merely to its allocation, ensuring that it is enjoyed by the owner spouse, not a third party. However, the contribution in this sense is not related to the definition of active or passive appreciation.

The judicial practice in China does not support the classification of the mortgage house's appreciation as an active appreciation, either. According to the Supreme Court commentaries and articles written by its judges, the SPC never addressed the issue, let alone admitted such a

[28] See Pei Hua, 'On the Classification of the Gains of One Spouse's Premarital Property during Marriage' ('论夫妻一方婚前财产于婚后所生利益的归属') (2008) 5 *Contemporary Law Review* (当代法学) 121.

[29] See Liying Fan, 'Property Transfer Rules and the Ownership of Spousal Property' ('物权变动模式与夫妻财产归属') (2010) 2 *Journal of Yantai University (Philosophy and Social Science Edition)* (烟台大学学报[哲学社会科学版]) 45.

[30] See respectively, Wenling Yu, 'On the Distribution of Mortgage Houses in a Divorce' ('试论离婚案件中按揭房屋的处理') (2005) 4 *People's Judicature* (人民司法) 24; Qiang Pan and Zhoubin Zhang, 'Appreciation Attributable to the Copayment of a Mortgage Shall be Shared' ('共同还贷,增值部分共有') (21 September 2008), p. 7.

classification.[31] Moreover, some lower courts held expressly that the appreciation of a mortgaged home is a passive appreciation and shall be deemed a separate property of the owner spouse. Of course, these rulings were later all reversed at the second instances (the appeals), based on some special provisions (e.g., art. 10 of Interpretation III of Marriage Law).[32] Still, the existence of such special rules themselves does not deny the theoretical definition that the appreciation of a mortgaged home is a passive appreciation, rather than an active appreciation.

Instead, if we admit that passive appreciation can also be partly classified as community property,[33] the tension between the proportional approach and the definition of passive appreciation could be solved. As a matter of fact, that is exactly what the American family law says in this regard, from which the distinction between active and passive appreciation under Chinese family law draws.

In the United States, with no doubt, the appreciation of a separate property during marriage attributable to the market is a passive appreciation and therefore the owner spouse's separate property.[34] Nevertheless, under certain circumstances, the passive appreciation may also partly be classified as marital property or community property. The Supreme Court of Florida once made it very clear in a case:[35]

> In sum, when a marital home constitutes nonmarital real property, but is encumbered by a mortgage that marital funds service, the value of the *passive, market-driven appreciation* of the property that accrues during the course of the marriage is a *marital asset* . . .. (emphasis added)

[31] See Wanhua Du, Xinwen Cheng and Xiaofang Wu, 'Understanding and Applying Interpretation III of Marriage Law' ('"关于适用婚姻法若干问题的解释(三)" 的理解与适用') (2011) 17 *People's Judicature* (人民司法) 25–26; Xi, 'Understanding Interpretation III', pp. 161–67; Wu, 'Hard issues', 58; Senate I of the SPC (eds.), *Understanding and Applying Interpretation I of the SPC on the Application of Book of Marriage and Family of the Chinese Civil Code* (最高人民法院民法典婚姻家庭编司法解释(一)理解与适用) (Beijing: People's Court Press, 2021), pp. 664–69.

[32] See *Liu* v. *Zhao*, Civil Judgment of Beijing No. 2 Intermediate Court, Jing 02 Min Zhong [2016] No. 980 (柳×与赵×离婚后财产纠纷上诉案，北京市第二中级人民法院(2016)京02民终980号民事判决书); *Wang* v. *Zhao*, Civil Order of Dalian Intermediate Court of Liaoning Province, Da Min Yi Zhong [2015] No. 01988 (王某某诉赵某某离婚后财产纠纷上诉案，辽宁省大连市中级人民法院(2015)大民一终字第01988号民事裁定书).

[33] Some judges have been aware of this possibility, see Lv Cheng and Xiaofang Wu, 'On the Gains of Separate Property during Marriage' ('一方个人财产婚后收益问题探析') (2013) 12 *Journal of Law Application* (法律适用) 116.

[34] See Brett R. Turner, 'Unlikely Partners: The Marital Home and the Concept of Separate Property' (2006) 20 *Journal of the American Academy of Matrimonial Lawyers* 104–5.

[35] *Kaaa* v. *Kaaa*, 58 So. 3d 867, 872 (Fla. 2010).

It seems that the majority view in China is very likely based on a *misunderstanding* of American family law. In contrast, the proportional approach as reflected in art. 10 of Interpretation III of Marriage Law, accords exactly with the rules in American family law.

Of course, even in the United States, scholars and courts do not always share the same view as the Supreme Court of Florida. Actually, definitions and classifications on active appreciation and passive appreciation, similar to the *negative* approach, could be seen in the American literature.[36] The very same misunderstanding could also be found among foreign lawyers who study American family law.[37]

10.4 The Theory of Joint Investment: A Case for the Proportional Approach

This section first provides a doctrinal construction of the proportional approach and thereby a preliminary explanation of why and how the passive appreciation of one spouse's separate property during marriage could be shared by both spouses. Further, it will examine two potential arguments from the perspective of value judgments, namely a fairness argument and an efficiency argument (i.e., the hypothetical intention argument), and the latter will be preferred.

10.4.1 The Theory of Joint Investment: A Doctrinal Construction

The theory of joint investment focuses on the fact that during the marriage a specific asset from one type of property could be used in the interests of another specific asset from another type. For example, the money from the community property would be used during the marriage to pay the mortgage in the interests of the husband's separate property.

[36] See American Law Institute, *Principles of the Law of Family Dissolution: Analysis and Recommendations* (Saint Paul, MN: American Law Institute, 2002), pp. 740–41; John DeWitt Gregory, Janet Leach Richard and Sheyl Wolf, *Property Division in Divorce Proceedings: A Fifty State Guide* (New York: Aspen, 2006 supplement), § 3.06[C]; Suzanne Reynolds, 'Increases in Separate Property and the Evolving Marital Partnership' (1989) 24 *Wake Forest Law Review* 284–86; Turner, 'Unlikely Partners', 104.

[37] See Robert Battes, 'Echte Wertsteigerungen im Zugewinnausgleich' (2007) 54 *Zeitschrift für das gesamte Familienrecht* 315; Zhengyan Ke, 'On the Classification of Marital Property and Separate Property in the Case of an Equalization Claim of Accrued Gains' ('*剩余财产分配请求权中婚前财产与婚后财产认定之研究 – 美国共同财产制为借镜*'), Master's thesis, Taipei University, 2011, p. 186.

In this case, the act of using the money in the interest of the husband's mortgage house would be regarded as an equity investment made between the community property and the husband's separate property, and thereby these two types of assets become joint investors (or more accurately, joint owners) over the mortgaged house. Consequently, any gains in connection to the house, including the market-led appreciation, shall be shared between the two types of property (as investors) according to their ownership shares. In this theoretical framework, the group of property providing the equity investment is entitled not only to what it actually contributed (i.e., active appreciation in most cases) but also to a part of all the gains available, such as the 'corresponding appreciation' of a mortgage house (i.e., passive appreciation). In the end, the gains can be shared between the spouses.

In American family law, the theory of joint investment is the fundamental idea in classifying the passive appreciation of separate property during marriage partly as marital property or community property.

The Minnesota Supreme Court held exactly so in *Antone* v. *Antone*. In this case, the mortgage of one spouse's separate-property house was paid with marital property, 'a portion of the market-related appreciation during the marriage is marital property'; by doing so, the law avoided 'depriving the marital estate of any *return on its investment*'.[38]

A more detailed illustration can be found in a case of the California Supreme Court:[39]

> Where community funds are used to make payments on property purchased by one of the spouses before marriage, the rule developed [28 Cal.3d 372] through decisions in California gives to the community *a* pro tanto *community property interest* in such property in the ratio that the payments on the purchase price with community funds bear to the payments made with separate funds ... the community is entitled to a minimum interest in the property represented by the ratio of the *community investment* to the total separate and community investment in the property. In the event the fair market value has increased disproportionately to the increase in equity [the community property and hence] the wife is entitled to participate in that increment in a similar proportion. (emphasis added)

Similarly, in China the SPC also adopted a certain version of the theory of joint investment. According to art. 10 of Interpretation III of

[38] *Antone* v. *Antone*, 645 N.W.2d 96, 103 (Minn. 2002).
[39] *In re Marriage of Moore*, 28 Cal. 3d 366, 372 (1980).

Marriage Law, the mortgage house is coined a 'hybrid property', a mixture of the separate property (e.g., down payment made by the owner spouse before marriage) and the community property (i.e., mortgage payment during the marriage with the community property).[40] Based on the idea of hybrid property (or co-ownership), the separate property and the community property concerned can share the value of the house based on its internal share, which continuously changed, particularly in accordance with the amount of the mortgage payment during marriage!

The SPC's invention of hybrid property is very similar to the '*pro tanto* community property interest' as dubbed by the California Supreme Court as cited above. In fact, the latter is known as the 'shared investment approach'[41] or related to an 'equity investment',[42] because, for example, it allows the separate property and the community property to share the mortgage house's appreciation as joint investors.

In sum, the proportional approach that allows the sharing of passive appreciation could doctrinally rest upon the theory of joint investment. However, that is only a preliminary step. For the proportional approach, the theory of joint investment is merely a doctrinal construction, not an ultimate justification or argument. Terms such as equity investment, joint investment, joint investors etc. are just doctrinal illustrations rather than justifications, given that no agreement of joint investment is actually reached between the spouses or between the different groups of property. The argument for the theory of joint investment remains to be explored.

10.4.2 Potential Arguments for the Theory of Joint Investment

Fairness

The first potential argument for the theory of joint investment is fairness. In fact, in order to justify the idea of hybrid property, the SPC held that it is 'a bit unfair' to simply classify the mortgaged home either as the community property or as the separate property of the owner spouse.[43]

40 See Du et al., 'Understanding Interpretation III', 26; Xi, 'Understanding Interpretation III', pp. 161–66.

41 See Louise E. Graham, 'Using Formulas to Separate Marital and Nonmarital Property' (1985) 21 *Kentucky Law Journal* 63, 67. See also, Turner, 'Unlikely Partners', 90 ('joint investors').

42 *In re Estate of Kobylski*, 178 Wis. 2d 158, 180 (Ct. App. 1993). For related comments, see David R. Knauss, 'What Part of Yours Is Mine?' (2005) *Wisconsin Law Review* 887.

43 See Du et al., 'Understanding Interpretation III', 26.

Similar fairness arguments could also be found under Swiss law[44] and American law. For example, the Supreme Court of Florida reasoned as follows:[45]

> Because paying the mortgage is a prerequisite to enjoying the appreciation in value of the marital home, we conclude that *principles of equity* do not allow an owner spouse to receive the full benefit of the passive appreciation when the non-owner spouse contributed to the property, and marital funds were used to pay the mortgage. (emphasis added)

Despite its popularity, the plain fairness argument that rests on the contribution or 'sacrifice' of the community property in paying the mortgage for one spouse's separate property is fairly weak. It is indeed unfair, if the community property were merely entitled to the original sum of the mortgage payment during the marriage, without any additional compensation or reimbursement. Then it would function as an interest-free loan. However, if any additional reimbursement is possible, such as a restitution of the mortgage payment plus the statutory interests, it is difficult to say which model of reimbursement is fairer than others.

Imitating What Most Spouses Would Have Wanted

Let me put forward another argument for the theory of joint investment in support of the proportional approach. That is, the proportional approach, as a default rule of a statutory matrimonial regime, is just what most (rational) spouses would have wanted if transaction costs are low enough to allow them to contract in this regard.[46]

One important insight of the hypothetical intention argument concerns the aforesaid fact that, during the course of the family life, many assets from one type of property would be used or contributed in the interests of another type of property. The spouses' salaries during marriage would be used to pay the mortgage of the husband's premarital house, the wife's premarital savings would be used to pay the down payment of the community family home, so on and so forth.

In all these occasions, if the transaction costs were low enough the spouses would easily reach an agreement on any asset contribution, whether it is for free or if not, what its 'price' or consideration is. In

[44] BGE 96 II 305 ('recht und billig').

[45] *Kaaa* v. *Kaaa*, 58 So. 3d 867, 871 (Fla. 2010).

[46] See generally, Horst Eidenmüller, *Effizienz als Rechtsprinzip*, 2nd ed. (Tübingen: Mohr Siebeck, 1998), p. 65; David Campbell, 'Welfare Economics for Capitalists: The Economic Consequences of Judge Posner' (2012) 33 *Cardozo Law Review* 2250.

the real life, however, such an agreement is rare and hardly possible due to extremely high transaction costs. The causes include the ignorance of the legal issue that matters only if the marriage ends in a divorce and emotional barriers that make a negotiation on this issue embarrassing or even weird for a normal or healthy marriage relationship. Given these extremely high transaction costs, the law has to solve the problem by prescribing what most spouses would have wanted in this case as a default rule. The decisive question would therefore be: what would most spouses (in a jurisdiction) have wanted?

The answer offered by the proportional approach is that most spouses would like to treat the groups of property concerned as joint investors, so that the one contributing the specific asset – the equity investment – is entitled to the passive appreciation and any other gains of the asset receiving the contribution thereafter. In such an (equity investment) agreement, both groups of property are appropriately protected. In particular, for the group of property receiving the contribution, it obtains the ordinary investment proceeds based on its actual contribution.[47]

The hypothetical intention argument has two important implications.

First, the asset contribution or the equity investment could occur between the two types of property. Therefore, for example, not only the community property, but also one spouse's separate property, may be able to share the passive appreciation of the other spouse's separate property during marriage.

Second, as long as an asset contribution is made by one type of property in the interests of another, a sharing of the passive appreciation (and any other gains) of the specific asset receiving the contribution thereafter is justified. Therefore, it does not matter whether the passive appreciation is attributable to the asset contribution. Consequently, for example, the critical asset contribution does not have to be paying the mortgage, which prevents the enforcement of the mortgage and ensures the owner spouse's entitlement to the house's appreciation. The asset contribution could also be in many other forms, such as funding the renovation or construction of a mortgage house.

To illustrate, suppose the renovation of the husband's premarital mortgaged house was funded with the wife's premarital property. In this case, the house's increase in value directly due to the renovation shall be classified as active appreciation and belong to the type of property that

[47] See Turner, 'Unlikely Partners', 107.

provided the funding (i.e., the wife's separate property). Moreover, the funding constitutes an asset contribution from the wife's separate property in the interests of the husband's premarital mortgage house. In regard to the mortgage house, both groups of separate property became joint investors after the funding as an equity investment. Consequently, although the house's appreciation attributable to the market shall be classified as passive appreciation, it could be shared by each spouse's separate property according to the investment share.

10.5 A Revised Hypothetical Intention Argument for the Affirmative Approach

This section reconsiders the analysis in Section 10.4 on what most spouses would have wanted regarding the appreciation issue. Based on a revised (corrected) version of the hypothetical intention argument, this section will argue in support of the *affirmative* approach that any passive appreciation of one spouse's separate property during marriage shall be classified as community property and shared by both spouses.

The hypothetical intention of most spouses in Section 10.4 merely focuses on the asset contribution from one type of property in the interests of a specific asset that belongs to another group of property and appreciates after the contribution during marriage. However, other circumstances that also affect the hypothetical intention are ignored.

First, the specific asset receiving the contribution may rarely or never appreciate, but generally tends to depreciate, just as in the case of motor cars and most other kinds of moveable property. In this case, there is no appreciation to be shared.

Second, what benefits from the asset contribution may not be an asset in specific but a group of property in general. For example, it is very often the case that one spouse's premarital savings is consumed in the family daily life and thereby generally in the interests of the community property. In this case, there is no appreciation from a specific asset to be shared, either.

Given all these circumstances, it is the affirmative approach, not the proportional approach, that accords with most spouses' hypothetical intention.

Under the proportional approach, a spouse would still be encouraged – or induced – to act 'selfishly', namely to follow the motto, that one spouse's own separate property shall be used for appreciation, while the community property or the other spouse's separate property shall be used for consumption or depreciation.[48] For example, bearing even the tiny risk of a divorce in the far future, it is rational for a husband to use his premarital savings to pay his premarital mortgage exclusively, rather than to use it to pay the daily bills. Generally, for a rational spouse who considers the risk of divorce, the proportional approach yields a bad incentive: a spouse is incentivized to allocate all the assets at his or her disposal to maximize his or her individual wealth, rather than for any other purpose that might be pursued in a marriage. Given the fact that people get married not exclusively for the purpose of maximizing the individual's prospects upon a divorce, it is clear that the proportional approach does not accord with most spouses' hypothetical intention over the distribution of the appreciation.

On the other hand, the *affirmative* approach should prevail. It would be what most spouses would have wanted *ex ante* marriage if we treat all passive appreciation of separate property as community property equally owned by both spouses. An equal distribution of all the passive appreciation eliminates the difference a spouse would face in a divorce. Any passive appreciation from any asset during marriage would now be classified as community property and equally shared by both spouses. It does not matter in which way a specific asset from a group of property is used or allocated. Even a rational spouse bearing the risk of divorce in mind will not mind at all which asset is used for the family daily life and which is used for appreciation and depreciation, and so on and so forth. That is exactly what a marriage is in most cases and thereby what most spouses would have wanted.

In accordance the hypothetical intention of most spouses, the *affirmative* approach also has two important implications.

Firstly, even for an asset that appreciates passively during marriage that is not related to any specific asset contribution (from another type of property), the passive appreciation arising thereof during marriage shall be classified as community property and shared by both spouses. The appreciation's classification depends only on what most spouses would have wanted, not anything else.

Also, besides passive appreciation, passive *depreciation* shall also be similarly shared by both spouses.[49] As indicated above, a default rule that

[48] See Thomas R. Andrews, 'Income from Separate Property' (1993) 56 *Law and Contemporary Problems* 211.

[49] This also accords with the SPC's opinion in the case of depreciation of a mortgage house. See Xi, 'Understanding Interpretation III', pp. 165–66. See similarly, Zhuqing Wang,

allows the sharing of appreciation, but denies the sharing of depreciation, would also yield a bad incentive that runs against most spouses' hypothetical intention.

Technically, the sharing of passive depreciation means that the appreciation of a specific asset shall be 'set off' by the depreciation of another. In other words, only the *overall net (passive) appreciation* matters. Basically, German family law has for a long time adopted a similar approach as advocated here that both spouses shall share the overall net (passive) appreciation of separate property during marriage, yet excluding the sharing of passive appreciation due to inflation. And it shall be noted, interestingly, that the original underlying argument for such an approach was fairness, not the revised hypothetical intention argument as proposed in this chapter.[50] As regards Chinese family law, the idea that only the overall net (passive) appreciation shall be shared is also possible. Technically or doctrinally, the passive appreciation shall be narrowly interpreted not as that of a specific asset but as the overall net passive appreciation of all the assets of both spouses' separate property respectively.

10.6 Conclusion

There are three main approaches in classifying passive appreciation of separate property during marriage. Interestingly and paradoxically, they all coexist under Chinese family law. This chapter analyzes them and reaches the following conclusions.

The *negative* approach where passive appreciation of separate property during marriage cannot be shared by both spouses is simply wrong. It derives partly from the idea of community of labour and partly from a misinterpretation of American family law. In American family law,

'Classifying and Distributing a Premarital Mortgage House' ('婚前按揭房产的归属及分割') (2010) 18 *People's Judicature* (人民司法) 64.

50 The rule is said to be 'simple and clear, and in line with the essence of the theory of marriage as a community of fate'. See Schriftlicher Bericht, zu BT-Drucks. II/3409, p. 11 ('daß die Regelung einfach und klar sei und dem Wesen der Ehe als einer Schicksalsgemeinschaft entspreche'). For other justifications in the German literature, see Nina Dethloff, 'Unterhalt, Zugewinn- und Versorgungsausgleich', in Ständige Deputation des Deutschen Juristentages (Publ.), *Verhandlungen des 67. Deutschen Juristentages*, Bd. 1 (München: C. H. Beck, 2008), pp. A 88 ff., A 92 ff.; Joachim Gernhuber and Dagmar Coester-Waltjen, *Lehrbuch des Familienrechts*, 6th ed. (München: C. H. Beck, 2010), pp. 368, 419 ff.

passive appreciation of separate property during marriage would usually be classified as separate property and enjoyed by the owner spouse. However, it could also be classified as marital property or community property and thereby shared by both spouses under certain circumstances.

The proportional approach, under which passive appreciation of separate property during marriage could be proportionally classified as community property and shared by both spouses based on certain criteria, is very popular in many jurisdictions, such as in China, Switzerland and the United States. But it cannot stand, either. None of the existing arguments, which regard the proportional sharing of passive appreciation as a compensation for the non-owner spouse's loss of opportunity to acquire the sole ownership of the house, an offset for high inflation rates or a restitution of active appreciation, is successful. In addition, the theory of joint investment aims to provide a doctrinal construction for the proportional approach. According to this theory, the asset contribution from one group of property in the interests of a specific asset from another type of property is regarded as an equity investment, and thereby the different types of property involved become joint investors of the specific asset receiving the asset contribution. However, neither the doctrinal theory itself nor the fairness argument or the hypothetical intention argument may justify the proportional approach.

The affirmative approach, that all the passive appreciation of separate property during marriage shall be classified as community property and shared by both spouses, could be justified based on a revised version of the hypothetical intention argument. Moreover, technically, the passive appreciation subject to a sharing shall be narrowly interpreted as the overall net passive appreciation, so that not only passive appreciation but also passive depreciation of a specific asset will be shared by both spouses.

11

The Rule of Law in Traditional China

JAMES GORDLEY[*]

11.1 The Chinese Legal Tradition

It is often said that while the West recognized the rule of law, China did not. The discussion has been biased by ideas about the meaning of the rule of law that have become popular in the West since the rise of legal positivism in the nineteenth century.

In the nineteenth century, jurists came to believe that they should interpret texts without regard to any higher principles on which they might rest. If there were such principles, it was not the task of a jurist to investigate and apply them. Legal texts such as codes or court decisions were authoritative simply because they were the law of a particular region, enacted or accepted by those with authority in that region. If the texts were the ultimate source of law, then a jurist must be able to derive his conclusions from the texts somewhat as a mathematician could derive conclusions from axioms and postulates. A jurist who could not do so would be presenting his own opinions as if they were law. He would be usurping legal authority. Many people still conceive of the rule of law in that way.

If that is what is meant by the rule of law, it never existed, neither in China nor in the West, as Western jurists now recognize. In France, François Gény criticized the mistake of thinking that the law consisted of rules whose "consequences should be deduced by logically necessary reasoning," a view that "could not be justified unless law were an exact science, such as mathematics."[1] In Germany, Rudolf von Ihering wrote a satire in which he visited the heaven of the jurists, which contained concepts so rarefied that they could never exist in our world and devices

[*] My thanks to Tong Xu for her help with the classical Chinese texts.

[1] François Gény, *Method d'interpretation et sources en droit privé positif* (Paris, 1899), no. 62.

Ibid., no. 64.

for exploring them such as a hair-splitting machine. As Matthias Reimann observed, Oliver Wendell Holmes' position was like that of Ihering.[2] Holmes denied that legal questions can be "settled deductively, or once for all."[3] He criticized those who think "that the only force in the development of law is logic," "that a given system, ours, for instance, can be worked out like mathematics from some general axioms of conduct."[4]

Yet the principle that cases should be decided in accordance with definite preestablished norms is not the creature of positivism. It is a staple of the Western tradition stretching back to Roman law. If that is what is meant by the rule of law, the rule of law was recognized in traditional China as well. Indeed, as we will see, the method used to decide cases in traditional China was like that of the Roman jurists.

This method was not deductive. It rested on a belief that a person familiar with prior law could judge accurately how a new case should be decided, even though his conclusion was not backed by a formal proof. The Roman method, like that of the Chinese, was to compare one particular case with another rather than to propose abstract rules. If you asked a Roman jurist about the meaning of negligence, he would answer by giving particular examples of conduct that is negligent. If asked about the meaning of consent, he would answer by giving particular examples in which a party did not consent to a contract because he was mistaken as to what he contracted to receive.[5] As we will see, the Chinese method was similar.

The difference is that the Roman jurists used the particular cases to elucidate the meaning of legal concepts such as negligence and consent. These concepts concerned substantive law: the law that determines a person's obligations to others. For the most part, they concerned private law: the law of torts, contract, and property. Chinese law was principally concerned with the punishment of crimes. It was concerned less with norms of conduct than with the penalties that should be imposed on those who violate them.

[2] Mathias W. Reimann, "Holmes's *Common Law* and German Legal Science," in Robert W. Gordon (ed.), *The Legacy of Oliver Wendell Holmes* (Stanford: Stanford University Press, 1992), pp. 101–3.

[3] Oliver Wendell Holmes Jr., "The Path of the Law," in *Collected Legal Papers* (New York: Harcourt, Brace and Howe, 1920), p. 182.

[4] Ibid., p. 180.

[5] James Gordley, *The Jurists: A Critical History* (Oxford: Oxford University Press, 2013), pp. 7–12.

The Chinese put great intellectual effort into determining what the penalties should be for different crimes, as the Roman jurists did in determining the scope of obligations. As Langlois said, the question of the appropriate degree of punishment received "the attention of the greatest legal minds and aroused equally deep intellectual discussion."[6] Yet "[t]he primary issue in traditional Chinese jurisprudence was the setting of punishments."[7]

Many scholars agree with Derek Bodde and Clarence Morris, "the law in imperial China became the embodiment of the ethical norms of Confucianism."[8] At a later point, we will see that this view goes too far. Be that as it may, the two characteristics of traditional Chinese law that we have just described – its concern with penalties and its method of reasoning by the comparison of particular cases – were not Confucian in origin. They began in the state of Qin 秦, which reunified China in 221 BC, founding a short-lived dynasty that was overthrown in 206 BC.

The Qin dynasty was anti-Confucian. Its leading philosophers belonged to the anti-Confucian Legalist school (法家 *fajia*). They taught that law was purely an instrument of power. After reunifying China, the first Qin emperor, Qin Shi Huang 秦始皇, persecuted Confucian scholars and burned their books. Evidently, the Qin founders of the Chinese legal tradition did not think that law was purely an instrument of power. They were concerned with a question of justice: the fairness of punishments.

We would know nothing about the origins of this tradition had it not been for the discovery in 1975 of the tomb of a third-century official who had his law book buried with him written on strips of bamboo (秦簡*qin jian*).[9] When Liu Bang 劉邦 overthrew the Qin, he promised to abolish their laws. Instead, he adopted a collection of laws or code that was largely based on them. According to the dynastic history of the Han, in about 200 BC, "Hsaio Ho [Xiao He] gathered together the laws of the Qin . . . choosing those which were suitable for those times."[10] After the fall of the Han dynasty, the king of one of the surviving kingdoms, the

[6] John D. Langlois, "Living Law' in Sung and Yüan Jurisprudence" (1981) 41 *Harvard Journal of Asiatic Studies* 165–217 at 165.

[7] Ibid.

[8] Derk Bodde and Clarence Morris, *Law in Imperial China* (Philadelphia: University of Pennsylvania Press, 1967), p. 5.

[9] A. F. P. Hulsewé, *Remnants of Ch'in Law* (Leiden: E. J. Brill, 1985), E 20, p. 198.

[10] *Han shu* 23.12a, quoted in A. F. P. Hulsewé, *Remnants of Han Law* (Leiden: E. J. Brill, 1955), p. 26.

Wei 魏, ordered two Confucians to revise the Han Code. He promulgated their new code, the Xin Lü 新律 or Wei Lü 魏律, which has been lost. It reduced the severity of punishments. It also added a section called the "Eight Deliberations" (八議 *ba yi*), which survived into later codes and which we will discuss later.[11] The law was modified again in the Northern Wei 北魏 dynasty (386–584) when Emperor Yuan Hong 元宏 (孝文帝*Xiao Wen Di*) modified the punishments for certain crimes to reflect Confucian principles: for example, breaches of filial piety were punished more severely.[12] It was modified again by the promulgation of the Kai-Huang Code (開皇律*Kai Huang Lü*) by Emperor Yang Jian 楊堅 (隋文帝*Sui Wen Di*) when China was reunified under the short-lived Sui 隋dynasty (581–618). That code further reduced the severity of punishments. It extended the "Eight Deliberations" to "Ten Abominations (十惡 *shi e*)".

These developments culminated in the Tang Code (唐律*tang lü*), which, as Geoffrey MacCormack observed, "in essentials survived until the end of the imperial period."[13] As John Head and Yanping Wang noted, "[T]he Song, the Yüan, the Ming and the Qing . . . each . . . added its own stitches to the pattern set by the Tang Code."[14] As Brian McKnight said, the "laws of the Song . . . are virtually identical in style and form with their predecessors and their successors"[15] despite reorganization and revision by the Ming 明 and Qing 清. Thirty to forty percent of the articles of Qing Code (大清律例 *Da Qing Lü Li*) were borrowed unchanged from the Tang.[16]

We can see the influence of Qin law by comparing the provisions of Tang Code with those remnants of Qin law that survive. The drafters and commentators in the Qin and Tang dynasties put much hard thought into determining when one person was more deserving of punishment than another. In the surviving fragments of Qin law and in the Tang

[11] John W. Head and Yanping Wang, *Law Codes in Dynastic China A Synopsis of Chinese Legal History in the Thirty Centuries from Zhou to Qing* (Durham, NC: Carolina Academic Press, 2005), p. 109.

[12] Ibid., pp. 111–12.

[13] Geoffrey MacCormack, *Traditional Chinese Penal Law* (Edinburgh: Edinburgh University Press, 1990), p. 13.

[14] Head and Wang, "Law Codes," p. 137.

[15] Brian E. McKnight, "Patterns of Law and Patterns of Thought: Notes on the Specifications (shih) of Sung China" (1982) 102 *Journal of the American Oriental Society* 323–31 at 323.

[16] Wallace Johnson, "Introduction," in Wallace Johnson (trans.), *The Tang Civil Code* (Princeton: Princeton University Press, 1979), vol. I, p. 9.

Code, the fruit of their efforts was presented in much the same way: as a description of cases, each with a conclusion as to the appropriate punishment. There is no systematic organization in these cases. There is no attempt to group them under principles that are arranged hierarchically under higher level principles. Principles are stated infrequently, and they are not presented as reasons why one offense deserves greater punishment than another. The texts contain generalizations based on specific cases, and the results appropriate in these cases are worked out by comparison and analogy to others.

For example, in the texts concerning theft, the punishment deemed to be appropriate depends on the "illegitimate profit (贓 *zang*)" made by the thief. The texts do not define "illegitimate profit" or explain how it is to be determined. They describe specific cases. They ask what is to be done if the object stolen by the accused was worth over 660 units (錢 *qian*) at the time of the theft but worth only 110 at the time of trial. The answer: the accused was to be punished for a theft of over 660.[17] Suppose the value was 110 at the time of the theft 660 at the time of trial. Then the accused should suffer the lesser punishment, and officials who had punished him to a greater extent were themselves to be punished for doing so.[18] The Tang Code provided more generally: "All cases of assessing the value of illicit goods do so according to the value of the articles at the time and place of the offense in terms of the set price of the highest grade of silk."[19] In particular: "Assessment of the value of such things as boats, grinding mills, warehouses, and wholesale stores is according to the rent at the time of the offense."[20]

A more difficult question was whether the punishment of a thief should depend on the value of what the thief actually stole or what he intended to steal. Neither Qin law nor the Tang Code posed the question in general terms. They described how a thief was to be punished in particular cases, and their answers differed. Suppose someone stole a goat with a rope attached and that the value of the goat warranted one punishment while the value of the goat and the rope combined warranted another more severe one. According to the Qin texts, he should receive the lesser punishment if his "attention was on the goat he stole, not the

[17] Hulsewé, 'Remnants of Ch'in Law," D 27.
[18] Ibid., D 28.
[19] Tang Civil Code art. 34.1
[20] Ibid., art. 34.3.

rope."[21] Suppose "there is a robbery of a mare and her foal follows her." According to the Tang Code, "the foal's value is included in the punishment."[22]

Since the punishment depended on the harm done by the perpetrator, when several perpetrators were responsible, the question arose how much of the harm to attribute to each. Suppose A and B steal 800 cash from C. According to the Qin texts, if they planned the crime together, each is to be punished as though he had stolen 800. But if A and B each went to rob C, and met for the first time just before the robbery, and each took 400 from C, then A and B are to be punished as though each had stolen 400.[23] Suppose A, B, C, and D planned together to beat or wound someone. According to the Tang Code, the punishment of each person is based on the harm done by the heaviest blow struck. If the heaviest blow broke a limb, the one who struck that blow receives the punishment from breaking a limb, which is three years of penal servitude. For the original plotter, if he did not strike that blow, the punishment is one degree less: two and a half years. For the others, it is two degrees less: two years.[24] But suppose they did not plot together. Then each person is liable for the harm that he did himself: the person who broke a limb is punished by three years of penal servitude, the one who broke a finger by one year; the one who beat him without causing a wound with forty blows with the light stick.[25]

Most of the texts deal with how the perpetrator of a crime is to be punished. A few deal with what the perpetrator owes the victim. Again, that question was addressed by describing particular cases. A robber must give back what he stole, but suppose "he sells what he had robbed, thereby buying other things?" If so, according to the Qin texts, "all are given back to the owner" of the stolen goods.[26] Suppose the robber stole the victim's clothes, sold them for money, and used it to buy cloth. Can the owner claim both the cloth and the clothes? He can only claim the cloth.[27] According to the Tang Code, in "all cases . . . in which the illicit goods are still in existence, return them to the . . . owner."[28] "If there has

21 Hulsewé, "Remnants of Ch'in Law," D 24.
22 Tang Civil Code Commentary 300.2.
23 Hulsewé, "Remnants of Ch'in Law," D 10.
24 Tang Civil Code Subcommentary to art. 308.1.
25 Ibid., to art. 308.2.
26 Hulsewé, "Remnants of Ch'in Law," D 20.
27 Ibid., D 20.
28 Tang Civil Code art. 33.1a.

been an exchange for other goods . . . the illicit goods are still considered to be in existence."[29] Suppose, however, "a robber takes another's goods and articles through trade or loan and gets a profit." The profit does not go to the original owner because "this is due to the efforts of the later possessor and not the original owner."[30]

The texts do not state the principles at stake or explain why they should be applied to reach a certain result. Yet the texts show, not the absence of legal reasoning but a method of reasoning that rests on recognizing similarities without analyzing why they are important. Those who formulated the texts decided, after careful thought, what punishment is appropriate to a particular offense by considering those prescribed for others. The magistrate deciding a new case would consider which texts described a case most like his own.

MacCormack correctly noted that the "comprehensiveness, clarity and precision" of the codes reflect "drafting techniques . . . developed principally by the legalist officials of the state of Qin."[31] It has often been assumed that Qin law was the legal expression of the legalist philosophy endorsed by the regime.[32] Hulwesé said the "primary motive" was "raison d'état" and "maintaining the stability of government and . . . increasing its power."[33] But that motive does not explain the concern with consistency in punishment. A better explanation is a concern with fairness. It was the prime concern of the Tang Code and those of later dynasties, but it was neither in conflict with Confucian principles nor the result of their influence.

MacCormack concluded that because of "legalist influence," the codes tried to "ensure that for every situation there should be a rule specifically stated or clearly inferable" to keep "judicial discretion . . . to a minimum."[34] On the contrary, the object of the codes was not to provide rules for determining what conduct would be deemed wrongful. Indeed, one of the offenses in the Tang and later Codes was "doing that which ought not to be done." According to art. 450 of the Tang Code, "All cases of doing what ought not to be done are punished by forty blows with the light stick." A subcommentary explained that "If there is no provision in

[29] Tang Civil Code Commentary to art. 33.1a.

[30] Tang Civil Code Query & reply to art. 33.1a.

[31] MacCormack, "Traditional Chinese Penal Law," p. 39.

[32] Hulsewé, "Remnants of Han Law," p. 13; Bodde and Morris, "Law in Imperial China," p. 27; Head and Wang, "Law Codes," pp. 73–75.

[33] Hulsewé, "Remnants of Han Law," p. 5.

[34] MacCormack, "Traditional Chinese Penal Law," p. 39.

either the Code or the Statutes . . . and there is no text to which analogy can be made, then . . . the circumstances of the crime are weighed to decide a punishment. So this article was established with a view to supplementing omissions and deficiencies."[35] The concern of the codes was consistency in punishing different offenses.

We can now better understand the traditional Chinese view that there was no need for the people to know the provisions of the law or to consult lawyers who knew them. In the Song dynasty, private persons were prohibited from printing or copying the code or any other laws, although the prohibition was lifted by Wang Anshi王安石. According to Ichisada Miyazaki, "[t]he theory was that, if the people knew the law, they could devise ways to circumvent it. The people's duty was simply to obey the doctrines of Confucianism."[36] By consulting the Code, however, a person was unlikely to find loopholes in the definitions of what conduct could be punished. There were few definitions. He could, however, calculate and minimize the risk of being severely punished. He could determine the largest amount he could steal without incurring a greater punishment or whether he would be punished less if he stole secretly or by force or by fraud. Chinese lawmakers saw little point in informing wrongdoers how to get off more lightly. In the United States, where all laws must be made public, and ex-post facto laws are constitutionally prohibited, a criminal may still receive a greater punishment that was prescribed by a statute enacted after the crime was committed. He has no right to know in advance how much he will be punished.

He does have a right to know in advance what conduct is prohibited, and in the United States and in many other countries, that right is regarded as part of the rule of law. The traditional Chinese attitude toward the rule of law was different. The Chinese subject was not informed in advance of what sort of wrongdoing was subject to punishment. He was supposed to know without consulting the law whether he was behaving rightly or wrongly. But by the same token, in China, unlike the United States, he was unlikely to be punished for breaking a law he had never heard of that prohibited seemingly innocent conduct and to be told that his ignorance of that law is no excuse. According to the traditional Chinese view, to be treated fairly, a rule of law must prescribe

[35] Tang Civil Code Subcommentary to art. 450.

[36] Ichisada Miyazaki, "The Administration of Justice during the Sung Dynasty," in Jerome Alan Cohen, R. Randle Edwards, and Fu-Mei Chang Chen (eds.), *Essays on China's Legal Tradition* (Princeton: Princeton University Press, 1980), p. 58.

a punishment so that the punishment is proportional to the wrong committed. Under the traditional English common law, all felonies were punishable by hanging. In the United States, the punishment today depends on a vague set of sentencing guidelines and the discretion of a parole board, except in states that have adopted the "three strikes and you're out" rule, by which a person convicted of three felonies, even if they are comparatively minor, loses his freedom for life. Both traditions rest on underlying ideas of fairness and the need for legal rules, but these ideas are different.

11.2 The Influence of Confucianism

As mentioned earlier, scholars such as Bodde and Morris have described traditional Chinese law as "the embodiment of the ethical norms of Confucianism."[37] According to Tung-tsu Ch'ü (瞿同祖 *Qu Tongzu*), "[a]fter Han times, the formulation and revision of the law fell into the hands of Confucian scholar-officials who seized the opportunity to incorporate as many as possible of the essentials of Confucianism (*li*) into the codes."[38] MacCormack claimed that "[i]n their content, the ... codes give effect to the Confucian system of values."[39] According to Jean Escarra, "[d]espite the influence of the Legalists ... the Confucian conception came to dominate all ancient Chinese legislation."[40]

Too much has been made of the "Confucianization of the law."[41] Although the Tang Code was acceptably Confucian, it was not tightly integrated with Confucian thought. The codes incorporated some Confucian ideals. The scale of punishment was gradually reduced. Moreover, the severity of punishment was increased or decreased to reflect Confucian ideas of the seriousness of an offense. As we have seen, the underlying idea of fairness in the severity of punishments, on which so many provisions depended, went back to the Qin.

Some scholars have thought that this idea of fairness was due to a Confucian view of law. According to Wallace Johnson, "the purpose of law is to maintain a harmony between the human and the natural

[37] Bodde and Morris, "Law in Imperial China," p. 5.
[38] Ibid., p. 276.
[39] MacCormack, "Traditional Chinese Penal Law," p. 39
[40] Jean Scarra, "Law, Chinese," in E. R. A. Seligman et al. (eds.), *Encyclopedia of the Social Sciences* (New York: Macmillan, 1933), vol. IX, p. 251.
[41] T'ung-tsu Ch'ü, *Law and Society in Traditional China* (The Hague: Mouton & Co., 1961), p. 267.

worlds." Like Hulwesé, he traces that idea to the Han Dynasty philosopher Dong Zhongshu 董仲舒. According to Johnson, "An offense was regarded as a disruption in society that must be restored by the proper punishment. But punishments in the human sphere that are too heavy can bring about a reaction in the natural world – epidemics, floods and draughts are commonly mentioned."[42] This concern, he claimed, explains the "lack of flexibility afforded in sentencing by the Code." "[T]hroughout the empire a particular crime would be met with exactly the same punishment. The theory behind this is that if a certain punishment has been decided upon for a crime, then assigning a lesser punishment would not be a sufficient response and a heavier punishment might well provoke some natural disaster."[43] "In the final analysis," according to Bodde and Morris, "a disturbance of the social order really meant, in Chinese thinking, a violation of the cosmic order."[44]

MacCormack observed that "such a view of the relationship between crime and punishment is nowhere explicitly stated in the legal sources."[45] There was "a widespread belief . . . that gross cases of injustice are likely to lead to a visitation of evil on the part of Heaven." Sometimes, as Johnson noted, when natural disasters occurred, the emperor would "take steps to reduce punishments."[46] But the overriding concern, for Han, the Tang, and later dynasties was not the absolute severity of a punishment: whether, for example, a robber should be punished by 100 blows of the heavy stick or 50. As we have seen, the scale of punishments was changed across the board from one dynasty to the next. What mattered was consistency among the punishments administered for different offenses, so if one offense was so grave as to merit 100 blows with the heavy stick, equally grave offenses would be punished in the same way. The bulk of the Tang Code is concerned with determining the seriousness of an offense so that this consistency can be maintained. That concern was not the result of Confucian influence. It was the chief concern of the law under the Qin.

The traditional law was modified under the influence of Confucian principles. The severity of punishments was reduced. The Qin punished crimes by fines, mutilation – which ranged from having one's head and

42 Johnson, "Introduction," p. 10.
43 Ibid., p. 11.
44 Bodde and Morris, "Law in Imperial China," p. 4.
45 MacCormack, "Traditional Chinese Penal Law," p. 42.
46 Johnson, "Introduction," p. 10.

beard shaved off to the loss of one or both feet or castration – hard labor, exile, and the death by decapitation or by "cutting asunder (斬)."[47] In later dynasties, it was said that the Qin dynasty fell because of the severity of its punishments. The Tang Code, like the Sui Code, recognized five: beating with a light stick (10, 20, 30, 40 and 50 blows), beating with a heavy stick (60, 70, 80, 90, and 100 blows), penal servitude (1, 1½, 2, 2½, and 3 years), life exile (at a distance of 2,000, 2,500, and 3,000 li), and death (by strangulation or decapitation).[48] Some of the lighter punishments could be "redeemed" by paying a fine. Punishments further decreased in the Song. They sharply increased during the Ming, a step that coincided with a retreat from Confucian principles as they had previously been understood.

Also under Confucian influence, punishments were changed to reflect Confucian ideas concerning the seriousness of an offense. Some of the punishments for particular offenses were modified, especially when they concerned family members. Various articles of the Tang Code define the punishments for "cursing with bad language," beating, wounding or killing one's wife, one's husband, one's parent or grandparent, one's elder brother or sister, one's younger brother or sister, one's elder brother's wife or husband's younger brother or sister, a relative who is older but within the fifth degree of mourning, and so forth.[49] Nevertheless, to allow the punishment to depend on the family relationship of the parties was not a Confucian innovation. Although Qin philosophers deprecated the importance of this relationship, punishments in Qin law depended on whether a man beat one's grandparents or great-grand parents[50] or his wife,[51] that is, on whether a person accused another of unfilial behavior.[52] In the Tang Code, concerns with the family relationship of the parties were more pervasive.

In addition, as in the Northern Wei, the Tang Code contained "Eight Deliberations (八議*ba yi*)"[53] or circumstances in which a punishment should be deceased, and, as in the Sui Code, "Ten Abominations (十惡 *shi e*)"[54] or particularly serious circumstances in which the punishment

47 Hulsewé, "Remnants of Ch'in Law," pp. 14–18.
48 Johnson, "Introduction," pp. 14–15.
49 Tang Civil Code arts. 325–35.
50 Hulsewé, "Remnants of Ch'in Law," D 63.
51 Ibid., D 64.
52 Ibid., D 85.
53 Tang Civil Code art. 7.
54 Ibid., art. 6.

should be increased. They do reflect Confucian influence. The official explanations of these provisions often cite the Confucian classics. Yet in many ways the Eight Deliberations and the Ten Abominations are not a straightforward application of Confucian teachings.

Of the Eight Deliberations, which concern the reason for reducing the normal punishment, five concern the virtues of the person guilty of an offense: the "deliberations" "for the morally worthy," "for ability," "for achievement," "for high position," and "for diligence." The others favored relatives and old retainers of the emperor and guests of state. It is hard to see on Confucian principles why the "morally worthy" should be punished less rather than more, or why the punishment of imperial relatives and retainers or those in "high position" should be mitigated.[55]

The Ten Abominations also show a Confucian influence. They are described as "the most serious of those offences that come within the five punishments. They injure morality and destroy propriety (*li* 禮)."[56] All but one of them are offenses against relationships that on Confucian principles are worthy of special respect: against the emperor, against hierarchical superiors, and against family members. Nevertheless, if one began with Confucian principles and considered which offenses against them should be considered the most severe, one would be unlikely to end up with the items on this particular list.[57] If there is a connection with

[55] The Subcommentary cites the Confucian classic, the *Book of Rites* (禮記 *li ji*): "Punishments do not extend up to the great officers." *Li ki* I.53 cited in Tang Civil Code Subcommentary to art. 7. Yet they are the very sort of people whose misbehavior Confucius and Mencius denounced and which, they believed, had caused the ruin of dynasties.

[56] Tang Civil Code Subcommentary to art. 6.

[57] Four concern harm or disrespect to the state or the emperor: "plotting rebellion" (謀反 *mou fan*), "plotting treason" (謀叛 *mou pan*), "plotting great sedition" (謀大逆*mou da ni*), and "great irreverence" (大不敬*da bu jing*). One concerns harm or disrespect toward one's hierarchical superiors such as a department head, district magistrate, prefect, or teacher. Four concern offenses within family relationship. One is "lack of filial piety" (不孝*bu xiao*). Another is "to beat or plot to kill . . . one's paternal grandparents or parents; or to kill one's paternal uncles or their wives, one's elder brothers or sisters, or one's maternal grandparents, or one's husband, or one's husbands maternal grandparents, or his parents" (惡逆*e ni*). Tang Civil Code Commentary to art. 7. Another is "discord" (不睦*bu mu*), which is committed by plotting to kill relatives within the fifth degree of mourning and beating relatives within the fourth degree. Another is incest (內亂*nei luan*). The remaining "abominations" are "unrighteousness" (不義 *bu yi*) and "depravity" (不道*bu dao*), which is committed by killing three members of a single household, sorcery, and making *ku* poison, which was used in black magic.

Confucian principle, it is not one that Confucius or Mencius themselves would easily recognize.

11.3 The Moral Authority of the Rule of Law

For most of Western history, it was believed that there is natural law governing human conduct that is reflected in the law that is administered by courts. The Roman jurists had said, "law is the art of goodness and fairness. Of that art we [jurists] are deservedly called priests. For we … claim awareness of what is good and fair, discriminating between fair and unfair."[58] In the Middle Ages, Thomas Aquinas (1225–74) had used the term "natural law" to describe the ethical norms by which a person would act who possessed the Aristotelian virtues of justice and practical reason. In the sixteenth and seventeenth century, a group of philosopher-jurists, centered in Spain, and known to historians as the "late scholastics," synthesized Roman law, as interpreted by medieval jurists, with Aristotelian philosophy, as interpreted by Aquinas. They gave Roman law a systematic doctrinal structure that it previously had lacked.[59] They tried to find a philosophical justification for the rules of Roman law. When they succeeded, they said that the rule was one of natural law. When they did not, they ascribed the rule to Roman positive law. It was established for some good reason, no doubt, but it did not state a universal principle. Hugo Grotius (1583–1645), the founder of the northern natural law school, borrowed many of the conclusions of the late scholastics without grounding them expressly in Aristotelian philosophy. Among them was the conviction that the human law was grounded on the higher principles of a law of nature.[60]

So long as that view prevailed, the rule of law as administered by the courts was regarded as the embodiment of principles of human conduct grounded in human nature. It derived its moral authority from those principles. This view was not confidently rejected until the rise of positivism in the nineteenth century. For the positivists, there was no natural law or, at least, no natural law sufficiently definite to provide standards for human conduct. The law derived its authority from the those who had the authority to adopt or enact it. The rule of law, however, became all the more critical. If there were no higher principles to which the law

58 Dig. 1.1.1.pr., 1.
59 Gordley, "Jurists," pp. 82–101.
60 Ibid., pp. 128–40.

must conform, a principal limit to the authority of those in power was that they rule through law. Indeed, the recognition by jurists in the twentieth century that all cases could not be decided by logical inference from authoritative texts touched off a crisis that has never been resolved.[61]

In traditional China, the rule of law was never regarded as having moral authority for either reason. Confucians believed in higher norms grounded in human nature. They taught that those in power should exercise their authority in accordance with these norms. The law administered by the courts, however, was concerned with the penalties for wrongful conduct.

Because Roman law was concerned with norms of conduct, in the West, it was possible to regard Roman law as an embodiment of higher principles that should govern conduct. In China, it was not. Confucianism was never fused with the Qin legal tradition in the way the Roman law was combined with Aristotelian philosophy. The late scholastics had sought a philosophical principle that would justify particular Roman rules. Traditional Chinese law sought to provide appropriate penalties for different wrongs. But no one sought a Confucian principle that would justify each distinction in the severity of penalties.

Moreover, because traditional Chinese law was concerned with penalties, and penalties are not norms of conduct but sanctions for the breach of such norms, the role of law was seen differently. Law was necessary in a well-administered state. Nevertheless, it would be far better if people would act out of respect for the higher norms, not out of fear of the law. As Confucius said, "If people are led by command and regulated with punishment people will avoid it and become shameless. If people are led by virtue and regulated by propriety, they will have a sense of shame and restrain themselves."[62]

Chinese courts respected the rule of law. They were supposed to decide according to preexisting legal rules. Their decisions could be reversed by higher courts if they failed to do so. Great intellectual effort was put into establishing and applying these rules. But the concern of law was not to promulgate just norms of conduct. It was to ensure that the penalties for violating norms of conduct were just. Hence it played a different role in practice and in the way in which the rule of law was conceived.

[61] See Roberto Mangabeira Unger, *Knowledge and Politics* (New York: The Free Press, 1975).

[62] *Analects* 2.3.

12

The Private Law Influence of the Great Qing Code

ZHANG TAISU

12.1 Introduction

This chapter considers the socioeconomic functionality of legal codes and codification through the lens of late imperial Chinese legal history. Specifically, it asks whether formal legal codes can wield significant influence over private socioeconomic behavior despite being poorly enforced – or even unenforced – and whether such influence derives, in part, from the symbolic value of codification itself. It argues that the answer to both questions is likely "yes," at least in the context of Qing Dynasty private law. This contains potentially generalizable insights into the nature of legal authority and prestige, some of which may potentially be applied to the recent passage of the Chinese Civil Code in 2020.

The core of the chapter is situated in mid-to-late Qing history, which spans the later eighteenth century and the entirety of the nineteenth. During this period, Chinese coercive state capacity sank to arguably its lowest point in history, driven primarily by severe decay in the state's fiscal capacity, which hit rock bottom in the mid-nineteenth century at barely 1 percent of estimated GDP.[1] As a result, the state's control over sub-county localities plummeted, and law enforcement capacity plummeted with it. The center of gravity of socioeconomic regulation – at least in the realms that we commonly attribute to "private law" – shifted to local custom, rather than formal laws: when local property or contract customs substantively clashed with laws, a fairly frequent occurrence, local courts tended to defer to custom, rather than attempt to enforce formal law. By the nineteenth century, Chinese "private law" had, as a

[1] This is discussed in some detail in Taisu Zhang, *The Ideological Foundations of Qing Taxation* (Cambridge: Cambridge University Press, forthcoming), ch. 1. See also Loren Brandt, Debin Ma, and Thomas G. Rawski, "From Divergence to Convergence: Reevaluating the History Behind China's Economic Boom" (2014) 52 *Journal of Economic Literature* 45; Jason Qiang Guo, "A Quantification of Fiscal Capacity of Chinese Government in the Long Run" (2019) Working Paper, New York University.

matter of substantive content, almost certainly become highly fractured and localized.

The formal coercive authority of central legal codes, most notably the *Great Qing Code*, which supplied much of the country's formal socioeconomic legislation, therefore deteriorated sharply over the course of late imperial Chinese history. This does not imply, however, that they somehow became socioeconomically insignificant. The persistent sociointellectual influence of formal legal codes is seen, in fact, in almost every corner of local economic customs and perhaps most obviously in property and contract customs.

Despite Qing China's enormous ecological, sociocultural, economic, and even political diversity, the functional structure of property and contract relations were remarkably uniform across nearly all Han Chinese-settled parts of the empire, even in highly intricate and therefore highly variable legal relationships like mortgage transactions. The substantive regulatory details of property use, ownership, and transaction varied from region to region, even from village to village, but the general architectural framework of these legal institutions – the basic legal nature of private economic relationships – did not. Moreover, these customary frameworks were all broadly consistent with those provided in the *Qing Code*.

These observations are inconsistent with either a purely bottom-up account of social norm formation or a purely materialistic account of institutional path-dependency and instead point to *Qing Code* as an external source of intellectual influence and institutional focus. The *Code* could not have had much coercive power by the time these customs were surveyed in the dynasty's final decade (1901–1911), nor did there seem to be a very large amount of economic reliance on its substantive rules. Nonetheless, it seemed to retain a significant amount of noncoercive authority and prestige, enough to serve, on more abstract issues of legal architecture, as the dominant focal point for local customary self-regulation. This likely explains why customary private law shared core structural features across China, even as regional differences led to significant differences in substantive regulatory content.

The natural follow-up question to these claims is whether the act of codification itself enhanced the *Qing Code*'s noncoercive authority in any substantial fashion. Although the lack of clear historical counterfactuals makes it impossible to answer this question with any level of certainty, the answer is very likely "yes." Codification in Qing China was less an act of substantive lawmaking than an assertion of political authority and an attempt to lower the information costs related to law enforcement. The state eventually lost its grip on the substantive dimensions of law enforcement, and the *Code* did relatively little to delay that decline, but the socio-intellectual prestige and salience of the *Code* were nonetheless very substantial – far higher than other government-issued legal rules that covered the same substantive ground. Among other things, it occupied an outsized position in the commercial printing industry's legal publishing business.

In fact, the *Code* retained a considerable amount of its socio-intellectual prestige even after the dynasty's final decline and fall. For example, British colonialists recognized it as the formal source of civil and criminal law in Hong Kong after their takeover in 1841 and would continue to do so in some capacity for much of the twentieth century. Similarly, many rules in the *Code* retained some measure of influence in Republican China, serving as default blueprints for new statutes and regulations right up to the issuance of the Republican *Civil Code* in 1929. Its socio-intellectual longevity seemed to far exceed that of other sets of Qing legal rules.

The *Qing Code* therefore offers a major example of what might be called the "prestige effect" of codification: the act of legal codification typically carries a large amount of socio-intellectual prestige and influence that operates somewhat independently of its actual legal significance, or even of its legal enforceability. The compilation of legal rules into a single unified text creates significant economies of scale when it comes to the social salience of those rules, lending them a stronger veil of authority and prestige. This effect is widely observed in modern legislative contexts, and may very well have been the primary driving force behind the issuance of the 2020 Chinese *Civil Code*. The Qing example, among many others, shows that the effect also exists in premodern sociolegal contexts and may well be even stronger there due to the greater costs of premodern legal communication and education.

The remainder of the chapter is organized as follows: Section 12.2 gives a very brief summary of the *Qing Code*'s initial drafting process and basic functionality. Section 12.3 discusses the sharp decline of the Qing state's formal administrative and legal capacities in the later eighteenth and nineteenth centuries, which severely eroded the *Code*'s functional authority. Section 12.4 argues that, despite such erosion, the *Code* nonetheless retained a significant amount of socio-intellectual prestige and influence. It further proposes that the *Code*'s status as a *code* strongly enhanced its ability to retain prestige in the face of functional decline.

Section 12.5 concludes with some general thoughts about the "prestige effect" of legal codification and how it may apply to the 2020 Chinese *Civil Code*.

12.2 Creating the *Great Qing Code*

For most of imperial Chinese history, dynasties had a habit of issuing major law codes – criminal law codes, in particular – in the decades after their establishment. For example, in 583, the Sui dynasty issued the *Kaihuang Code* shortly after the formal ascension of its founding emperor. Similarly, the Tang dynasty began work on the *Wude Code* immediately after its founding, and issued it seven years later in 624.[2] Work on the Song Dynasty's criminal code, the *Song Xing Tong* (*Unified Criminal Laws of the Song Dynasty*), began three years into the dynasty in 962.[3] In comparison, work on the *Great Ming Code* moved more slowly, and the code was only formally completed in 1397, three decades after the dynasty's founding.[4] The Qing, too, fell into this general pattern, beginning work on the *Great Qing Code* almost immediately after taking control of Beijing in 1644, and issuing the first formal version of the code in 1646.[5]

In many of these cases, the newly issued code would simply be a moderately or lightly modified version of the previous dynasty's code: the *Kaihuang Code* was, substantively and structurally, a direct predecessor to the *Wude Code*, as was the *Great Ming Code* to the *Great Qing Code*, and so on. The reasons for this are relatively straightforward: the new dynasty was rushing to establish its authority as quickly as possible under conditions of significant political uncertainty, and insofar as the issuance of a new code was an important part of that, it could not afford a

[2] Zhang Xianchang, "*Kaihuang Lü* de Xiuding ji qi zai Zhongguo Fazhi Shi shang de Diwei" ("开皇律》的修订及其在中国法制史上的地位") ["The Revision of the Kaihuang Code and its Significance in Chinese Legal History"] (2002) 4 *Faxue Yanjiu* (法学研究) 154; Xu Hanyan, "'Zhenguan' Fazhi Qiantan"("'贞观法治' 浅谈") ["A Brief Discussion of the 'Zhenguan Rule of Law Debate'"] (1981) 3 *Faxue Yanjiu* (法学研究) 54.

[3] Guo Dongxu, "*Song Xing Tong* de Zhiding ji qi Bianhua" ("宋刑统的制定及其变化") ["The Creation and Evolution of the Song Xing Tong"] (1991) 4 *Hebei Xuekan* (河北学刊) 84.

[4] See Yonglin Jiang, "Introduction: The Making of the *Great Ming Code*," in Yonglin Jiang (trans.), *The Great Ming Code* (Seattle: University of Washington Press, 2012), p. xxxiii.

[5] Qu Tongzu, "Qing Lü de Jicheng he Bianhua" ("清律的继承和变化") ["The Inheritance and Revision of Ming Law in the Qing"] (1980) 4 *Lishi Yanjiu* (历史研究) 32.

careful and systemic drafting process that would take a very long time to finish.[6]

This tells us something important about the functions of these codes: very often, they were not employed to make substantive legal changes but rather to send various political signals. Most notably, they functioned as a symbol both of the new dynasty's legal authority and capacity and of its commitment to some measure of institutional and socioeconomic continuity and stability. It therefore communicated a "credible commitment," to employ the language of New Institutional Economics, to the population on the dynasty's basic legal vision.

The act of codification – that is, of the issuance of a *comprehensive* legal code purporting to regulate nearly all areas of private activity – was centrally important to this "symbolism function": the comprehensive nature of the new legislation conveyed political messages much more effectively than a more limited bundle of laws could. The sheer scale of the code, along with its unified, concentrated structure, gave it an outsized amount of sociopolitical salience, helping the new dynasty effectively communicate its claim to authority and its commitment to institutional stability. To some extent, the code's symbolic functions were not all that different from those of a major physical monument, except that, with the advent of commercial legal printing in later imperial history, it was even easier to disseminate and publicize: most people in Ming or Qing China would never be able to lay eyes on the Imperial Palace, but they could be taught the basic contents of the dynastic criminal code.[7]

The existence of symbolism function does not imply, of course, that these dynastic codes were somehow unimportant as sources of substantive law. Quite the opposite, as the new dynasty solidified its coercive powers and general state capacity, the codes were usually quite functional as substantive legal regulation, often enjoying – for a time – relatively robust enforcement and somewhat widespread socioeconomic compliance. The point here is simply that, from the perspective of substantive law enforcement and socioeconomic regulation, there was rarely a terribly urgent need to issue a new code after the dynasty's formal establishment, especially if the new code was largely a regurgitation of the

6 See discussion in sources in notes 2–5.

7 On local legal education in the Qing, see, e.g., Ting Zhang, *Circulating the Code: Print Media and Legal Knowledge in Qing China* (Seattle: University of Washington Press, 2020).

previous dynasty's criminal code. A simple declaration that the previous code would continue to function – which the Mongol-ruled Yuan Dynasty issued upon consolidating its rule over Northern and Central China in the mid-thirteenth century – would have served largely the same legal functions.[8] Instead, the primary rationale for rushing to issue a new code was likely to make use of its political symbolism.

In all likelihood, this was also the dominant political rationale behind the *Great Qing Code*'s issuance in 1646. The so-called drafting process produced, at this time, a document that almost completely copied the *Great Ming Code*, with only minor adjustments: apart from a few reorganizational moves, the only substantive changes were the removal of three statutes related to paper currency and the addition of one statute on military service exile.[9] The new dynasty therefore reaped very few substantive legal benefits from this process, and yet the code's political symbolism was nonetheless significant: it was simultaneously a claim to legal authority, a call for law and order, and an explicit commitment to maintaining the basic legal structure of Chinese society. For an ethnically foreign conquest dynasty looking to solidify and legitimate its rule over an often hostile Han Chinese population, these symbolic benefits were undoubtedly enormous and more than justified the decision to rush out the new code despite the almost complete lack of new legal material.

Once Qing rule had been solidified – a process that took until the later seventeenth century to complete – the Court began to make substantive changes to the *Code* at a more leisurely pace.[10] The *Code* underwent two formal revisions over the course of the next century, once in 1727 under the Yongzheng emperor, and once in 1740 under the Qianlong emperor. Unlike the rushed nature of the initial *Code*, these later revisions took much longer to complete and made somewhat larger changes to legal structure and content. The Yongzheng revision actually began under his father, the Kangxi emperor, in 1679, but dragged on for decades until it finally picked up speed after 1725. The Qianlong revision, in comparison, took only five years to complete but nonetheless represented a far more measured legal approach than what the court could muster back in 1644. Beyond these formal revisions to the *Code*'s primary statutes, the

[8] See, e.g., Huang Shijian, "*Da Yuan Tongzhi* Kaobian" ("大元通制考编") ["On the Evolution of the Da Yuan Tongzhi"] (1987) 2 *Zhongguo Shehui Kexue* (中国社会科学) 157.

[9] Qu Tongzu, "Qing Lü," 32.

[10] Ibid.

Imperial Court also added a very large amount of substatutes that clarified, interpreted, and sometimes expanded upon the broader legal principles laid out in the statutes. This process, which began soon after the *Code*'s issuance in 1646 and continued throughout the dynasty at regular five- or ten-year intervals, eventually produced a legal corpus of nearly 2,000 substatutes, which, by the nineteen century, had arguably superseded the primary statutes in legal significance.[11]

Besides the *Great Qing Code*, which covered criminal punishment and socioeconomic regulation, the Imperial Court also issued another major law code in the seventeenth century, the *Great Qing Administrative Code* (*Da Qing Huidian*), which laid out the basic structures and rules of governmental operation.[12] Comparing the legislative histories of the two codes reveals some significant differences in their underlying political logic: after the 1644 conquest,[13] work on issuing a new *Administrative Code* did not commence until 1684 and only produced a formal product in 1690. From then on, apart from receiving a somewhat steady stream of new substatutes, the *Administrative Code* underwent four major revisions, in 1732, 1764, 1819, and 1890, which largely involved the compilation and formal reorganization of substatutes accumulated over previous decades.

Why did the Qing Court rush to issue the *Great Qing Code* immediately after its 1644 conquest but not the *Great Qing Administrative Code*? The most likely answer once again comes down to symbolic value: the criminal code – which actually covered all areas of private activity, including those that modern legal systems would recognize as criminal, such as homicides, but also those that they would insist are civil, such as

[11] See Lü Li, "Lun *Da Qing Lüli* 'yi Li Fu Lü' de Tili Yuanze" ("论大清律例 '以例辅律' 的体例原则") ["On the Systemic Use of Precedent and Interpretation in the Application of the Great Qing Code"] (1999) 4 *Jilin Daxue Shehui Kexue Xuebao* (吉林大学社会科学学报) 36.

[12] See Macabe Keliher, "Administrative Law and the Making of the First *Da Qing Huidian*" (2016) 37 *Late Imperial China* 55.

[13] Some scholars, most notably Zhang Jinfan and Guo Chengkang, argue that, prior to the conquest, the Manchu state had already issued a rudimentary *Huidian* in 1636, although this is under dispute. Zhang Jinfan and Guo Chengkang, "Qing *Chongde Huidian* Shixi" ("试析清崇德会典") ["A Tentative Analysis of the Qing Dynasty's Chongde Huidian"] (1983) 3 *Faxue Yanjiu* (法学研究) 69. Assuming this earlier *Huidian* did exist, it nonetheless covered a qualitatively lesser amount of legal and regulatory ground than the administrative codes issued after 1644 and probably cannot be considered a direct functional predecessor.

contractual breaches – was socially salient and therefore symbolically important in a way that the administrative code was not.

Although the latter also carried enormous amounts of functional importance, its center of legal gravity lay in the internal organization and regulation of governmental action, rather than the external regulation of socioeconomic activity by the general population. There were plenty of statutes in the *Administrative Code* that substantially affected the population's everyday life – for example, its rules on tax collection and local governance – but they did so in a somewhat less direct fashion than the penal punishments laid out in the *Great Qing Code*. The latter, not the former, was the general population's most immediate and perhaps extensive encounter with formal law and therefore carried a measure of social salience that the former simply did not.[14] For a conquest dynasty that needed to quickly establish its rule over a Han Chinese population that vastly outnumbered Manchu bannermen, the symbolic value of an authoritative criminal code was almost certainly much higher than that of an administrative code.

The relatively weaker social salience, and therefore weaker symbolic value, of the administrative code may also help explain why it continued to be formally revised in the late Qing, whereas the criminal code was not. The state may well have perceived a need to signal institutional stability to the general population through "locking in" the *Qing Code*'s primary statutes, but no such need to lock in the less socially salient *Administrative Code*. Indeed, such a move would fit well into the general pattern of political conservatism, reduced state capacity, and institutional decentralization that dominated later Qing political and legal history – as Section 12.3 will discuss in greater detail.

12.3 Institutional Erosion in the Later Qing

Scholars who study late imperial Chinese history widely recognize the Qing state as an unusually weak one, at least in terms of its formal and coercive capacities. By the most direct and most easily quantified measure of state capacity – fiscal capacity – the Qing was not only the weakest of any major Chinese dynasty but also probably the weakest state among all major powers in the early modern world.[15] Across most of imperial

[14] On different levels of public exposure to legal codes, see discussion in Zhang, "Circulating the Code."

[15] See discussion in Zhang, "Ideological Foundations," ch. 1.

Chinese history, such as during the Tang or Ming dynasties, the state tended to fiscally extract in the range of 5 percent of estimated GDP. During the Song and Yuan dynasties, it extracted significantly more than that, peaking at over 10 percent in the thirteenth century. The Qing, in contrast, started out at around 4–5 percent in the late seventeenth century, but quickly fell to less than 2 percent in the late eighteenth, and to 1 percent or occasionally even lower in the nineteenth century. This was shockingly low by the global standards of eighteenth and nineteenth century taxation, which saw major Eurasian powers extract as little as around 5 percent, which represented the norm for Ottoman tax rates, or as high as over 20 percent in smaller, more compact island states such as England or Japan.

The reasons for the Qing's unusual fiscal weakness range from geopolitics to bureaucratic management to ideology and are far too complex to discuss in this chapter. The point here is simply that its low – and generally declining – fiscal capacity was enormously detrimental to its formal state capacity and particularly its legal capacity. The Chinese population more than doubled from the early eighteenth century to the mid-nineteenth, but the state's total income remained largely stagnant in total volume. In fact, even in the late seventeenth and early eighteenth century, the Qing's fiscal capacity, as measured by the percentage of gross production it fiscally extracted, was already lower than late Ming levels and far lower than Song or Yuan levels.

By the late eighteenth and early nineteenth century, the Qing state consciously withdrew from the everyday administration of sub-county governance, recognizing that its constantly shrinking fiscal capacity simply could not keep up with the institutional needs of its still-growing population.[16] As a result, the state's formal coercive control over sub-county entities eroded to levels perhaps not seen at any other point in the second millennium, locking it into a self-reinforcing cycle of political conservatism: fiscal weakness led to administrative decline, which made it even harder for the state to muster the political resolve to raise taxes.

Scholars have sometimes disputed the claim that Qing state capacity declined in the nineteenth century by pointing to the rise of state-coordinated local self-governance, which filled in much of the administrative and even legal gap left open by the state's formal erosion.[17] Unlike

[16] Ibid., ch. 5.

[17] E.g., He Wenkai, "Caizheng Zhidu, Guojia Quanli Zhengdangxing yu Guojia Nengli: Qingdai Guojia Nengli de Zai" ("财政制度, 国家权力正当性与国家能力 清代国家能

its predecessors, who were at best lukewarm to sharing sociopolitical power with local lineages, the Qing actively encouraged lineage formation and self-governance, especially from the late eighteenth century onwards. Certainly this institutional decentralization posed significant risks for state control and political stability, but it was made necessary by the erosion of fiscal capacity: the state effectively faced an either/or choice between aggressively raising taxes or allowing, even encouraging, more local self-governance, and it had no appetite for the former.

Whether these developments successfully substituted for the state's institutional retreat – which they likely did in some dimensions, such as the provision of local public goods or dispute resolution, and almost certainly did not in others, such as large-scale famine relief or industrial investment – is, for our present purposes, largely beside the point. If we define state capacity to incorporate both formal and informal capacity, then perhaps we can argue that, to some extent, state capacity did not seriously suffer from fiscal decline, but there is no logical way to argue that formally coercive state capacity did not seriously suffer. Replacing formal capacity with informal capacity nonetheless implies that the former is in decline, and while the formal–informal distinction may not be terribly critical for some other institutional topics, it is unavoidably central to any discussion of *codification*, in which the formal, coercive enforcement of a law code is fundamentally different from the code's informal intellectual or social influence.

Along those lines, there can be no doubt that, by the nineteenth century, the Qing state's formal law enforcement capacities were very limited, especially in the area of substantive private law. Despite being a criminal code, the *Qing Code* actually recognized a sort of public law/private law distinction: serious offenses against the state and public – homicides, assaults, moral crimes – were punished with higher sentences and required at least one level of formal review beyond the initial trial court.[18] In contrast, "minor offenses related to household affairs, marriage, tax payment, and landed property" (*hu hun tian tu xigu*) were

力在考察") ["Fiscal System, State Legitimation, and State Capacity: A Reevaluation of the State Capacity in Qing China"] (2021) 1 *Zhongguo Jingji Shi Yanjiu* (中国经济史研究) 18.

[18] Da Qing Lüli (大清律例) [The Great Qing Code], sec. 334.05 (1768); Jonathan Ocko, "I'll Take It All the Way to Beijing: Capital Appeals in the Qing" (1988) 47 *Journal of Asian Studies* 291, 295 ("[N]o appeals of minor civil cases could be accepted"); Qiang Fang, "Hot Potatoes: Chinese Complaint Systems from Early Times to the Late Qing" (2009) 68 *Journal of Asian Studies* 1105, 1121.

almost entirely the domain of local county courts, and, by design, generally could not be appealed to a higher legal authority. Functionally speaking, the latter constituted the bulk of what modern lawyers might recognize as "private law," covering most private disputes in everyday life.

While the Qing state seemed to maintain a reasonable amount of coercive and information capacity over serious criminal offenses throughout its 268 year existence, by the nineteenth century, it had largely ceded control over these "private law" issues to local communal self-governance and self-regulation, routinely allowing local customary rules to supersede formal laws, including those provided by the *Qing Code*, in general socioeconomic significance.

This was not merely true in private life, where most interactions and transactions were governed by local customs and norms far more extensively and intensively than by any set of formal legal rules, but even in local courts, where magistrate judges routinely punted disputes back to community mediation and, in some cases, directly disregarded formal law in favor of customary rules.[19] Surveys of eighteenth and nineteenth century county case archives from North China, Sichuan, Taiwan, and the Lower Yangtze reveal a very significant number of "private law" disputes that never produced any formal criminal sanctions. The great majority of these cases were simply settled out of court, often at the judge's explicit behest. The comparatively small number of formal judgments that were issued were frequently consistent with formal legal rules but also frequently not. There was, after all, a large amount of substantive common ground between formal law and local customs, which generally eliminated any incentive for judges to diverge from formal legal dictate, but if a clear divergence between, say, the *Qing Code* and local customs did emerge on any substantive issue – and there were many of these in the regulation of property rights, monetary transactions, and family relations – then most county courts were probably more likely to follow the latter than the former.

The reasons for such behavior are not hard to understand: county magistrates almost always had very strong incentives to maintain positive relations with the local population, especially as the amount of coercive

19 See discussion in Taisu Zhang, *The Laws and Economics of Confucianism: Kinship and Property in Pre-Industrial China and England* (Cambridge: Cambridge University Press, 2017), ch. 1; Philip C. C. Huang, *Civil Justice in China: Representation and Practice in the Qing* (Stanford: Stanford University Press, 1996).

force they possessed declined precipitously after the late eighteenth century. It was therefore rarely in their personal interests to openly enforce formal law against inconsistent local customs.[20] Not only were they not rewarded for doing so, but they risked official censure from their superiors if the enforcement action triggered any significant amount of social unrest and protest. Moreover, because most "private law" cases could not be appealed beyond the county level, there was very little risk, and virtually no records, of higher authorities punishing a county magistrate for failing to follow formal legal rules.

What this meant, for our present purposes, is that, by the late eighteenth century at the latest, and perhaps even since the early eighteenth or even late seventeenth century, formal legal documents like the *Qing Code* could not be consistently enforced at the local level. Within the private law domain, they very often could not be enforced at all against substantively inconsistent local customs and had clearly taken a back seat in everyday socioeconomic life to those customs. Some of this was by design, as the state consciously withdrew from local administration and governance, but it nonetheless represented a fundamental erosion of the *Code*'s formal legal authority. For the latter half of its existence, the *Code* simply was not a functionally reliable source of socioeconomic regulation.

12.4 The *Code*'s Socio-Intellectual Prestige

Despite the serious erosion of its functional enforceability and therefore legal authority after mid-dynasty, the *Great Qing Code* nonetheless continued to enjoy a significant measure of socio-intellectual influence and prestige, even after the dynasty's collapse in 1911–12. There are several different ways to observe this "prestige effect" at work. The most systemic one is to take a look at the content of customary law across the country: in the absence of any functionally enforceable central legal authority, one might expect it to splinter and diverge in innumerable locally specific ways. To some extent, this is exactly what happened, and yet there were also significant common legal structures, transcending local idiosyncrasies, that seemed to suggest the continued existence of some centralizing force – an influence-based one, not a coercive one.

[20] Zhang, "Laws and Economics of Confucianism," ch. 1.

It is, in fact, possible to obtain a usable, if ultimately crude, sense of the content of late Qing customary law. After 1900, the Qing Court conducted a nationwide survey of local private law customs, as part of its preparation for systemic legal modernization in the European model: the idea was that any new legal code must be the synthesis of outside influences and domestic realities, and insofar as the old Qing Code no longer accurately reflected those realities – a point that the Court was keenly aware of – new surveying needed to be done.[21] Following the dynasty's end, successor regimes in the Republican era continued to pursue this project, until a published report was issued in 1930, at around the same time – perhaps not by coincidence – that the new *Republican Civil Code* went into effect.

What this survey reveals is that most local customs, while varying significantly on the finer points of legal substance, seemed to share a basic functional architecture. For example, in customary property law, the specific rules governing land redemption following a collateral transaction or rent negotiation under "permanent tenancy" arrangements varied greatly from place to place, but the core structure of property ownership, use, and transfer was largely consistent: land was generally privately owned, either by a household or by a lineage collectively – much more often the former than the latter – and was used primarily at the household-level. It could be rented, collateralized, gifted, sold, or forfeited in structurally similar ways across most of the country.[22]

For a very specific illustration of these institutional circumstances, consider the act of collateralized lending: in nearly every locality covered by the survey, local customs recognized and protected the use of land as collateral, generally through a "conditional sale" (*dian*) that gave the creditor both nominal title and usage rights over the land until the debtor redeemed.[23] Conditional ownership acquired in this fashion could be sold or rented out (including to the debtor), subject to the debtor's right

[21] Sui Hongming, *Qingmo Minchu Minshangshi Xiguan Diaocha zhi Yanjiu* (清末民初民商事习惯调查之研究) [A Study on Commercial and Civil Customs Surveys in the Late Qing and Early Republic] (2005), pp. 18–76.

[22] Zhang, "Laws and Economics of Confucianism."

[23] Taisu Zhang, "Land Law in Chinese History," in *Routledge Companion to Chinese Legal History* (London: Routledge, forthcoming), https://papers.ssrn.com/sol3/papers.cfm?abstract_id=3547494; Thomas Buoye, *Manslaughter, Markets and Moral Economy: Violent Disputes over Property Rights in Eighteenth Century China* (Cambridge: Cambridge University Press, 2000); Kenneth Pomeranz, "Land Markets in Late Imperial and Republican China" (2008) 23 *Continuity & Change* 101.

of redemption. In the great majority of localities – but not all of them – the right of redemption did not automatically terminate after any specific period of time, but it was subject to significant limitations at the other end of the time spectrum: the debtor could not redeem until *after* a certain number of years had passed, thereby guaranteeing the creditor at least some significant amount of use value. On this latter point, local customs varied greatly in the length of this "guaranteed usage period," ranging from a year to over a decade. Further customary variation was seen in other technical details of use and redemption, including whether it could be done between seeding and harvest and whether the creditor would also have to assume tax liability for the collateralized land.

Other local variations of collateralized lending existed in some regions, under a variety of names, but in nearly all documented regions, the conditional sale, under the basic transactional structure described above, was the central mechanism through which relatively large amounts of long-term credit were extended.[24] One might wonder whether this structural uniformity was simply a product of its instrumental superiority – that, in other words, it simply represented the most obvious and most efficient way to set up a collateralized loan. Such a claim would likely seem far-fetched to any comparative scholar: alternative legal arrangements that have been employed in early modern human history include those that give the creditor a right to be repaid from the proceeds of a foreclosure sale, but not any actual title over the collateral, or perhaps give him nominal but not actual title. There is no obvious reason why either of these arrangements would have been functionally inferior to the dominant Qing mechanism, which gave the creditor actual title, subject to a possibility of redemption. Relatedly, there is also no obvious reason why the optimal use arrangement would have been to transfer usage rights to the creditor until redemption: commonly used alternatives in other countries include keeping usage rights with the debtor but giving the creditor a right to collect interest or rent. In fact, given the enormous socioeconomic variation in China, it is very difficult to imagine how *any* one-size-fits-all institutional arrangement could have been definitively instrumentally superior across all regions, or even most of them.

Instead, the better explanation for the structural uniformity of conditional sales was that there were some standardizing forces at work across all, or nearly all, of Qing society. For most of the common structural

[24] Zhang, "Laws and Economics of Confucianism."

features described above, formal legal recognition in the *Qing Code* was almost certainly one of the most important forces that drove their cross-regional entrenchment. It is important to note that the conditional sale predates the *Qing Code* by at least several centuries and that the *Code* never explicitly defines what a conditional sale is, but it nonetheless contains multiple statutes and substatutes that clearly recognize the basic structure of such transactions: a loan, a transfer of title and usage rights, and a right of redemption.[25] It seems very likely that such recognition helped sustain the structure against the erosion of regional socioeconomic variation – if not through formal legal authority, then at least through socio-intellectual salience and prestige.

One might ask, of course, why these codified structural features were able to maintain cross-regional uniformity, while other *Qing Code* rules concerning conditional sales – including those concerning redemption deadlines and procedures – were frequently ignored in local practice and therefore subject to more regional variation.[26] The most plausible answer is that some rules are more sociopolitically controversial and contested than others and that specific rules concerning redemption rights were probably more intensely contested than the basic legal structure of a conditional sale. The latter might merely have created moderate functional inconveniences in some localities, whereas the former had serious consequences for wealth distribution and household welfare across the country. Local communities might therefore have been content to follow what they considered standard practice on the structure features, even as they constantly negotiated and renegotiated the rules of redemption based on their specific sociopolitical conditions. In other words, the standardizing force of the *Code* was certainly not immune to local erosion on instrumental grounds, but it may have provided an additional layer of "protection" that only more socioeconomically charged issues could breach.

These institutional dynamics are hardly limited to the conditional sale context but are instead generally observable across most of Qing "private law": in tenancy, contract, family law, and so on. It was, in general, possible to travel from one corner of the empire "Chinese core" to another, and perhaps even to Manchuria, and still come across basic

[25] Ibid. See also Lin Feng, "Qingdai Zhengfu ruhe Jianguan Tudi Jiaoyi" ("清代政府如何监管土地交易") ["How the Qing State Oversaw Land Transactions"] (2019) 9 *Renmin Luntan* (人民论坛) 141, https://core.ac.uk/download/pdf/343509667.pdf.

[26] Zhang, "Laws and Economics of Confucianism."

customary legal structures that were recognizably similar to those in one's place of origin, even if the substantive details differed significantly. It was therefore possible to speak of "the Qing legal system" in some generalized, structural sense, even though whatever "system" there was contained thousands of regional variations at finer levels of functionality.

Given that, after mid-dynasty, the formal legal system in general, and the *Qing Code* in particular, possessed very little coercive force at the sub-county level, the *Code*'s standardizing force could only have come from some noncoercive mechanism. One possibility is that, once a basic structural framework was in place, given the costs of institutional change, local communities were simply unlikely to diverge from it unless it became *very* onerous or sociopolitically contested. The problem with a theory of pure path-dependency is that China is unusually large and regionally diverse – China's core macroeconomic regions are approximately the size of Western, Central, and Southern Europe combined and comparably diverse in socioeconomic or geographical terms – and the history of Qing legal decentralization was unusually long – at least a century and a half and quite possibly much longer. The likelihood that at least some regions would deviate from the standardized structure seems quite high simply due to geographical size and temporal length involved. Moreover, it is not clear how large the costs of structural change actually were: would it really have been that costly to, for example, give creditors nominal title, instead of actual title in a conditional sale, or, in the many regions where most creditors were in the habit of renting out their usage rights back to the debtor anyway, to convert their usage rights into a simple right to collect a fixed amount of the land's annual produce? Relying solely on a theory of path-dependence seems altogether too intellectually passive, and likely too thin, in the face of the enormous socioeconomic forces working in favor of regional legal variation in Qing China.

A better approach would be to affirmatively acknowledge that the *Code* retained a substantial amount of socio-intellectual influence and prestige even after the functional erosion of its legal authority. Even in the nineteenth century, it continued to be widely printed and distributed by commercial publishers across the country,[27] and its intellectual mark is easily seen even in areas and historical eras fully beyond the control of the Qing state. For example, when the British assumed control over Hong

[27] See discussion in Zhang, "Circulating the Code."

Kong, they quickly recognized the *Code* as the primary legal authority of the region, rather than any set of local customs – even though the latter were, in all likelihood, much more closely attuned with actual socio-economic practice in the colony.[28] Similarly, the *Code* continued to serve as a basic template for the various attempts at civil codification that the Qing and its successor regimes made in the early twentieth century, which preserved large segments of its family, property, and contract law well into the 1920s.[29]

Recognizing this continued socio-intellectual influence would allow us to make easy sense of the *Code*'s ability to exert a considerable standardizing force over the basic structure of private legal relations, well after it had lost its coercive authority: individuals and communities do not draw up customs from scratch but instead employ models or templates to guide and streamline their decision-making whenever possible. Rulemaking is, as many have argued, as reliant on prestige-oriented considerations as it is on functionalist ones, and there was, of course, no legal template in Qing society that was more socially salient and prestigious than the *Great Qing Code*.

One final question is whether the *Qing Code*'s socio-intellectual prestige derived, at least partially, from its status as a *code* – a nominally comprehensive, coherently organized collection of durable legal rules covering nearly all aspects of individual behavior. While this effect is, by nature,[30] almost impossible to directly observe, there is some circumstantial evidence for its existence. Although the *Qing Code* was perhaps the most important source of substantive "private law" issued by the state, it was by no means the only source: the *Administrative Code*, for one, contained some legal rules that directly controlled private behavior, especially insofar as it affected the use and transaction of "banner land"

[28] On the enduring influence of Qing law in Hong Kong courts, see, e.g., Jérôme Bourgon, "Historians at the Court: How Cultural Expertise in Qing Law Contributes to the Invention of Hong Kong 'Chinese Customary Law'" (2020) 1 *Law and History Review* 38, 85–98.

[29] Li Xiandong, *Cong Daqing Lüli dao Mingguo Minfa Dian de Zhuanxing* (*从大清律例到民国民法典的转型*) [*The Transition from the Great Qing Code to the Civil Code of the Republic of China*], 中国人民公安大学出版社(Beijing: Press of People's University of Public Security of China, 2003).

[30] A direct observation would require documents that directly show local socioeconomic elites directly discussing the importance of the *Qing Code*, relative to other legal documents. Unsurprisingly, there is very little known material of this sort, if any.

(*qi di*) held by Manchu or Han bannermen.[31] Perhaps more importantly, several of the Six Ministries in Beijing routinely issued their own legal rules, many of which directly overlapped with the *Qing Code* in terms of subject matter.[32] For example, the Ministry of Finance issued a fairly large number of regulations, collected into the *Ministry of Finance Regulations* (*Hubu Zeli*), that overlapped with the private law portions of the *Qing Code* and in many cases significantly updating them. Likewise, the Ministry of Punishment also issued regulations that dealt with more serious criminal offenses, and these, too, overlapped substantively with the *Code*. Both sets of ministry regulations were systemically issued to all local magistrate courts, who were expected to enforce them as rigorously as any other legal text.

Despite their nominal legal importance, neither the *Administrative Code* nor the *Ministry of Finance Regulations* ever came close to matching the socio-intellectual prominence of the *Qing Code*. Recent scholarship on legal publishing suggests that, while commercial presses published a considerable number of legal texts in the Qing, the *Qing Code* far outpaced other formal legal statutes in its popularity and volume of distribution. Literati writings from the eighteenth and nineteenth centuries also single out the *Qing Code* as the most important legal text to master for officials. As Tian Wenjing, a prominent official of the Yongzheng reign, stated, "the *Qing Code* is the foundational legal text of our dynasty, representing the fixed rules of ten thousand generations . . .. Any new local official . . . should become intimately familiar with every chapter of the *Great Qing Code*."[33] Similarly, an essay on local

[31] Yang Xuechen, "Qingdai Qidi de Xingzhi ji qi Bianhua" ("清代旗地性质及其变化") ["The Character of Banner Land during the Qing and Its Evolution"] (1963) 3 *Lishi Yanjiu* (历史研究) 78.

[32] E.g., Lin Qian and Zhang Jinfan, "Zailun *Chongde Huidian*, *Hubu Zeli* de Falü Shiyong" ("再论崇德会典、户部则例的法律适用") ["Restudying the Legal Application of the Chongde Huidian and Hubu Zeli"] (2003) 5 *Faxue Qianyan* (法学前沿) 197; Zhang Jinfan (ed.), *Zhongguo Fazhi Tongshi* (中国法制通史) [*History of Chinese Law*] (Beijing: Falü Press, 1999), vol. XIII, p. 436; Kong Qingming, Hu Liuyuan, and Sun Jiping (eds.), *Zhongguo Minfa Shi* (中国民法史) [*The History of Chinese Civil Law*] (Changchun: Jilin People's Press, 1996), pp. 602–3.

[33] These materials are cited in Wang Zhiqiang, "Zhiding Fa zai Zhongguo Gudai Sifa Panjue Zhong de Shiyong" ("制定法在中国古代司法判决中的使用") ["The Uses of Formal Statutory Law in Traditional Chinese Adjudication"] (2006) 5 *Faxue Yanjiu* (法学研究) 136.

administration from the late Qing states that, "the only way [to curb the evils of local corruption] is to familiarize oneself with the *Great Qing Code*."[34]

While it might be tempting to believe that the *Qing Code*'s socio-intellectual prominence stemmed directly from its greater functional importance, that was not necessarily the case: the *Administrative Code* may well have been less functionally important for local administration due to its greater focus on internal bureaucratic organization, but the ministry regulations covered as much substantive ground as the *Code* itself, often in much greater detail and with superior adaptability to changing socioeconomic circumstances. Given that they carried a comparable expectation of formal institutional enforcement, the best explanation for their noticeably lower socio-bureaucratic salience seems not to be functional insignificance but instead lower levels of social prestige and intellectual stature. The *Code*'s more concentrated form, its veil of comprehensiveness, its clearer internal organization, its greater substantive stability – all of these institutional features that we associate with formal codification almost certainly enhanced its socio-intellectual prominence vis-à-vis the more piecemeal, fluid, and structurally disorganized ministry regulations. The former was institutionally packaged to maximize social visibility and transmission, whereas the latter closely tracked the substantive disorder of everyday governance and rulemaking.

The *Great Qing Code* was, in the end, the principal legal monument of the dynasty, the socio-intellectual focal point of the Qing legal apparatus, if not necessarily its substantive focal point. While that may very well have hindered its substantive legal adaptability – which created an institutional need for the more structurally flexible and easy-to-update ministry regulations – it greatly enhanced the *Code*'s socio-intellectual prestige. The erosion of formal state capacity in the eighteenth and nineteenth centuries rendered formal legal rules largely ineffective in a functional sense, but the *Code*'s prestige probably outlived its functional enforceability by many decades.

12.5 Conclusion: The "Prestige Effect" of Codification

The primary goal of this chapter, apart from illustrating some segments of the *Great Qing Code*'s 326-year history – it was not formally abolished

[34] Ibid.

in Hong Kong until 1972 – has been to highlight and analyze the "prestige effect" of codification. Law codes can, depending on the circumstances, bring quite a bit of legal functionality to the political regimes that issue them, but very often their sociopolitical impact goes well beyond that. The *Qing Code* is a perfect example of this: not only was its initial issuance in 1646 driven largely by social signaling considerations, but its broader socioeconomic impact in the eighteenth and nineteenth centuries was, in all likelihood, far more reliant on socio-intellectual prestige than on formal legal functionality. In fact, its socio-intellectual prestige was apparently instrumentally distinct from its legal functionality and could exist – thrive, even – in the latter's absence.

There are some potentially usable theoretical insights in this historical narrative for our understanding of more recent acts of codification. The 2020 Chinese *Civil Code*, in particular, seems like an excellent candidate for prestige-oriented analysis: despite the enormous amount of excitement it seemed to generate within the legal profession – of which this volume is an example – the *Civil Code* ultimately made only relatively minor changes to legal substance.[35] Moreover, as far as anyone can tell, there was no obvious internal inconsistency within Chinese private law prior to 2020 that only codification could fix. So what, in the end, was the primary motivation for civil codification, especially for Chinese lawmakers?

This is a question for another time, or perhaps for the other contributing authors to this volume, but it would not be unreasonable to suspect that lawmakers were at least as enamored of the prestige benefits of codification as they were motivated by its legal functionality. The government repeatedly hailed the issuance of the *Civil Code* as a major milestone in China's legal development, a testament to its institutional maturity, and something that would command respect from other nations. In the midst of a long-term economic slowdown, the COVID-19 pandemic, and rising geopolitical tensions with developed countries, the government may very well have pursued codification *primarily* for its prestige effect, so as to help shore up its domestic popularity and perhaps signal the regime's commitment to legal stability. If so, that would give the *Civil Code* much in common with the *Great Qing Code*.

[35] These changes are summarized in the document prepared by the Shanghai Lawyers Association, and published in numerous major Chinese newspapers, for example in *Pengpai* (澎湃) [*The Paper*], May 30, 2020, https://m.thepaper.cn/baijiahao_7635602.

13

The New Validity Rules in Chinese Civil Code and Chinese State-Owned Enterprises' Freedom in Contracting

One Step Too Far

HAO JIANG AND ANTONIA VON APPEN*

13.1 Introduction

In virtually all major civil codes, rules concerning the validity of contracts serve the same purpose: they are in place to ensure that the contract is legal and the consent is valid. They afford remedies when there are defects concerning the legality and consent. Such rules were written with private parties and a free market in mind. When the market is free and consent was obtained free from fraud, duress, and mistake, a contract is valid regardless of its economic fairness. The new Chinese Civil Code is no exception.

Nevertheless, when it comes to state-owned enterprises (SOEs) in a less than free and competitive market, as in both China and the former Soviet Union, however, such rules would lead to ridiculous outcomes. SOE managers will naturally be inclined to strip state assets when market information indicators are missing and, in the effort to eliminate such managerial opportunism, the state usually retains an enlarged power to declare a contract null and void in the name of protection of the state interest. Meanwhile, in asserting such a power, the state will have encouraged the SOEs to renege on a bad bargain.

This two-pronged problem will not be solved simply by providing validity rules that treat the state interest and the private interest alike.

* Hao Jiang is responsible for the whole chapter while Antonia von Appen's research is reflected on the part of the German regulations on the trading of state assets.

The difficulty arises because the normal market information indicators such as price and profit fail. When the price no longer reflects value and profit no longer reflects managerial performance, there will not be enough information to judge the performance of the SOEs, the SOE managers will have an information advantage over the state. Normal validity rules that only assure autonomy will give SOE managers incentives to trade state assets at a price that is significantly lower than their value. Such a practice is called asset stripping. Therefore, traditional Chinese contract rules both before and after the economic reform were, under Soviet influence, more paternalistic in nature in order to curb the managerial opportunism.

Both the Chinese law before the 2020 Civil Code and Soviet civil law before 1989 allowed the state to curb freedom of contract: contractual autonomy was limited and the state exercised an enlarged power to annul contracts that harm the state interest through the means of fraud or duress or conspiracy.[1] Here, the state interest is not to be confused with the public interest; rather, it is precisely the financial interest of the SOEs. Such a paternalistic power was in place to curb the SOE managers' incentive to strip state assets and divert them into their own pockets. In fact, such devices allowed SOEs to renege on a bargain that turned out to be less profitable.

Following the introduction of a private market and the principle of freedom of contract, in China, a logic dilemma arose. According to the principle of freedom of contract and pro-market rules, courts are not supposed to examine the adequacy of the bargain, which would encourage asset stripping; on the other hand, the state's power to annul transactions that harm state interests continue to permit reneging on a bad bargain on the part of the state. Ironically, both the problems of asset stripping and reneging continue to exist despite the modernization of the law.

Upon the enactment of the Chinese Civil Code, the previous rules that allowed for enlarged state power to annul contracts such as General

[1] See Article 52 of the Chinese Contract Law (1999). For example, Article 52(1)–(2), (4)–(5) provide that a contract is "null and void" if "either party enters into the contract by means of fraud or coercion, undermining the state interests; through malicious conspiracy that harmed state, collective and third party interest . . . social and public interests are undermined; or . . . mandatory provisions of laws and administrative regulations are violated." See also Article 58(3) of the General Principles of Civil Law (1987) (providing that a civil juristic act is null and void [not voidable] if it was concluded through the means of fraud and duress; all translations are done by the first author unless otherwise stated).

Principles of Civil Law Article 58 §3 and Contract Law Article 52 §1–§2 were dropped. Chinese law has gone one step further in promoting freedom of contract. The validity rules now have been streamlined and the previous contradictory and inconsistent treatment between civil juristic acts and contracts, state and private parties, was eliminated.[2] Now the rules are concise, transparent, and pro-market. The previous paternalistic rules that allowed the state to exercise an enlarged power to annul a contract are now gone. There are no longer any distinct treatments of public and private interests in the validity rules. On this point, Chinese law now looks exactly like German law. However, the new legislative technique does not resolve the problem that was created initially to deal with an entirely different economic structure. Given the fact that one-third of the Chinese economy is still owned and run by SOEs,[3] and that SOEs are subject to a market that is still not the same as the private enterprises, the very problem that the old rules set out to prevent still exists: the SOE managers are incentivized to divert the assets to their own pockets through related-party transactions. This practice is difficult for the state to curb due to the information asymmetry between the managers and the state in the absence of a competitive market and the incompatible incentives again between the two.[4] The new rules unavoidably will facilitate the stripping of state assets. It is true that there are administrative regulations that require trading of state assets to be fair. However, such regulations only bind the SOEs and have no authority over private parties. As a result, contracts that would effectively strip state assets are held to be binding despite the violation of SOE regulations.[5] The Chinese Supreme People's Court traditionally distinguishes

[2] Articles 143–57 of the Chinese Civil Code (2020).

[3] The private sector makes up 60 percent of the Chinese gross domestic product, see Amir Guluzade, "The Role of China's State-Owned Companies Explained," World Economic Forum, May 7, 2019), www.weforum.org/agenda/2019/05/why-chinas-state-owned-companies-still-have-a-key-role-to-play/, https://perma.cc/67R2-B7JH.

[4] See Hao Jiang, "The Making of a Civil Code in China: The Promises and Perils of a New Civil Law" (2021) 95 *Tulane Law Review* 777, 790–91.

[5] 张杰与侯效锋、*涡阳县青町粮食购销有限公司确认合同无效纠纷二审民事判决书* [*Zhang Jie* v. *Hou Xiaofeng & Woyang County Grain Trading Company LLC*] (2014) 亳民一终字第01081号 [(2014) Guo Min Yi Zhong Zi No. 01081];上海国信捷报实业有限公司与海南东方风力发电有限公司确认合同无效纠纷二审民事判决书 [*Shanghai Guoxin Holding Company* v. *Hainan Dongfang Windpower Company*] (2019) 琼民终108号 [(2019) Qiong Min Zhong No.108]; 哈尔滨市自然资源和规划局、*张凯确认合同无效纠纷二审民事裁定书* [*Harbin Bureau of Natural Resources and Planning* v. *Zhang Kai*] (2020) 黑01民终2805号 [(2020) Hei 01 Min Zhong No. 2805].

mandatory rules on validity from mandatory administrative rules in order to safeguard the safety of transactions and prevent courts' abuse of judicial power to randomly annul contracts.[6] Therefore, based on this distinction, only the violation of the former will result in illegality.[7] As we will see, courts had ruled that violation of asset valuation rules, for example, is merely a violation of administrative rules that does not result in illegality and nullity of the contract.[8] Through this technicality, SOEs are able to effectively violate the asset appraisal rules yet still have a valid contract despite the presence of gross disparity between market price and the contract price. In fact, as we will see, German law, through both the BGB and public statutes, would effectively require state assets to be traded at the market value despite having the same validity rules.

Through a historical, doctrinal, and logical lens, we will show why there can be no effective model of a neutral set of validity rules that could deal with SOEs in a less than free and competitive market. The only way to make it work is to have SOEs exit most of the competitive industries and focus on areas that serve the policy goals. Also, paternalistic rules concerning the validity of a contract in trading state assets should be enacted either in the Civil Code or through special legislation and applicable to government, SOEs, and private parties alike.

13.2 Preventing Asset Stripping: A Paternalistic Approach

The logical starting point for having a paternalistic approach in dealing with validity of contract concerning SOEs is to prevent asset stripping. When private ownership is by and large replaced by state ownership and the market by central economic planning, private parties no longer have

[6] "审理民商事合同纠纷案件指导意见." ["Guidance on the Adjudication of Civil and Commercial Contract Disputes"], 法发〔2009〕40号 [Fa Fa (2009) No. 40] Articles 15–16 (noting that transaction safety is an element to consider in identifying mandatory rules on validity).

[7] See Article 153 of the Chinese Civil Code ("A civil juristic act in violation of the mandatory provisions of laws or administrative regulations is void, unless such mandatory provisions do not lead to invalidity of such a civil juristic act"). See also Chinese Supreme People's Court's Judicial Interpretations (I) on Contract Law Article 4, according to which only violation of administrative regulation issued by the State Council and national statutes enacted by National People's Congress will lead to illegality and nullity of contract. See also SPC's Judicial Interpretations (II) Article 14, clarifying that the violation of mandatory rules under Article 52(5) of the Chinese Contract Law only referred to rules on validity.

[8] See *Zhang Jie* v. *Hou Xiaofeng & Woyang County Grain Trading Company LLC et al.*

an interest in contracting. Consequently, if only the state interest would be at stake, contract law would not be necessary. If we allow private interests in an overwhelmingly state-run socialist economy, contract law's main concern becomes curbing the practice of asset stripping, which does not exist in the normal contract law model. Necessarily, the state needs to assume a more paternalistic power in annulling contracts that might harm the state's financial interest. However, the result is often to allow the state to renege on a bad bargain at the cost of the private parties.

13.2.1 The Paternalistic Approach of Soviet Law

The Soviet Union went through rapid nationalization that completely wiped away the private ownership and private economy during the period of militant communism (1917–1922). The first and fundamental premise of Western law that Soviet law challenged was the impartiality of law. Supposedly, law should be applicable to all regardless of the social status and protect the interests of all. However, in the Marxist theory of law, law is only the law of the ruling class that represents only the latter's interests. Law therefore became a means that the ruling class uses to exploit the oppressed classes. Under this view, bourgeois law was not impartial but rather it represented only the interests of the bourgeois class and allowed the bourgeois to exploit the proletarian class. Not only was law not supposed be impartial, but the judiciary was also not allowed to be independent. Since 1917, courts were rebranded as "people's courts" that represented only the interests of the proletariat. They were instructed to "apply the hitherto existing law but only insofar as they were not abrogated by the revolution and did not contradict the revolutionary conscience and revolutionary concept of law."[9]

According to Karl Marx, law was considered a by-product of economic conditions. Law is a superstructure with an economic basis.[10] Therefore, legal relationships are "rooted in the material production of a given society"[11] and law is the reflection of "the material production of a given society."[12] The forms and contents of the law therefore differ according to the economic conditions of the society. According to Marx and Engels,

[9] Item 50, § 5 of the R.S.F.S.R Laws (1917–1918).

[10] See Vladimir Gsovski, "The Soviet Concept of Law" (1938) 7 *Fordham Law Review* 1, 5.

[11] Ibid.

[12] Ibid.

all the other elements in the society were elevated to superstructures that were based on the economy.[13] The concept of law that is consistent with this perspective is defined by a communist lawyer, Stuchka, as "[a] system (order) of social relations corresponding to the interests of the ruling class and protected by the organized force of this class (the State)."[14]

This ideological definition of law was criticized by other communist lawyers. The main criticisms were that the interests of the ruling class were not only protected by law but also by other means in the society. Such interests were not the only interests the law protects.[15] There are laws that were not merely protecting the interests of the ruling class, and laws will not cease to be law if they protect also the interests of the oppressed class. For example, traffic regulations do not only serve the interest of the ruling class but also protect other classes. Labor law in a bourgeois system protects the interests of the oppressed proletariat. A Marxist should find "the specific criteria of law different from other ideological superstructures."[16]

Such a reaction met with the criticism that it is "an undue attempt to develop the Marxist theory of law along the lines of idealistic, bourgeois philosophy."[17]

In fact, the withering away of law and disappearance of government was deemed to be an inevitable consequence in realizing communism.[18] According to the leading Soviet theorist Evgeny Pashukanis, capitalist law was merely a reflex of the capitalism economic conditions due to economic necessities, rather than "a manifestation of justice."[19] "Only capitalism creates the conditions necessary to enable the juridical element to obtain its highest development in social relation .... When the whole economic life is based on the principle of the free agreement of wills, then every social function in some way or other obtains a legal characteristic, that is to say, becomes not a mere social function, but the right of him who exercises the function."[20]

[13] Ibid.

[14] Item 590, § I(1) of the Fundamentals of Criminal Law in the R.S.F.S.R. Laws (1919).

[15] See Gsovski, "The Soviet Concept of Law," 9.

[16] Mikhail A. Reisner, "Theory of Law by Comrade Stuchka" (1922) 1 *Messenger of the Communist Academy* 173.

[17] Gsovski, "The Soviet Concept of Law," 9.

[18] Ibid.

[19] Ibid., 11.

[20] Ibid., quoting Evgeny Pashukanis, Общая теория права и марксизм [The General Theory of Law and Marxism], 1st ed. (Moscow: Sotsiahsticheskoi Akademii, 1924), pp. 19, 57.

He did not try to introduce a socialist law that would reflect the new economic conditions but advocated the abolition of law. According to him, "[t]he withering away of the categories of bourgeois law (exactly the categories, and not of this or that particular rule) can under no circumstances mean their replacement by some new categories of proletarian law."[21]

However, the paradigms changed with the enactment of the 1922 Russian Civil Code, the first Russian Civil Code, which was largely influenced by the German Civil Code and by the New Economic Policy that realized the indispensability of private ownership and private economy in a socialist country.

Even though the majority of the code articles resemble a typical Western civil code, the supremacy of the state interests over private interests was obvious. As a result, a clear paternalistic approach was taken to curb asset stripping. To be more specific, the law allowed the state to assume an enlarged power to avoid a contract that would otherwise harm its interest. Section 30 of the 1922 Civil Code of R.S.F.S.R. was a prime example of enabling the state to effectively combat asset stripping. It provided that "[a] civil juristic act made for a purpose contrary to law, or in fraud of law, as well as a transaction directed to the obvious prejudice of the State, shall be invalid."

Clearly, this provision seeks to protect the financial interest of the state and SOEs. Soviet case law and jurisprudence suggest that the range of contracts that were deemed to be directed to the obvious prejudice of the state was larger than those covered by the recently repealed Chinese Contract Law Article 52 §1– §2.[22]

Most scholars have agreed that it was a device to guard against the undesirable growth of private business and that it was enacted in conformity with Lenin's instruction "to enlarge the interference of the State with the relations pertaining to private law and to enlarge the right of the government to annul, if necessary, private contracts."[23] Another scholar, Tatiana E. Novitskaya, referred to this device as "an effective weapon in the hands of the Soviet state."[24] The right of the state to interfere with any contracts made in any area of civil law was a tool created to avoid

[21] Ibid.

[22] Hao Jiang, "Enlarged State Power to Declare Nullity: the Hidden State Interest in the Chinese Contract Law" (2014) 7 *Journal of Civil Law Studies* 147.

[23] See Vladmir Gsovski, *Soviet Civil Law* (Ann Arbor: University of Michigan Press, 1948), p. 426.

[24] Tatiana E. Novitskaya, Гражданский кодекс [*Grazhdanskiy Kodeks, Civil Code of the R.S.F.S.R.1922*] (Moscow: Moscow State University, 2002), p. 86.

consequences disadvantageous for the socialist economy. In a Russian Supreme Court case, the court annulled sales contracts solely because SOEs had an interest in the objects for sale.[25] Such annulments were based on the "socially announced purpose of use" of the object.[26] In another case, the high court annulled a lease and thereby interfered with a party's property right. The court held that the property right is not absolute under the Civil Code, and the economic interest of the SOE prevailed over the private party's property right.[27] It can be inferred that had the SOE been defrauded or the contract had been made under duress, the Soviet courts would have annulled it to protect the financial interests of the SOE. Also, it should be noted that when a contract is annulled under § 30, damages would be recovered by the state rather than the aggrieved party. This also serves a disincentive for SOEs to use this doctrinal device to renege on a bad bargain since it clearly would not serve their financial interest either when what is due under the contract is forfeited to the state.

As a result, SOEs would not be able to renege on any bad bargains caused by market fluctuation. Some bargains were fair upon conclusion of the contract but become less advantageous to one contracting party due to market price fluctuation. This is an inherent risk of the market that ought to be borne by the contracting parties. Even Vladimir Gsovski, an adamant critic of the Soviet government, admitted that the state was not allowed to renege on a rental contract when the price went up.[28] The court did not side with the state because the obvious prejudice under § 30 must be detrimental to the state upon conclusion and it was not the case here.[29]

This enlarged state power in contracting to prevent asset stripping outlived the 1922 Civil Code. In the 1964 Russian Civil Code, the nullity of a contract would normally result in bilateral restitution. However, when a transaction was intended for a purpose known to be contrary to the interests of the socialist state and society, § 30's special effect continued: the properties received by the parties will be forfeited to the state including both goods received or returned and payment due.[30]

[25] Ibid.
[26] Ibid.
[27] Ibid, p. 87.
[28] Gsvoski, "Soviet Civil Law," p. 427.
[29] Ibid.
[30] Article 49 of the R.S.F.S.R. Civil Code (1964).

Ye Fleishits, a jurist from within Soviet Union, acknowledged that this provision was rarely used.[31] However, he did explain what qualifies as contrary to the state interest: when the contract enriches private parties at the expense of the state and co-operative organizations:[32] for example, private citizens renting collective farm-land against the law or transactions concealing the sale of land.[33]

Since the massive privatization that took place at the end of the 1980s and early 1990s, there simply is no more special state interest that contract law needs to identify and protect. This paternalistic approach was abandoned by the 1994 Russian Civil Code.

Unlike America where state-ownership in business was rejected early on, other European countries that have had a communist regime such as the German Democratic Republic also went through a phase where SOEs played an important role in the national economy. Unsurprisingly, a similar set of rules aiming at protecting socialist property were in place in the Civil Code ZGB to prevent privatization and to limit the trading of state assets.[34] Privatization of SOEs and sale of state assets were deemed illegal unless through special legislation.[35] As a result, sales of state assets could likely be avoided and the proceeds be forfeited by the state. As we will see, such a distinct treatment is no longer in the BGB.

13.2.2 Paternalism in Traditional Chinese Economy and Chinese Contract Law

Extreme Paternalism: Contract as Mere Documentation of Transactions

Starting in the 1950s, following the gradual nationalization of the Chinese economy, SOEs along with government agencies and village collectives were the only parties legally allowed to contract. The normative system of contract law was nowhere to be found in the official literature of the law except for an eleven-article contract regulation, the *Provisional Methods*.[36] Yet it only prescribed the procedural steps to be

[31] Ye A. Fleishits and A. L. Makovsky, *The Civil Codes of the Soviet Republic* (Moscow: Progress, 1976), p. 94.

[32] Ibid.

[33] Ibid.

[34] § 20, §§ 68, 69 ZGB (Civil Code of the GDR).

[35] BVerwG, judgment from March 31, 2004 – 8 C 5/03 – BVerwGE 120, 246–55.

[36] 机关 、国营企业、合作社签订合同契约暂行办法' [Interim Measures for the Signing of Contracts by Government Agencies, State-owned Enterprises, and Cooperatives],

taken in order to properly document the transactions and seek legal remedies for breach of contract.[37] No normative contract rules were introduced until the 1981 Economic Contract Law (ECL). The rationale for this extreme paternalism was straightforward: when private interests no longer exist and market information is not available to monitor the SOE managers, any autonomy would result in an incentive for the managers to engage in opportunistic conduct to strip state assets.

With the *Provisional Methods*, the purpose of the regulation was "to facilitate the normal business relations among all the work units such as government organs, state enterprises and cooperatives in order to prevent one party causing the other loss through breaking its credit and further affecting the implementation of economic plans."[38] A government organ that engages in production activities, meets the production criteria, and has qualified itself as an independent business should be considered a state enterprise.[39] The *Provisional Methods* regulate the contracting activities among government organs, state enterprises, and cooperatives. Under the 1950 Regulations, contracting was required in the following transactions such as loans, sales of goods, product ordering, exchange of goods, commissioned purchase, commissioned processing, commissioned capital or equipment loan, commissioned transportation, construction, commercial rental, joint venture, etc.[40] All contracts, when the payment could not be processed immediately, had to be registered at the People's Bank, and contracts, upon conclusion, had to be filed with the higher level government agency and its economic commission and also filed in the record of the ministry of finance.[41] Payment could only be in the form of checks issued by a People's Bank's local branch. When applying for bank loans, such loans had to be qualified for the purpose of carrying out projects or financial plans that had been approved by superior government agencies or the agencies with appropriate authority.[42]

promulgated by the Fin. & Econ. Comm. Cent. People's Gov't Admin. Council, September 27, 1950.

37 Ibid.

38 Ibid., Article 1.

39 Ibid.

40 Ibid., Article 2.

41 Ibid.

42 Ibid., Article 3.

The *Provisional Methods* provided that contracts could only be entered by legal persons represented by their chief administrators.[43] When there is change of legal representative, such change cannot serve as a defense to the performance of contract.[44] Bank loan agreements required the borrower to post security and name a guarantor. As a rule of thumb, guarantors were usually the supervising government agency of the state enterprises or cooperatives.[45] When a high value or important contract is entered into by an agency under the central government, the department of treasury must serve as the guarantor.[46] The guarantor is obligated to supervise the performance of the contract.[47] Furthermore, the guarantor is jointly liable for the default of contract.

Compulsory dispute resolution mechanisms were in place before a contract dispute could be adjudicated by a court. For example, disputes regarding to nonperformance or breach of contract would have to be first submitted to a higher governmental authority for mediation. If both parties were from the same province or circuit, their disputes had to be submitted to the higher level government's economic commission.[48] If the parties were from different provinces or circuits, the disputes had to be submitted to the economic commission under the central government.[49] A suit could only be filed in court when such arbitration or mediation from the higher authority could not solve the disputes.[50]

Limited Paternalism: An Enlarged State Power to Annul Contracts

Extreme paternalism was a simple approach that curbed the problem of asset stripping. However, the cost of constant monitoring and planning was high, and evaluation of managerial performance was difficult when effective market indicators such as profitability and price were simply not available in the planned economy. The alternative indicators such as industrial output were misleading and hindered contract fulfilment.[51]

[43] Ibid., Article 5.
[44] See ibid.
[45] Ibid., Article 6.
[46] Ibid.
[47] Ibid.
[48] Ibid., Article 10.
[49] Ibid.
[50] Ibid.
[51] As a result, SOEs had the reasonable incentive to produce a high quantity of output at the expense of the costs, productivity, product quality, and research and development etc.

As Pitman B. Potter described, when there was a late delivery, the remedy always took the form of an apology and a promise to deliver later.[52] Even if the performance could be further delayed indefinitely, the non-breaching party would not have an incentive to pursue the most efficient remedy, which might risk damaging the personal relationships with colleagues at the other SOE. Also, it would be too expensive for the state itself to monitor the performance of every contract.

In the 1960s, attempts were made to reintroduce autonomy and incentives by trial policies and administrative department rules such as *70 Articles on Industrial Enterprises* (*70 Articles*) and the *Tentative Rules on the Fundamental Provisions on Industrial and Mining Products Ordering Contracts* (*Tentative Rules*).

Both sets of rules were intended to introduce autonomy, incentives, and accountability in running SOEs. The *70 Articles* created, for the very first time, the director responsibility system that would impose both responsibility on the directors and allow autonomy at the factory/enterprise level. It also introduced the idea of compensation based on merits and independent accounting. On the legal side, the *Tentative Rules* were the major source of authority in contract law before the Economic Contract Law became effective in 1982. *Tentative Rules* introduced autonomies in contracting and accountability for breach of contract and the subsequent non-fulfillment of state plans. Some autonomy was allowed outside the state plans. Strict penalty standards were introduced as non-fulfillment.[53] Only a few things were left for parties' mutual

Logically, if non-performance of contract could help increase the quantity of industrial output, SOEs would have the incentive to default their contractual obligations.

[52] See Pitman B. Potter, *The Economic Contract Law Of China: Legitimation and Contract Autonomy in the PRC* (Seattle: University of Washington Press, 1992), p. 42.

[53] For example, when specification and quality of products were nonconforming, if the buyer agreed to accept the products, suppliers were liable for the reduction in value. When the products were not needed, the supplier was obligated to reproduce conforming products and was liable for the loss caused. When the supplier could not produce the quantity of products under contract, 20 percent of the price of the nonconforming products would be imposed as penalties. When packaging was nonconforming, repackaging was the remedy. However, when such specific performance was not needed, 5 percent of the nonconforming packaging price would be imposed as penalty. For the delay of delivery, the supplier was to be charged 0.1 percent of the contracting price as penalty for each day of the delay. The supplier was liable for the storage fees for the nonconforming products that were placed in buyer's custody. Buyers were to pay penalties for modifying the specification or quality of products, for return of the conforming products, or failure to provide technical materials in time or to pick up the goods

consultations and negotiations such as technical specifications when no state implemented standards were available.

With no private interest in the picture, the clear goal of contract regulation was to minimize the financial loss to the state in case of non-performance despite the official rules that impose penalties. There were two distinct considerations in the regulation that were cited frequently in the 1980s' cases: loss splitting[54] and accommodation of other's difficulties.[55] They were introduced to allow flexibility in order to serve the collective interest of the state, which was the only legal interest in contracting. Some flexibilities were allowed in delivery dates and pricing when one party encountered difficulties. In that case, the other party was expected to accommodate them. As a result of such practices, SOEs that would have been closed down could stay in business, and the losses that the system suffered could be spread among a few SOEs.

The ECL was introduced soon after the economic reform that allowed private businesses to exist and compete with SOEs. Freedom of contract was not yet a fully developed idea and the law was still very paternalistic because the private interest was negligible compared to the state interest in contracting. Still, for the first time, parties' rights and interests were recognized by the ECL and their wills respected when not in conflict with law, public policies, and state economic plans.

The ECL was enacted with the purpose of "ensuring the fulfillment of state plans."[56] Further, complying with this particular purpose, the ECL

that were supposed to be picked up by the buyer in time or delay in payments etc., *Tentative Rules* Articles 33–34.

54 In a 1984 case, the defendant, an individual business household, refused to pay for the substandard silk weaving materials it had ordered from the plaintiff, a cotton factory. The official comment acknowledged the fact that the quality of the products was substandard and that liability should be borne by the plaintiff. However, through court-supervised mediation, the defendant agreed to pay for the material at a reduced price. The court's "careful and thorough work" on the case and the appropriate solution it provided were commended by the official comment. See Wang Zonghua and Yin Hongfeng (王宗华 殷红峰), "Jingji Hetong Jiufen Anli Xuǎnbian" ("经济合同纠纷案例选编") ["Selected Cases on Economic Contract Disputes"] [The Collection] (1987). See also Hao Jiang, "Freedom of Contract under State Supervision" (2016) 7 *George Mason Journal of International and Comparative Law* 202, 225–38.

55 In a case between two SOEs, where the defendant refused to pay for the cotton cloth they ordered from the plaintiff, the defendant's only argument was that it did not have the financial means to pay. Consequently, it only paid RMB 50,000 yuan out of the contract price at RMB 1,398,268.65 yuan one year after the partial payment of RMB 1,211,353.78 yuan was due. Jiang, "Freedom of Contract," 225–38; The Collection, 80.

56 See Article 1 of the Economic Contract Law of the People's Republic of China.

allowed only legal persons to be the parties to the contract.[57] Under this article, economic contracts were defined as "agreements between legal entities for the purpose of realizing certain economic goals and specifying each other's rights and obligations."[58] While maintaining the concern with economic law, certain features of civil law emerged for the first time in the legislative history of the People's Republic of China. The contracting parties, for the first time, had a lawful interest in contracting,[59] enjoyed equal status, and parties' autonomy in contracting was recognized and protected.[60] However, SOEs' managerial autonomy varied according to the specific rights they had acquired through their separate negotiations with the state, the scope of which could change overnight as the economic reform progressed. Contractual autonomy was always linked to the managerial autonomy. Still, the rising contractual autonomy was enjoyed by not only SOEs but also by township and village owned enterprises (TVEs), private enterprises, and private business households. The non-SOE sector soon became the driver of economic growth and started competing with SOEs in many industries. The state was still responsible for setting the market prices for some products according to its plans. Pursuant to the ECL, the contract price could only be negotiated if permitted by the state policy.[61] The only form of contracting was the written form. An economic contract had to include terms specifying the object, the price, the quantity and quality, the duration, location and methods of performance, and remedies for breach.[62] When it comes to remedies, monetary damages supplemented the previously dominant form, specific performance.

The validity rules first appeared in Article 7 of the ECL. A contract was void when it was concluded through the use of fraud or duress or violated state economic plans and policy. No room was made for relative nullity. The predominance of the state interest in contracting deprived a contracting party of the option of not invalidating when he was defrauded or

57 See ibid., Article 2.

58 Ibid.

59 Ibid., Article 1.

60 Ibid., Article 5. This article provides: "Economic contracts must be made according to the principles of equality and mutual benefit, agreement through consultation and compensation of equal value. Neither party is allowed to impose its will on the other, and no unit or individual is allowed to interfere illegally."

61 Ibid., Articles 17(3), 23. Prices for both sales and lease contracts can be negotiated by parties when prices are not set by the state.

62 See ibid., Article 12.

entered the contract under duress. Again, the very incentive for this paternalistic approach was to prevent SOE managers who engaged in self-dealing and defrauded the state from exercising their freedom of contract by keeping such a contract alive. The same rule was carried over to the 1986 General Principles of Civil Law (GPCL) and was applied to all civil juristic acts (Rechtsgeschäfte) where the existence of fraud and duress in contract formation would only lead to absolute nullity.[63]

Paternalism waned to an even lesser degree when the Contract Law was enacted in 1999. Freedom of contract was formally introduced as a basic principle of contract law. For the first time, relative nullity was recognized in Article 54 – fraud, duress, and mistake would only render a contract voidable rather than void.[64] However, consistent with the Soviet practice, as in the 1922 Civil Code and 1964 Civil Code, under Articles 52 § 1 and 52 § 2, the state retained the power to declare a contract void when the state interest was harmed by a contract that was induced by fraud, duress, or malicious collusion. As the first author has shown elsewhere,[65] similar to Soviet law, here, the state interest that was protected by paternalistism was not the normal public interest but the financial interest of the SOEs.

The State Interest in Article 52 The state interest in Articles 52 § 1 and 52 § 2 differs from social or public interest in Article 52 § 4 or legality in 52 § 5. Harming state interests through fraud, duress, and collusion will produce the same legal effect as illegality and violation of public interests – it will lead to absolute nullity of the contract. Just as in Soviet law,

[63] Article 58 of the General Principles of Civil Law of the People's Republic of China (GPCL, adopted April 12, 1986 and effective January 1, 1987) provides that:

> Civil juristic acts in the following categories shall be null and void: (1) those performed by a person without legal capacity for civil conduct; (2) those that according to law may not be independently performed by a person with limited capacity for civil conduct; (3) those performed by a person against his true intentions as a result of fraud, duress or exploitation of his unfavorable position by the other party; (4) those performed through malicious collusion are detrimental to the interest of the state, a collective or a third party; (5) those that violate the law or the public interest; (6) economic contracts that violate the state's mandatory plans; and (7) those performed under the guise of legitimate acts conceal illegitimate purposes. Civil acts that are null and void shall not be legally binding from the very beginning.

[64] See Article 52 of the Chinese Contract Law.

[65] Generally Jiang, "Enlarged State Power."

this is a financial interest that the state has in the supposedly private transactions because of the overwhelming presence of state-owned and state-holding enterprises.

Though it is not always easy to draw the distinction between the two interests, some courts have openly admitted that the state interest is harmed when an SOE interest is harmed.[66] One case showed how malicious collusion as in Article 52 § 2 could be carried out to harm the state interest: the plaintiffs were state-owned pharmaceutical companies that entered into an agreement with two advertising firms after the two firms prevailed in the bidding process. However, the plaintiff's employees had leaked the confidential information in the course of the bidding process to help the defendants succeed. The court, in its opinion, stated that "the employees of the two plaintiffs and two defendants committed malicious collusion and therefore harmed the two plaintiffs' interests. Given the fact that the two plaintiffs are state-owned enterprises, when their interests are harmed, the state interest is harmed."[67] Perhaps, the contract could be avoided at the request of the SOE under Article 54 but the powerful tool provided by Article 52 § 2 renders the contract null and void *ab initio*. Here, the validity of the contract is no longer subject to the will of the SOE because of the state financial interest involved. Freedom of contract is trumped by the state interest in contractual transactions as it was under Soviet law.

Another illustration of this enlarged state power is a case when the SOE was defrauded and sued for breach of contract because of the default of the private party. Citing Article 52 § 1, the court dismissed the breach of contract claim and voided the contract, without any request to do so by the aggrieved party.[68]

Another doctrinal difficulty, in the pre–Civil Code era, was raised by Article 58 § 3 of GPCL, which regulated the validity of civil juristic acts including contracts. Under this provision, civil juristic acts induced by fraud and duress were deemed void rather than voidable. This doctrinal construction severely contradicted Article 54. Given the jurisprudence that special rules prevail over general rules (*specialia generalibus*

[66] *San X Pharmaceutical JSC* v. *Ya Advertising LLC.* 2010, Shen Luo Min Er Chu Zi No. 3X4X (citation partially omitted).

[67] Ibid.

[68] *Henan Middle Pharmaceutical Company* v. *Dong Xueling & Hubei Hualong Pharmaceutical Company* 2011, 郑民二终字第1327号 [Zheng Min Er Zhong Zi No.1327].

derogant), only non-contract civil juristic acts would be governed by Article 58 § 3. However, the reality was, as the first of us showed elsewhere,[69] that it was either used as an extension of protection of SOE's financial interest in Article 52 § 1 or misused by courts that were not aware of the existence of Article 54.[70]

13.3 Equal Treatment of Private and Public Interests: Back to Square One?

The entanglement, confusion, and contradictions created by Article 52 of the Contract Law and Article 58 § 3 of the General Principles of Civil Law were finally removed by the Civil Code where the validity of contracts was dealt with exclusively in the general part of the Code.[71] Now, there is one set of rules that deals with the validity of civil juristic acts in general. Moreover, no state interest calls for additional protection by the validity rules just as one would expect in a Western civil code. Therefore, according to the Civil Code, an act to defraud SOEs will only render the contract voidable.[72] This means that a non-contracting party, even as powerful as The State-owned Assets Supervision and Administration Commission (SASAC), will not have standing to sue to have a contract avoided. From this point on, at least in its form, Chinese codification of private law has moved toward a body of law that does not subscribe to a particular political ideology and that levels the playing field between state and private enterprises.

Our concern is that, without a significant reform of the corporate governance structure of SOEs, it is likely that the equal treatment of state and private interests will exacerbate the very problem the paternalistic approach was adopted for originally in both Soviet law and Chinese law: SOEs' opportunistic behavior in stripping state assets. Our contention is based on the premise that SOEs still dominate a significant portion of the Chinese economy, and as a result, transactions involving SOEs are pervasive; also, that market SOEs are subject to is still not free and competitive.

69 See Jiang, "Enlarged State Power," 191.

70 Ibid.

71 The General Provision of Civil Law was first introduced in 2017 before the enactment of the Civil Code. For nearly three years, there were competing rules regarding validity in three major statutes: General Principles of Civil Law, General Provisions of Civil Law, and Contract Law.

72 Articles 147–51 of the Civil Code of the People's Republic of China.

As Justin Yifu Lin argued: SOEs can still succeed in the market economy without privatization, but the key is to subject SOEs to a competitive market without policy-induced burdens and soft budget constraints.[73] In reality, both still exist. SOEs still carry out policy goals that are nonprofit-driven, and SOE managers make business decisions that are in alignment with their political responsibilities. Such decisions enhance the political legitimacy of the Communist Party of China and, at the same time, serve to advance the managers' bureaucratic careers. Conversely, in order for SOEs to survive, the state must provide direct and indirect subsidies. As a result, SOEs will continue to have information advantages over the state. Moreover, an effective corporate governance structure for SOEs is still missing. Freedom of contract only works when parties act in their own best interest and corporate governance only works when the agency problem can be solved by using the market to make incentives compatible between the state as shareholder and managers as agents. It is only reasonable that other paternalistic measures are taken to curb the managerial opportunism when market mechanisms fail.

As things stand now, it appears that asset stripping could take place through violation of the so-called managerial rules such as asset valuation standards. Neither the state, SASAC, nor any third party would have the standing to sue to annul the contract, as the contract is not deemed illegal anymore.

Several regulations issued by SASAC and the treasury department require administrative filing and approval before SOEs trade state assets. These regulations would prescribe acceptable accounting methods in evaluation,[74] public disclosure process,[75] and mandatory approval procedure for major transactions.[76]

One major difficulty in preventing the stripping of state assets has been the binding force of such regulations issued by SASAC. They are considered administrative rules rather than mandatory rules, the violation of which would lead to the illegality of the transaction. Here, most courts

[73] Generally on this point: Justin Yifu Lin, Fang Cai, and Zhou Li, *State-Owned Enterprise Reform in China* (Hong Kong: Chinese University Press, 2001), pp. 125–53.

[74] 国有资产评估管理办法 第23条 [Article 23 of the Methods on Valuation of State-owned Assets].

[75] 企业国有资产交易监督管理办法 第13条，第15条，第16条 [Articles 13, 15–16 of the Supervisory Methods on Enterprise State Assets Trading].

[76] 企业国有资产交易监督管理办法 第7–8条 [Articles 7–8 of the Supervisory Methods on Enterprise State Assets Trading].

hold that violation of SASAC rules will not lead to illegality as they do not bind the private parties. Therefore, freedom of contract wins and contracts that might lead to the loss of state assets are legally binding despite the violation of administrative rules.

In a 2013 case that concerned a dispute over the sale of an SOE, the court abstained from assessing the fairness of the price in a stock purchase agreement even when 69 percent of a RMB 3.8 million yuan company was sold for a mere RMB 300,000 yuan to some former employees who won the public bid. The party who lost the bid sued to have the contract annulled under Article 52.[77] It was alleged that the accounting method adopted in valuation of the assets was not among the ones permitted under *the managerial methods in state asset valuation*. When dealing with the potential harm to a state interest and explicit violation of regulatory rules, the court expressly limited its role to examining the external forms of a commercial transaction rather than its substance. The court reasoned that the rule on valuation methods is not a mandatory one, thus its violation does not lead to illegality and nullity of the contract. Here, the court prioritized the public policy to ensure the safety of the transaction over a paternalistic approach to curb asset stripping even when it could have rescinded the transaction under Contract Law Article 52. Moreover, the Law on State-owned Assets in Enterprises expressly declared that malicious collusion in trading state assets would leave the transaction void.[78] Here, freedom of contract allowed state assets to be sold to former state employees at a bargain price.

In another case, when the SOE violated procedures prescribed by the regulatory rules in trading state assets, the court again opined that such regulatory rules are managerial in nature rather than mandatory and therefore the noncompliance will not affect the validity of the contract.[79] In this case, the wholly state-owned enterprise defaulted on the 500,000 yuan loan. The lender sued the SOE and the court tried to seize three storefronts that it owned. It turned out that the three stores were already sold to a private individual. These transactions did not comply with the

[77] 张芸诉江苏演艺集团公司诉江苏华扬公司 [*Zhang Yun* v. *Jiangsu Performing Arts Group & Jiangsu Huayang Corp*]白商民初字第231号 [(2013) Bai Shang Min Chu Zi No. 231].

[78] See 企业国有资产交易监督管理办法 第7–8条 [Article 72 of the Supervisory Methods on Enterprise State Assets Trading].

[79] See note 5; (2014) 亳民一终字第01081号 [(2014) Guo Min Yi Zhong Zi No. 01081].

procedures (public auction and disclosure) prescribed under the regulatory rules for the trading of state assets and was never approved by the SASAC. The trial court ruled that the transaction was void citing Article 52. Due to the fact that the state interest was maliciously harmed by the transaction, the individual to whom the storefronts were transferred was not entitled to receive a refund.[80]

The appellate court reversed the decision and took a pro-transaction stand by saying that SOEs have a status independent of the government. If SOEs cannot freely trade their own assets, they cannot function as an independent enterprise. The noncompliance did not amount to illegality of the contract as the rules on required procedures leading up to the transaction were not mandatory rules. In another case,[81] a state-owned power company sued to rescind a joint venture agreement and a stock purchase agreement selling 60 percent of the equity interests to a private company at a bargain. They alleged that the original agreements did not go through the appropriate procedures. The court held that it was the SOE's own fault that the procedural requirements were not met. Using procedural defects as excuses to annul the contracts, in the court's view, deviates from the principle of good faith. Therefore, the contracts were held binding. Again, the court rejected the use of Article 52 because they placed a higher premium on freedom of contract than the protection of a state interest.

Even when confronting the most blatant attempt to strip state assets, courts still hesitated to use Article 52 to avoid contracts.[82] In a fairly recent case decided after the passage of the Civil Code, the court refused to step in to set aside a contract that sold a formerly state-owned urban designing firm to its former manager for free (the price was set at RMB 0 yuan). Though the original appraisal suggested the firm was 2 million yuan in debt, a new appraisal put the market value of the firm at a solid 70 million yuan. Still, the court preserved the sanctity of the contract and avoided deciding whether the transaction harmed the state interest as provided by Article 52. The court merely said that it was an administrative action in disposing state assets and it is not a civil court's jurisdiction to determine the validity of such a contract.

In another case, a trial court annulled a related-party transaction where a 100 percent state-owned enterprise was dealing with a private

[80] It could well be that the sale price was nominal compared to the market price.

[81] See note 5; (2019) 琼民终108号 [(2019) Qiong Min Zhong No. 108].

[82] See note 5; (2020) 黑01民终2805 号[(2020) Hei 01 Min Zhong No. 2805].

company owned by its own managers and where the SOE was overbilled to pay an assembly line worth 180 million yuan at a hefty price tag of 201 million yuan.[83] The decision was reversed by the Supreme Court, which ruled that the contract can stand because the price had been lowered to 180 million later based on an appraisal and that a violation of the SASAC trading rules did not necessarily lead to nullity of the contract.[84] Here, it was a strong pro-transaction stance that was quite encouraging to the SOE managers' stripping efforts.

As we have seen, Article 52 has been the main vehicle in combating asset stripping. Without a free and competitive market and the removal of the normative remedial channel that Articles 52 §1 and 52 § 2 of Contract Law afford, the Civil Code can only leave the state interest under protected. Equal protection of private and state interests is not equal. The pro-transaction approach only promotes sham transactions.

In dealing with similar situations, even German law sets limits to the freedom of contract when government is involved with private transactions concerning the disposition of state assets. On the one hand, there are far fewer market players who qualify as state-owned,[85] and the relevant government agencies such as municipalities and states do enjoy decentralized managerial autonomy in trading state assets. On the other hand, such autonomy is subject to the requirement that state assets must be traded at the full value under the principle of economic and efficient budgeting (*Grundsatz der Sparsamkeit und Wirtschaftlichkeit*) contained in the federal budget law (BHO).[86] Consequently, courts have confirmed the nullity of contracts on the grounds of a gross disparity between the

83 河南颂春实业开发有限公司确认合同无效纠纷再审审查与审判监督民事裁定书 [*Henan Songyue Corp.* v. *Henan Songchun Corp.*] (2017) 最高法民申1968号 [(2017) Zui Gao Fa Min Shen No.1968].

84 Ibid.

85 According to the Beteiligungsbericht des Bundes 2021 (State Report of participation), in 2020, the federal government was invested in 506 private enterprises, only in 116 of these directly, Bundesministerium der Finanzen, "Beteiligungsbericht des Bundes" (2021), p. 12, www.bundesfinanzministerium.de/Content/DE/Downloads/Broschueren_Bestellservice/beteiligungsbericht-des-bundes-2021.pdf?__blob=publicationFile&v=4 (accessed May 1, 2022).

86 This principle is indicated in Article 114 paragraph 2 sentence 3 of the Constitution (Grundgesetz, GG) as well as mentioned in § 7 of the Federal Budget Code (Bundeshaushaltsordnung, BHO) and § 6 of the Law on the Principles of Federal and State Budgetary Law (Haushaltsgrundsätzegesetz, HGrG); the BGH has recognized the legal obligation to dispose of state property only at full value according to § 63 para. 3 BHO in its decision from 12 July 2013 – V ZR 122/12 = NJW 2013, 3779.

trading price of the state assets and the actual market value.[87] Moreover, courts did so both on the grounds of the violation of budgetary law and public policy. In the latter case, courts could declare the transaction immoral according to § 138 para. 1 BGB.[88]

It is also difficult to tackle this problem through public policy grounds or the doctrine of obvious unfairness. As the first of us argued elsewhere, traditionally the state's financial interest in SOEs was not considered a public interest.[89] That is why it was governed under Contract Law Article 52 § 1 rather than Article 52 § 5. Also, obvious unfairness does remedy economically unfair contracts but, as the American doctrine of unconscionability, it does require one party's exploitation of another's vulnerability,[90] which is generally lacking in SOE-related transactions.

Still, it is only logical for Chinese law to adopt a rule that would allow the courts to examine the contracts and avoid contracts when the price value disparity cannot be explained in the trading of state-owned assets even if no mandatory rules on validity are violated. As things stand now, it appears that asset stripping could take place through violation of the so-called managerial rules such as asset valuation rules, while neither the state nor the SOE would have the standing to sue to annul the contract, as the contract is not deemed illegal anymore.

13.4 Conclusion

A state-owned economy logically runs counter to a competitive market and freedom of contract. The lack of market information indicators gives SOE managers the information advantage and incentives to strip state assets for their personal gain. As we have seen, when there was no private economy, freedom of contract was not permitted for the very purpose of preventing the stripping of state assets. Both the pre-1922 Soviet Union and pre-1982 China banned private transactions all together.

Things get more complicated when the state-owned economy becomes a state-run economy that also allows private businesses and a market. Necessarily, private law is needed. Yet the state retains a larger power to

[87] BGH, judgment from July 12, 2013 – V ZR 122/12 = NJW 2013, 3779; BGH, judgment from January 30, 1967 – III ZR 35/65 = BGHZ 47, 30 (39) = NJW 1968, 726.

[88] BGH, judgment from January 25, 2006 – VIII ZR 398/03 = NZM 2006, 707; see also OVG NRW, decision from October 26, 1990 – 15 A 1099/87 = DÖV 1991, 611.

[89] See Jiang, "Enlarged State Power."

[90] Han Shiyuan (韩世远) and Hetong Fa Zong Lun (合同法总论), *The Law of Contract*, 4th ed. (Beijing: Law Press China, 2018), p. 292.

avoid contracts that would normally be valid in a typical Western economy to curb SOE managers' opportunistic behaviors. Again, both Soviet law post-1922 and Chinese law post-1982 went down the same path. Such a paternalistic approach was abandoned in Russian law after the massive privatization following the major change in economic structure.

The Chinese Civil Code also removed the enlarged state power to annul contracts and streamlined the rules. The technical quality of the Civil Code has improved as a result. Nevertheless, absent structural change in the economy, asset stripping, the very problem the paternalistic approach was set up to prevent, will continue to exist. Now, however, the problem has been exacerbated because the law took freedom of contract and the security of transactions one step too far, which led to a dilemma. The state no longer has the power to step in and courts no longer have the power to decide whether a contract can be rescinded because of the state interest that was harmed by the transaction. Consequently, courts shall be allowed to examine a contract concerning an SOE's trading of state assets and determine if the transaction is a sham transaction when state-owned asset valuation rules are violated or when there is a gross disparity between the contract price and the market value.

14

Chinese Civil Law and Soviet Influences

What Is Left?

GIANMARIA AJANI

To better understand the actual role of the law within the PRC, Western observers have made use, over time, of different filters: Chinese traditions, Confucianism, observance of Soviet patterns, independent Marxist-Maoism, legal transplants from the West, and so forth. This paper aims to investigate the role played by some Soviet theories in the making of Chinese civil law.

In particular, it recalls the tension between formalism and Anti-formalism in the making of a civil law with Chinese characteristics, from the times of incumbering Soviet models to the most recent era of (re)codification.

14.1 The "Myth of the Civil Code" between Decline and Resurgence

14.1.1 A Traditional, Western Approach to Codification

Why is there a need for a Civil code?

The question is not a minor one if we consider that the conception and importance of civil codes within many countries has changed during the last decades of the twentieth century.

In fact, there has been a widely recognized decline in the importance of the Civil code as the main source of private law. This does not seem to be outweighed by the appearance of new Civil codes in Brazil (2002), Quebec (1994), and The Netherlands (1992). Rather, the attempt and subsequent failure to adopt a Civil code for the European Union has shown that, at least within the EU Member States, the conditions necessary to adopt a general codification of civil law[1] have faded away.

[1] "Codification of civil law" is a multi-semantic expression. Not to mention, here, the numerous uses of the word "Code," one can simply consider that a Civil code can include family and labor relationships, or leave them aside, to be governed by separate statutes or codifications (all former Socialist Civil codes made this choice, and some post-socialist

Nevertheless, for more than a century, within the Western legal tradition and elsewhere, the Code, and in particular its prototype, the Civil code, has been the quintessential component, a path of legal modernization undertaken by many sovereign states. Many positive characteristics have been attributed to the codification of civil law, which has helped to create a "mythology of codification."

It is easy to recall the principal elements of this myth, some of which are derived from the positivist optimism that characterized the nineteenth century. For example, according to the myth of *completeness* of the Code, the Code becomes the center for a rational reorganization of the entire system of rules related to property, contracts, torts, family, and inheritance laws. A corollary to this idea is the principle that the Code represents a "closed" and self-contained system of norms.

We know that those ideas failed to survive the evolution of social and market relationships; nonetheless, despite all of the corrections introduced during the twentieth century (e.g., the recourse to open, vague, formulas of interpretation exemplified by both the German and the Swiss codifications), the very idea of codification as the master project of modernization of a legal system continued to influence political leaders as well as law scholars.

As Professor Wang Liming said: "If the advent of the French Civil code in the early 19th century and the one of the German civil code in the early 20th century were significant achievements in the history of development of civil law, then the promulgation of the Chinese Civil code in the 21st century will surely be meaningful and momentous chapter in the history of civil law."[2]

Another myth attached to the Code is the idea of its "educational function." The illusion that codification can bring simplicity is an old one; following a common understanding, in codifications, as well as in consolidations and restatements, there is an element of democracy in

codifications have confirmed it). Also, a Civil code can contain regulations on commercial companies, or leave it to separate statutes, or to commercial codes. Other matters of variation can affect the regulation of copyright and industrial property, of private international law, as well as of topics belonging to the realm of civil procedure (such as, e.g., the law of evidence). From those considerations one can deduct that there is a special power in the word Code, which attracts lawmakers and commentators: even a limited set of regulations, dealing with only a portion of the totality of "private law," provided that it is systematically organized, can seek to be named as a "Code."

[2] Wang Liming's keynote speech at the Bocconi Law School Conference: The Making of the Chinese Civil Code on June 22, 2021.

allowing easier access to the sources of law. Ever since the mythical twelve tables of Roman law, it has been commonplace to insist on the "egalitarian" outcome resulting from the publication of entire *corpuses* of regulation. However, we know that, in practice, the first codifications adopted in the nineteenth century did not contribute to a vulgarization of the juridical message. They were, instead, a necessary point of departure in taking political responsibilities away from interpreters, and particularly judges, while at the same time increasing the technical skills of jurists. Quite often, new codifications have resulted in a situation in which jurists' action could be shaped in technical-cognitive and not practical-valuational terms.[3] This is even more evident in both civil and criminal law if we consider that the Codes adopted under fascist regimes have persisted, with slight modifications, as these regimes transitioned into parliamentary democracies (for example, in Germany, Italy, Spain, Portugal), or that other Codes adopted during the nineteenth century have been maintained despite the advent of Soviet-like political systems (Hungary, until 1977, Romania). This challenges the ideal of "*la plus parfait simplicité*," which Sieyes hoped for the French *Code Civil*,[4] as only the hermeneutical support performed by Supreme courts could tune-up the contents of regulations with dramatic changes to the political order.

Within the chorus that sang the decay of codification in the West, different voices have been heard. According to some, the idea of codification is never gone but only the conditions for its orderly and systematic interpretation. According to other, more radical opinions, the crisis of codification was due, in reality, to the ending of the myth of the "general interest" and to the growing complexity of contemporary technological societies. The hurdles to codification have been made even more stringent by the increase of sectoral normative systems, based on contingent interests that are not related to the general principles contained in the Civil codes. Moreover, wherever a Constitution is enforced by a dedicated court, the historical authority of the Civil code has been quite often overtaken by the authority of constitutional jurisdictions. Finally, underneath or beside the Civil code, para-legal sources, such as collective labor agreements, soft law regulations, and the like, have also eroded the all-encompassing normative capacity of the Codes.

[3] Gianmaria Ajani, "The Soviet Experience with Codification: Theoretical and Comparative Perspectives," in R. Buxbaum and K. Hendley (eds.), *The Soviet Sobranie of Laws* (Berkeley: University of California Press, 1991), pp. 185–96.

[4] Ibid., p. 187.

14.1.2 Soviet-Like Attitude toward Codification

Until the dissolution of the Soviet Union, Soviet-type legal systems shared with the West all the positive features that had been said about codifications. The Socialist world, however, had no chance to experience the so called age of decodification that characterized the legal debate by the end of twentieth century.

Despite the decline of civil law codification in Western Europe, the myth endured and proved to be vital and strong among most Central and Eastern European countries. It is not redundant to say that the process of re-privatization of post-Soviet economies has set at its end the adoption of new (or renewed) civil codes.[5]

Soviet-like legal systems never experienced the crisis of general codification of civil law denounced by Western legal literature (and amplified by politicians). Quite the opposite: the myth of the Code had an overwhelming impact on Soviet-like legal cultures. Evidence of this is given by the widely respected and pioneer comparativist Vladimir Tumanov (former chairman of the Russian Federation Constitutional Court [1995–97] and then first Russian judge to be appointed to the European Court for Human Rights); he wrote in the 1970s, observing the crisis of codifications in the West: "Statute, by itself, may play either a static or a dynamic role, and the law of socialist countries shows that codification may be a valid instrument, able to ensure unity, consistency and fullness of legislation."[6]

In the Soviet and Soviet-like legal orders, codification has been considered, first and foremost, as the most suitable tool to fill the many gaps left by pre-socialist lawmakers in their systematization and modernization of the sources of civil law. And, second, codification has been considered as the most suitable means for achieving a uniform and standardized set of rules governing property, contracts, and torts.

One of the many myths about the Civil code absorbed by the socialist legal culture is that of simplicity.[7] In fact, the recourse to a simplified

[5] Donald D. Barry, George Ginsburgs, and William B. Simons, *The Revival of Private Law in Central and Eastern Europe* (Leiden: Brill, 1996).

[6] Vladimir A. Tumanov, *Contemporary Bourgeois Legal Thought* (Moscow: Progress, 1976), p. 60.

[7] An example has been the Civil code of the GDR (ZGB, 1975), which had in part satisfied some propositions of the German "*Juristensozialismus*" (end of the nineteenth century), calling for the use of nontechnical terms comprehensible to the layman (such as *Anderen* instead of *Dritten*, *Betrieb* instead of *Unternehmen*, and so forth).

vocabulary has been quite sporadic. Socialist lawmakers have usually achieved brevity and simplification by recourse to general clauses. Hence, the motto "for the greater ease and clearer understanding of the people," which has accompanied most codifications in the world (with the exception of the German BGB) was transformed into vagueness caused by a resort to general formulas and to the technique of *renvoi* to sub-legal sources (such as Supreme courts guiding directives and administrative regulations). And where there is no legal scholarship qualified and recognized as a guide for uncertain judges, vagueness cannot but turn into administrative discretion.

Finally, and on a different note, there is another myth about codification that has not reached the Communist world: that of its *universal* and *lasting character*.

In fact, the movements toward codification, which at their outset had been characterized by a spirit of cosmopolitanism and long-lasting duration, has rapidly become a bastion of nationalism. The ideal of universalism, steeped in the values of the Enlightenment, which inspired the first codifiers between the end of the eighteenth and the beginning of the nineteenth century, declined in the West and never developed in the East. As to the "aspiration to eternity" proclaimed by the first Codes, there has therefore been a total divergence from the two sides of the iron curtain.

Several factors explain the frequency of codification and re-codification that affected most Communist countries during their existence. In a nutshell, they can be summarized by the fast erosion of their contents due to changes in ideology and to the political hostility directed toward the frequent maintenance and readjustment made in the West by judges and other interpreters. Lawmakers in the area, therefore, felt free from the need to preserve the clarity of the Civil code as an unchangeable *ordo rationalis*.

As another eminent comparativist, the Hungarian Gyula Eörsi has observed, "when confronted by social reality, the reaction of socialist lawmakers is not Napoleon's 'Mon Code est perdu,' but, perhaps, somewhat overstated, this watchword: 'Le Code est mort; vive le Code!'"[8]

14.1.3 Post-Soviet Approaches to Codification

In the experience of the post-Soviet states, the adoption of a new Civil code has represented not only a formal change in the body of rules

[8] Gyula Eörsi, *Comparative Civil (Private) Law* (Budapest: Akademiai Kiadó, 1979), p. 549.

governing freedom in contracting and acquiring alienating property rights, it has also embodied the political design to adopt a "constitution" for the organization of the market. A symbolic value of Civil codes, which dates to the French Revolution, has been transmitted to post-socialist lawmakers together with an emphasis on the Civil code as a major trait of discontinuity between old regimes and new legal orders.

It must also be considered that the attribution of political significance to Civil codes blurs the differences between the role played in the regulation of economic freedoms by the Constitutions and the one played by the codes themselves; this may result in forgetting the "neutrality of private law rules" that has been considered a major trait of the "Roman-Germanic" family of legal systems.

Searching for reasons why there is so much emphasis on the drafting of Civil codes, one must think first to the interdependence between economic and legal reforms.

Among economists and social scientists, there is general agreement that, although structural market-oriented reforms could not be introduced simultaneously, a critical mass of comprehensive reforms had to be introduced at the outset of the transition period to create basic conditions for the development of market relations. Substantive legislation, such as those on property, contract, and corporate laws, needed to be introduced to prevent traders, consumers, and farmers from adopting a wait-and-see attitude in the expectation that policies of liberalization could be reversed unexpectedly by governments. The population, as well as all economic agents, needed to be reassured that there was an irrevocability in the gradual process of reforming the mechanisms of production.

Two main key concepts can drive us – I believe – in understanding why the crisis of the (Western) Civil code turned, during the last decade of the twentieth century, into a renewed triumph of codifications over the post-Communist area.

Firstly, remodeling the whole infrastructure of production and distribution of goods required the repeal of a huge body of preexisting legislations. For the organization of a new hierarchy of the sources of law, it was necessary to give an equal status to all owners (individuals and entities) who were entitled to manage the means of production.

Secondly, to avoid inconsistency and contradiction among the rules, a comprehensive modern codification of civil law is the best tool to prevent chaos and provide the technical guarantees for the further development of both civil and commercial legislation. In this respect, a Code appears as the necessary complement to political guarantees made in Constitutions and international conventions. Therefore, far from being a simple legislative act, a Civil Code can also be considered as a depository of fundamental rules for new economic freedoms and commercial relations.

Historically, in the European continental experience, Civil Codes have contained the fundamental legal decisions supporting private initiative and autonomy. The following set of provisions and rights that were not fully recognized under the feudal system were embodied in the "classical" Civil codes of continental Europe:

(a) the recognition of a general legal capacity of individuals and legal entities (see, for instance, Art. 1 of the 1804 French Civil Code, par. 17 of the 1811 Austrian Civil Code);
(b) the abolition of restraints on the free trade of goods and on the sale of land and property within the State (see Arts. 537, 544 of the French Civil Code, par. 308 of the Austrian Civil Code);
(c) the acknowledgment of a wide degree of autonomy in contractual relations (Arts. 1107–34 of the French Civil Code);
(d) unlimited debtors' liability.

Under the planned economy, all the principles just mentioned were subordinated to the paramount principles of Marxism-Leninism as interpreted by the Communist Party leadership. With the creation of a market economy, all agents in the market are treated equally under the law, and these principles have reacquired their "classical" meaning.

14.2 The New Civil Code of the PRC

14.2.1 Codification or Consolidation?

Codification and consolidation are historically interrelated in scholarly analysis even if they respond to different questions.

"What is the rule like?" is the demand to which codification responds. "Where is the rule?" is the demand to which consolidation responds. Both the Code and consolidations are fostered by the myth of the perfect statute, by the belief in a state monopoly in the production of rules.

A project of codification entails rejection of particularism and the implementation of wide-ranging rules and definitions to drive comprehensive solutions for diverse cases. During the last decades, the rebirth of juridical particularism has proved to be incompatible with the traditional idea of codification: one may recall the experience of consumer law within the EU, where inputs provided by a set of directives has been not evenly received within the structure of civil law codifications.[9]

Today, the proliferation of regulations in the fields of private and commercial law shows a preference for sectoral interests, and this generates a loss of coherence within codifications. Sectors flanking civil law codifications, such as labor and agrarian laws, have been filled up by administrative procedures, emergency or temporary regulations that have shrunk what were once the grand ideas and ruling principles of the Civil code.

The crisis of classical codifications has not, however, quelled the aspiration to a systematic *corpus* of laws. The fulfilment of this desire is entrusted to different tools, such as sectoral collations, often labeled as "code," designed to contain all rules related to a specific field (the contract of sale, public procurements, consumers protection, and so on).

Following the deterioration of the idea and of concrete possibilities for general codifications, the practice of sectoral consolidation has gained favor. Although such compilations are phrased differently (the American restatements of law or, in Italian, *Testo unico*), those recollections have been enacted worldwide thanks to their capacity to respond to the new fragmentation of the sources of law.

The PRC has made, in the last twenty-five years, a gigantic effort in legislating, appropriate to the transformation of the once totally state-owned economy. How is the newly enacted Civil code situated within the system of the sources of Chinese law? Can we adapt to China the narration on codifications I have made right now? Can we find some remnants of Soviet patterns within the new Code?

In the following pages, I will try to answer these questions.

Let us begin by observing how the Code is positioned within the sources of Chinese civil law.

Art. 1260 ends the seven books that compose the Code. According to it, and following its coming into force on January 1, 2021, the Marriage Law, the Succession Law, the General Principles of Civil Law, the Adoption Law, the Guarantee Law, the Contract Law, the Property Law, the Tort Law, and the General Provisions of the Civil Law of the People's Republic of China have been repealed.

9 See Mateusz Grochowski, "European Consumer Law after the New Deal: A Tryptich" (2020) 39 *Yearbook of European Law* 387–422.

Quite clearly, January 1, 2021, has marked the end of a long era of transitional legislation, which was opened in the year 1986 with the promulgation of the General Principles of Civil Law. Twenty-five years of experiments, attempts, and sectoral lawmaking have reached their conclusion. The system is now stable and in tune with constitutional provisions.

It is in the same transitional nature of the aforementioned laws that we find a first answer to the question: code or consolidation?

As the first Chinese law to carry the title "Code" since the founding of the People's Republic of China in 1949, the Civil Code (*Minfa Dian*, 民法典) is without a doubt more than a mere consolidation.

It is true that its main parts (like the General Provisions, Property, Contract, Torts Laws, as well as the Family and Inheritance Laws) had already been adopted, also beyond formal limits set by the PRC Constitution.[10] The nature of "work in progress" of most of those statutes, however, required an all-compassing revision, aimed to fix what had been experimented upon and to give an internal coherence to the whole structure. This considerable work of rewriting, quite more challenging than a mere restyling, also somewhat explains why so much time has been spent between the first promises to have a new Civil Code by the year 2010 and the actual promulgation.

I said "somewhat," as it is also evident that the Communist Party leadership paid much attention to the political nature of some of its parts, such as those related to property law. Only today, after more than fifteen years of preparation and draft Codes, does China seem to be ready to absorb the (many) rules of the Code based on an irreversible commitment to a regulated market.

14.2.2 Sovietism Is Not Necessarily Socialism

The belief that the label "Soviet Law" was nothing but an oxymoron was deeply rooted, not only in the Western political milieu but also within a certain legal literature.[11]

Somehow, the profound distrust toward Soviet-like legal systems has been passed on to Chinese law.

[10] Tong Rou and Jonathan K. Ocko, "The *General Principles of Civil Law of the PRC*: Its Birth, Characteristics, and Role" (1989) 52 *Law and Contemporary Problems* 151.

[11] Ugo Mattei, "The Cold War and Comparative Law" (2017) 65 *American Journal of Comparative Law* 3, 567.

Following more sophisticated approaches, both Soviet law and Chinese law deserve the "law" label but also incorporate elements of contradictions, particularly as to their external compatibility with the main principles of democratic parliamentarism and to their internal (lack of) coherence in regard to the respect and implementation of the rule of law.

The problem is well known and resides in the supremacy of a ruling Communist Party, which causes a kind of schizophrenia between respect for the law in the books (socialist legality) and a practice of implementation driven by the Communist Party.

In fact, both Communist Russia and Communist China have chosen to express their political will through formalized acts (laws, decrees, regulations), adopted via a procedure activated by State organs (governments and lawmaking assemblies). Pure Party-driven discretion is not excluded, but it is more of an exception rather than a rule.

In 1949, the new Communist China could bypass any temptation to declare the incompatibility between a State-ruled economy and the law that circulated in the first years of the Soviet governments, since all those proposals had been wiped out, quite often together with their proponents, by the firm establishment of a Stalinist doctrine: the "originality of Soviet Civil Law," characterized by "new contents in old forms" (1936). Between 1954 and 1957, therefore, it appeared as easy and necessary to Chinese Communist leaders to establish an original, revolutionary but formalized legal system. Following a quick but intense training in the basics of Soviet institutions and law, Party officials and social science scholars headed toward the adoption of a new constitution and codes of laws.

Quite similar to other Soviet-like countries, the PRC started to develop a strategy of re-codification, grounded on the progressive repealing of "bourgeois laws" of the Guomindang period[12] and the adoption of new enactments based on the ideal of the revolution. Some peculiarities of the Chinese revolutionary experience, however, made problematic an immediate acknowledgment of civil law as a "branch of Socialist law regulating patrimonial-type and personal relations, in a context of exchange of goods."[13] The link between the concept of civil law and the politically orthodox concept of "economy based on an exchange of goods" was quite an obstacle for the development of a (Soviet-like) civil law in the PRC, as

[12] Jianfu Chen, *Chinese Law: Context and Transformation* (The Hague: Brill, 2016), pp. 41ff.

[13] This was the official definition of civil law as from the Soviet textbooks of civil law published in the USSR in the 1950s.

the existence, in the Chinese context, of an economic system based on the exchange of goods did not appear to be tuned with the main tenets of President Mao's thinking. Consequently, the development of Chinese law in the PRC was, during the first years of formation of the revolutionary regime, rather a practical issue, focused on the need to take the most urgent issues opened by the demolition of the old system.

Some relevant enactments, such as the agrarian reform or the Marriage Law, were adopted, together with a myriad of minor regulations. Such regulations were quite narrow in area, but at the same time very relevant as to their economic impact (e.g., the "Provisional regulations on the conclusion of contracts by administrative bodies, state enterprises and cooperatives", adopted by the State Council Committee for finance and economics [1950], or the "Resolution on the vigilant and accurate conclusion of contract", approved by the Ministry of Commerce [1950]).[14]

The necessity to establish a complete legal order in the new context of a state economy was acknowledged already in the early 1950s, together with the adoption of a central planning system.[15] In those years, the cultural influence of Soviet legal scholarship became dominant. Soviet legal texts were translated and the presence of Soviet experts in the fields of economics, law, and management became the norm. New legal periodicals, like *Zhengfa Yanjiu* (政法研究) and *Faxue* (法学), containing translations from the Soviet legal literature and original essays, were published. In the next few years, the dichotomy emerged, already experienced in the Soviet Union in the late 1930s, between the practice of economic law, based on countless sub-legal regulations and administrative orders, and the theory of civil law. Efforts were made at overcoming the redundant system of sources of law and at bringing the regulation of real rights and obligations within a unitary frame, based on the structure of (Soviet) civil law.

Notwithstanding the adoption by the 8th Congress of the Communist Party of a resolution supporting the "Strengthening of the democratic legal system of the people"(1956) and the subsequent declaration of the already very influential Prime Minister Zhou Enlai, anticipating the

[14] See Arthur Stahnke, "The Background and Evolution of Party Policy on the Drafting of Legal Codes in Communist China" (1966) 15 *The American Journal of Comparative Law* 3, 506.

[15] A State Committee for Planning was established in 1952, following the Soviet *Gosplan* architecture, while the first five-year plan was adopted in 1953 (but approved by the National Assembly only two years later).

preparation of a new Civil Code Draft lasted only until the launch of the "anti-rightist campaign" (1957). It was not yet a massive destabilization of the system, as any project to establish a formalized legal system was suppressed for ten years by the red guards. But it heralds a period of shaming and delegitimizing the law, its interpreters, and the legal culture in general.

Following the movements of a wavering ideology, a short window of opportunity was open again in the early 1960s when a short draft of a Civil Code (242 Arts.) was made public (1962–64).[16] The historical significance of the project resides in the original attempt made by its drafters to make use of very simplified language readable by any layman, while emancipating the regulation from the already rejected Soviet model.

It was only after the end of the "Cultural Revolution" and the death of President Mao that, within a renewed climate of partial openness, some Soviet concepts, based on the re-emerging theory of "Economic law"[17] as an autonomous branch of law, independent from Civil Law, ignited the interest of Chinese scholars.

Those favoring the idea of separating economic law (经济法) from civil law (民法) had good reasons. The same notion of civil law seemed to be deprived of any connection with Chinese economy where, notwithstanding the first experiment to loosen planning directives in favor of timid decentralization, the prevalence of vertical relationships between the administrative planning system and the productive units remained quite prevalent toward the end of the 1970s.

But the doctrine of "economic law" in its Chinese version was destined to have, as within the USSR, modest fortune. With the adoption of the "short codification," namely the General Principles of Civil Law (1986), the supporters of a unitary civil law prevailed. Art. 2 of the General Principles hailed their success:

> The Civil Law of the People's Republic of China shall adjust property relationships and personal relationships between civil subjects with equal status, that is, between citizens, between legal persons and between citizens and legal persons.[18]

[16] See Zhang Lihong, "The Codification of Civil Law in China: History, Current Situation and Perspectives" (2004) 10 *Studium Juris* 896.

[17] See Witold Małecki, "The Scholar Discussion on the Theory of Economic Law in the Soviet Union" (2017) 9 *Cracow Studies of Constitutional and Legal History* 111, www.ejournals.eu/Krakowskie-Studia-z-Historii-Panstwa-i-Prawa/.

[18] Rou and Ocko, "The General Principles."

A reconciliation of economic law (vertical) regulations and the civil law (horizontal) ones within the General Principles of 1986 also meant a final reconciliation with some Soviet legal classifications. In the 1980s in China, like in the USSR, state enterprises received assets from the state (land, buildings, raw materials, and money) and sold outputs produced like a private enterprise sells products. To circumvent the concept of state enterprise "ownership" of this property, which was not accepted by the ideology, Soviet lawyers had defined the relationship between state enterprise and property as the right of the state enterprise to operate and manage property. Another example is the concept of strict liability, or liability without fault, which was maintained as an ideological choice rooted in the first years of Soviet law.[19]

The return to a formalized set of civil law principles, however, did not mean a return to a coherent and methodical set of sources of civil law.

For more than twenty years, the role played by civil law regulations in post-Maoist China had been directed to setting the borders between an emerging private economic initiative and a residual state economy based on planning and local administrative bodies guidance. At the same time, during the Deng Xiaoping era (1980–92), the dominant tenet was to adopt any statutes or regulations that might facilitate the new economic development.

Having departed from the Soviet model, but still influenced by the political driven search for a fruitful coexistence between the two sectors of the economy (the private, and the public one), Chinese civil law has seen the urgent need to modernise legislation from the planned economy era based on thematic, expansive areas of law, such as Contracts, Property, Torts, and looking to a forward-looking and coherent codification of civil law.

14.2.3 *A Code with a Unique Theme: Socialism as Solidarity*

The 2021 Civil Code is new, original, and innovative. It is not a completely new draft with a severe departure from the earlier drafts produced between 1979 and 2002. These earlier drafts, in fact, represented a break from their respective times when compared to the regulations on civil law and economic relations in force.

[19] Jewoo Lee, "Two Defining Features of Russian Tort Law: Their Rationale and Legal Effect" (2014) 39 *Review of Central and Eastern European Law* 109.

In our case, the 2021 Code collects what had been consigned to its drafters by the positive law and the practice of the last twenty years (as counted from the adoption of the 1999 Contract law).

In doing so, it is in line with the new Constitutional amendments; also, as a sign of innovation, it makes clear how property titles will be regulated at the lapse of time limits set by Property law.[20] The usufruct of residential housing will be automatically renewed while renewal of other kinds of land use rights will follow separate statutes.[21] Thus, residential land use right holders will enjoy a right that approximates full land ownership.

Among the many myths embodied by classical codification during the last two centuries, it seems to me that the 2021 Code maintains the character of being a "didactic law."

This might be the best way to explain some redundancies present in its Introductory Part. *Repetita iuvant*, as the Romans said. It is also quite useful whenever new ideas are introduced into legislation, such as the new tendency to connect regulations to the respect for the environment.[22]

The Code is original as it may have abandoned, consistent with the actual context of the mixed economy of China, all those features that represented, in some way, remnants of a Soviet-like economy. Many of these features were still present in the 1999 Contract Law, as well as within the General Principles of Civil Law. It is true that the general design of Chinese Civil Law within a single regulated domestic market still identifies large areas where state interest prevails. Still, undeniably, a dramatic reduction in the interference of administrative guidance in the formation and performance of contracts has returned the basic functions of contract law to what we know in the West. While most of the more than 200 amendments to the text of the 1999 Contract law do not

[20] See Art. 327 of the Civil Code: "Where a right to usufruct is extinguished or adversely affected due to expropriation or requisition of the immovable or movable property, the usufructuary has the right to compensation according to the provisions of Art. 243 and 245 of this Code."

[21] Art. 359 of the Civil Code: "The right to use a lot of land for construction of residential buildings is automatically renewed upon expiration of the term .... The renewal of the right to use a lot of land for construction of buildings other than residences, upon expiration of the term, shall be dealt with in accordance with the provisions of the laws."

[22] See, e.g., Art. 9 of the Civil Code: "When conducting a civil activity, a person of the civil law shall act in a manner that facilitates conservation of resources and protection of the ecological environment."

necessarily reflect substantive changes, some do. Notably, previously paternalistic rules such as Art. 44[23] and Art. 52[24] of the 1999 Contract law have been set aside. Nor can the adoption of the new Art. 534 be considered a choice in continuity with a past when binding planning directives were imperative and could supersede the wills of contracting parties.[25]

The Civil Code has reorganized the rules concerning validity and eliminated the differences in the treatment of contracts and legal transactions (*Rechtsgeschäfte*). (See, e.g., its Art. 5: "The parties to civil legal relations shall conduct civil activities under the principle of free will, and create, modify, or terminate civil legal relations according to their own wills.")

According to the Civil Code, illegality, sham transactions, and violation of good morals will render a civil juristic act null and void.[26]

Victims of fraud, duress, mistake, and obvious unfairness have the option to challenge the transaction by filing a claim before a court or arbitration institution. Thus, the Civil Code no longer has distinctive rules that give to state interests better protection. Chinese Civil law, in other words, has moved toward a system of rules of law that is apolitical and levels the playing field between state and private firms.

Solidarity represents a common theme connecting different parts of the Code. Its fabric is evident through the texture of many chapters, and within the lines of many general clauses which disseminate the Code.[27]

[23] Art. 44 noted that contracts that require state approval or registration might not take effect until such approval or registration is obtained. Such contracts are categorized as effect-to-be-determined contracts. See Hao Jiang, "The Making of a Civil Code in China: Promises and Perils of a New Civil Law" (2021) 95 *Tulane Law Review* 777, 805, 806.

[24] Art. 52 pronounced an enlarged state power to declare a contract void when the state interest in contracting is harmed. See generally Hao Jiang, "Enlarged State Power to Declare Nullity: The Hidden State Interest in the Chinese Contract Law" (2014) 7 *Journal of Civil Law Studies* 147.

[25] Art. 534 of the Civil Code reads: "Where the parties take advantage of the contract to commit an act that endangers the State's interests and public interests, the market regulatory authority and other relevant administrative authorities shall be responsible for supervising and handling it in accordance with the provisions of laws and administrative regulations."

[26] See Chinese Civil Code Arts. 153–57.

[27] Art. 6 Civil Code: "The parties to civil legal relations shall conduct civil activities under the principle of fairness, and rationally determine the rights and obligations of each party"; Art. 7 Civil Code: "The parties to civil legal relations shall conduct civil activities under the principle of good faith, adhere to honesty, and fulfill their promises"; Art. 8 Civil Code: "The parties to civil legal relations shall not conduct civil activities in violation of the law, nor contrary to public order and good morals."

This regards some parts of the Book on Torts,[28] as well as the new signals on environmental protection.[29] Perhaps times are not yet ready to connect transgenerational duties to specific regulations on environmental protection, but we can identify the first signs.[30]

The People's Republic of China is pursuing the construction of a "harmonious society" and has connected this path to the UN 2030 sustainability goals.

A "harmonious society" is originally Confucian.[31] Clearly, it has no direct connections with the Marxist-Soviet old class-conflict doctrine,[32] nor with the theoretical view of the classless society.[33]

[28] See, e.g., Art. 1180 Civil Code, which reads: "Where the same tortious act causes multiple deaths, the same amount of death compensation may be applied to all of them."

[29] Art. 1233 of the Civil Code: "Where environmental pollution or ecological damage is caused owing to the fault of a third person, the infringed person may claim compensation against either the tortfeasor or the third person. After making compensation, the tortfeasor has the right to indemnification against the third person."

[30] See Arts. 9 (expressing the duty to exercise civil law rights in a manner that is compatible with the preservation of a sustainable environment), 286 (asking the owners of a building unit to conserve resources and protect the ecological environment), 346 (establishes that the right to use a lot of land for construction purposes shall be used in conformity with the requirements for conservation of resources and protection of the ecological environment), 509 Civil Code (according to which parties of a contract shall avoid wasting resources, polluting the environment, or damaging the ecology in the course of the performance of a contract).

[31] The idea of a harmonious society comes from the Confucian idea of a society of great unity (大同社会). The concept was introduced by President Hu Jintao (2002–12) as a vision and objective for the country's future socioeconomic development

[32] According to Karl Marx, all history is the history of class conflict. Different epochs are characterized by an oppressed class seizing power and defeating an oppressor class.

[33] The "classless society," in Marxism, is the ultimate condition of social organization, expected to occur when true communism is achieved.

15

The Connections between Roman Law and Chinese Civil Law

Traditions, Innovations and Environmental Protection

ENRICO TOTI

15.1 Introduction

This chapter is about the complex relationship between Roman law and Chinese civil law. I will discuss the historical roots of the Westernization of Chinese civil law, the particular influence of Roman law and Italian academia, and the innovations and nuances in the new Chinese Civil Code with an emphasis on the new green principle and its surprising connections to Roman law.

On the one hand, the sources of the majority of the Chinese Civil Code can be traced to ancient sources. On the other, after forty years of unprecedented economic growth, China seems to have switched gears and started to focus on other important, more contemporary aspects of civilian life, such as social justice, administration of law, and, most notably, environmental protection.[1] Surprisingly, we can tie Chinese civil law to Roman law from both ends.

15.2 The Rise and Fall of Roman Law in China

Since the early 1900s, China opted to modernise its law and institutions through codification. Such an effort led to the organisation of private law that is modelled on the Roman legal system. Let us start with a set of historical facts that cemented the tie between Roman law and Chinese law.

[1] S. Schipani, 'Diritto Romano in Cina' in *Treccani* (XXI Secolo, 2009), www.treccani.it/enciclopedia/diritto-romano-in-cina_%28XXI-Secolo%29/.

Though the first Civil Code in PRC was just recently enacted, the journey towards civil codification goes back more than a century. In fact, 6 April 1902 is considered the date when the decision to model Chinese law after the West was made. By an imperial Decree, the Qing government appointed a commission to codify first criminal law and then civil law. This effort soon led to a full-scale modernisation of Chinese law and Chinese institutions.

It took four years (1907–11) for the first draft of the Civil Code to be compiled. This draft of the Qing civil code was modelled after the Japanese-German model. Japanese jurist, Matsuoka Yoshitada worked closely with a group of Chinese jurists in drafting the Code; but this draft, despite being published, was never enacted. When the last imperial dynasty fell in 1911, the Republic of China followed. Nevertheless, the draft was highly influential in the development of the modern day legal system in China. For instance, for the first time, legal doctrines and concepts were organised in a pandect structure as in German law, which is rooted in the Roman legal system. Significant importance has been attached to this choice, which later proved to be irreversible, to link Chinese civil law with the Romanist juridical family through the German legal model.[2]

Such a legal transplant from Roman law to Chinese law was also made possible by way of Japan. Starting in 1868, Japan modernised its law by modelling it after the Romanist juridical family. The close historical, geographical and cultural ties between China and Japan made Japanese influence practical and readily available. The main practical reason of such an influence was the linguistic similarities between the two languages: 'Japanese is a language that develops from Chinese . . . China could use the Japanese legal concepts . . . through Japan, the Roman legal model entered the Chinese legal life.'[3]

[2] Y. Xingzhong, 'Legal Pragmatism in the People's Republic of China' (1989) *Cornell Law Faculty Publications*, Paper 993, http://scholarship.law.cornell.edu/facpub/993; W. Zhenmin, 'The Roman Law Tradition and Its Future Development in China' (2006) 1 *Frontiers of Law in China* 72; X. Zhang, 'The New Round of Civil Law, Codification in China' (2016) 1 *University of Bologna Law Review* 106; J. Gordley, H. Jiang and A. Taylor Von Mehren, *An Introduction to the Comparative Study of Private Law: Readings, Cases, Materials*, 2nd ed. (Cambridge: Cambridge University Press, 2021), pp. 48–50. Concerning the study of Chinese law by Japanese jurists, see D. F. Henderson, 'Chinese Legal Studies in Early 18th Century Japan: Scholars and Sources' (1970) 30 *The Journal of Asian Studies*, p. 21.

[3] X. Jun, 'La codificazione del diritto civile cinese e il diritto romano' (2016) 110 *Bullettino dell'Istituto di Diritto Romano Vittorio Scialoja*, p. 73.

Despite the civil war and two world wars, the modernisation process eventually led to the 1930 Civil Code of Republic of China. The Code is considered a milestone in the reform path of the Chinese legal system, both for its official entry into the Romanistic family and its structure.

The similarities between this Code and Roman law are quite revealing. For example, article 1 states: '[i]n the absence of the express provisions for a civil case, the case will be decided according to customs. In the absence of customs, then according to the jurisprudence'. This provision followed Article 1 of the Swiss Civil Code, which included the entire legislation within the legal system, as provided for in the structure of *Corpus iuris civilis*, thus, avoiding any legal gaps. All in all, this Code resembled a typical European Civil Code with inspirations from both French and German models. It was abolished after the end of Communist China, yet it continues to be the Civil Code in Taiwan to this day.

It would be an understatement to say that the relationship between the state and private law has seen its ups and downs in China. Here is a brief chronology.

1949–57, mass nationalisation and attempt to design a socialist legal system following the Soviet model;
1958–66, legal nihilism and political disorientation when virtually all private laws were abolished except for the marriage law;
1966–79, cultural revolution and class persecution;
1980–2010, economic reform and creation of socialist market economy and a new round of private and commercial law legislations based on legal transplants from both European civil law and Anglo-American law.

The political turmoil of the period 1966–79 saw the complete denial of private law and the abolition of legal institutions and law schools. The entire legal profession disappeared. Soon after, economic reform restarted economic activities, and private law was revived in China with a strong tie to Roman Law.

Early on, Professor Jiang Ping reminded everyone coming out of this dark period of the importance of Roman law in China in two of his works: 'The Revival of the Spirit of Roman Law in China'[4] and 'Roman

[4] J. Ping, 'Il risorgere dello spirito del diritto romano in Cina', in L. Formichella, G. Terracina and E. Toti (eds.), *Diritto Cinese e sistema giuridico romanistico* (Torino: G. Giappichelli, 2005), pp. 49–56.

Law in the People's Republic of China'[5]. Jiang Ping's first book utilized Western methodologies to explain law and its doctrinal topics through deductive reasoning. This creates a 'connection' between Western law and the spirit of contemporary Chinese law. The starting point was to identify a 'Chinese legal renaissance' and connect it with the spirit of Roman law. The book states: 'the development of socialist reforms of the market economy has led, even in China, a gradual transformation of the legal system and doctrine; this transformation is the consequence of the rebirth of the spirit of Roman law and humanism . . .. The foundation and development of the market economy necessarily require the rebirth of the Roman law spirit . . .. [O]f course, the feudal legal system that had lasted for two thousand years cannot still be applicable in modern China'.

One of the possible contributing factors that made Roman law a reference model in China[6] since the early 1900s is the natural law philosophy embedded in Roman law. This does not mean that natural law was the only influence upon Roman law, but Roman law was certainly the most important, most radical and most effective model. The legacy of the Stoic theories of the natural law of Panezio (185–109 BCE) was carried on by Cicero who elevated the philosophical thinking of the Romans to an even higher level. Thanks to his influence, natural law prevailed and Roman law became the common law of Western Europe until the rise of conceptualism in the nineteenth century. In the sixth century CE, Justinian's *Corpus iuris civilis* accepted the definition of natural law as that which nature teaches to all animals (D.1.1.3. and I.1.2 pr.): this law is or should be the logical foundation of any legal norm. In this way, not only would the concept of law become more exact, but even more important was the possibility of carrying out a deeper theoretical critique in the light of which any actual norm, or custom, could appear unjust or irrational, even if it were a generally accepted practice.

Jiang Ping's second book, *Roman Law in the PRC*, published in 1988, states in the preface that during this period of formulation of the Chinese legal system (1978–88), we recognized that 'the legal culture including the Roman law, represents an essential part of the culture of humanity. Just as legal cultures can be inherited, the Roman law legacy can also be

[5] Ibid., pp. 57–68.

[6] N. Ho, 'Natural Law in Chinese Legal Thought: The Philosophical System of Wang Yangming' (2017) 8 *Yonsei Law Journal* 1; Z. Shoudong, 'Chinese Natural Law Tradition and Its Modern Application: A Response to Hon Rollin A. Van Broekhoven' (2018) 13 *Frontiers of Law in China*, p. 86.

inherited and used in modern China'. He further identified the fundamental issues relating to Roman law research: (a) when we admit that the law of the pre-socialist period can be inherited and used by socialist law, we also admit the influence of Roman law on socialist law; (b) as we are developing market economy in China, Roman law is useful because it has given, and still gives us, a rich experience and legal solutions for market oriented societies. Roman law, as in the past, has a general social significance.

As we have seen, China has always embraced the 'civil law' tradition and this trend was cemented by the enactment of the Civil Code. Naturally, the Code resorts to the experience handed down from the *ius romanum* and developed a structure based upon both Roman law and the German Pandectist Model. Rightfully, the Code is divided into a general part including the fundamental elements of the legal relationships and a special part endorsing the drafting of an 'open' code, liberal and permissive, so as to avoid the risk of a closed structure and embrace the need to adapt.

15.3 The Code: Between Tradition, Innovation and Political Context

The Chinese Civil Code became effective on 1 January 2021. This is the first legislative text in Chinese history to be titled as a "Code" (典 *diǎn*) and abrogated nine separated statutes.[7]

The Code (at the present) includes 1,260 articles gathered in seven books: General Provisions, arts. 1–204; Real Rights, arts. 205–462; Contracts, arts. 463–988; Personality Rights, arts. 989–1039; Marriage and Family, arts. 1040–1118; Succession, arts. 1119–63; Tort Liability, arts. 1164–1260. Without a doubt, it represents an event of historical character, both for China and for the entire world.

Some of the main features can be summarised as follows: greater protection of transaction safety was implemented through a streamlined

[7] Article 1260 provides: '[t]his Code shall come into force on January 1, 2021, upon which the Marriage Law of the People's Republic of China, the Succession Law of the People's Republic of China, the General Principles of the Civil Law of the People's Republic of China, the Adoption Law of the People's Republic of China, the Guarantee Law of the People's Republic of China, the Contract Law of the People's Republic of China, the Property Law of the People's Republic of China, the Tort Law of the People's Republic of China, and the General Provisions of the Civil Law of the People's Republic of China shall be repealed'.

set of validity rules in contracts. Personality rights became an independent subject from tort law. Some pressing issues of our time such as data protection and privacy, e-commerce and health emergency have been addressed.

The objectives and meanings of this Code are numerous not only from a legal point of view but also with respect to political, social and systemic considerations. The intention emerges to act as a declaration of Chinese civil rights, to set a boundary between government and market, between public power and the private rights of individuals, to provide a solid legal basis for the social stability and economic prosperity of the country, as well as to promote the guarantee of quality economic development, to improve public welfare, to improve civil law, commercial law and the rule of law.

At the ideological level, the conclusion of the codification itself exemplifies the Chinese government's commitment to the rule of law in the civil and commercial spheres. Also, according to Xi Jinping, China's law has to be based on China's own social conditions, it moral standards and, at the same time, practical.

This can be seen from Xi Jinping's own words:

> We have adopted at this plenary session, which is the necessity of keeping to and expanding the path of socialist rule of law with Chinese features. This path constitutes an overall guideline. That is to say, China has achieved dozens of successes in its efforts to establish the rule of law, some large and some small. But ultimately these achievements boil down to one thing, and that is the path of socialist rule of law with Chinese features .... On the fundamental issue of keeping to and extending the path of socialist rule of law, we need to demonstrate both confidence and resolve .... Firstly, we must uphold the leadership of the CPC .... Secondly, we must uphold the principal position of the people .... China's socialist system also ensures that the people are the primary actors in advancing the rule of law. This is a strength of our system and the fundamental distinction between socialist rule of law with Chinese features and capitalist rule of law. To uphold the principal position of the people, we must develop the rule of law for the people and rely on them, and it must benefit and protect them .... Third, we must uphold the principle that all are equal before the law .... It is essential that we are earnest in our efforts to promote and enforce the rule of law. Officials at all levels must have a reverence for the law, lead the way in handling affairs in accordance with the law, and set a good example on observing the law .... Fourth, we must integrate the rule of law with the rule of virtue. Laws are ethics that have been written down, while ethics are laws that we follow in our hearts. Both functions to regulate social behavior

> and maintain social order. Therefore, in running our country and society, we need to lay emphasis on both the rule of law and the rule of virtue, ensuring both the role of the law in regulating behavior and the role of ethics in shaping the mind, so that law and virtue promote and enhance each other and rule of law and rule of virtue complement each other .... Fifth, we must base our work on the prevailing conditions in China .... To base our work, in reality, we need to lay emphasis on who is practical, what is contemporary, and what is quintessentially Chinese.[8]

15.4 The Roman Law Influence and Its Practical Implications

Historical contexts aside, the specific links between Roman law and contemporary Chinese civil law can be seen by a comparison of the statutory texts. For example, let us look at arts. 2, 6, 7 and 9 of the General Part of the Chinese civil code that in Book I, Chapter I (arts. 1–12) are classified as 'basic provisions' (基本规定, *jīběn guīdìng*) that form the basis of the Code.

Article 2 provides: '[c]ivil law regulates personal relationships and property relationships among natural persons, legal persons, and unincorporated organizations, as equal parties'; the direct reference can be found in I.1, 2, 12 where '[a]ll the rights we use pertain to persons, or things, or actions'. So let us look at persons first. 'It is indeed not enough to know the law if one does not know the persons for whom it is established', and in Gaio inst. I. 8: 'All our laws concern persons, things, or actions. We address persons first.'[9]

Article 6 states: '[t]he parties to civil legal relations must conduct civil activities according to the principle of fairness and rationally determine the rights and obligations of each party'. An important aspect is a proportion in the distribution of risks between the parties. Article 604 of the Chinese civil code states: 'The risk of damage or loss of a subject matter shall be borne by the seller prior to the delivery of the subject matter and by the buyer after delivery unless otherwise stipulated by law or agreed upon by the parties.' The modern doctrine of the risk of damage of the thing is lost to the owner, *res perit domino*; every person

[8] Xi Jinping, 'Promote Socialist Rule of Law, October 23, 2014', in *The Governance of China II* (Beijing: Foreign Language Press, 2017). For more on the Rule of law in China, see Vai Io Lo, *Law and Society in China* (Cheltenham, UK: Edward Elgar, 2020); and Weidong Ji, *Building the Rule of Law in China: Procedure, Discourse and Hermeneutic Community*, 1st ed. (Milton Park, UK: Routledge, 2017).

[9] F. de Zulueta, *The Institutes of Gaius, Part II, Commentary* (Oxford: The Clarendon Press, 1953), pp. 23–24.

must bear the damage he suffers, that is, according to which the damage by chance or force majeure falls on the present owner or possessor of the thing, with the consequent passage of the risk from the seller to the buyer not before the delivery of the thing (the theory of the passage of the risk from delivery, on the other hand, had its basis in the sources: see, for example, Julian's D. 18.5.5.2). Based on these considerations, it may be said that Chinese law also follows the scheme *res perit domino*, which is in conformity with the English, French and German systems.

Article 7, where '[t]he parties to civil legal relations shall conduct civil activities according to the principle of good faith adhere to honesty and fulfil their promises', can find its roots in I. 3, 22, 3. It provides '[i]n these contracts, each is obliged to the other for what each must render to the other according to honesty and equity, whereas in verbal obligations one stipulates and the other promises'. And in Gai. 4, 47: 'Good faith requires a balance between the interests of the two parties in an obligatory relationship, as followed by the French Civil Code and the German Civil Code but in recent time the principle of good faith has become a basic principle of civil law that must be extracted from the law of obligations and applied to the whole field of civil law where it is applicable.'[10]

Regarding the meaning of this principle, we have recourse to Han Shiyuan's engaging and convincing interpretation, who, as for other principles, went back to the Confucian tradition and prioritises the human factor in its morality. Considering that good faith constitutes in modern civil law a fundamental principle to exercise the power to fulfil obligations, the jurist asks to evaluate its effects: 'it has created a moral order in the economic activities of the market ... moreover, it induces the parties involved in commercial activities to maintain their commitments, to be honest, not to deceive, not to pursue their interests to damage the interests of others; it has, therefore, created ethical parameters for honest traders and workers. Ultimately in this respect, the law rises to a moral value'.[11]

[10] Xu Guodong, 'La base romanistica della Parte generale del Codice civile cinese' (2017) 6 *Bullettino dell'Istituto di diritto romano 'Vittorio Scialoja'*, p. 48; Xu Guodong, Minfa jibenyuanze jieshi – chengxin yuanze de lishi, shiwu, fali yanjiu [*Explanation of the Fundamental Principles of Civil Law: Research into the History and Practical Aspects of the Principle of Good Faith; Rationale for the Fundamental Principles of Civil Law*] (Beijing: Beijing daxue chubanshe, 2013).

[11] Han Shiyuan, 合同法总论 [*The Law of Contract*], 3rd ed. (Beijing, s.n., 2011), p. 41.

It is comparable with the Roman experience, where the operation of *bona fides* in an objective sense[12] represents one of the most important moments in the historical development of *ius civile* and *honorarium.*

Though, there is a difference between modern law and Roman law; as we have just seen in the Chinese code concerning good faith, the latter is a general standard of conduct as well as a general standard of interpretation of contractual clauses. In Roman law, the scope of application of good faith was more restricted, being limited to some typical contractual figures, those assisted by judicial protection through the so-called *iudicia bonae fidei*, that is, actions based on the clause *oportere ex fide bona.*[13]

It is of interest to investigate the origin of *bonae fidei iudicia* using the famous text of Cicero's De officiis D 3.70, which provides: '[h]ow much weight do those words have: as long as I am not taken and defrauded because of you and the trust placed in you!' As golden as the other words: 'One must act well and without fraud as among honest men!' But the primary issue is to understand what is being honest and what is acting well. The supreme pontiff Q. Scevola stated that all the *arbitria* to which the clause *ex fide bona* is added are of great importance, and he thought that the concept of *bona fides* had an immense extension, concerning guardianships, companies, trust deposits, power of attorney, purchases and sales, contracts and leases, in which social life consists; in these relationships, especially since in most of them there are 'direct and contrary actions, a true judge must determine what each person must "lend" to the other'.[14]

[12] Cf. M. Talamanca, 'La bona fides nei giuristi romani: "Leerformeln" e valori dell'ordinamento', in L. Garofalo and A. Burdese (eds.), *Il ruolo della buona fede oggettiva nell'esperienza giuridica storica e contemporanea atti del Convegno internazionale di studi in onore di Alberto Burdese Padova, Venezia, Treviso, 14–15–16 giugno 2001* (Padova: CEDAM, 2003), vol. III, pp. 3–17.

[13] Ibid., pp. 42–52. On page 60, the author speaks explicitly of the 'sectoral' nature of the operation of objective good faith in the Roman legal system as regards the contractual system. Lists of *iudicia bonae fidei* are found in Gai 4.62 and I. 4.6.28. A list may also be considered Cic. De off. 3.17.70, su cui cfr. L. Lombardi, *Dalla fides alla bona fides* (Milano: Giuffrè, 1961), pp. 167–83; for a contrary opinion, see R. Fiori, 'Bona fides. Formazione, esecuzione e interpretazione del contratto nella tradizione civilistica (parte seconda)', in *Modelli teorici e metodologici nella storia del diritto privato* (Napoli: Jovene Editore, 2011), vol. IV, p. 107 n. 27; A. Schiavone, *Giuristi e nobili nella Roma repubblicana* (Roma-Bari: Laterza, 1992), pp. 68–73. On good faith in China, see R. Cardilli, 'Precisazioni romanistiche su "hetong" e "chengshi xinyong"', in *Il Libro e la Bilancia. Studi in memoria F. Castro* (Napoli: ESI, 2011), pp. 551–72.

[14] The translation is a liberal elaboration of the translation contained in M. Tullio Cicerone, *Opere politiche e filosofiche* (Torino: UTET, 1995), vol. II, pp. 797–99, from which I have

The relationship between usefulness and honesty is resolved by Cicero by shifting the focus from the philosophical to the legal-social level, that is, exalting the duty not to harm others as a limit to the pursuit of profit in the sphere of intersubjective relations. Therefore, Cicero's solution meant the exaltation of a Roman 'model', which emerged in legal practice, thus giving rise to a legally sanctioned duty to enrich the more purely philosophical perspectives.[15]

15.5 The Green Principle: An Unexpected Connection between Roman Law and Chinese Law

Another example of the connections between Chinese law and Roman law is surprisingly in the area of environmental protection. Article 9 of the Chinese Civil code for the first time established a green principle. It provides: '[w]hen conducting a civil activity, a person of the civil law shall act in a manner that facilitates conservation of resources and protection of the ecological environment'. It is necessary to analyse the specific problems and treat the specific cases to understand its greatest role in introducing an interesting and innovative principle in the civil law – of functionalising all private law activities and negotiations to the need for environmental conservation.

Roman law also enabled some institutions, especially procedural ones, to deal with the protection of the natural environment without having to speak of environmental law.[16] In general, it can be argued, following the indications of scholars who have dealt with this subject, that in Rome, there were procedural instruments aimed directly or by extension at protecting the *salubritas* of goods such as water or air. But by accepting this statement, one could respond positively to the question 'did the Romans provide means of protection to the environment?' on the sole condition of demonstrating in advance that such means had the specific

kept my distance, especially in the rendering of legal terms and expressions in English. A translation of reference adapted to the legal aspect is the R. Fiori, *Bonus vir. Politica, filosofia, retorica e diritto nel de officiis di Cicerone* (Napoli: Jovene Editore, 2011), p. 334.

15 R. Cardilli, *Bona fides tra storia e sistema*, 2nd ed. (Torino: G. Giappichelli Editore, 2010), p. 32.

16 For this discussion, for all, cf. A. Di Porto, *La tutela della* salubritas *fra editto e giurispridenza I. Il ruolo di Labeone* (Milano: Giuffrè, 1990), *passim*; M. Bretone, *I fondamenti del diritto romano. Le cose e la natura* (Roma-Bari: Laterza, 1998), pp. 102–21; M. Fiorentini, *Precedenti di diritto ambientale a Roma? I. La contaminazione delle acque*, in *Index* (Napoli: Jovene Editore, 2006), vol. XXXIV, pp. 353–400.

purpose to protect the ecosystem, that is, to defend nature as a value in itself and not to postulate uncritically that any procedural means, for the sole fact of being intended to protect a portion of the environment (quality of air and water, keeping rivers running, preventing water stagnation etc.). For this reason, it was introduced for environmental protection.[17]

As far as the protection of water safety is concerned, the Romanist doctrine discusses the scope of certain procedural instruments, among which it is worth mentioning those who led themselves most to a reflection on the relevance of Roman legal schemes concerning the interaction between man and the environment. The first case is that of the role of the *actio aquae pluviae arcendae*. In general, this civil action *in personam*, which was based on the Law of the XII Tables (Table 7.8a),[18] was given to the owner of a property against his neighbour when, due to a work carried out by the same neighbour or by a third party, the fear arose that rainwater would cause damage to the property itself.

The sources[19] make it clear that the work on the neighbouring property had to create a situation of the danger of damage by rainwater (or rainwater mixed with other water) and not actual damage.[20] With this action, the plaintiff could demand that the neighbour should personally take care of the restoration of the places to remove the danger if the work had been done by him or that he should allow the restoration to be carried out by the plaintiff, in the case of work done by third parties.

[17] Fiorentini, 'Precedenti di diritto ambientale a Roma?', pp. 355–56. This is the writer's preamble rightly posed to the analysis of Zamora Manzano's book, which highlights the forced study of a series of procedural means of the Roman praetor's edict – *actio iniuriarum, actio aquae pluviae arcendae*, interdetto *quod vi aut clam*, up to the point of stating that they were aimed at the ecosystem. Having said this, once the issue has been cleared of a simplistic approach to a 'Roman law of the environment', it is of considerable interest, more appropriately, to reflect on the technical solutions that the Romans adopted to contain phenomena and behaviour that directly or indirectly had the effect of altering the balance of nature or putting people's health at risk.

[18] *Fontes Iuris Romani Anteiustiniani (FIRA)* (Firenze: Florentiae, 1968), vol. I, p. 50. The fact that the XII Tables dealt with this action is certainly known from a statement accidentally made by the jurist Pomponius in D. 40.7.21.pr. (Pomp. 7 *ex Plautio*): 'sic et verba legis duodecim tabularum veteres interpretati sunt "si aqua pluvia nocet", id est "si nocere poterit"' (the *veteres* have also interpreted the words of the law of the Twelve Tables in this way: 'if rainwater does harm', that is, 'if it can harm'). This leads to the hypothesis that the verse of the Twelve Tables began with the words: *Si aqua pluvia nocet*. See Di Porto, 'La tutela della *salubritas*', p. 57 n. 179.

[19] D. 39.3, the passage ulpianeo in D. 39.3.1.1.

[20] D. 39.3.1.1 (Ulp. 53 *ad edictum*).

Obligatio propter rem is the obligation deriving from the action that was borne both by the *dominus fundi*, creator of the property, and by all those who had current ownership of the property. For the latter, unlike the *dominus fundi*, who had the obligation to restore the place to its original condition, the obligation[21] was limited to *patientiam praestare* – it allowed the neighbour who feared the damage to stem the water. Now, a wide discussion among Romanists concerning the role of the *actio aquae pluviae arcendae* in environmental matters has been aroused by the following Ulpian fragment (in a free translation of mine):

> D. 39.3.3.pr. (Ulp. 53 *ad edictum*): Apud Trebatium relatum est eum, in cuius fundo aqua oritur, fullonicas circa fontem instituisse et ex his aquam in fundum vicini immittere coepisse: ait ergo non teneri eum aquae pluviae arcendae actione. Si tamen aquam conrivat vel si spurcam quis immittat, posse eum impediri plerisque placuit.[22]

It is known that the *fullonicae*, the workshops for washing, treating and dyeing clothes and used pollutants, and for this reason, in the city, they were connected to a system of public and private sewers to canalise the water used there to ensure protection of the health of the environment.[23] They were also part of the economy of the villas in the late Republican age and at the beginning of the Principality period, generating a considerable need for water accompanied by risks to the *salubritas* of the water resources.[24]

For the exegesis of the fragment, I refer to Andrea di Porto's rich examination.[25] Here, it is sufficient to recall how scholars dealt with this fragment in the context of the problem of whether the *actio aquae pluviae arcendae* required rainwater. The first part of the text seems to

[21] For the formula of the *a.a.p.a.*, see D. Mantovani, *Le formule del processo privato romano* (Padova: Cedam, 1999), p. 59. This was a civil action *in personam* with the sentence of *quanti ea res erit* (a sum that was in accordance with the interest of the plaintiff) and with arbitrary formula, example, an action that gave the judge the power (*arbitrium iudicis*) to acquit the defendant who was found to have restored the situation in the prior state to that which had given rise to the lawsuit.

[22] D. 39.3.3.pr.: 'At Trebazio, it was reported that one, where the water originated, had installed fullonicas near a source and that from these sources he began to introduce water into the ground of a neighbour: Trebazio, therefore states, that one is not held with the action *aquae pluviae arcendae*. If, however someone collects water or if he introduces dirty water "the jurist" affirms that he can be prevented, and this pleased most.'

[23] A. Di Porto, *Salubritas* e forme di tutela in età romana. Il ruolo del *civis* (Torino: G. Giappichelli Editore, 2014), p. 4.

[24] Di Porto, 'La tutela della *salubritas*', pp. 68–73.

[25] Ibid., pp. 56–91.

say that Trebatius denied the action in a case where spring water was used for the fullyonic. The second part, on the contrary, admits the possibility, or at least a remedy, when dirty water or collected water was involved (either spring water or rainwater?). This second hypothesis has led some scholars, those who consider rainwater to be an essential requirement of the action, to say either that the text has been revised or that the hypothesis of the collection of water for fullyonic included the collection of rainwater as well.[26]

Other academic theories, on the other hand, admitted the possibility that the Roman jurisprudence extended the possibility of the *actio aquae pluviae arcendae* beyond the case of rainwater. In this way, interestingly, the action becomes an instrument of environmental protection. If we read the fragment in the way it has been read by this second strand of opinion, we arrive at the hypothesis that the action that we are examining was extended, perhaps on the direct impulse of the jurist Trebazio, as well as to hypotheses of non-rainwater, which proved to be dangerous for *salubritas*.

The requirement of harm would be at the basis of these applicative extensions of the procedural instrument well beyond rainwater and to protect health. The jurists that Andrea Di Porto identifies as possible authors of such applicative innovations are Trebatius, as we have seen, and Labeon, for his well-known scientific activity in the field of water flow.[27]

A different interpretation of the problem of fullonics in D. 39.3.pr. is provided by Mario Fiorentini.[28] The example of the *actio aquae pluviae arcendae* and the variety of doctrinal interpretations that we have briefly outlined allows us to propose, as of now, the first evaluation of how, in ancient Rome, the effect – to prudently use a term that does not lead to conclude, too hastily, for the existence of Roman environmental law – of environmental protection was achieved. It seems to me to be able to say that classical jurisprudence, rather than devising specific instruments on the environment, could, if anything, adapt the various procedural instruments of Roman law to environmental requirements.

Having examined the procedural elements in Roman law, it is fair to argue that they are adequate to deal with the situations of today without

[26] Ibid., pp. 57–59.
[27] A text concerning this theme is by Ulpiano-Labeone in D. 39.3.1.22–23.
[28] Fiorentini, 'Precedenti di diritto ambientale a Roma', pp. 360–61.

resorting to particular procedures.[29] For example, an interdictal instrument was of fundamental importance in combatting air and water pollution due to waste.[30]

Interdicts were orders to do or not to do something issued by the magistrate to a private individual based on a request from another private individual; such orders were provisional and based on factual circumstances pled by the claimant, the truthfulness of which could only be ascertained definitively following the opening of an ordinary trial.[31]

The specific function of interdicts, according to the doctrine that appears to be better,[32] seems to be attributable to public orders, which preserve the status quo against possible disturbances (prohibitory interdicts), return something or restore a place or property to the state before the disturbance (restitutory interdicts, or decrees) and, finally, exhibit something before the magistrate (exhibiting interdicts, or decrees).[33]

Prohibitory interdicts could be directed towards only one party and were called *simplicia*, or they could be directed towards both parties and called *duplicia*, whereas interdicts *esibitori* and *restitutori* were always *simplicial*.[34]

This doctrine is used to render a further distinction between private interdicts and popular interdicts, the latter having regime-like popular

29 On the question of whether the interdicts, the effectiveness of which we are about to examine in terms of environmental protection, were administrative or jurisdictional instruments, see, for all, L. Capogrossi Colognesi, 'Interdetti', in *Enciclopedia del diritto* (Milano: Giuffrè, 1971), vol. XXI, pp. 913–16.

30 Di Porto, '*Salubritas* e forme di tutela', pp. 3–16.

31 Gai 4.141.

32 Capogrossi Colognesi, 'Interdetti', p. 904.

33 See ibid. pp. 901–5. See Gai. 4.140: Vocantur autem decreta, cum fieri aliquid iubet, uelut cum praecipit, ut aliquid exhibeatur aut restituatur, interdicta uero, cum prohibet fieri, uelut cum praecipit, ne sine uitio possidenti uis fiat, neue in loco sacro aliquid fiat. unde omnia interdicta aut restitutoria aut exhibitoria aut prohibitoria uocantur ('They are called decrees, when they order something to be done, for example, when they order something to be produced or returned; they are called interdicts, when they forbid the doing of something, for example, when they order that no action shall be taken against the possessor without fault, or that nothing shall be done in a sacred place.').

34 Gai 4.156–60. see Capogrossi Colognesi, 'Interdetti', p. 906. In the Institutions of Gaius, three distinctions of interdicts are expressly made: in addition to the distinction between prohibitory, exhibiting and restitutory interdicts, and the distinction just mentioned, in Gai 4.143–55 interdicted persons are identified *adipiscendae, retinendae* and *reciperandae possessionis causa*. This last classification concerned specifically possessory interdicts, relating to things belonging to private individuals, which are less relevant for us here. It should be noted, however, that the interdicts referred both to *res divinae* and *res humanae*; the latter, in turn, could concern both public and private things.

actions[35] that could be brought by *quivis* and *populo* for situations relating to public things or things for public use.[36] It was precisely the so-called popular interdicts that came into play in a series of hypotheses in which the good to be protected was *salubritas*. The doctrine identified a series of areas of application of the interdicts that affected environmental protection.

In the Republican age, the *praetor* introduced the prohibitory interdicts *de rivis purgandis* and *de fonte purgando*, aimed respectively at the purgatory – that is, the maintenance of healthiness – of water pipes and sources.[37] The interdicts *de cloacis* were devised by the *praetor* against acts of discharge into *cloacae* (private or public) that resulted in air pollution.[38] The jurist Labeon then developed extensive applications of these interdicts.[39]

As Andrea Di Porto's studies show, the Augustan jurist Labeo also made further contributions to the application of interdicts for the protection of human health. The application of the interdict *quod vi aut clam* was proposed against the water pollution of the fund, as can be deduced from D. 43.24.11. pr.[40] Labeo would have, moreover, widened the application of the interdicts concerning the navigability of the rivers, revealing that he had – at heart – interests related to the healthiness of the river

[35] On these, for all, it remains fundamental F. Casavola, *Studi sulle azioni popolari romane. Le actiones populares* (Napoli: Jovene Editore, 1958), *passim*, which highlighted that the person entitled to bring an action was the citizen as such, as a member of the populus, in situations where the enjoyment of public goods was restricted *populus*, in situations where the use of public property was restricted (*rectius*: *res in usu publico*). Cf. A. Di Porto, *Res in usu publico e 'beni comuni'. Il nodo della tutela* (Torino: G. Giappichelli Editore, 2013), p. 41: 'The citizen as such is responsible for a large part of the protection of this category of persons, which is achieved through the instrument of popular interdicts.'

[36] Capogrossi Colognesi, 'Interdetti', p. 907.

[37] Di Porto, '*Salubritas* e forme di tutela', p. 10; cf. Di Porto, 'La tutela della *salubritas*', pp. 91–98.

[38] Di Porto, '*Salubritas* e forme di tutela', pp. 51–64. Cf. Di Porto, 'La tutela della *salubritas*', pp. 114–38.

[39] D. 43.23.1.8; D. 43.23.1.9; D.43.23.2. see Di Porto, '*Salubritas* e forme di tutela', pp. 64–75.

[40] Di Porto, 'La tutela della *salubritas*', pp. 3–53. Observations in Fiorentini, 'Precedenti di diritto ambientale a Roma?', p. 365. D. 43.24.11.pr.: Is qui in puteum vicini aliquid effuderit, ut hoc facto aquam corrumperet, ait Labeo interdicto quod vi aut clam eum teneri: portio enim agri videtur aqua viva, quemadmodum si quid operis in aqua fecisset ('He who has put something into the well of his neighbour, so as to corrode the water with this fact, Labeon states that he is held with the interdict quod vi aut clam: in fact, the aqua viva seems to be a portion of the property, as if he did some work in the property.'). On the concept, *aqua viva*, see L. Capogrossi Colognesi, *Ricerche sulla struttura della servitù d'acqua in diritto romano* (Milano: Giuffrè, 1966), pp. 6–11, and, in particular, p. 8 n. 16. It can be said that the Romans meant by *aqua viva* the water of the earth as opposed to rainwater, and for this reason included in the concept of *aqua perennis*.

waters.[41] Further intervention by Labeo would have taken place, about the healthiness of public places, through a broad conception of the applicability of the interdict *ne quid in loco publico vel itinere fiat*.[42]

Admittedly, even without a body of environmental law, Roman law provided an effective procedural model for environmental protection. The most powerful of such techniques is its system of disqualification of people through temporary injunctions.[43] On the one hand, there is an action given to *quivis de populo*; on the other hand, an order to do or not to do was issued by the magistrate on the summary knowledge of the facts, which could lead to a subsequent trial (if the addressee of the order considered his actions to be legitimate).

The Civil Code must be read in its entirety. In the Book of Contracts, the green principle is fully implemented through Article 509, para. 3. Although this is a provision that comes with a set of guidelines, which therefore do not impose specific obligations between the parties. However, if the contents of the contract were to violate mandatory rules set forth in laws or regulations on environmental protection, the contract could be null and void; if the parties in the contract performance commited waste, polluted the environment or damaged the ecosystem, they could be held liable under the rules in this regard set forth in the Seventh Book, Tort Liability.[44]

It is considered also the period of time after the termination of an obligation, Arts. 558[45] and 625.[46]

41 Di Porto, '*Salubritas* e forme di tutela', pp. 13–14, 27–48; Cf. Di Porto, 'La tutela della *salubritas*', pp. 99–113.

42 Di Porto, '*Salubritas* e forme di tutela', pp. 75–81; Di Porto, 'La tutela della *salubritas*', pp. 141–51.

43 The interdictal procedure is described by Gai 4.161–70. See C. A. Cannata, *Istituzioni di diritto romano* (Torino: G. Giappichelli Editore, 2001), vol. I, pp. 239–41; Capogrossi Colognesi, 'Interdetti', pp. 909–13, 916–18. This procedure, which is quite complex, is the one that Gaius refers to interdicted possessors.

44 Article 509 provides '[e]ach party shall fully perform its own obligations as agreed. The parties shall abide by the principle of good faith, and perform obligations of notification, assistance, and confidentiality, etc. in accordance with the nature and purpose of the contract and the transaction practice. When performing a contract, the parties shall avoid wasting resources, polluting the environment, and destroying the ecology'.

45 Article 558 provides '[a]fter the termination of an obligation, the parties shall observe the principles such as good faith and perform obligations such as notification, assistance, confidentiality, and recycling of used things in accordance with the relevant transaction practices'.

46 Article 625 provides '[w]here any law or administrative regulation requires, or the parties agree, that the subject matter should be recovered after the expiration of its useful life, the

The Roman experience has, perhaps, bent normal procedural instruments to environmental protection purposes, but what stands out is the wide use of interdictal protection. As in contemporary experience, some essential elements emerge in Rome: procedural legitimacy appropriate to the presence of widespread interests to justify the use of popular interdicts. Above all, it is not the search for compensatory remedies with financial rewards, but instruments that specifically inhibit the damaging acts, through prohibitions or orders to restore the places.

What emerges, therefore, appears to be an approach aimed at restoring the environment, a superior asset belonging to the entire community, rather than the prevalence of a compensatory profile aimed at the individual.

15.6 Concluding Remarks

As we have seen since the early 1900s, China has charted the path of codification as a careful approach towards a scientific system of private law.

As Jiang Ping argued, among the various factors, it is the systematic nature, the scientific nature, the universality of *ius Romanum*, in its component of *ius gentium*, which have contributed to the development of Chinese civil law and, more specifically, the Chinese Civil Code.[47] Still, as we have seen, in order for the comparison between the two to stay current and relevant, we ought to study the ancient sources in the historical context and look for the relevance through a developmental view.

The new civil code speaks to us in a language in which we can no longer limit ourselves to a formal acknowledgement of one reference model or another. We must now resort to historical comparison to cast a new glance toward the East and place ourselves in a dialogue that is authentically intercultural with Chinese law.

seller shall have the obligation to recover the subject matter in person or authorize a third party to do so'.

47 See E. Toti, 'La Legge sul trust della Repubblica Popolare Cinese' (September 2004) *Giustizia Civile*, pp. 447–67, (para: 1, 2, 6, 8); Yu Xingzhong, 'Legal Pragmatism in the People's Republic of China', in *Chinese Law and Legal Theory* (Trowbridge, s.n., 2001), p. 60, spec. 73.

INDEX

absolute rights, 154–57
abuse of rights, 115, 124–27, 130
accessory principle, 135–40, 149, 152
actio aquae pluviae arcendae, 318–20
active appreciation, 224–26
Anthony v. *Anthony*, 222
Antone v. *Antone*, 227
apology, 154, 156–57, 206, 280
Aquinas, Thomas, 247
asset stripping, 13, 270–71, 273, 275–77, 279, 285–91
autonomy, sexual, 55–58
awareness, 194, 247

Bai Junying v. *Tumertzuo Banner People's Government*, 85
Bank of Montréal v. *Bail Ltée*, 126
Beijing Tianqi Weiye Mun. Eng'g Co., Ltd. v. *Beijing Nanyuan Vegetable Oil Factory*, 30
Bhasin v. *Hrynew*, 126
bonae fidei iudicia, 316
Book of Contracts, 323
Book of Han, 34
Book of Marriage and Family, 216
Book of Personality Rights, 6, 17–18, 44, 45, 46, 50–57, 59, 61–62, 64–65, 66, 70, 71, 73–76, 154–56, *See also* personality rights
Book on Contracts, 94, 115
Book on Property, 133
Book on Tort Liability, 46, 70, 153–56, 178, 179, 181, 199, 307, 323, *See also* Tort Liability Law (TLL)

C.M. Callow Inc. v. *Zollinger*, 126
cannot perform test, 82–83, 88–92
causation
  adequacy theory, 184
  in civil codification, 180–86
  comparative law and, 180–83
  cumulative, 193–94
  in eggshell-skull cases, 187–89
  flexibility of, 186, 193–94, 196
  force majeure and, 181–83, 185
  intentional acts and, 186–87, 194, 196
  legislative restraint and, 185–86
  multiple tortfeasors and, 179, 181–83, 184, 190–96
  necessity theory, 184
  third parties' act and, 181, 184
  victim's comparative/contributory fault and, 186–90
change of consequences, doctrine of, 77–93
Charlebois v. *Baril*, 117
Chengdu Pengwei Industrial Co Ltd v. *The People's Government of Yongxiu County, Jiangxi Province and Yongxiu County Poyang Lake Sand Mining Management Leading Group Office*, 80
Chinese judicial practice, 85
Chinese legal tradition
  development of, 235–43
Chinese Property Law, 132–34, 136, 141–45, 305
Chinese Security Law, 132–33, 135–36, 142–44
Chongqing Changhong Plastic Factory v. *Chongqing Tianlong Real Estate Development Co Ltd*, 82
Cicero, 311, 317

circumstance, change of, 21–23, 26, 77–96, 97, 98, 100, 107, 109, 113, 122
Civil Code of the ROC, 6
civil interests, 5, 21, 29, 40, 176, 177
Civil Procedure Law, 61, 206
codification
  causation and, 180–81
  consolidation and, 133, 164, 293, 298–300
  Great Qing Code, 267–68
  post-Soviet approaches to, 296–98
  socialism and, 304–7
  Soviet-like approach to, 295–96
  Western approach to, 292–94
commercial risk, 80–81, 109, 113
communitarian value, 31–32
community property, 214, 217–22, 223, 225–32, 234
comparative law, 45, 72, 180–83
compensation
  based on merits, 280
  contracts and, 103
  joint mortgages and, 143
  for lost opportunity, 222–23
  mortgages and, 151
  passive appreciation and, 234
  as pecuniary equivalent, 324
  property rights and, 163–64
  punative damages and, 153–59
  in tort law, 29, 123, 124, 149, 167–71, 178, 203, 206, 210, 211
Confucianism, 32, 37, 55, 237–38, 241–46, 248, 292, 307, 315
consciousness, rights, 43, 44, 46–47, 50, 75–76
consent, 32, 50, 60, 63, 65, 68, 70, 76, 137, 140, 148, 236–37, 269
consent, contractual, 114–16, 117, 119–22, 124–30
consolidation, 133, 164, 293, 298–300
contract law, state interest in, 10–14
contract purpose test, 82–84, 88, 89, 90–91, 93
contracts
  adaptation of, 84–85
  annulment of, 270–73, 275–76, 279–87, 288, 290, 291
  breach of, 28, 83, 100, 102, 105, 109, 126, 129–30, 164, 223, 278, 279, 280, 284
  deadlock in performance of, 94–96, 101, 104, 106
  effect-to-be-determined, 27–28
  formation of, 116–20, 129, 130, 283
  freedom of, 270–71
  frustration of purpose, 22, 23, 111
  fulfillment of, 83–84, 87, 91, 100, 102, 113
  interpretation of, 115, 119–21, 130
  judicial termination of, 97, 98, 100, 103, 104–11, 112
  performance of, 77, 91–92, 94, 97–100, 101, 323
  renegotiation of, 86
  standard form, 127–29
  termination of, 23, 84–86, 90–91, 94–113
COVID-19, 12, 65, 71, 79, 86–92, 268
credit, 131, 148, 262, 278
Cui Jianyuan, 97, 104
Cultural Revolution, 303
cybertort liability, 159–62

Davis Contractors Ltd v. *Fareham*, 122
deadlock in performance, 94–96, 101, 104, 106
despatch theory of acceptance, 117–18
deterrence, 156, 158, 203, 211
di Porto, Andrea, 319–20, 322
Dickinson v. *Dodds*, 118, 121
Du Moumou v. *Chen Moumou et al.*, 188
duty to act, 35–39
duty to perform, 22

economic law, 282, 303–4
eggshell-skull rule, 187–89
environmental law, 158–59, 164, 178, 317–24
environmental protection, 158, 307, 317–24
Eörsi, Gyula, 296
ethical norms, 237, 243, 247
exemption of liability, 85–86, 90, 92

fairness
  commutative justice and, 5
  contractual, 115, 130
  economic, 269
  joint investment and, 228–29
  of judicial system, 205
  justice and, 77
  law as art of, 247
  liability and, 194
  obvious unfairness and, 24–27
  principle of, 38, 85, 87, 88, 96–97, 98, 103, 125, 134, 145, 218, 226, 234, 241, 243, 314
  of punishment, 237
  of stock purchase agreement, 13
family law, 214, 216–19, 222, 225–26, 233
fate, 209–11
fault
  contributory, 181–83
  delictual, 123–26
  victim's comparative/contributory, 186–90
fault liability, 6, 17, 28, 32–35, 37–39, 111, 112, 123, 149, 159, 161, 165–73, 180, 210, 212, 304
fault principle, 155, 165, 199–202
favor contractus, 84
Feststellungsklage, 107
force majeure, 77–93, 100, 102, 109, 112, 122
  causation and, 181–83, 185
Foreign Investment Law, 28
freedom of contract, 270–71
French Civil Code, 4, 17, 28, 128, 293, 298, 315
frozen embryos, ownership of, 72–73
frustration of purpose, 22, 23, 111

Gallen v. *Allstate*, 120
gender equality, 55–58
General Principles of Civil Law, 11, 20, 26–27, 39, 48–49, 131–32, 156, 283, 284, 299, 303
German Civil Code, 4, 22, 25, 29–30, 110, 128, 275, 293, 315
Geschäftsgrundlage, 22
Gestaltungsklagerecht, 103, 107
Gestaltungsrecht, 107
Gestaltungsurteil, 107
good faith, 96–97, 98, 103, 104, 115, 121, 124–27, 130, 147–48, 288, 314–16
Great Peace Shipping Ltd v. *Tsavliris (International) Ltd*, 122
Great Qing Code, 238, 249–68, 309
  socio-intellectual prestige of, 260–67
green principle, 317–24
Gu Zhengkang v. *Shiyan Ronghua Dongfeng Automobile Ltd*, 144–45
Guangzhou Xianyuan Real Estate Co., Ltd. v. *Guangdong Zhongda Zhongxin Inv. Plan. Co., Ltd., Guangzhou Yuanxing Real Estate Co., Ltd., & China Inv. Grp. Int'l Fin. Mgmt. Co., Ltd.*, 28
Guarantee Law, 140–42, 144–45
guarantees, 135, 137, 138–42, 145–47, 172, 262, 297–98
  personal, 131–32, 134, 140–42, 144–45
Guo Yuefeng and Zhang Hongzhao v. *Liu Yanwei*, 83

Hai Rui, 34
Han Shiyuan, 25, 26, 315
Harbin Bureau of Natural Resources and Planning v. *Zhang Kai*, 271
harmonious society, 307
Henan Middle Pharmaceutical Company v. *Dong Xueling & Hubei Hualong Pharmaceutical Company*, 284
Henan Songyue Corp. v. *Henan Songchun Corp.*, 289
Hongfei Xie, 106
Houle v. Canadian National Bank, 126
Hua Ken International Trade Co Ltd v. *Shanxi Lunda Meat Industry Co Ltd*, 89
human flesh search, 60–61
hypothetical intention argument, 218, 226, 229–33

imperial China, 34, 237, 249–50, 252, 257
impossibility, 83, 89, 99, 109, 183, 194
industrialization, 48, 199, 200
inflation, 223–24

intellectual property, 157, 161, 164, 175–76
intentional acts, 111–12, 157, 158, 171, 173, 175, 177–78, 186–87, 194, 196
interdicts, 321–23
Interfoto Picture Library Ltd v. *Stiletto Visual Programmes*, 126
Investors Compensation Scheme Ltd v. *West Bromwich Building Society*, 128

Japanese Civil Code, 111
Japanese law, 309
Jean Coutu Group (PJC) Inc v. *Canada (Attorney General)*, 120
Jhering, Rudolf von, 106
Jiang Ping, 310–12, 324
Jia-shan Jingxin Film Co Ltd v. *Jia-shan Luo Shang Metal Products Co Ltd*, 82
joint investment, theory of, 226–31
joint security, 142–46
Judicial Interpretation of the Security Law, 132
justice, 77, 99, 103, 120, 237, 247, 274
  access to, 203
  commutative, xiii, 2, 3, 5–6, 33
  distributive, 2, 5–6, 33, 34, 40, 169, 201, 212
  equity and, 97–98
  social, 308

Kaaa v. *Kaaa*, 225, 229
Kaihuang Code, 252–53
Kant, Immanuel, 50, 116
Krell v. *Henry*, 21

L'Estrange v. *F Graucob Ltd*, 128
land use rights, 14–16, 131
Lauritzen AS v. *Wijsmuller BV (The 'Super Servant Two')*, 111
Law of the XII Tables, 318
law, as superstructure, 15, 273–74
legal transplants, xiii, 2, 4, 6, 17, 40, 292, 309–10
Lei Chen, 31
lenders, 131, 137, 287
liability, 4–6, 62, 64, 128
  for breach of contract, 94, 100, 102, 109
  civil, 20, 39, 57–58, 65, 154–57, 167, 196
  for compensation, 222–23
  compensatory, 68
  concurrent, 163
  contractual, 28, 183
  contributory, 171–73
  cybertort, 159–62
  for damages, 22–23
  defendant, 184–88
  delictual, 115, 118, 123–26, 130
  in equity, 6, 32–39, 40, 212
  exemption of, 90, 92–93
  fate and, 209–11
  guarantees and, 137–42
  joint and several, 190–96
  multiple tortfeasors and, 190–96
  multi-tier, 169–73, 178
  for negligence, 181
  for nonperformance, 82, 89, 91–92
  security, 142–49, 151
  social costs and, 203–4
  strict, 34, 109, 159, 165–66, 169–73, 191, 201–2, 212, 304
  tax, 262
Liang Huixing, 10, 18, 44, 155
Liu Minglian, Guo Lili and Guo Shuangshuang v. *Sun Wei & Lanting Property Management Co. Ltd*, 189
Liu v. *Zhao*, 225

mainfest unfairness test, 83–84
manifest unfairness test, 82, 90, 93
Marbury v. *Madison*, 19
marital property, 214–34
marriage, 214–34
marriage law, 216–17, 299, 302, 310
Marx, Karl, 15, 273
Marxist theory of law, 15, 274
McCoy v. *Ware*, 223
McCutcheon v. *David Macbrayne Ltd.*, 128
Meng Qiang, 5, 18

Mid Essex Hospital Services NHS Trust v. *Compass Group UK and Ireland Ltd*, 126
the Minutes 2019, 101, 104, 108, 112
mistake, 12, 115–16, 121–24, 126, 130, 269, 283, 306
moral philosophy, xiii, 2, 6, 32–33, 40
mortgage house, 220–21, 224, 227–28, 231
mortgages, 131–40, 143–44, 149–51, 215, 220–32, 250
MSC Mediterranean Shipping Company SA v. *Cottonex Anstalt*, 126
multiple tortfeasors, 170–72, 179, 181–83, 184, 190–96

National Bank v. *Soucisse et al.*, 126
natural increase, 215–16, 218–19, 224
natural law, 247–48, 311–12
necessity theory, 184
negligence, 33, 190, 236
  comparative, 182, 183
  contributory, 173
  gross, 39, 163, 171, 178
  intention and, 40
  liability and, 170, 180, 184
  medical, 165
  tort of, 202
non est factum, 120
non-monetary obligation, 96, 97–102, 105, 112, 113, 136
numerus clausus, 123, 133

Pa De Ke Ya Ku Pu Yaqup v. *Abliz*, 91
pacta sunt servanda, 99
Parker v. *The South Eastern Railway Co*, 120
parol evidence rule, 120
passive appreciation, 214–34
  affirmative approach to, 219–20, 231–33
  negative approach to, 218–19, 231–33
  proportional approach to, 220–31, 234
paternalism
  in Chinese contract law, 277–85
  in Soviet law, 273–77
Peng Yu case, 36–39
People's Ins. Co. of China Tangshan Branch v. *Ju Zhenhua, Tangshan Lunan Hexin Feight Co., Ltd.*, 31
personal attributes, commoditization of, 50–55
personal interest, 42, 49
personal sphere, 41, 46, 51, 52, 73, 75
personality rights, 1, 6, 17–21, 41–57, 59–76, 154–57, 176, 313
  biomedical threats to, 67–73
  data-based threats to, 62–67
  internet-based threats to, 59–62
prestige effect, 251–52, 260, 267–68
prevention, 57, 58, 70, 158
Principles of International Commercial Contracts (PICC), 96
privacy, right to, 45, 48–49, 62, 64–66, 75
  hierarchical needs and, 49–50
private law, 5, 39, 64, 125, 180, 198, 236, 268, 275, 290, 292, 297, 308, 310, 317, 324
  codification of, 12, 285
  German, 124
  Great Qing Code and, 249–52, 258–60, 263–67
  legitimatation of, 9–10
  Western, 2–3, 5, 6, 14
private ownership, 2, 6–10, 14–15, 272–73, 275
Provisional Methods, 277–79
punative damages, 157–59
punishment, 34, 60, 98, 203, 211, 237–46, 248, 255–56, 266
pure economic loss, 28–31

Qi Yuling v. *Chen Xiaoqi*, 19–21
Qing dynasty, xiv, 249–68
Québec (Agence du Revenu) v. *Services Environnementaux AES inc*, 120

real security, 132–33, 135, 140–42, 145
reasonableness, 124–25
Rechtsgeschäfte (civil juristic acts), 17, 283

rectification, 120
remedies, 74, 85, 92, 98, 115, 129–30, 154–56, 181, 186, 208–9, 269, 278, 282, 324
Ren Weijun v. *Zhang Xiang*, 80
Republican China, 261
reputation, right to, 59–62
right of recourse, 142–46
Roman law, 135, 236–37, 247–48, 294, 297, 305, 308–24
Rong v. *Wang & Yongcheng Insurance Company*, 187–89
rule of law, 115, 121, 129, 235–36, 242, 301, 313–14
  moral authority of, 247–48
Russian Civil Code, 32, 275, 276–77

San X Pharmaceutical JSC v. *Ya Advertising LLC*, 284
Sanya Changyuan case, 90
security interest, 131–52
  termination of, 149–51
separate property, 215, 217–34
Severe Acute Respiratory Syndrome (SARS), 71, 78, 79, 86–92
Shaanxi Zhongbei case, 85
Shaanxi Zhongbei Real Estate Development Co Ltd v. *Xi'an Tongfang Real Estate Development Co Ltd*, 85
Shanghai Guoxin Holding Company v. *Hainan Dongfang Windpower Company*, 271
Shields v. *Gross*, 50
shopping mall management contract, 96–110
Smith v. *Hughes*, 126
social harmony, 198, 212–13
social loss, 203–5
solidarity, 304–7
Soviet influence, 270, 273–77, 283–85, 295–96, 300–4
Sovietism, 300–4
SPC Interpretation on Security, 138, 147–49
state assets, trading of, 272, 287, 289
state interests, 3, 269–73, 275, 277, 285, 287–89, 291, 305–6
  in article 52, 285
  in contract law, 10–14
  in contracts, 281–83
state-owned enterprises (SOE), 7, 9, 11–14, 39, 269–72, 275–77, 279–91
statutory matrimonial regime, 214, 215, 217, 229
Storer v. *Manchester City Council*, 120
Su Yongli v. *Yunnan Gaosheng Lianhe Touzi Youxian Gongsi*, 176
Sun Liangguo, 97
surrogacy, 54–55

Taylor v. *Cardwell*, 112
technology, 41–46, 51, 58–59, 73, 75–76
  biomedical, 67–73
Tentative Rules, 280–81
third parties' acts, 181, 184
Thornton v. *Shoe Lane Parking Ltd.*, 120
Tianjin Second Harbour case, 79–80
Tilden Rent-A-Car v. *Clendenning*, 127
tort law, 153–56
  aims of, 197–213
  causation and, 179–96
  compensation in, 29, 123, 124, 149, 167–71, 178, 206, 210, 222–23
  deterrance in, 156, 158
  empirics of, 199, 202–5
  extra-judicial dynamics of, 205–9
  fate and, 209–11
  fault liability and, 6, 17, 28, 32–35, 37–39, 111, 112, 123, 149, 159, 161, 165–73, 180, 210, 212, 304
  judicial interpretations of, 171–73
  in law and economics, 203
  plurality of, 199
  social harmony and, 212–13
  strict liability and, 34, 109, 159, 165–66, 169–73, 191, 201–2, 212, 304
  Western development of, 199–202
tort liability, 18, 19, 43, 70, 153–57, 176–77, 181–83

Tort Liability Law (TLL), 4–5, 8, 29–30, 39, 43, 46, 49, 61, 64, 68, 154, 156, 157, 159, 163, 164, 166, 176–77, 179, 181, 184, 186–87, 190–92, 198
tradition
  Chinese imperial legal, 40
  Chinese legal, 208, 237
  civil law, 180, 312
  German, 3
  Qin legal, 248
  Western, 236
  Western legal, 293
Transfield Shipping Inc v. Mercator Shipping Inc (The Achilleas), 129
translation, 179, 302, 319
Tumanov, Vladimir, 295

unconsciousability, 23–27
unfairness, obvious, 12, 24–27
unjust enrichment, 1, 8, 136, 222
usufruct, 16, 29, 305

validity rules, 269–91, 313
Vertrauensschaden, 123

Wang Liming, 29, 293
Wang Ting et al v. *The Business Department of the Agricultural Bank of China Guangdong Branch et al*, 89
Wang v. *Zhao*, 225
Wen Qiong v. *Li Hongbin, Li Guanlin, Miaomingshi Dianbaqu Diyitan Youle Zhongxin and Miaomingshi Dianbaiqu Binhai Lvyou Fuwu Youxian Gongsi*, 172
'will theory' of legal doctrine, 3
Willenserklärung, 107
Wuhan Gas Company v. *Chongqing Testing Instrument Factory*, 78

Xi Jinping, 313–14
Xia Yun v. *Jiangsu Performing Arts Grp. Co., Ltd. & Nanjing Dafeng Venture Cap. Mgmt. Co., Ltd.*, 14
Xinjiang Yakun Commercial Trade Co Ltd v. *Xinjiang Jinghe Kangrui Cotton Processing Co Ltd*, 83
Xinyu case, 22, 98–100, 102, 106, 109, 112, 113
Xinyu Co. v. *Feng Yumei Store*, 23
Xu XX v. *Peng Yu*, 36

Yam Seng Pte Ltd v. *International Trade Corporation Ltd*, 126
Yang Jiang, 61
Yao Sheng (Xiamen) Property Management Co Ltd v. *Qingdao Haixie Trust Investment Co Ltd*, 82
Yifu Lin, Justin, 13
Yin Wenmin v. *Sanya Changyuan Property Development Co Ltd*, 90
Yumen City Xi Gui Renewable Resource Recovery Co Ltd v. *Yumen Oil Field Branch of China National Petroleum Co*, 85

Zhang Jie v. *Hou Xiaofeng & Woyang County Grain Trading Company LLC*, 271
Zhang Lin case, 86–88
Zhang Pinghua, 47, 51, 185
Zhang Qun v. *Foshanshi Xinyijia Supermarket Co., Ltd.*, 42
Zhang Yun v. *Jiangsu Performing Arts Group & Jiangsu Huayang Corp*, 287
Zhongguo Changcheng Zichan Guanli Gufen Youxian Gongsi Jilinsheng Fengongsi v. *Jilinshi Zhongxiao Qiye Xinyong Danbao Jituan Youxian Gongsi*, 177
Zhongji General Import & Export Co v. *Tianjin Port No. 2 Port & Harbor Co Ltd*, 79
Zhou Youjun, 5, 21
Zhu Guangxin, 105–7
Zuh Suli, 208–9

www.ingramcontent.com/pod-product-compliance
Lightning Source LLC
LaVergne TN
LVHW052033200926
848481LV00005B/1666
* 9 7 8 1 0 0 9 3 3 6 6 3 5 *